MY SiDEWALKS ON
SCOTT FORESMAN
READING STREET
Intensive Reading Intervention

Welcome to
MY SIDEWALKS

ISBN-13: 978-0-328-45330-6
ISBN-10: 0-328-45330-7

10   13

PEARSON
Scott
Foresman

pearsonschool.com

Glenview, Illinois • Boston, Massachusetts • Chandler, Arizona •
Upper Saddle River, New Jersey

Welcome to MY SiDEWALKS

Motivating text.

Explicit
instruction.

Accelerated
learning.

With *My Sidewalks*, you will take your
intensive intervention students through a program
that starts where they are, builds skills step-by-step,
and helps them progress to on-level reading.

This book will give you the
professional support you need to
get started.

Contents

Overview

What can you do when a core reading program with small-group instruction isn't enough for your struggling students? You can give them *My Sidewalks*.

My Sidewalks is a research-based, intensive reading intervention program. It is designed for students who are unable to read and comprehend grade-level material and who are unable to benefit adequately from the strategic intervention that supports their core classroom reading instruction. *My Sidewalks* should be used along with a scientifically research-based comprehensive classroom reading program. It can be used with both native English speakers and English learners.

3 TIERS OF INTERVENTION

TIER I PRIMARY

Comprehensive **Core** Program

TIER II SECONDARY

Core Program Plus **Strategic** Intervention

TIER III TERTIARY

Intensive Reading Intervention

My Sidewalks follows the **Response to Intervention** model. This model is based on the **3 TIERS OF INTERVENTION:**

1 Primary Intervention consists of high-quality, research-based classroom reading instruction. It includes assessment at least three times a year to determine if children are meeting grade-level benchmarks.

2 Secondary Intervention consists of small-group strategic intervention that supports and complements classroom reading instruction. It is designed to prevent at-risk readers from falling behind.

3 Tertiary Intervention consists of small-group intensive intervention designed to accelerate struggling readers' acquisition of priority skills (phonemic awareness, phonics, fluency, vocabulary, and text comprehension).

Focus on Priority Skills

The ultimate goal of *My Sidewalks* is to improve students' reading and comprehension abilities. To reach this goal, *My Sidewalks* is built on instruction in **priority skills**. *My Sidewalks* provides instruction in phonemic awareness (Levels A–B), phonics, fluency, vocabulary, and comprehension skills and strategies.

• **Phonemic Awareness** is one of the strongest predictors of a child's future reading ability. Levels A and B of *My Sidewalks* include daily phonemic awareness activities that incorporate teacher modeling and scaffolding.

• **Phonics** instruction in Levels A and B of *My Sidewalks* is based on core phonics elements, blending strategies, and daily practice with these skills in decodable texts. Instruction at Levels C, D, and E focuses on decoding multisyllabic words.

• **Fluency** instruction in *My Sidewalks* includes teacher modeling, student practice with repeated readings, and teacher feedback. Beginning in the middle of Level A, teachers and students track and monitor progress.

• **Vocabulary** instruction is focused on vocabulary that is thematically related to the weekly science or social studies concept. Instruction includes multiple exposures to each word in the context of reading and multiple opportunities to practice the words.

• **Comprehension Skills and Strategies** instruction includes those skills that struggling readers need to become proficient readers: main idea, compare and contrast, sequence, and drawing conclusions. Strategy instruction includes strategies such as previewing and setting purposes, asking and answering questions, and summarizing text.

Instructional Features

Levels A–E of *My Sidewalks* each include 150 lessons that

• provide 30 to 45 minutes of instruction each day

• are intended for small groups of two to five students

• may be used during group time in a regular classroom, as a pull-out intervention program, or as a before or after school program

LEVEL ⟷ GRADE	
A	1
B	2
C	3
D	4
E	5

Research-Based Intervention

My Sidewalks was built upon the foundational research provided for Scott Foresman ***Early Reading Intervention*** by Project Optimize.

The following research findings from **Project Optimize** informed the instructional design of Levels A–E of *My Sidewalks*:

Instructional Emphasis

Emphasizing the essential elements of reading affects outcomes. *My Sidewalks* teaches strategically, focusing on the priority skills that are critical for student success.

Specificity

Highly specified instruction accomplishes more than less specific instruction. *My Sidewalks* Teacher's Guides feature explicit, consistent, easy-to-follow lessons.

Intensity

Fast-paced instruction should be delivered to small groups of two to five students for at least thirty minutes per day in addition to their core classroom instruction. *My Sidewalks* small-group instruction provides struggling students with additional teacher modeling and feedback, more scaffolding, multiple opportunities for practice, and more time on task.

Progress Monitoring

Frequent progress monitoring keeps learning on track. In *My Sidewalks*, students' progress is monitored daily, weekly, and at the unit level. Assessment informs instruction. Students exit the program when they are able to read classroom material with ease and understanding.

Level A3 Student Reader

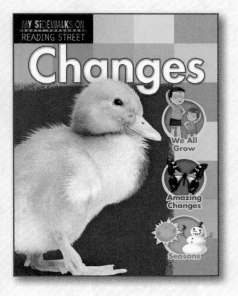

Level D4 Student Reader

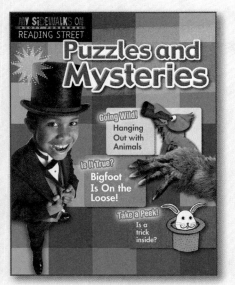

Hallmarks of My Sidewalks

In addition to the research features cited on p. 6, *My Sidewalks* possesses these distinguishing characteristics:

- **An acceleration plan** prioritizes skills and teaches less, more thoroughly.

- **An abundance of student reading material**— four selections each week—allows students to spend half their small-group time engaged in reading. Students apply their skills and build stamina for reading.

- **An emphasis on oral language, vocabulary, and concept development** is central to the instruction. Lessons are designed to develop deep meaning for key concepts and vocabulary and to elicit extended language from children. *My Sidewalks* addresses the fact that children's comprehension is inextricably tied to their vocabulary knowledge.

- **A focus on word-reading strategies** for multisyllablic words at Levels C–E teaches students to decode the words they struggle with the most.

- **Integrated instruction meets the needs of English language learners** who need to hear and practice oral language, read and write English words and sentences, and experience language devoted to exploring concepts.

- **Alignment with Scott Foresman *Reading Street*** offers students a consistency of instructional routines and terminology. In addition, the oral language, vocabulary, and concepts developed in *My Sidewalks* parallel those in the core program, *Reading Street*.

MY SIDEWALKS ON
SCOTT FORESMAN
READING STREET
Intensive Reading Intervention

Authors

My Sidewalks was created by the leading researchers in the area of reading intervention instruction. Their work has helped struggling readers and is the basis for the 3-Tier model of instruction.

"Research shows that for students to make significant progress, they need systematic and intensive instruction that is tailored to their current instructional level."

Sharon Vaughn

Connie Juel, Ph.D.
Professor of Education
School of Education
Stanford University

Jeanne R. Paratore, Ed.D.
Associate Professor of Education
Department of Literacy
and Language Development
Boston University

Deborah Simmons, Ph.D.
Professor
College of Education and
Human Development
Texas A&M University

Sharon Vaughn, Ph.D.
H.E. Hartfelder/Southland
Corporation Regents
Professor
University of Texas

Effective Classroom Practices

How Can I Teach Effectively?

Provide fast-paced, high-density instruction. Students should be on-task throughout the lesson. Planning is key to keeping students actively engaged in learning. The daily lessons in *My Sidewalks* offer suggested time frames to help you keep instruction focused.

Use explicit and systematic instruction. Predictable, explicit instructional routines appear throughout *My Sidewalks*. The routines incorporate practices such as these:

- Connect to what students already know; build on their prior knowledge.

- Introduce a small amount of new information at a time. Break tasks down into smaller steps.

- Always model a new skill before asking students to use it.

- Provide ample practice first for the group and then for individuals.

- Use visuals and graphic organizers to clarify instruction.

- Systematically review previously learned skills.

- Regularly check English language learners' understanding of instruction.

Scaffold students' learning by providing support. Offer modeling and prompts frequently as students learn new skills. In reading, thinking aloud is often the best way to model skills and strategies.

Establish routines so that students know what they're supposed to do. Use the Routine Cards to help you establish routines for intensive intervention.

Routine Card 1

Blending Strategy

Teach children to blend words using this Routine.

1 Connect Relate the new sound-spelling to previously learned sound-spellings.

2 Use Sound-Spelling Card Display the card for the sound-spelling. Say the sound. Have children say it.

3 Listen and Write Have children write the letter(s) as they say the sound.

4 Model Demonstrate how to blend words with the sound-spelling. Have children blend a word with you.

5 Group and Individual Practice Have children work together to segment and blend several words with the sound-spelling. Then have each child blend two words individually. Provide corrective feedback.

Routine Cards are located in the back of the Teacher's Guide.

Provide ample time for reading every day. Students should be reading for approximately half of your intensive intervention time block.

Monitor students' progress regularly. Reteach skills when necessary.

Provide immediate corrective feedback if a student makes an error.

Create high expectations that students can and will learn.

Reinforce achievement with praise and recognition.

Encourage self-regulation. Praise students often for making their own decisions.

Differentiating Instruction

The charts on these pages show instruction during a week in *My Sidewalks*. The charts can also be used as guides for **reteaching** or **accelerating** through parts of the lessons. In addition, the ***If... then...*** directions will help you identify how to customize instruction for your students.

Reteaching To meet the needs of the lowest performing readers, it may be necessary to modify the pacing and intensity of instruction. Activities shown in blue boxes on the charts may be repeated for these students.

Accelerating A child who shows mastery of skills following initial instruction may be ready for instruction at a faster pace with fewer repetitions. Activities shown in pink boxes might be omitted for these students.

Levels A–B

	PHONEMIC AWARENESS	PHONICS	HIGH-FREQUENCY WORDS	CONCEPTS/ ORAL VOCABULARY	PASSAGE READING	FLUENCY	WRITING
Day 1	Phonemic Awareness	Blending Strategy	High-Frequency Words	Concepts/ Oral Vocabulary	Read a Passage	Reread for Fluency	
Day 2	Phonemic Awareness	Blending Strategy	High-Frequency Words		Read a Passage	Reread for Fluency	Write
Day 3	Phonemic Awareness	Blending Strategy	High-Frequency Words	Concepts/ Oral Vocabulary	Read a Passage	Reread for Fluency	
Day 4		Fluent Word Reading		Concepts/ Oral Vocabulary	Read Together	Reread for Fluency	Write
Day 5		Assess Word Reading	Assess Word/ Sentence Reading	Check Oral Vocabulary	Assess Passage Reading/ Reread		Write

☐ **Reteach**   ☐ **Omit for acceleration**

If... a child is struggling with word reading, ***then...*** reteach Word Work activities and include More Practice extensions.

If... a child lacks oral language, ***then...*** elicit extended language from the child, provide ample opportunities for the child to respond when building concepts, and expand the structured picture walks before reading each selection.

If... a child's reading is so slow that it hinders comprehension, ***then...*** provide additional models of fluent reading, give more corrective feedback during fluency practice, and include More Practice extensions when rereading for fluency.

If... an English learner struggles with sounds, ***then...*** repeat appropriate practice activities.

Levels C–E

	VOCABULARY	COMPREHENSION	PASSAGE READING	PHONICS	FLUENCY	WRITING
Day 1	Vocabulary		Read a Passage	Blending Strategy (Level C)	Reread for Fluency	Write (Levels D–E)
Day 2	Vocabulary	Comprehension Skill	Read a Passage	Phonics	Reread for Fluency	Write (Levels D–E)
Day 3	Vocabulary	Comprehension Skill Assess (Levels D–E)	Read a Passage	Phonics	Reread for Fluency	Write
Day 4	Vocabulary	Comprehension Skill/Strategy Assess (Levels D–E)	Read Together (Level C) Read a Passage (Levels D–E)	Phonics Review (Level C)	Reread for Fluency	Write
Day 5	Vocabulary	Assess Comprehension	Read Together (Levels D–E) Reread (Level C)	Assess Sentence Reading (Level C)	Assess Fluency	Write

If... a student is struggling with word reading, **then...** reteach Vocabulary and Phonics activities and include More Practice extensions.

If... a student lacks oral language, **then...** elicit extended language from the student, provide ample opportunities for the student to respond when building concepts, and expand the After Reading discussion for each selection.

If... a student's reading is so disfluent that it hinders comprehension, **then...** provide additional models of fluent reading, give more corrective feedback during fluency practice, and include More Practice extensions for fluency.

If... a student lacks comprehension and is unable to retell or summarize, **then...** reteach comprehension skills and strategies, provide additional modeling of retelling and summarizing, and give more corrective feedback during practice.

If... an English learner lacks English vocabulary for known concepts, **then...** say the unknown English word, have the student repeat it, and ask questions that will allow the student to use the word in a meaningful context.

4-Step Assessment Plan

1 **Diagnosis and Placement**
2 **Monitor Progress**
3 **Evaluate Student Progress**
4 **Exiting the Program**

The assessments in the Assessment Book will enable you to gather valuable information about your students' understanding and mastery of reading skills before, during, and after instruction.

Screening and Benchmark Assessment

For a screening test at the beginning of the year or for grade-level benchmark testing, you may want to use **DIBELS**—Dynamic Indicators of Basic Early Literacy Skills. This test may be downloaded from the Internet for free. For the test and scoring information, see the DIBELS website at the University of Oregon.

MY SIDEWALKS ON
SCOTT FORESMAN
READING STREET
Intensive Reading Intervention

Assessment Book

• Program Placement Tests

• Individual and Group Unit Tests

• Guidelines for tracking and evaluating student performance

Level **C**

Step 1 Diagnosis and Placement

Use the Placement Test in the Assessment Book with individual at-risk students who have been identified through baseline test performance, work in the core reading program, and observation. Administer the *My Sidewalks* Placement Test to determine the level at which to begin children in *My Sidewalks* and to identify the areas of literacy that are problematic for each child.

Placement Test

Placement Test Overview

The Level C Placement Test is designed to help you identify the appropriate level at which to begin students who will be using the *My Sidewalks*.

The five subtests are to be administered sequentially. The chart below shows the number of items in each subtest. Estimated times are given for planning purposes only. Allow as much time as needed for each student to complete the test. You may administer this test in two or three sittings.

Subtest	Number of Items	Estimated Time
1 Consonant Letter-Sounds	25	2 minutes
2 Word Reading Part I	20	1 minute
3 High-Frequency Words	20	1 minute
4 Word Reading Part II	20	2 minutes
5a and 5b Fluency and Comprehension	WCPM Retelling	10 minutes
Total	**85**	**16 minutes**

Directions for Administering the Test

The directions in **bold** type are to be read aloud. Item numbers appear in the directions for your convenience and for use in scoring. They do not appear on students' pages.

Make two copies of the student's test, p. 22—one for the student and one on which to mark the student's responses. Also make a copy of the Evaluation Chart, p. 19, for each student. Have Benchmark Readers B2 and B6 on hand. For your convenience, the Level A Benchmark Readers are reproduced on pp. 85–108.

Begin with Subtest 1. If the student scores less than 80% on Subtests 1–3, discontinue testing. If the student scores 80% or better on Subtests 1–3, continue testing.

Scoring

Record scores on the Evaluation Chart. Correct answers are given with the directions. There is also an Answer Key on pp. 109–112.

Interpreting the Scores

• If the student scores less than 80% on Subtests 1–3, he or she may be more appropriately placed in Level B of *My Sidewalks* or may require further testing.

• If the student scores 80% or higher on subtests 1–4 but less than 80% on Subtest 5, have the student read Benchmark Reader B2. Students who can read Benchmark Reader B2 with 95% accuracy and retell with a summative score of 2 may be placed in Level C of *My Sidewalks*.

• Students who score 80% or higher on Subtests 1–4 should be asked to read Benchmark Reader B6. If they can read Benchmark Reader B6 with 90% accuracy and retell with a summative score of 3, they may be capable of working in the core third-grade reading program with instructional emphasis in the areas of need and with strategic intervention.

18　　Placement Test Overview

Step 2 Monitor Progress

Use the ongoing assessments found on Day 5 each week in the Teacher's Guides to identify individual instructional needs and to provide appropriate support. Use the Sentence Reading Charts (Levels A–C) and the Fluency Progress Chart found in the Teacher's Guides to track each child's progress.

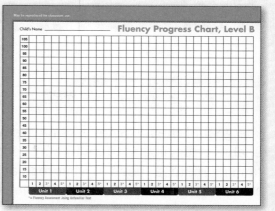

Step 3 Evaluate Student Progress

Administer the Unit Tests in the Assessment Book to check mastery of unit skills. To make instructional decisions at the end of a unit, use end-of-unit assessment results, which include children's performance on Day 5 assessments for that unit, on the Unit Test, and on reading of the unit Benchmark Reader. (Use of the Benchmark Reader is optional.) Use the Fluency Progress Chart, the Retelling Progress Chart, and the Record Chart for Unit Tests in the Assessment Book to gather complete end-of-unit information.

Level A1 Benchmark Reader

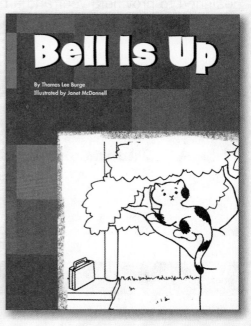

Step 4 Exiting the Program

There are two opportunities for children to exit the program—at midyear and at the end of the year. To exit the program, a child must show progress toward grade-level goals. Use the Midyear and End-of-Year Exit Criteria on p. 17 of the Assessment Book as your guide.

Exit Criteria

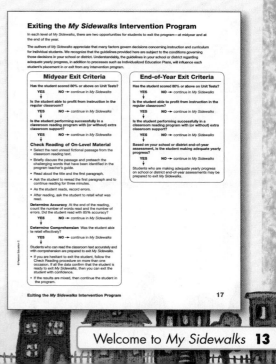

Distinctions Between Levels

Understanding the Levels of *My Sidewalks*

The goal of the *My Sidewalks* program is to enable struggling readers to succeed with the reading material used in their regular classrooms. To achieve this, *My Sidewalks* focuses on accelerating students' acquisition of priority skills. Each level of *My Sidewalks* is designed to provide a year and a half of reading growth. Consequently there is an overlap of skills between one *My Sidewalks* level and the next.

These pages describe the skills students should have to successfully begin each level of *My Sidewalks* and what they will learn in that level. Use the Placement Tests to help you determine the correct level at which to enter each student.

To begin this level a child should know:	**In this level**, the instructional focus is on:
Early Reading Intervention (Grade K)	
	• Phonological and phonemic awareness
	• Letter names and sounds
	• Blending regular short-vowel words
	• Sentence reading
Level A (Grade 1)	
• Some phonological awareness	• Phonemic awareness
	• Letter names
	• Consonants: Individual letter-sounds, blends, and digraphs
	• Vowels: Short, long (CVCe), and *r*-controlled
	• Blending words and fluent word reading
	• High-frequency words
	• Oral vocabulary and concept development
	• Building fluency (40–60 WCPM)
	• Passage reading and retelling

To begin this level a student should know:	In this level, the instructional focus is on:

Level B (Grade 2)

- Letter names
- Individual consonant letter-sounds
- Some basic high-frequency words
- And be able to read Benchmark Reader A2 with accuracy and comprehension

- Phonemic awareness
- Letter names and sounds
- Blending words and fluent word reading
- High-frequency words
- Oral vocabulary and concept development
- Building fluency (70–90 WCPM)
- Passage reading and retelling

Level C (Grade 3)

- Consonants: Individual letter-sounds, blends, and digraphs
- Vowels: Short and long (CVCe) and be able to distinguish between them
- A wider range of high-frequency words
- And be able to read Benchmark Reader B2 with accuracy and comprehension

- Blending words and fluent word reading
- Decoding multisyllabic words, including words with one or more affixes
- Phonics: Vowels
- Concept vocabulary
- Building fluency (100–120 WCPM)
- Passage reading and summarizing

Level D (Grade 4)

- Consonants: Individual letter-sounds, blends, and digraphs
- Vowels: Short and long (CVCe) and be able to distinguish between them
- How to decode regular VC/CV words with short and long (CVCe) vowels
- Many high-frequency words
- And be able to read Benchmark Reader C1 with accuracy and comprehension

- Decoding multisyllabic words, including words with one or more affixes
- Phonics: Less frequent vowel patterns, such as vowel diphthongs
- Concept vocabulary
- Building fluency (110–130 WCPM)
- Passage reading and summarizing

Level E (Grade 5)

- Consonants: Individual letter-sounds, blends, and digraphs
- Vowels: Short and long (CVCe) and be able to distinguish between them
- How to decode regular VC/CV words with short and long (CVCe) vowels
- Many high-frequency words
- And be able to read Benchmark Reader D1 with accuracy and comprehension

- Decoding multisyllabic words, including words with one or more affixes
- Phonics: Less frequent vowel patterns, such as vowel diphthongs
- Concept vocabulary
- Building fluency (120–140 WCPM)
- Passage reading and summarizing

Managing Daily Instruction

To make your daily preparation easier, each week of instruction starts with an overview with this important planning information:

Overview page in Teacher's Guide

The week's concept and focus question

Each week an essential question is introduced to develop one aspect of the unit theme. This question guides instruction as students explore new concepts and literature. Each unit theme connects to learning in science or social studies.

Research Says "Perhaps the most compelling reason to teach with themes is that, done well, they promote a view of both teaching and learning as meaningful enterprise.... themes can 'provide a framework for the children's discoveries of the connections among the literature selections.'"

Lipson, Marjorie Y., Sheila W. Valencia, Karen K. Wixson, and Charles W. Peters. "Integration and Thematic Teaching: Integration to Improve Teaching and Learning." *Language Arts*, vol. 70, April 1993.

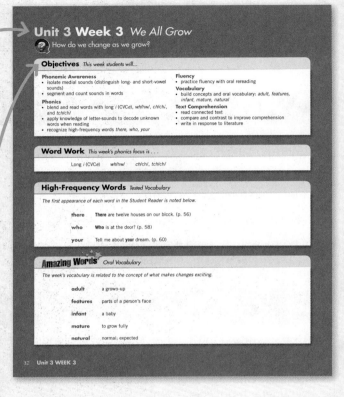

Unit 3 Week 3 *We All Grow*

How do we change as we grow?

Objectives *This week students will...*

Phonemic Awareness
- isolate medial sounds (distinguish long- and short-vowel sounds)
- segment and count sounds in words

Phonics
- blend and read words with long *i* (CVCe), *wh/hw/*, *ch/ch/*, and *tch/ch/*
- apply knowledge of letter-sounds to decode unknown words when reading
- recognize high-frequency words *there, who, your*

Fluency
- practice fluency with oral rereading

Vocabulary
- build concepts and oral vocabulary: *adult, features, infant, mature, natural*

Text Comprehension
- read connected text
- compare and contrast to improve comprehension
- write in response to literature

Word Work *This week's phonics focus is . . .*

Long *i* (CVCe)   *wh/hw/*   *ch/ch/, tch/ch/*

High-Frequency Words *Tested Vocabulary*

The first appearance of each word in the Student Reader is noted below.

there	**There** are twelve houses on our block. (p. 56)
who	**Who** is at the door? (p. 58)
your	Tell me about **your** dream. (p. 60)

Amazing Words *Oral Vocabulary*

The week's vocabulary is related to the concept of what makes changes exciting.

adult	a grown-up
features	parts of a person's face
infant	a baby
mature	to grow fully
natural	normal; expected

32   Unit 3 WEEK 3

Objectives for the week

The priority skills of phonemic awareness (at Levels A–B), phonics, fluency, vocabulary, and comprehension are covered daily. Progress in the priority skills is monitored frequently.

Research Says "Systematic evaluation of each student's progress is characteristic of classrooms in which students make the most progress."

Gaskins, Irene W. "A Multidimensional Approach to Beginning Literacy." *Literacy and Young Children: Research-Based Practices.* The Guilford Press, 2003.

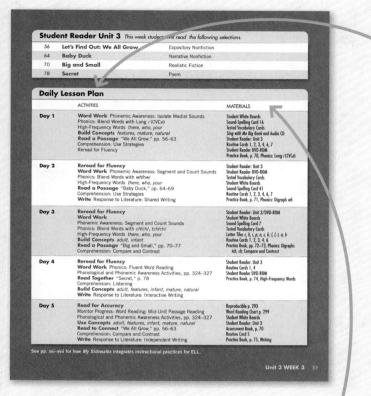

A Daily Lesson Plan that lists each day's activities

Every activity in *My Sidewalks* was designed with struggling and at-risk students in mind. Instruction is intended for small groups. The activities last only five to ten minutes and are organized in a carefully planned sequence of skills.

Research Says "Smaller group ratios increase likelihood of academic success through student-teacher interactions, individualization of instruction, student on-task behavior, and teacher monitoring of student progress and feedback."

Vaughn, Sharon, Sylvia Linan-Thompson, Kamiar Kouzekanani, Diane Pedrotty, Shirley Dickson, and Shelly Blozis. "Reading Instruction Grouping for Students with Reading Difficulties." *Remedial and Special Education*, vol. 24, no. 5, September/October 2003.

A Materials list

All the materials you need for each day's activities are listed here.

Research into Practice
Word Work

Phonemic Awareness

Each phonemic awareness lesson is tied to phonics instruction and prepares children for the blending lesson that follows. Phonemic awareness activities incorporate letters and focus on blending and segmenting sounds. Children write the letters as they say the sounds. Including letters in phonemic awareness activities helps children develop the skills they need to benefit from phonics instruction.

Research Says "Our analysis showed that PA [Phonemic Awareness] instruction was more effective when it was taught with letters. Using letters to manipulate phonemes helps children make the transfer to reading and writing words (Adams, 1990)."

Ehri, L. C., et al. "Phonemic Awareness Instruction Helps Children Learn to Read: Evidence from the National Reading Panel's Meta-Analysis." *Reading Research Quarterly*, vol. 36, no. 3, 2001.

"Segmenting words into phonemes and blending phonemes into words contributes more to learning to read and spell well than any other phonological awareness skills."

Vaughn, Sharon and Sylvia Linan-Thompson. *Research-Based Methods of Reading Instruction.* Association for Supervision and Curriculum Development, 2004.

ACTIVITY 1 **Word Work**

Phonemic Awareness Isolate Medial Sounds

2 minutes

	To Do	To Say
Scaffold instruction.	Distribute white boards. Write *hid* and *hide*.	**Model** Listen to the sounds in *hid*. Stretch the sounds /hhh/ /iii/ /d/ as you write *h, i, d*. Repeat, having children write the letters that go with each sound. Now listen to the sounds in *hide*. Stretch the sounds /hhh/ /ī/ /d/ as you write *h, i, d, e*. Repeat, having children write the letters that go with each sound. Now listen to both words: *hid, hide*. Which word has the sound /i/? (*hid*) Which word has the sound /ī/? (*hide*)
Lead the activity.	Lead children in isolating medial sounds as they write.	**Teach and Practice** Have children say the sounds with you as you point to the letters in the pairs of words. Listen to both words. Which word has the sound /i/? Which word has the sound /ī/? pin—pine bit—bite kit—kite Tim—time

Blending Strategy Long *i* (CVCe)

5–10 minutes   Routine

	To Do	To Say
Use the blending routine.	Write *age* and *make*.	**1 Connect** You already can read words like these. What are the words? What is the vowel sound in *age*? (/ā/) in *make*? (/ā/) Both words have silent *e* at the end. Now let's look at words with long *i*.
	Display Sound-Spelling Card 16.	**2 Use Sound-Spelling Card** This is ice cream. What sound do you hear at the beginning of *ice cream*? (/ī/) Say it with me: /ī/. The sound you hear at the beginning of *ice cream* is long *i*. When you see the letter pattern *i*–consonant–*e*, the *i* says its name, and the *e* is silent.
Scaffold instruction.		**3 Listen and Write** Write *hide, h, i, d, e*. What vowels do you see in *hide*? (*i, e*) *Hide* has the long *i*, /ī/. (*i*-consonant-*e*) As you write, say the sound to yourself: /ī/. Now say the sound aloud.
	Write *hide*.	**4 Model** When I add *e* to *hid*, it makes the *i* say its name. The *e* in this word is silent. This is how I blend this word: /h/ /ī/ /d/, *hide*. Now you try: /h/ /ī/ /d/, *hide*. h i d e
CORRECTIVE FEEDBACK	Write each practice word. Monitor student practice	**5 Group Practice** Let's try the same thing with these words. Give feedback using the *if . . . then* statements on Routine Card 1. like wide ripe prize* nine mice
		6 Individual Practice Write the words. Have each child blend two of them. smile kite wipe bike price* dime
	Check understanding of practice words.	*Children need to make sense of words that they segment and blend. If needed, help children with meanings. A *prize* is something you get when you win. A *price* is how much money someone must pay for something.
MORE PRACTICE	Model spelling long *i* words.	**Spell and Write** What sounds do you hear in *hide*? (/h/ /ī/ /d/) What is the letter for /h/? Let's all write *h*. What is the letter for /ī/? Write *i*. What is the letter for /d/? Write *d*. What letter must we add to the end of a word to make *i* say its name? Write *e*. Continue practice as time allows. Have children confirm their spelling by comparing it to what you've written. mine side nice line smile drive

34   **DAY 1** We All Grow

A Note on Pronunciation

Consonant phonemes are divided into those with a **continuous sound** (a sound that can be pronounced for several seconds without distortion) and a **stop sound** (a sound that can be pronounced for only an instant). In this program, we recommend stretching vowel sounds and continuous consonant sounds (/mmm/ /aaa/ /nnn/), but stop sounds cannot be stretched in this way (/b/ /aaa/ /t/). When pronouncing stop sounds, try to drop any vowel sound in order to avoid distorting the sound: /b/, not "buh."

Continuous sounds: /f/, /l/, /m/, /n/, /r/, /s/, /v/, /w/, /y/, /z/
Stop sounds: /b/, /d/, /g/, /h/, /j/, /k/, /p/, qu/kw/, /t/, x/ks/

A guide to explaining sound production to children is printed on pp. 31–32.

Phonics

In Levels A–C, initial instruction for phonics skills uses a Blending Strategy Routine. The Routine provides explicit instruction for letter-sounds and word parts and includes connecting to previous learning, writing for sounds, modeling, group practice, corrective feedback, and individual practice.

Research Says "The very process of sounding a word out requires controlled attention to its separate letters and letter-sound correspondences as well as to the relationships among them that collectively determine the word's overall pronunciation and meaning."

Adams, Marilyn J. "Alphabetic Anxiety and Explicit, Systematic Phonics Instruction: A Cognitive Science Perspective." *Handbook of Early Literacy Research.* The Guilford Press, 2002.

"The phonics instruction in the two most successful classrooms for 'low' reading group students was very 'hands-on' and included 'writing for sounds'…. Thus, active decision making and thought is required to compare and contrast sounds and spelling patterns…."

Juel, Connie and Cecilia Minden-Cupp. "Learning to Read Words: Linguistic Units and Strategies." CIERA/University of Michigan, 1999.

Decodable Text

Student Readers for Levels A, B, and the first half of C provide children with immediate practice in reading words with the phonics elements they have just learned. Children apply these skills in connected, meaningful text that is constructed to have 100% potential for accuracy, that is, no untaught word types appear in the selections.

Research Says "As students learn the strategy for sounding out and blending words, it is crucial that they read these decodable words in stories."

Chard, David, Deborah C. Simmons, and Edward J. Kame'enui. "Word Recognition: Instructional and Curricular Basics and Implications." *What Reading Research Tells Us About Children With Diverse Learning Needs: Bases and Basics.* Lawrence Erlbaum, 1998.

Level A Student Reader

Swish! Swish! Ducks swim in a line.
Is Baby Duck with them? Yes!
Kick your legs, Baby Duck!

67

Research into Practice
Word Work

Fluent Word Reading

In Levels A–C, a Fluent Word Reading Routine is used each week to encourage children to preview, or think about all the sounds or word parts in a word, before they read the word. The routine and related activities give practice in all the week's phonics skills.

Research Says "To read new words in or out of text, children need to be taught how to decode the words' spellings. As students practice reading words, connections between letters and sounds are formed for those words in memory and students become able to read those words by sight rather than by decoding. As students practice reading words, they become able to read them automatically."

"[S]ight word learning depends upon the application of letter-sound correspondences. These provide the glue that holds the words in memory for quick reading."

Ehri, Linnea C. "Teaching Phonemic Awareness and Phonics: An Explanation of the National Reading Panel Meta-Analysis." *The Voice of Evidence in Reading Research.* Paul Brookes, 2004.

"Fluency is important because it exerts an important influence on comprehension; that is, to experience good comprehension, the reader must be able to identify words quickly and easily."

Samuels, S. Jay. "Reading Fluency: Its Development and Assessment." *What Research Has to Say About Reading Instruction,* 3rd ed. International Reading Association, 2002.

Level A Teacher's Guide

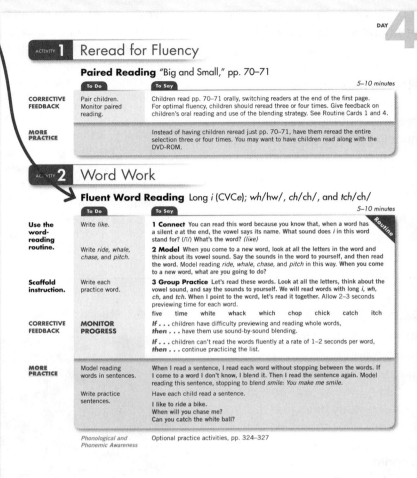

High-Frequency Words

The high-frequency words taught in this program are both irregular words and regular words that are not decodable at the point of introduction. A routine for learning these words involves saying the word, spelling it aloud, and then saying it again. Children are encouraged to decode the parts of the words that are decodable. (See the teacher's page reproduced on p. 22.)

Research Says "Since approximately 300 words account for 65% of the words in texts, rapid recognition of these words during the primary grades forms the foundation of fluent reading."

Hiebert, E. H., et al. "Every Child a Reader, Topic 4: High-frequency Words and Fluency." *Every Child a Reader: Applying Reading Research in the Classroom.* CIERA/University of Michigan, 1998.

2

ACTIVITY 1 Word Work

Phonics Long *i* Spelled *igh, ie,* Final *y*

	To Do	To Say	5–10 minutes
Teach long *i* spelled *igh, ie,* final *y.*	Write on the board or a transparency: *Why might you lie down?*	Read the sentence. Listen for the vowel sounds. How many words contain the sound long *i?* (3) How is the sound long *i* spelled in those words? (*y, igh, ie*) When *ie* or *igh* appear together, these letters usually stand for the sound long *i.* The letter *y* at the end of a word or syllable stands for either long *i* (as in *cry*) or long *e* (as in *baby*).	
Scaffold instruction.	Write *frightened* and *python.* Develop word meaning.	Would you feel like this if one of these came by? Let's read the words together. Remember to look for meaningful parts when you read a long word. Do you see any parts you know in these words? (Students may notice *fright* in *frightened.*) If you don't see any meaningful parts, you can look for chunks. Think about how you pronounce the vowel in each chunk. Model reading the chunks *py* and *thon* in *python.* Clarify that although the word *python* does not end in *y,* its first syllable does. Then help students read the chunks *fright* and *ened* in *frightened.*	
CORRECTIVE FEEDBACK	Write each practice word.	Have students practice reading these long *i* words. Correct any words students miss and have them reread the list. sighing nighttime fighting crying hydrant fireflies skylight	
MORE PRACTICE	Write more practice words.	Have students practice reading these additional words with long *i.* higher brightest lullaby shyness dragonfly replied terrified	

Amazing Words **Vocabulary**

	To Do	To Say	5 minutes
Review vocabulary.	Review the homework.	Ask students to go over answers and share their writing from Practice Book, p. 65. See Routine Card 1 for the multisyllabic word routine.	
	Deepen understanding of *protect.*	Remember, to *protect* means "to keep safe from harm or danger." Think about how the homes of the beaver and hermit crab *protect* them. What behaviors do you know that animals use to *protect* themselves?	

ACTIVITY 2 Comprehension

Compare and Contrast

	To Do	To Say	5 minutes
Scaffold instruction.	Introduce compare and contrast.	Today you will read about how animal parents keep their young safe. You already know that humans and animals have many similar behaviors. As you read, look for ways to compare and contrast animal behaviors with human behaviors. The compare and contrast strategy helps you make sense of the text and link it to what you already know. Look for clue words, such as *both, like, similar, but, however, unlike.*	
	Model the skill.	For example, if I read *both care for their young,* I know that here is something humans and animals do that is alike.	
	Distribute Graphic Organizer 4.	As you read "Keeping Baby Safe," look for ways that animals and humans are alike and different. Record likenesses and differences and words that signal them *(both, but)* on your graphic organizer. See Routine Card 7.	

Phonics

In Levels D–E, phonics skills are taught within the context of decoding multisyllabic words. Word parts and syllable patterns are explicitly taught, and vowel sounds are taught within syllables. Word meaning instruction is integrated into every lesson.

Research Says "Many poor decoders, even those who can read single-syllable words, have difficulty with multisyllabic words (Just & Carpenter, 1987). . . . An emphasis on multisyllabic word reading is critical because of the number of novel words introduced in intermediate and secondary textbooks and the potential for failing to learn from material if the words cannot be read. From fifth grade on, it is estimated that the average student encounters approximately 10,000 words per year that they have never previously encountered in print (Nagy & Anderson, 1984). Most of these new words are multisyllabic words."

Archer, Anita L. "Decoding and Fluency: Foundation Skills for Struggling Older Readers." *Learning Disability Quarterly,* vol. 26, no. 2, March 22, 2003.

Research into Practice
Vocabulary

Oral Vocabulary

Each week in Levels A and B children learn a set of conceptually related Amazing Words. These are words that are beyond children's reading ability. An Oral Vocabulary Routine introduces each word with a child-friendly definition, gives one or two examples, demonstrates the word's meaning, and gives children an opportunity to apply the word. Words are then displayed and used throughout the week in multiple contexts.

Research Says "A robust approach to vocabulary involves directly explaining the meanings of words along with thought-provoking, playful, and interactive follow-up."

Beck, Isabel L., Margaret G. McKeown, and Linda Kucan. *Bringing Words to Life: Robust Vocabulary Instruction.* The Guilford Press, 2002.

"Students learn word meanings when vocabulary is taught directly and explicitly through a variety of instructional strategies."

Edwards, E. C., G. Font, J. Baumann, and E. Boland. "Unlocking Word Meanings: Strategies and Guidelines for Teaching Morphemic and Contextual Analysis." *Vocabulary Instruction: Research to Practice.* The Guilford Press, 2004.

Level A Teacher's Guide

DAY 1

High-Frequency Words *there, who, your*

To Do	To Say
Teach high-frequency words. Display *there.*	**1 Say, Spell, Write** Use the Tested Vocabulary Cards. Display *there.* Here are some words that we won't sound out. We'll spell them. This word is *there, t, h, e, r, e* (point to each letter). What is this word? What are the letters in the word? Now you write *there.*
Point to the initial digraph in *there.*	**2 Identify Letter-Sounds** Let's look at the sounds in *there* that you do know. What are these letters? What is the sound for these letters? (*th*/th/) Continue with *r.*
Display *who* and *your.*	**3 Demonstrate Meaning** Tell me a sentence using *there.* Model a sentence. Repeat the Routine with *who* and *your.* Children can identify these letter-sounds: *your* (*y*/y/, *r*/r/). Have children write the words in their word banks. Add the words to the Word Wall. Point out that the words they are learning are on p. 79.

ACTIVITY 2 Build Concepts

Amazing Words Oral Vocabulary *features, mature, natural* — 5–10 minutes

To Do	To Say
Introduce oral vocabulary. Display p. 15 of *Sing with Me Big Book.* Play audio CD.	This week you will learn about how we change as we grow. Listen for the Amazing Words *features, mature,* and *natural* as I sing this song. Play or sing the song. Then have children sing it with you.
Scaffold instruction. Follow the Routine to teach *features, mature,* and *natural.*	**1 Introduce, Demonstrate, and Apply** **features** This song is about a growing puppy with cute *features.* A *feature* is a part of your face. Have children say the word. A person's eyes, nose, and chin are *features.* What other *features* can you name? **mature** The song says that as the puppy *matures,* he gets much bigger. When you *mature,* you grow fully. Have children say the word. People get taller as they *mature.* What is a way you are changing as you *mature?* **natural** The song says it's as *natural* as can be for the puppy to grow and grow and grow. *Natural* means normal or expected. Have children say the word. It is *natural* for babies to learn to walk after they crawl. If you are cold, what is the *natural* thing to do?
Display the words on the Amazing Words board.	**2 Display the Words** Have children say each word as they look at it. You can find sounds you know in big words. Read *fea/tures* as you run your hand under the letters. Find *f.* What sound does the *f* stand for? (/f/) Children can identify these letter-sounds: *mature* (*m*/m/), *natural* (*n*/n/, *a*/a/, *l*/l/).
Monitor understanding.	**3 Use the Words** Ask children to use each word in a sentence. Model a sentence if children need help.
MORE PRACTICE	Use oral vocabulary to discuss the song. What do you think might be cute about the puppy's *features*? How does the puppy change as he *matures*? What things does the puppy do that are *natural* for dogs?

WEEK 3 DAY 1 We All Grow   35

The vocabulary (oral in Levels A–B, written in Levels C–E) taught each week reflects the science or social studies concept for the week. Vocabulary was selected to build broad knowledge for understanding grade-level text and content area concepts.

Research Says "Much of the trouble students have comprehending informational material relates to the specific vocabulary that communicates major concepts. Research has documented that students' active involvement in identifying and learning vocabulary is critical to vocabulary learning and related content learning."

Ogle, Donna, and Camille L. Z. Blachowicz. "Beyond Literature Circles: Helping Students Comprehend Informational Texts." *Comprehension Instruction: Research-Based Best Practices.* The Guilford Press, 2002.

Concept Vocabulary

In Levels C–E, the teacher first uses a concept web to build understanding of the meanings and relationships among words in the lesson. The teacher then addresses decoding the word by modeling the multisyllabic word strategy and guiding students to look for meaningful parts and then chunking words with no recognizable parts.

Research Says "While a semantic map addresses the relationships between words, it allows students to generate new information based on their reading and learning. In this way, it expands their understanding of central concepts in the content areas."

Blachowicz, Camille and Peter J. Fisher. *Teaching Vocabulary in All Classrooms*, 2nd ed. Merrill Prentice Hall, 2002.

"Provide struggling readers a systematic and sustained program of vocabulary instruction that teaches them more important words and efficient strategies in less time."

Edwards, E. C., G. Font, J. Baumann, and E. Boland. "Unlocking Word Meanings: Strategies and Guidelines for Teaching Morphemic and Contextual Analysis." *Vocabulary Instruction: Research to Practice.* The Guilford Press, 2004.

"In our research we found rich instruction led not only to knowledge of word meanings but also to improved comprehension of stories containing those words."

McKeown, Margaret G. and Isabel I. Beck. "Direct and Rich Vocabulary Instruction." *Vocabulary Instruction: Research to Practice.* The Guilford Press, 2004.

ACTIVITY 1 Build Concepts

Amazing Words Vocabulary

	To Do	To Say	10–15 minutes
Develop oral vocabulary.	See Routine Card 6 and p. 198.	Introduce the Concept/Amazing Words with an oral routine prior to displaying them in print. Page 198 in this Teacher's Guide provides specific guidelines for introducing each word.	
Develop word meaning.	See Routine Card 5. Discuss pp. 7–9.	Have students read p. 7 and then look at the pictures on pp. 8–9. **Look at the pictures. What do you notice?** (People seem to be leaning in strange directions.) **Can you use the word** *perception* **to describe what's happening?** (Example: Our *perception* that people are tilting may be mistaken.)	
Scaffold instruction.	Create a concept web.	In the center of a web, write *Perception.* **This week's concept is** *perception. Perception* **is being aware through the senses.** Provide an example to demonstrate meaning. Our *perception* of a kitten comes from seeing (and perhaps touching) it.	
	Add the other vocabulary words.	Discuss the meaning of each word as it relates to perception, using the glossary as needed. (See p. 2 in this Teacher's Guide for definitions.)	

Concept and Language Goals

Model the multisyllabic word strategy.	Display each word. Say it as you display it.	Use Tested Vocabulary Cards. Follow this routine for each word: • **Look for Meaningful Parts** Do you recognize any parts of this word? What do these parts mean? Use the parts to read the word. As you introduce each word, be sure students notice the following: *in-* ("not"), *visible, magic, mystery.*	
	Think aloud.	• **Model** I see *in* at the beginning of *invisible.* I know *in* can mean "not." I also recognize the word *visible.* I know *visible* means "able to be seen." So I think *invisible* must mean "not visible, or not able to be seen." Point out the Latin root *vis* ("see") in *invisible.* Discuss other words with this root. *(visible, vision, visor)*	
	Point to *vanish.*	• **Chunk Words with No Recognizable Parts** Model how to chunk the word *vanish.* I see a chunk at the beginning of the word: *van.* I see a part at the end of the word: *ish.* I say each chunk slowly: *van ish.* I say the chunks fast to make a whole word: *vanish.* Is it a real word? Yes, I know the word *vanish.*	
		• Have students practice reading each word.	
Preview.	Read p. 6 with students.	Do you see any of the words we just learned on this page? Together with students, read the sentences on p. 6 describing each selection. Talk about how the vocabulary words might be used in the selections.	
MORE PRACTICE	Deepen understanding of *perception.*	Have students demonstrate understanding by answering questions. When you see something from a distance, can your *perception* be wrong? Why? Can you believe everything you *perceive,* or see? Give an example.	

4 **DAY 1** Perception

Level C Routine Card 2;
Levels D–E Routine Card 1

Routine Card 1

Multisyllabic Word Routine

Teach students this Routine for reading long words.

1 Look for Meaningful Parts Think about the meaning of each part. Use the parts to read the word. Help students analyze long words for base words, endings *(-ing, -ed, -s),* prefixes *(un-, re-, dis-, mis-, non-),* and suffixes *(-ly, -ness, -less, -ful,* and so on).

2 Chunk Words with No Recognizable Parts Say each chunk slowly. Then say the chunks fast to make a word.

Build Concepts

Build Background

Each week, the Student Reader selections focus on one aspect of the unit theme. The first selection every week is nonfiction. Its purpose is to increase students' background and concept knowledge for the topic of that week's reading selections. Children's text comprehension depends on their having some relevant prior knowledge.

> **Research Says** "Children's understanding of what they read is based on their experiences and knowledge; thus, teachers must do whatever they can to help children fill the gaps in their background knowledge."
>
> Gaskins, Irene W. "A Multidimensional Approach to Beginning Literacy." *Literacy and Young Children: Research-Based Practices.* The Guilford Press, 2003.

Informational Text

Two main selections follow the background building selection each week. They consist of one informational text and one narrative text. This high proportion of nonfiction is intended to help struggling readers build the concepts they need to succeed with content area materials.

Level A Teacher's Guide

ACTIVITY 3 Read a Passage

Build Background "We All Grow," pp. 56–63

	To Do	To Say	10 minutes
Develop language and concepts.	**Concept and Language Goals** See Routine Card 7. Read aloud p. 55 of the student book.	**Preview the Book** The selections this week are about how we change as we grow. Use p. 55 to preview. Ask children what they think each selection will be about.	
Scaffold instruction.	See Routine Card 6. Display pp. 56–63. Ask questions and elaborate on answers to develop language. Key concepts: *adult, baby, bird, change, duck, eggs, fins, fish, grow, hatch, little*	**Before Reading** Read the title aloud. Do a structured picture walk with children. pp. 56–57 What animal do you see? (a duck) Is a *duck* a *bird*? Yes, a duck is a bird because it has feathers and wings. Where did the *little* duck come from? (an egg) Like all birds, ducks *hatch* from *eggs*. pp. 58–59 The pictures show a *baby* duck and *adult* ducks. Point to the adult ducks. How do ducks *change* as they *grow*? (They get bigger. Their color changes.) pp. 60–61 What do you see? (fish) Where do *fish* live? (in water) The adult fish has *fins*. Point to fins. Fish use their fins for swimming. How do these fish change as they grow? (They get bigger and grow fins.) pp. 62–63 What else do you see? (a baby and mother) How do people change as they grow? (They get bigger and can do more.) Let's read to find out how some animals and people grow.	
Teach story words.	Write *baby* and *day*.	You will read these words in the selection. They are *baby* and *day*. Have children say the words and spell them. Review their meanings.	
Guide comprehension.	Read pp. 56–63. Model strategic reading. Use Routine Card 2.	**During Reading** Ask children to read along with you. As we read, ask yourself: What did I learn? What is this mainly about? Read pp. 56–63 aloud with the group. Stop on each page to model asking questions. For example, for p. 59: After I read, I ask myself, "What is this mainly about?" The author says, "In time, Baby Duck will get just as big." I think this part is mainly about how ducks grow and get big.	
Monitor independent reading.	Use Routine Card 3.	**Reread** Have children read the selection aloud together without you. Then have them read it on their own in a whisper. Listen in on each child. Monitor reading using Routine Card 3.	
Summarize.	Use oral vocabulary to develop the concept.	**After Reading** What did you learn about how ducks, fish, and people *mature*? What *features* change on ducks, fish, or people as they *mature*? Is it *natural* for you to get taller as you *mature*? What other changes are *natural*?	

Reread for Fluency "We All Grow," pp. 56–59

	To Do	To Say	5–10 minutes
CORRECTIVE FEEDBACK	Monitor oral reading.	Read pp. 56–59 aloud. Read them three or four times so your reading gets better each time. Give feedback on children's oral reading and use of the blending strategy. See Routine Cards 1 and 4.	
MORE PRACTICE		Instead of having children reread just pp. 56–59, have them reread the entire selection three or four times. Children can read along with the DVD-ROM.	
Homework		Practice Book, p. 70, Phonics: Long *i* (CVCe)	

36 **DAY 1** We All Grow

> **Research Says** "By the end of grade 1, children in [the] experimental group [those using the most informational texts] . . . were better writers of informational text than children in the control groups, had progressed more quickly in reading level, and had shown less decline in attitudes toward recreational reading. Experimental classes that entered school with relatively low literacy knowledge showed higher overall reading and writing ability by the end of grade 1 than comparable control classes."
>
> Palincsar, A. S. and Nell K. Duke. "The Role of Text and Text-Reader Interactions in Young Children's Reading Development and Achievement," *Elementary School Journal*, vol. 105, no. 2, 2004.

Develop Concepts

The Student Readers for Levels C–E have the same organizational structure as Levels A–B. Instruction for the background-building selections in these levels includes genre and text structure.

Research Says "An important feature of good reading instruction that needs to be present in the classroom is providing students with experience reading the range of text genres that we wish them to comprehend. Students will not learn to become excellent comprehenders of any given type of text without substantial experience reading and writing it."

Duke, Nell K. and P. David Pearson. "Effective Practices for Developing Reading Comprehension." *What Research Has to Say About Reading Instruction,* 3rd ed. International Reading Association, 2002.

"Students who learn to use the internal organization and structure of informational text are more able to comprehend and retain key ideas."

Ogle, Donna and Camille L. Z. Blachowicz. "Beyond Literature Circles: Helping Students Comprehend Informational Texts." *Comprehension Instruction: Research-Based Best Practices.* The Guilford Press, 2002.

Reproduced Teacher's Guide Page

DAY 1

ACTIVITY 2 Read a Passage

Develop Concepts "Mystery Spots," pp. 8–9

	To Do	To Say	10–15 minutes
Practice strategic prereading.	See Routine Card 2. Think aloud.	**Discuss Genre** Read the title on p. 8 and have students look at the illustrations on pp. 8–9. Model determining genre. The photographs are a clue that this is nonfiction. They look like photos of real places. I think this article will tell me what "mystery spots" are.	
Scaffold instruction.	Review text structure.	**Ask Questions** What questions do you ask yourself to help you understand nonfiction? (What did I learn? What is this mainly about?) As you read this article, ask these questions and look for the answers.	
Guide comprehension.	Read pp. 8–9 aloud.	**Read** Read the article as students follow along. Then read it a second time, having students join in. If necessary, stop at the end of each paragraph to check comprehension. Ask questions to promote discussion and develop the concept.	
Develop language and concepts.		• What is a mystery spot? • What happens at these mystery spots? • Do you believe these things really happen, or are they illusions? • What words on the concept web could help you describe a mystery spot?	
MORE PRACTICE		Have students reread "Mystery Spots." As they read, tell them to make a list of all the strange things that can happen in a mystery spot to share with family members tonight.	

Reread for Fluency "Mystery Spots," p. 9

	To Do	To Say	5 minutes
CORRECTIVE FEEDBACK	Monitor oral reading.	Read p. 9 aloud. Reread the page three or four times so your reading gets better each time. Give feedback on students' oral reading, using the *if . . . then* statements on Routine Card 4. Model fluent reading if necessary. You may want to have students read along with the DVD-ROM.	

ACTIVITY 3 Write

Response to Literature

	To Do	To Say	5 minutes
Prompt journal writing.	Write on the board or a transparency: *Can you always believe what you see?*	Take out your journals. This week we are reading about perception. Our question for this week is: *Can you always believe what you see?* Write an answer to this question based on what you read today. Have students write about the topic, using what they read and their own experiences.	
	Homework	Practice Book, p. 61, Vocabulary	

DAY 1 Perception   5

Research into Practice
Comprehension

Read a Passage

The week's comprehension skill is taught on Day 3 in Levels A–B. The teacher begins by introducing and then modeling the skill and asking children to apply it to a familiar example.

As children read the selection in the Student Reader, they answer questions that focus on the comprehension skill. After rereading, children retell the story, with a focus on the same comprehension skill.

Research Says "Comprehension improves when teachers design and implement activities that support the understanding of the texts that students will read in their classes."

Pearson, P. David and Nell K. Duke. "Comprehension Instruction in the Primary Grades." *Comprehension Instruction: Research-Based Best Practices.* The Guilford Press, 2002.

"Research has demonstrated that instruction and practice in retelling are likely to result in the development of comprehension, a sense of story structure, and oral complexity in a child's use of language."

Morrow, Leslie M. "Story Retelling: A Discussion Strategy to Develop and Assess Comprehension." *Lively Discussions! Fostering Engaged Reading.* International Reading Association, 1996.

3

Continued Oral Vocabulary

MORE PRACTICE

Use oral vocabulary to discuss growing and changing. **How do you know when a child is not an** *infant* **anymore? How are** *infants* **different from** *adults***?**

ACTIVITY 4 Read a Passage

Reading "Big and Small," pp. 70–77

10 minutes

To Do	To Say
Teach compare/ contrast. Introduce the skill.	Today you are going to learn how to compare things as you read. Comparing is saying how things are alike or different. Things that are alike are the same. Things that are different are not the same. For example, I can compare my shoes to yours. Point to one student's shoes. They are alike because they both keep our feet safe and dry. But they are different sizes and colors.
Scaffold instruction. Model the skill.	
Apply the skill.	Compare two objects in the room. **How are these two chairs alike?** (Both have legs, a place to sit, and a back.) **How are they different?** (different sizes, colors, and so on)
Develop language and concepts. See Routine Card 6. Display pp. 70–77. Model using key words and concepts.	**Before Reading** Read the title. Do a structured picture walk with children.
	pp. 70–71 The children are *measuring* how *tall* they are. Which one is taller? As children get older, they grow bigger and learn new things. The girl is learning to walk. When she was an *infant*, she couldn't walk at all.
Key concepts: *champ, infant, measuring, pool, smile, stack, tall*	pp. 72–73 I see a *smile* on the boy's face. What is he doing? Yes, he is reading and helping the girl stack blocks. To *stack* is to put things on top of one another.
	pp. 74–75 The boy can swim in a *pool* really well. He swims like a *champ*. Why do you think the girl isn't swimming?
	pp. 76–77 The girl and boy look bigger. How has the girl changed?
Monitor children's use of vocabulary.	Now turn to your partner and talk about the pictures, using the words I used.
Teach story words. Write *baby* and *new.*	You read this word yesterday. It is *baby.* You will read it again in today's story. You will also read the word *new.* Have children say and spell the words.
Guide comprehension. Use Routine Card 2. Read pp. 70–77.	**During Reading** Ask children to read along with you. As we read, ask yourself: How are the two children alike and how are they different? Read pp. 70–71 aloud with the group. Then ask: **How are Mitch and Liz different?** (Mitch is big; Liz is small. Liz can walk a little; Mitch walks well.)
	Read pp. 72–75 aloud with the group. Then ask: **How are Mitch and Liz alike?** (They have fun together. They like to play.) **How are they different?** (Mitch can stack blocks; Liz needs help stacking blocks. Mitch can swim; Liz cannot.)
	Read pp. 76–77 aloud with the group. Then ask: **What will happen to Liz when she gets big like Mitch?** (She will be able to do the things Mitch can do.)
Monitor independent reading. Use Routine Card 3.	**Reread** Have children read the selection aloud together without you. Then have them read it on their own in a whisper. Listen in on each child. Monitor reading, using Routine Card 3.
Guide retelling. Prompt children as they retell the story.	**After Reading** Have one child retell the story while the others assist. What did we learn about Mitch and Liz? How are they alike? How are they different? What is the big idea? (Little children grow and change.) See Monitoring Retelling, p. 292.
Homework	Practice Book, p. 72, Phonics: Digraphs *ch, tch* Practice Book, p. 73, Compare and Contrast

42   **DAY 3** We All Grow

2

ACTIVITY 1 Word Work

Phonics Compound Words

	To Do	To Say	5–10 minutes
Teach compound words.	Write on the board or a transparency: *How long can he hold his breath underwater?*	Remember, when you read a long word, look for meaningful parts. What parts do you see in this word? Frame *under* and *water*.	
		This word is a compound word. Compound words are made of two smaller words. To read a compound word, find the two smaller words. Put them together to read the word. The two smaller words in this word are *under* and *water*. The word is *underwater*.	
Scaffold instruction.	Develop word meaning.	Have students think and converse. If you're *underwater*, you must hold your breath. Why? What kinds of ships can travel *underwater*? Why do they do that?	
	Write *handcuffs*.	Here is another compound word. What are the two smaller words in this word? (*hand* and *cuffs*) Guide students in blending the word parts into the whole word. Develop word meaning by pointing to the handcuffs pictured on p. 13. Why do the police use handcuffs? How do handcuffs work?	
CORRECTIVE FEEDBACK	Write each practice word.	Have students practice reading these compound words. Correct any words students miss and have them reread the list.

cannot   something   tabletop   sometimes   watercolor | |
| **MORE PRACTICE** | Write more practice words. | Have students practice reading these compound words.

anything   stovetop   waterfall   underground   handmade | |

Amazing Words ★ Vocabulary

	To Do	To Say	5 minutes
Review vocabulary.	Review the homework.	Ask students to go over answers and share their writing from Practice Book p. 61. See Routine Card 1 for the multisyllabic word routine.	
	Deepen understanding of *illusion*.	Remember, an *illusion* is something that appears to be different from what it actually is. When you put a stick in the water, it sometimes looks as if it bends. Why is this an *illusion*? What else is an example of an *illusion*? Why?	

ACTIVITY 2 Comprehension

Sequence

	To Do	To Say	5 minutes
Scaffold instruction.	Introduce sequence.	Today you will read about a real person, Harry Houdini. When you read about a person's life, it's important to keep track of the sequence, or order, of events, because it may help you understand the person. Words like *first*, *next*, and *finally* give you clues to the sequence.	
	Model the skill.	For example, if I read that *at first* this person was terribly shy, but *later* she became a famous public speaker, I need to pay attention to the sequence to help me understand how this person changed.	
	Distribute Graphic Organizer 5.	As you read "Harry Houdini Escapes," look for words that help you track the sequence of events in Houdini's life. Add these words to your graphic organizer. See Routine Card 7.	

6 **DAY 2** Perception

Comprehension Skills

In Levels C–E a comprehension skill is taught each week on Day 2. The teacher defines the skill, explains why it is important, models his or her thought process by thinking aloud, and provides a graphic organizer to help students practice using the skill.

Read for Comprehension

As students read the day's selection, the teacher guides reading through the use of questions that help students practice using the comprehension skill.

Research Says "Diverse learners typically lag behind their peers in reading comprehension and demonstrate difficulty recognizing patterns in text, discerning relevant information, and recalling information. As a result, they require instruction that enables them to independently access text for comprehension and narrow the gap between themselves and their normally achieving peers."

Dickson, Shirley V., Deborah C. Simmons, Edward J. Kame'enui. "Text Organization: Instructional and Curricular Basics and Implications." *What Reading Research Tells Us About Children With Diverse Learning Needs: Bases and Basics.* Lawrence Erlbaum, 1998.

"Instruction and practice in summarizing not only improves students' ability to summarize text, but also their overall comprehension of text content."

Duke, Nell K. and P. David Pearson. "Effective Practices for Developing Reading Comprehension." *What Research Has to Say About Reading Instruction,* 3rd ed. International Reading Association, 2002.

Research into Practice
Fluency

Reread for Fluency

On Days 1–4, students reread a selection from the Student Reader to practice fluent reading. Rereading activities include choral reading, oral reading, paired reading, and reading along with the DVD-ROM. The Fluency Routine Card details ways to support students as they develop fluency by providing corrective feedback and modeling fluent reading.

> **Research Says** "Perhaps the best known of the strategies designed to support fluency development is that of repeated readings. . . . Generally, the students involved in using this strategy enjoy seeing the gains they make through their tracking of the changes in their reading and experience gratification when making visible improvement over a short period of time."
>
> Kuhn, Melanie. "How Can I Help Them Pull It All Together? A Guide to Fluent Reading Instruction." *Literacy and Young Children: Research-Based Practices.* The Guilford Press, 2003.

Model Fluent Reading

On Day 4, the teacher uses the Student Reader selection to model one aspect of fluent reading, such as rate, accuracy, expression, intonation, attention to punctuation, or characterization. Then children reread chorally for fluency.

> **Research Says** "The ability to read orally like a skilled reader after a few rereadings of a text is an important accomplishment and confidence builder for nonfluent readers, who are often embarrassed by their poor oral reading skills. [A] useful indicator of fluency is the ability to read a passage with expression."
>
> Samuels, S. Jay. "Reading Fluency: Its Development and Assessment." *What Research Has to Say About Reading Instruction,* 3rd ed. International Reading Association, 2002.

Level A Teacher's Guide

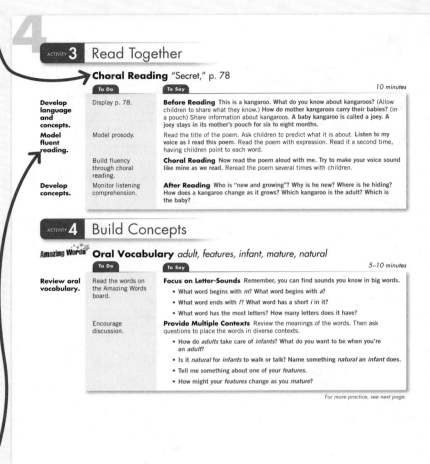

Level A Routine Card 4

Routine Card 4

Use these strategies to help children develop fluency.

- **Model Fluency** Model reading "as if you were speaking," attending to punctuation and phrasing and reading with expression (prosody).

- **Provide Corrective Feedback** Provide feedback on oral reading.

  If... students misread a word,
  then... help them decode it and have them reread the sentence.

  If... students read at an inappropriate or unsteady pace,
  then... model an appropriate pace, having children echo.

  If... students lack oral expression,
  then... model how to read based on the meaning of the passage. Tell students that their expression should show their understanding.

- **Monitor Fluency** See pp. 184–185 for assessment options.

DAY 4

ACTIVITY 3 Read a Passage

Read for Comprehension "Inside a Top Hat," pp. 18–25

10–15 minutes

	To Do	To Say
Scaffold instruction.	Monitor student engagement.	**Read** Have students read pp. 18–25 on their own and then discuss. For students who need more help, stop at the end of each page to discuss. After reading, ask questions.
	See Routine Card 3.	Who is telling this story? (Puff, a white rabbit) Who are the main characters? (the rabbit and Marva the Mysterious)
		What is the setting? Where is the rabbit? (inside a top hat, on a stage)
		What is the rabbit's goal? (to successfully complete the trick and amaze the audience)
		How does the rabbit get pulled out of the hat? (The rabbit is in a box hidden under a table, below the top hat. The magician reaches into the hat, opens the false bottom, and pulls the rabbit out of the box.)
	LOOK AT POINT OF VIEW	Explain whether you think the story would be as interesting if Marva had told it. (The rabbit's point of view makes it more interesting because you feel you are right there inside the hat during the trick.)
Assess comprehension.	Monitor understanding.	**After Reading** Have students discuss the What Do You Think? question. Prompt them to use sequence words in telling what steps the magician takes to prepare. Listen as they talk to assess comprehension.
MORE PRACTICE		**Reread** Have students reread pp. 23–24 and then explain the trick to a partner.

Reread for Fluency "Inside a Top Hat," pp. 21–24

5–10 minutes

	To Do	To Say
CORRECTIVE FEEDBACK	Pair students. Monitor paired reading.	Students read aloud pp. 21–24, switching readers at the end of each page. Have partners reread; now the other partner begins. For optimal fluency, students should reread three or four times. Give feedback, using Routine Card 4. You may want to have students read along with the DVD-ROM.
MORE PRACTICE	**READERS' THEATER**	Work with a group of three students to adapt pp. 21–24 as a radio play. Have students rehearse reading the parts, with one student being Puff, one a narrator, and one Marva.

ACTIVITY 4 Write

Response to Literature

5 minutes

	To Do	To Say
Prompt narrative writing.	Review pp. 22–24. Writing elements: organization, conventions	Tell how Marva performs the hat trick. Start with the sentence "First, Marva shows people that the hat is empty." Include other sequence words such as then and last to show the order of events. Use complete sentences to express your ideas.

DAY 4 Perception 11

Reread for Fluency

At Levels D–E, students continue to reread for fluency practice. On Days 1–4, students reread a selection from the Student Reader to practice fluent reading. Rereading activities include choral reading, oral reading, paired reading, reading along with the DVD-ROM, or Readers' Theater.

Research Says "The National Reading Panel report came out strongly in favor of repeated reading as a method for achieving fluency for nonimpaired students at least through grade 4, and on students with a variety of reading problems from elementary school through high school."

Samuels, S. Jay. "Reading Fluency: Its Development and Assessment." *What Research Has to Say About Reading Instruction*, 3rd ed. International Reading Association, 2002.

Level D Routine Card 4

Routine Card 4

Fluency Practice

Use one of these Routines for fluency practice. Provide corrective feedback as you listen to each child read.

- **Oral Reading** Have children read a passage orally. To achieve optimal fluency, children should reread the text three or four times.

- **Paired Reading** Reader 1 begins. Children read, switching readers at the end of each page. Then Reader 2 begins, as the partners reread the passage. For optimal fluency, children should reread three or four times.

- **Audio-Assisted Reading** The child reads aloud while listening to the recording. On the first reading, children point to words while they listen. On subsequent readings, they read along with the recording.

Research Bibliography

Adams, Marilyn J. "Alphabetic Anxiety and Explicit, Systematic Phonics Instruction: A Cognitive Science Perspective." *Handbook of Early Literacy Research.* The Guilford Press, 2002.

Archer, Anita L. "Decoding and Fluency: Foundation Skills for Struggling Older Readers." *Learning Disability Quarterly,* vol. 26, no. 2, March 22, 2003.

Beck, Isabel L., Margaret G. McKeown, and Linda Kucan. *Bringing Words to Life: Robust Vocabulary Instruction.* The Guilford Press, 2002.

Blachowicz, Camille and Peter J. Fisher. *Teaching Vocabulary in All Classrooms,* 2nd ed. Merrill Prentice Hall, 2002.

Chard, David, Deborah C. Simmons, and Edward J. Kame'enui. "Word Recognition: Instructional and Curricular Basics and Implications." *What Reading Research Tells Us About Children With Diverse Learning Needs: Bases and Basics.* Lawrence Erlbaum, 1998.

Dickson, Shirley V., Deborah C. Simmons, Edward J. Kame'enui. "Text Organization: Instructional and Curricular Basics and Implications." *What Reading Research Tells Us About Children With Diverse Learning Needs: Bases and Basics.* Lawrence Erlbaum, 1998.

Duke, Nell K. and P. David Pearson. "Effective Practices for Developing Reading Comprehension." *What Research Has to Say About Reading Instruction,* 3rd ed. International Reading Association, 2002.

Edwards, E. C., G. Font, J. Baumann, and E. Boland. "Unlocking Word Meanings: Strategies and Guidelines for Teaching Morphemic and Contextual Analysis." *Vocabulary Instruction: Research to Practice.* The Guilford Press, 2004.

Ehri, L. C., et al. "Phonemic Awareness Instruction Helps Children Learn to Read: Evidence from the National Reading Panel's Meta-Analysis." *Reading Research Quarterly,* vol. 36, no. 3, 2001.

Ehri, Linnea C. "Teaching Phonemic Awareness and Phonics: An Explanation of the National Reading Panel Meta-Analysis." *The Voice of Evidence in Reading Research.* Paul Brookes, 2004.

Gaskins, Irene W. "A Multidimensional Approach to Beginning Literacy." *Literacy and Young Children: Research-Based Practices.* The Guilford Press, 2003.

Hiebert, E. H., et al. "Every Child a Reader, Topic 4: High-frequency Words and Fluency." *Every Child a Reader: Applying Reading Research in the Classroom.* CIERA/ University of Michigan, 1998.

Juel, Connie and Cecilia Minden-Cupp. "Learning to Read Words: Linguistic Units and Strategies." CIERA/ University of Michigan, 1999.

Kuhn, Melanie. "How Can I Help Them Pull It All Together? A Guide to Fluent Reading Instruction." *Literacy and Young Children: Research-Based Practices.* The Guilford Press, 2003.

Lipson, Marjorie Y., Sheila W. Valencia, Karen K. Wixson, and Charles W. Peters. "Integration and Thematic Teaching: Integration to Improve Teaching and Learning." *Language Arts,* vol. 70, April 1993.

McKeown, Margaret G. and Isabel I. Beck. "Direct and Rich Vocabulary Instruction." *Vocabulary Instruction: Research to Practice.* The Guilford Press, 2004.

Morrow, Leslie M. "Story Retelling: A Discussion Strategy to Develop and Assess Comprehension." *Lively Discussions! Fostering Engaged Reading.* International Reading Association, 1996.

Ogle, Donna and Camille L. Z. Blachowicz. "Beyond Literature Circles: Helping Students Comprehend Informational Texts." *Comprehension Instruction: Research-Based Best Practices.* The Guilford Press, 2002.

Palincsar, A. S. and Nell K. Duke. "The Role of Text and Text-Reader Interactions in Young Children's Reading Development and Achievement," *Elementary School Journal,* vol. 105, no. 2, 2004.

Pearson, P. David and Nell K. Duke. "Comprehension Instruction in the Primary Grades." *Comprehension Instruction: Research-Based Best Practices.* The Guilford Press, 2002.

Samuels, S. Jay. "Reading Fluency: Its Development and Assessment." *What Research Has to Say About Reading Instruction,* 3rd ed. International Reading Association, 2002.

Vaughn, Sharon and Sylvia Linan-Thompson. *Research-Based Methods of Reading Instruction.* Association for Supervision and Curriculum Development, 2004.

Vaughn, Sharon, Sylvia Linan-Thompson, Kamiar Kouzekanani, Diane Pedrotty, Shirley Dickson, and Shelly Blozis. "Reading Instruction Grouping for Students with Reading Difficulties." *Remedial and Special Education,* vol. 24, no. 5, September/October 2003.

Sound Production Cue Chart

Letter	Phoneme	Teacher Says:
a	/a/	When you say /aaa/, your jaw and tongue are down. Say /aaa/ and feel your jaw and tongue go down.
b	/b/	When you say /b/, your lips start out together. Then they open and a tiny puff of air comes out of your mouth. Put your lips together and say /b/. Feel the tiny puff of air. Feel your voice box on when you say /b/.
c	/k/	When you say /k/, the back of your tongue is humped and in the back of your mouth. Say /k/ and feel that the back of your tongue is humped and in the back of your mouth.
d	/d/	When you say /d/, the tip of your tongue touches above your top teeth. Say /d/ and feel the tip of your tongue touch above your top teeth. Put your hand on your throat and see if your voice box is on when you say /d/. Yes, your throat moves when you say /d/ because your voice box is on.
e	/e/	When you say /eee/, your mouth is open and your tongue is behind your bottom teeth. Say /eee/. Did your mouth open? Yes, your mouth is open and your tongue is behind your bottom teeth. Say /eee/.
f	/f/	When you say /fff/, your top teeth touch your bottom lip. Say /fff/ and feel your top teeth touch your bottom lip.
g	/g/	When you say /g/, your mouth is open and your tongue is humped at the back of your mouth. Put your hand on your throat and see if your voice box is on. Yes, your throat moves when you say /g/ because your voice box is on.
h	/h/	When you say /h/, some air comes out of your mouth. Put your hand in front of your mouth. Say /h/ and feel the air. Say /h/.
i	/i/	When you say /iii/, your mouth is open and your tongue is slightly lowered. Say /iii/. Is your mouth open and is your tongue slightly lowered? Yes, your mouth is open and your tongue is slightly lowered. Say /iii/.
j	/j/	When you say /j/, your tongue is up and your lips are open. Watch, /j/. Open your lips and say /j/.
k	/k/	When you say /k/, the back of your tongue is humped and in the back of your mouth. Say /k/ and feel that the back of your tongue is humped and in the back of your mouth.
l	/l/	When you say /lll/, the tip of your tongue touches above your top teeth and stays there. Say /lll/ and feel the tip of your tongue touch above your top teeth and stay there.

Based on the Sound Production Cue Card developed by the team that created Project Optimize.

Letter	Phoneme	Teacher Says:
m	/m/	When you say /mmm/, your lips come together. Put your lips together and say /mmm/.
n	/n/	When you say /nnn/, your tongue is behind your top teeth and a little air comes out your nose. Say /nnn/. Was your tongue behind your top teeth and did a little air come out your nose? Yes, your tongue was behind your top teeth and a little air came out your nose. Say /nnn/.
o	/o/	When you say /ooo/, your mouth is open and your jaw drops. Put your hand under your chin and say /ooo/. See, your mouth opened and your jaw dropped.
p	/p/	When you say /p/, your lips start out together. Then they open, and a puff of air comes out of your mouth. Put your lips together and say /p/. Feel the puff of air that comes out of your mouth.
q	/kw/	When you say /kw/, the back of your tongue is humped and in the back of your mouth. Then your lips make a circle. Say /kw/.
r	/r/	When you say /rrr/, your voice box is turned on and the tip of your tongue goes up and toward the roof of your mouth. Say /rrr/ and feel the tip of your tongue go up and toward the roof of your mouth. Put your hand on your throat and see if your voice box is on when you say /rrr/; /rrr/. Yes, your voice box is on when you say /rrr/.
s	/s/	When you say /sss/, the tip of your tongue touches above your top teeth. It makes a snake sound. Say /sss/ and hear the snake sound.
t	/t/	When you say /t/, the tip of your tongue touches above your top teeth. Say /t/ and feel the tip of your tongue touch above your top teeth.
u	/u/	When you say /uuu/, your mouth is open and your tongue is down. Say /uuu/. Was your mouth open and tongue down?
v	/v/	When you say /vvv/, your top teeth touch your bottom lip and your throat moves a little. Say /vvv/ and feel your teeth touch your bottom lip.
w	/w/	When you say /www/, your lips make a circle. Say /www/ and feel your lips make a circle.
x	/ks/	When you say /ks/, it begins with the back of your tongue humped and in the back of your mouth. Then it makes a snake sound. Say /ks/.
y	/y/	When you say /yyy/, your tongue is behind your lower teeth and your mouth is open. Say /yyy/ and feel your tongue behind your lower teeth.
z	/z/	When you say /zzz/, the tip of your tongue touches above your top teeth and your voice box is on. Put your hand on your throat and see if your voice box is on when you say /zzz/; /zzz/. Yes, your voice box is on when you say /zzz/.

MY SiDEWALKS ON
SCOTT FORESMAN
READING STREET
Teacher's Guide

Level D
Volume 1

PEARSON
Scott Foresman

Glenview, Illinois • Boston, Massachusetts • Chandler, Arizona •
Upper Saddle River, New Jersey

Copyright © 2011 by Pearson Education, Inc., or its affiliates. All Rights Reserved. Printed in the United States of America. This publication is protected by copyright, and permission should be obtained from the publisher prior to any prohibited reproduction, storage in a retrieval system, or transmission in any form or by any means, electronic, mechanical, photocopying, recording, or likewise. For information regarding permissions, write to Pearson Curriculum Group Rights & Permissions, One Lake Street, Upper Saddle River, New Jersey 07458.

Pearson, Scortt Foresman, and Pearson Scott Foresman are trademarks, in the U.S. and/or other countries, of Pearson Education, Inc., or its affiliates.

ISBN-13: 978-0-328-45345-0
ISBN-10:   0-328-45345-5
7 8 9 10 V064 14 13

A Safe Place to Learn

Fit Your Framework

NO MATTER HOW YOU FRAME IT, IT FITS.

My Sidewalks provides the essential elements of Response to Intervention (RTI) in a validated instructional design for accelerating reading achievement.

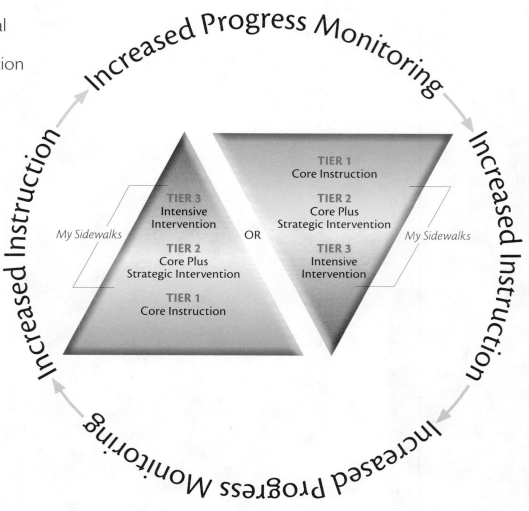

Increased Progress Monitoring

Increased Instruction

Increased Instruction

Increased Progress Monitoring

My Sidewalks

TIER 3
Intensive Intervention

TIER 2
Core Plus Strategic Intervention

TIER 1
Core Instruction

OR

TIER 1
Core Instruction

TIER 2
Core Plus Strategic Intervention

TIER 3
Intensive Intervention

My Sidewalks

iv

Three Steps Toward Creating a Safe Place to Learn

1 SUSTAINED INSTRUCTION

My Sidewalks contains lesson plans for 30 full weeks. Every day, for 30–45 minutes, you can put your struggling readers—monolingual and English Language Learners—on solid footing. With instruction that is systematic and explicit, *My Sidewalks* helps you create a learning environment that is both consistent and predictable so your students can sustain progress every day. Your students will make strides with:

- Increased time on task
- Explicit teacher modeling
- Multiple response opportunities
- Tasks broken down into smaller steps

2 INTENSIVE LANGUAGE AND CONCEPT DEVELOPMENT

Research shows that a child's vocabulary entering first grade is a strong predictor of comprehension at eleventh grade. This is a critical area where Tier III students are deficient. *My Sidewalks* helps build a foundation for future comprehension success with daily, intensive language and concept development:

- Unit themes organized around science and social studies concepts
- Five to seven new vocabulary words tied directly to the week's theme
- Four weekly selections that build on the unit concept
- Concepts that connect from week to week

3 CRITICAL COMPREHENSION SKILLS

Along with daily vocabulary instruction, *My Sidewalks* provides explicit and systematic instruction on the comprehension skills and strategies researchers have identified as being the most critical for developing reading success:

- Drawing Conclusions
- Compare/Contrast
- Sequence
- Main Idea and Supporting Details

Components

Student Readers

My Sidewalks takes high-interest reading selections and puts them in an engaging magazine format. Every week, your Tier III students read four different selections that work together to develop a science or social studies concept. Week in and week out, these fiction and nonfiction selections help your students get a better understanding of the overall unit theme (the same themes and concepts found in *Scott Foresman Reading Street!*). 30 lessons, organized into 6 units. (5 units at Level A)

Teacher's Guides

My Sidewalks keeps your intervention instruction running smoothly. The Teacher's Guides contain everything you need for Tier III instruction. Complete lesson plans focus on high priority skills and provide daily routines with suggested time frames to help you keep your instruction focused and on time.
2 Volumes per level

Practice Books

Finally, a practice book written specifically for Tier III students. These consumable workbooks/ blackline masters give your students additional practice in phonics, comprehension, vocabulary, and writing. Books are available for each level and have multiple practice selections for every lesson. Plus, each page contains a Home Activity to strengthen the school-home connection. *A Teacher's Manual with answer key is also available.*

Benchmark Readers

What's working for your students? Which students need more targeted instruction? Accurately assess your Tier III students' progress with these unit readers. Each 8-page book contains examples of all the skills targeted in the unit so you can find out instantly whether a student is ready to transition out of *My Sidewalks* or still needs additional intervention.

Alphabet Cards

Help your Tier III students practice letter names and sounds with these colorful cards. *(Level A)*

Assessment Book

All your assessment needs, all in one book. Along with assessment instruction, you'll find progress-monitoring forms, placement tests, unit assessments in individual and group formats, and guidelines for students to exit *My Sidewalks*.

Finger Tracing Cards

Hands-on Tracing Cards allow students to connect sounds to letters while they learn their letter shapes. *(Level A)*

Manipulative Letter Tiles

Sturdy, plastic, manipulative tiles are easy for little fingers to practice word building. *(Levels A–B)*

Student Readers DVD-ROM

Recordings of the Student Readers read at a fluent pace give Tier III students complete access to every selection.

Sing with Me Big Book

Large, illustrated Big Books develop oral vocabulary and build background. Pages inspire small group discussions using vocabulary words and include songs that demonstrate the words in context. *(Levels A–B)*

Sing with Me Audio CD

Song recordings accompany each Sing with Me Big Book. *(Levels A–B)*

Sound-Spelling Cards

Colorful cards with instructional routines introduce each sound-spelling in the intervention lesson. *(Levels A–C)*

Sound-Spelling Wall Charts

Large-size formats of the Sound-Spelling Cards are ideal for use in small-group instruction. *(Levels A–C)*

Tested Vocabulary Cards

Flash cards build important vocabulary knowledge and provide additional practice.

Welcome to *My Sidewalks*

This handy guide shows you how to provide effective instruction, manage your time, and help students catch up.

Write-On/Wipe-Off Cards

These cards have a write-on/ wipe-off surface and writing lines for practicing letter forms, letter-sounds, spelling, and writing.

Level	Grade
A	1
B	2
C	3
D	4
E	5

MY SIDEWALKS ON SCOTT FORESMAN READING STREET
Intensive Reading Intervention

Authors

My Sidewalks was created by the leading researchers in the area of reading intervention instruction. Their work has helped struggling readers and is the basis for the 3-Tier model of instruction.

"Research shows that for students to make significant progress, they need systematic and intensive instruction that is tailored to their current instructional level."

Sharon Vaughn

Connie Juel, Ph.D.
Professor of Education
School of Education
Stanford University

Jeanne R. Paratore, Ed.D.
Associate Professor of Education
Department of Literacy and
Language Development
Boston University

Deborah Simmons, Ph.D.
Professor
College of Education and
Human Development
Texas A&M University

Sharon Vaughn, Ph.D.
H.E. Hartfelder/Southland
Corporation Regents
Professor
University of Texas

Contents

Unit 1   Turning Points

Unit 2   Teamwork

Unit 3 Patterns in Nature

Resources

Distinctions Between Levels

Understanding the Levels of *My Sidewalks*

The goal of the *My Sidewalks* program is to enable struggling readers to succeed with the reading material used in their regular classrooms. To achieve this, *My Sidewalks* focuses on accelerating students' acquisition of priority skills. Each level of *My Sidewalks* is designed to provide a year and a half of reading growth. Consequently there is an overlap of skills between one *My Sidewalks* level and the next.

These pages describe the skills students should have to successfully begin each level of *My Sidewalks* and what they will learn in that level. Use the Placement Tests to help you determine the correct level at which to enter each student.

To begin this level a child should know:	In this level, the instructional focus is on:
Early Reading Intervention (Grade K)	
	• Phonological and phonemic awareness • Letter names and sounds • Blending regular short-vowel words • Sentence reading
Level A (Grade 1)	
• Some phonological awareness	• Phonemic awareness • Letter names • Consonants: Individual letter-sounds, blends, and digraphs • Vowels: Short, long (CVC*e*), and *r*-controlled • Blending words and fluent word reading • High-frequency words • Oral vocabulary and concept development • Building fluency (40–60 wcpm) • Passage reading and retelling

To begin this level a student should know:	**In this level**, the instructional focus is on:

Level B (Grade 2)

- Letter names
- Individual consonant letter-sounds
- Some basic high-frequency words
- And be able to read Benchmark Reader A2 with accuracy and comprehension

- Phonemic awareness
- Letter names and sounds
- Blending words and fluent word reading
- High-frequency words
- Oral vocabulary and concept development
- Building fluency (70–90 WCPM)
- Passage reading and retelling

Level C (Grade 3)

- Consonants: Individual letter-sounds, blends, and digraphs
- Vowels: Short and long (CVCe) and be able to distinguish between them
- A wider range of high-frequency words
- And be able to read Benchmark Reader B2 with accuracy and comprehension

- Blending words and fluent word reading
- Decoding multisyllabic words, including words with one or more affixes
- Phonics: Vowels
- Concept vocabulary
- Building fluency (100–120 WCPM)
- Passage reading and summarizing

Level D (Grade 4)

- Consonants: Individual letter-sounds, blends, and digraphs
- Vowels: Short and long (CVCe) and be able to distinguish between them
- How to decode regular VC/CV words with short and long (CVCe) vowels
- Many high-frequency words
- And be able to read Benchmark Reader C1 with accuracy and comprehension

- Decoding multisyllabic words, including words with one or more affixes
- Phonics: Less frequent vowel patterns, such as vowel diphthongs
- Concept vocabulary
- Building fluency (110–130 WCPM)
- Passage reading and summarizing

Level E (Grade 5)

- Consonants: Individual letter-sounds, blends, and digraphs
- Vowels: Short and long (CVCe) and be able to distinguish between them
- How to decode regular VC/CV words with short and long (CVCe) vowels
- Many high-frequency words
- And be able to read Benchmark Reader D1 with accuracy and comprehension

- Decoding multisyllabic words, including words with one or more affixes
- Phonics: Less frequent vowel patterns, such as vowel diphthongs
- Concept vocabulary
- Building fluency (120–140 WCPM)
- Passage reading and summarizing

Differentiating Instruction

The charts on these pages show instruction during a week in *My Sidewalks*. The charts can also be used as guides for **reteaching** or **accelerating** through parts of the lessons. In addition, the *If... then...* directions will help you identify how to customize instruction for your students.

Reteaching To meet the needs of the lowest performing readers, it may be necessary to modify the pacing and intensity of instruction. Activities shown in gray boxes on the charts may be repeated for these students.

Accelerating A child who shows mastery of skills following initial instruction may be ready for instruction at a faster pace with fewer repetitions. Activities shown in green boxes might be omitted for these students.

Levels A–B

	PHONEMIC AWARENESS	PHONICS	HIGH-FREQUENCY WORDS	CONCEPTS/ ORAL VOCABULARY	PASSAGE READING	FLUENCY	WRITING
Day 1	Phonemic Awareness	Blending Strategy	High-Frequency Words	Concepts/ Oral Vocabulary	Read a Passage	Reread for Fluency	
Day 2	Phonemic Awareness	Blending Strategy	High-Frequency Words		Read a Passage	Reread for Fluency	Write
Day 3	Phonemic Awareness	Blending Strategy	High-Frequency Words	Concepts/ Oral Vocabulary	Read a Passage	Reread for Fluency	
Day 4		Fluent Word Reading		Concepts/ Oral Vocabulary	Read Together	Reread for Fluency	Write
Day 5		Assess Word Reading	Assess Word/ Sentence Reading	Check Oral Vocabulary	Assess Passage Reading/ Reread		Write

■ **Reteach** ■ **Omit for acceleration**

If... a child is struggling with word reading,
then... reteach Word Work activities and include More Practice extensions.

If... a child lacks oral language,
then... elicit extended language from the child, provide ample opportunities for the child to respond when building concepts, and expand the structured picture walks before reading each selection.

If... a child's reading is so slow that it hinders comprehension,
then... provide additional models of fluent reading, give more corrective feedback during fluency practice, and include More Practice extensions when rereading for fluency.

If... an English learner struggles with sounds,
then... repeat appropriate practice activities.

Levels C–E

	VOCABULARY	COMPREHENSION	PASSAGE READING	PHONICS	FLUENCY	WRITING
Day 1	Vocabulary		Read a Passage	Blending Strategy (Level C)	Reread for Fluency	Write (Levels D–E)
Day 2	Vocabulary	Comprehension Skill	Read a Passage	Phonics	Reread for Fluency	Write (Levels D–E)
Day 3	Vocabulary	Comprehension Skill Assess (Levels D–E)	Read a Passage	Phonics	Reread for Fluency	Write
Day 4	Vocabulary	Comprehension Skill/Strategy Assess (Levels D–E)	Read Together (Level C) Read a Passage (Levels D–E)	Phonics Review (Level C)	Reread for Fluency	Write
Day 5	Vocabulary	Assess Comprehension	Read Together (Levels D–E) Reread (Level C)	Assess Sentence Reading (Level C)	Assess Fluency	Write

If... a student is struggling with word reading, **then...** reteach Vocabulary and Phonics activities and include More Practice extensions.

If... a student lacks oral language, **then...** elicit extended language from the student, provide ample opportunities for the student to respond when building concepts, and expand the After Reading discussion for each selection.

If... a student's reading is so disfluent that it hinders comprehension, **then...** provide additional models of fluent reading, give more corrective feedback during fluency practice, and include More Practice extensions for fluency.

If... a student lacks comprehension and is unable to retell or summarize, **then...** reteach comprehension skills and strategies, provide additional modeling of retelling and summarizing, and give more corrective feedback during practice.

If... an English learner lacks English vocabulary for known concepts, **then...** say the unknown English word, have the student repeat it, and ask questions that will allow the student to use the word in a meaningful context.

Meeting ELL Needs

My Sidewalks was developed to provide intensive reading intervention for Tier III students struggling to read and write. The program has been designed to reflect current research on literacy instruction for English language learners (ELLs)—not as additional notes, but integral to all elements of instruction. From its original conception, instruction to meet the needs of both native English speakers and English learners (who have some basic English conversational skills) has been integrated into the curriculum, teaching practices, and learning activities. Since English language learners acquire literacy skills in much the same way as their English-speaking peers, both will benefit from the same good instructional practices.

Research Says "ELLs at risk for reading problems profit considerably in their literacy skills from systematic and explicit interventions that address the core reading skills of beginning reading: phonemic awareness, phonics, fluency, vocabulary, and comprehension. . . . Our work with ELLs suggests that postponing interventions to wait for language to become more proficient is not necessary, and supporting literacy acquisition in the language of instruction provided by the school for students at risk is beneficial." Vaughn, S., Linan-Thompson, S., *et al.* 2005. "Interventions for 1st Grade English Language Learners with Reading Difficulties." *Perspectives*, 31 (2), p. 31–35.

English language learners need. . .	My Sidewalks provides. . .
Phonemic Awareness	
• to develop familiarity with the sounds of English	• explicit and systematic modeling of sounds in words
• to practice identifying, segmenting, and blending sounds in English words	• scaffolded instruction that evokes active responses by children
• to learn the sounds of English within words, in isolation and in meaningful contexts	• ample practice identifying, counting, segmenting, blending, adding, and deleting sounds in words
	• clear lessons that tie phonemic awareness to phonics
Phonics	
• to learn the letters and letter-sound correspondences of English	• explicit phonics instruction with regular practice
• to master identifying, segmenting, and blending the variety of sounds that letters represent in English words	• routines for practicing the core English phonics elements
• to understand how to complete phonics activities	• clear, step-by-step blending strategies understandable to students learning English as they learn to read
• to use the phonics they learn—seeing, saying, reading, and writing words—with growing proficiency	• active learning—hearing, speaking, reading, and writing—that ties phonics to decodable text (Levels A–C) and to decoding of multisyllabic words in text (Levels D–E)
• to learn the sounds and spellings of written English words in meaningful contexts	• practice decoding and reading words related to concepts explored in oral language and texts

English language learners need. . .	My Sidewalks provides. . .

Vocabulary

• to develop oral vocabulary in English, including words already familiar to English-speaking children • to learn functional English vocabulary, including high-frequency words • to encounter new words in meaningful oral and written contexts • to hear, see, and use new words repeatedly • to learn academic English vocabulary	• multiple exposures to each vocabulary word • a routine for learning high-frequency words (at Levels A and B) • a routine for learning oral vocabulary (at Levels A and B) • a focus on words related to science and social studies concepts • multiple opportunities to practice using and producing oral and written vocabulary, including academic English • development of deep meaning for key concepts and words

Comprehension

• to continually improve their comprehension of oral English • to read comprehensible texts and develop abilities to interpret more complex written language • to use their prior knowledge in order to comprehend texts • to acquire understanding of sentence structures and text organizations of academic English • to learn about cultural concepts embodied in the readings	• an emphasis on oral language and concept development, to improve students' English proficiency and comprehension • an abundance of comprehensible reading materials focused on science and social studies concepts • modeling, instruction, and practice of priority comprehension skills and reading strategies, including prereading routines • explicit instructional routines that model new skills, build on students' prior knowledge, use visual elements to clarify ideas, and incorporate ample practice and review • exposure to the structures of English, text organization, and cultural concepts of the readings and lessons

Fluency

• to hear models of fluent reading of instructional-level texts • to practice and improve their fluent reading • corrective feedback on their reading	• teacher modeling to familiarize students with expressive, meaningful reading of instructional-level academic texts • engaging practice opportunities that include choral reading, paired reading, and reading with AudioText, which provide many models for building fluency • instruction in reading rate, accuracy, expression, and intonation • repeated readings and corrective feedback, to help students see words in context and pronounce them • progress monitoring and assessments to aid in fluency growth

Writing

• to develop their English proficiency by writing as well as reading • to write about ideas related to reading topics • to practice communicating their ideas in English through manageable, interesting writing activities	• opportunities to respond to literature about themes • scaffolded writing instruction including sentence frames for young children, manageable writing prompts for all students, and self-checking activities • feedback for writers from teacher and fellow students

Unit 1
Skills Overview

Why These Skills? *My Sidewalks* focuses on the priority skills students need in order to succeed at learning to read. **Priority skills** are the critical elements of reading—phonemic awareness (Levels A–C), phonics, fluency, vocabulary, and text comprehension. Scientifically based research has shown that these skills are the foundations of reading and must be taught in a systematic sequence.

		WEEK 1 5–30 **Diversity**	**WEEK 2** 31–56 **Exploration**
Phonics	Decoding	Closed Syllables with Short Vowels	Closed Syllables with Long Vowels
	Spelling	Words with Closed Syllables and Short Vowels	Words with Closed Syllables and Long Vowels
Vocabulary	Concept	**What brings different people together?**	**What can we learn by exploring new places?**
Amazing Words	Vocabulary	*backgrounds, culture, ethnic, homesick, translated, understanding*	*area, confused, device, perspective, pioneers, territory, voyage*
Comprehension	Skill	Sequence	Draw Conclusions
	Strategies	Preview, Ask Questions, Use Story Structure, Summarize	Preview, Ask Questions, Use Story Structure, Summarize
	Writing	Response to Literature	Response to Literature
Fluency		Reread for Fluency Practice	Reread for Fluency Practice

57–82 **Travel America**	83–108 **The Southwest**	109–134 **The West**	
Plurals and Inflected Endings -s, -es, -ies	Verb Endings	Prefixes un-, re-, in-, dis-	
Words with Endings	Words with Verb Endings	Words with Prefixes	
What can we learn about the United States as we travel?	**What is special about the landscape of the Southwest?**	**What is special about the West?**	
itineraries, journey, miles, mode, route, transportation, views	arid, canyon, carved, cliffs, frontier, guide, hiking	astonishing, eruptions, formed, gigantic, naturally, unbelievable	
Sequence	Compare and Contrast	Main Idea	
Preview, Ask Questions, Use Story Structure, Summarize	Preview, Ask Questions, Use Story Structure, Summarize	Preview, Ask Questions, Use Story Structure, Summarize	
Response to Literature	Response to Literature	Response to Literature	
Reread for Fluency Practice	Reread for Fluency Practice	Reread for Fluency Practice	

Unit 2
Skills Overview

Why These Skills? *My Sidewalks* focuses on the priority skills students need in order to succeed at learning to read. **Priority skills** are the critical elements of reading—phonemic awareness (Levels A–C), phonics, fluency, vocabulary, and text comprehension. Scientifically based research has shown that these skills are the foundations of reading and must be taught in a systematic sequence.

		WEEK 1 5–30 **New Ideas**	WEEK 2 31–56 **Working Together**
Phonics	Decoding	*r*-Controlled Syllables *ar, or, ore*	*r*-Controlled Syllables *er, ir, ur*
	Spelling	Words with *ar, or, ore*	Words with *er, ir, ur*
Vocabulary	Concept	**What can we learn from the talents of others?**	**How can we work together to achieve a goal?**
Amazing Words	Vocabulary	*awareness, comprehend, exhibit, experience, horizons, interactive*	*accomplished, collaboration, cooperate, members, orchestra, teamwork*
Comprehension	Skill	Compare and Contrast	Draw Conclusions
	Strategies	Preview, Ask Questions, Use Story Structure, Summarize	Preview, Ask Questions, Use Story Structure, Summarize
	Writing	Response to Literature	Response to Literature
Fluency		Reread for Fluency Practice	Reread for Fluency Practice

WEEK 3	WEEK 4	WEEK 5
57–82	83–108	109–134
Team Effort	**A Job Well Done**	**Our Nation's Capital**
Comparative Endings *-er, -est*	Open and Closed Syllables	Suffixes *-ly, -ful, -ness, -less*
Words with *-er, -est*	Words with Open and Closed Syllables	Words with Suffixes
What can teams accomplish?	**How does working together get the job done?**	**What happens in our nation's capital?**
extraordinary, fantastic, inspiration, sculptures, skillful	*career, contribution, energy, gear, option, workers*	*capital, Capitol, dedicated, executive, memorabilia, museum*
Draw Conclusions	Sequence	Main Idea
Preview, Ask Questions, Use Story Structure, Summarize	Preview, Ask Questions, Use Story Structure, Summarize	Preview, Ask Questions, Use Story Structure, Summarize
Response to Literature	Response to Literature	Response to Literature
Reread for Fluency Practice	Reread for Fluency Practice	Reread for Fluency Practice

Unit 3

Skills Overview

Why These Skills? *My Sidewalks* focuses on the priority skills students need in order to succeed at learning to read. **Priority skills** are the critical elements of reading—phonemic awareness (Levels A–C), phonics, fluency, vocabulary, and text comprehension. Scientifically based research has shown that these skills are the foundations of reading and must be taught in a systematic sequence.

		WEEK 1 5–30 **Nature's Designs**	**WEEK 2** 31–56 **Animal Journeys**
Phonics	Decoding	Long *a* Spelled *ai, ay*	Long *e* Spelled *e, ee, ea*
	Spelling	Words with Long *a*	Words with Long *e*
Vocabulary	Concept	What can we learn from patterns in nature?	Why do animals migrate?
Amazing Words	Vocabulary	*arrangement, available, landscape, patterns, repeats, reveal, snowfall*	*migrate, observe, refuges, shelter, zones*
Comprehension	Skill	Sequence	Main Idea
	Strategies	Preview, Ask Questions, Use Story Structure, Summarize	Preview, Ask Questions, Use Story Structure, Summarize
	Writing	Response to Literature	Response to Literature
Fluency		Reread for Fluency Practice	Reread for Fluency Practice

WEEK 3	WEEK 4	WEEK 5	
57–82	83–108	109–134	
Our Spinning Planet	**Storms**	**Going Green**	
Contractions	Long *o* Spelled *oa, ow*	Prefixes *mis-, non-, over-, pre-, mid-*	
Contractions	Words with Long *o*	Words with Prefixes	
How do day and night affect people and animals?	**What can you learn about weather?**	**How can we protect nature?**	
dazed, hemisphere, nocturnal, revolution, rotation, vacation	*behavior, coast, inland, phenomenon, tsunami, unpredictable*	*benefits, cells, electricity, hydrogen, resources, solar*	
Draw Conclusions	Compare and Contrast	Main Idea	
Preview, Ask Questions, Use Story Structure, Summarize	Preview, Ask Questions, Use Story Structure, Summarize	Preview, Ask Questions, Use Story Structure, Summarize	
Response to Literature	Response to Literature	Response to Literature	
Reread for Fluency Practice	Reread for Fluency Practice	Reread for Fluency Practice	

Concept Development
to Foster Reading Comprehension

Theme Question: What can we discover from new places and people?

Concept: Turning Points

EXPAND THE CONCEPT

Week 1	Week 2	Week 3	Week 4	Week 5
Lesson Focus What brings different people together?	**Lesson Focus** What can we learn by exploring new places?	**Lesson Focus** What can we learn about the United States as we travel?	**Lesson Focus** What is special about the landscape of the Southwest?	**Lesson Focus** What is special about the West?

DEVELOP LANGUAGE

Vocabulary backgrounds culture ethnic homesick translated understanding **Background Reading** "Let's Explore: Diversity"	**Vocabulary** area confused device perspective pioneers territory voyage **Background Reading** "Let's Explore: Endless Discoveries"	**Vocabulary** itineraries journey miles mode route transportation views **Background Reading** "Let's Explore: Route 66"	**Vocabulary** arid canyon carved cliffs frontier guide hiking **Background Reading** "Let's Explore: Scenes from the Southwest"	**Vocabulary** astonishing eruptions formed gigantic naturally unbelievable **Background Reading** "Let's Explore: California"

READ THE LITERATURE

Expository Nonfiction "Beautiful Music" **Realistic Fiction** "Paper Birds and Plantains" **Annotated List** "What's for Supper?"	**Expository Nonfiction** "Look Inside Yourself!" **Animal Fantasy** "Danger in the Meadow" **Humorous Fiction** "Aliens from Idaho!"	**Expository Nonfiction** "A Cause for Walking" **Realistic Fiction** "The Longest Route" **Expository Nonfiction** "Odd Places, U.S.A."	**Expository Nonfiction** "Wild, Wild Westerns" **Realistic Fiction** "Searching for Sure Foot" **Poetry** "Desert Snow" "How the Maricopas Made Wishes Come True"	**Expository Nonfiction** "Surf's Up!" **Expository Nonfiction** "Natural Treasures" **Expository Nonfiction** "All Steamed Up"

TEACH CONTENT

Connect to Social Studies • Cultural Roots • Ethnic Instruments • Community Diversity	**Connect to Social Studies** • Shelter • Survival • Teamwork	**Connect to Social Studies** • Transportation • Volunteering • Time Zones • Tourism in America	**Connect to Social Studies** • Landforms • Geography of the Southwest • Western Films	**Connect to Science** • Surfing in California • National Parks of the West • Geysers

Unit 1 develops the same concepts and content-area knowledge as in Scott Foresman's *Reading Street*, Grade 4, Unit 1.

Concept Development
to Foster Reading Comprehension

Theme Question: What is the value of teamwork?

Concept: Teamwork

EXPAND THE CONCEPT

Week 1	Week 2	Week 3	Week 4	Week 5
Lesson Focus What can we learn from the talents of others?	**Lesson Focus** How can we work together to achieve a goal?	**Lesson Focus** What can teams accomplish?	**Lesson Focus** How does working together get the job done?	**Lesson Focus** What happens in our nation's capital?

DEVELOP LANGUAGE

Vocabulary awareness comprehend exhibit experience horizons interactive	**Vocabulary** accomplished collaboration cooperate members orchestra teamwork	**Vocabulary** extraordinary fantastic inspiration sculptures skillful	**Vocabulary** career contribution energy gear option workers	**Vocabulary** capital Capitol dedicated executive memorabilia museum
Background Reading "Let's Explore: Other Ways of Learning"	**Background Reading** "Let's Explore: Teamwork"	**Background Reading** "Let's Explore: Team Effort"	**Background Reading** "Let's Explore: Everyday Jobs"	**Background Reading** "Let's Explore: Birth of the Capital"

READ THE LITERATURE

Expository Nonfiction "Amazing Exhibits" **Realistic Fiction** "The Beast in Grandpa's House" **Expository Nonfiction** "Japanese Cartoons"	**Expository Nonfiction** "All Together Now" **Realistic Fiction** "Molly's New Role" **Expository Nonfiction** "Winning Teams"	**Expository Nonfiction** "Racing Art" **Humorous Fiction** "Sam and the Incredible Smash" **Photo Essay** "Sculptures in Sand"	**Expository Nonfiction** "The Big Dig of Boston" **Realistic Fiction** "All the Right Moves" **Expository Nonfiction** "Why Do We Work?"	**Expository Nonfiction** "Working in the White House" **Expository Nonfiction** "White House Pets" **Expository Nonfiction** "Washington's Wonderful Monuments"

TEACH CONTENT

Connect to Social Studies • Interactive Learning • Museums • Computer Literacy • Japanese *Anime* and *Manga*	**Connect to Social Studies** • Cooperation and Motivation • Teamwork and Collaboration • Winners in History	**Connect to Social Studies** • Creativity • Kinetic Art Racing • Teamwork and Collaboration	**Connect to Social Studies** • Unnoticed Workers • Transportation Project in Boston • Chores and Responsibilities • Values of Work	**Connect to Social Studies** • Washington, D.C. • White House Jobs • Executive Branch • Presidential Pets • Tourist Sights

Unit 2 develops the same concepts and content-area knowledge as in Scott Foresman's *Reading Street*, Grade 4, Unit 2.

Concept Development
to Foster Reading Comprehension

Theme Question: **What are some patterns in nature?**

Concept: Patterns in Nature

EXPAND THE CONCEPT

Week 1	Week 2	Week 3	Week 4	Week 5
Lesson Focus What can we learn from patterns in nature?	**Lesson Focus** Why do animals migrate?	**Lesson Focus** How do day and night affect people and animals?	**Lesson Focus** What can you learn about weather?	**Lesson Focus** How can we protect nature?

DEVELOP LANGUAGE

Week 1	Week 2	Week 3	Week 4	Week 5
Vocabulary arrangement available landscape patterns repeats reveal snowfall **Background Reading** "Let's Explore: Spectacular Snowflakes"	**Vocabulary** migrate observe refuges shelter zones **Background Reading** "Let's Explore: Animals on the Move"	**Vocabulary** dazed hemisphere nocturnal revolution rotation vacation **Background Reading** "Let's Explore: Night and Day"	**Vocabulary** behavior coast inland phenomenon tsunami unpredictable **Background Reading** "Let's Explore: Weird Weather"	**Vocabulary** benefits cells electricity hydrogen resources solar **Background Reading** "Let's Explore: Recycling"

READ THE LITERATURE

Week 1	Week 2	Week 3	Week 4	Week 5
Expository Nonfiction "Patterns Everywhere" **Realistic Fiction** "The Talking Pot" **Poetry** "I Wish I Knew" "Sunflakes"	**Expository Nonfiction** "Flight for Survival" **How-to Article** "Wildlife Welcome!" **Expository Nonfiction** "Where Birds Vacation"	**Expository Nonfiction** "The Amazing Skies of the North" **Realistic Fiction** "Plane Tired!" **Photo Essay** "Alaskan Animals"	**Expository Nonfiction** "How Did the Animals Know?" **Realistic Fiction** "Taito and the Gulls" **How-to Article** "Is It Going to Rain?"	**Expository Nonfiction** "Safer Energy" **Expository Nonfiction** "Racing with the Sun" **Expository Nonfiction** "Let's Save the Planet!"

TEACH CONTENT

Week 1	Week 2	Week 3	Week 4	Week 5
Connect to Science • Snowflakes • Patterns in Nature	**Connect to Science** • Migration • Survival of Migratory Birds • Outreach to Nature	**Connect to Science** • Day and Night • Time Zones • Alaska Sky Features • Alaskan Animals	**Connect to Social Studies** • Survival/Rescue • Tsunami • Family Responsibilities	**Connect to Science** • Recycling • Clean, Renewable Sources of Energy • Solar Cars • Environmental Awareness

 Unit 3 develops the same concepts and content-area knowledge as in Scott Foresman's *Reading Street*, Grade 4, Unit 3.

Unit 1 Week 1 *Diversity*

? What brings different people together?

Objectives *This week students will . . .*

Vocabulary
- build concepts and vocabulary: *backgrounds, culture, ethnic, homesick, translated, understanding*

Phonics
- read words with closed syllables (VC/CV and VCCCV) with short vowels
- apply knowledge of word structure to decode multisyllabic words when reading

Text Comprehension
- use sequence to improve comprehension
- write in response to literature
- make connections across text

Fluency
- practice fluency with oral rereading

Word Work *This week's phonics focus is . . .*

Closed Syllables with Short Vowels

Amazing Words Concept/Amazing Words *Tested Vocabulary*

The week's vocabulary is related to the concept of diversity.
The first appearance of each word in the Student Reader is noted below.

backgrounds	past experiences, knowledge, and training (p. 22)
culture	a way of life, including foods, celebrations, and languages (p. 11)
ethnic	a group of people of the same race and nationality who share common celebrations (p. 11)
homesick	very sad because you are far away from home (p. 22)
translated	changed something from one language into another (p. 26)
understanding	the act or fact of knowing something; knowledge (p. 13)

Student Reader Unit 1 *This week students will read the following selections.*

8	**Diversity**	Expository Nonfiction
12	**Beautiful Music**	Expository Nonfiction
20	**Paper Birds and Plantains**	Realistic Fiction
28	**What's for Supper?**	Annotated List
30	**4 You 2 Do**	Activity Page

Daily Lesson Plan

	ACTIVITIES	MATERIALS
Day 1	**Build Concepts** Weekly Concept: Diversity Vocabulary: *backgrounds, culture, ethnic, homesick, translated, understanding* **Read a Passage** "Diversity," pp. 8–11 Comprehension: Use Strategies Reread for Fluency **Write** Response to Literature	Student Reader: Unit 1 Routine Cards 2, 4, 5 Tested Vocabulary Cards Student journals Practice Book, p. 1, Vocabulary Student Reader DVD-ROM
Day 2	**Word Work** Phonics: Closed Syllables with Short Vowels Vocabulary: Deepen word meaning **Comprehension** Sequence **Read a Passage** "Beautiful Music," pp. 12–14 Reread for Fluency **Write** Response to Literature	Student Reader: Unit 1 Practice Book, p. 1, Vocabulary Graphic Organizer 6 Routine Cards 1, 2, 3, 4, 7 Practice Book, p. 2, Closed Syllables with Short Vowels Student Reader DVD-ROM
Day 3	**Word Work** Phonics: Closed Syllables with Short Vowels Vocabulary: Deepen word meaning **Comprehension** Sequence **Read a Passage** "Beautiful Music," pp. 15–19 Reread for Fluency **Write** Response to Literature	Practice Book, p. 2, Closed Syllables with Short Vowels Student Reader: Unit 1 Graphic Organizer 6 Routine Cards 1, 2, 3, 4, 7 Practice Book, p. 3, Sequence Student Reader DVD-ROM
Day 4	**Word Work** Vocabulary: Extend word knowledge **Comprehension** Skill and Strategy Practice **Read a Passage** "Paper Birds and Plantains," pp. 20–27 Reread for Fluency **Write** Response to Literature	Practice Book, p. 3, Sequence Student Reader: Unit 1 Routine Cards 2, 3, 4 Student Reader DVD-ROM
Day 5	**Read a Passage** "What's for Supper?" pp. 28–29 Comprehension: Sequence; Listening **Build Concepts** Vocabulary **Write** Response to Literature: "4 You 2 Do," p. 30 **Assessment Options** Fluency Comprehension	Student Reader: Unit 1 Routine Cards 3, 5, 6, 8 Fluency Progress Chart, p. 185 Practice Book, p. 4, Writing

See pp. xvi–xvii for how *My Sidewalks* integrates instructional practices for ELL.

Build Concepts

Amazing Words Vocabulary

| To Do | To Say | 10–15 minutes |

Develop oral vocabulary.

See Routine Card 6* and p. 198.

Introduce the Concept/Amazing Words with an oral routine prior to displaying them in print. Page 198 in this Teacher's Guide provides specific guidelines for introducing each word.

Develop word meaning.

See Routine Card 5.* Discuss pp. 7–11.

Have students read p. 7 and look at the pictures on pp. 8–11. **What do you notice?** (parades, celebrations) **Can you use the word** *diversity* **to describe what's happening?** (Example: There is a lot of *diversity* among these different celebrations.)

Scaffold instruction.

Create a concept web.

In the center of a web, write *Diversity.* **This week's concept is** *diversity. Diversity* **means "variety or difference."** Provide an example to demonstrate meaning. **America is a land of** *diversity* **because its people have come from many different places, with many different traditions and ways of life. As you read, think about what you know about** *diversity.*

Add the other vocabulary words.

Concept and Language Goals

Discuss the meaning of each word as it relates to diversity, using the glossary as needed. (See p. 2 in this Teacher's Guide for definitions.)

```
        backgrounds        culture

understanding     Diversity        ethnic

        translated         homesick
```

Model the multisyllabic word strategy.

Display each word. Say it as you display it.

Use the Tested Vocabulary Cards. Follow this routine for each word:

- **Look for Meaningful Parts** **Do you recognize any parts of this word? What do these parts mean? Use the parts to read the word.** As you introduce the words, be sure students notice *back, grounds, home, sick,* and ending *-ing.*

Think aloud.

- **Model** I see the word *home* at the beginning of *homesick.* I know that a *home* is where you live. I also recognize the word *sick.* So *homesick* is a compound word, made up of two smaller words. I think *homesick* must have to do with not feeling well because you miss your home.

Point to *ethnic.*

- **Chunk Words with No Recognizable Parts** Model how to chunk the word *ethnic.* I see a chunk at the beginning of the word: *eth.* I see a part at the end of the word: *nic.* I say each chunk slowly: *eth nic.* I say the chunks fast to make a whole word: *ethnic.* Is it a real word? Yes, I know the word *ethnic.*

- Have students practice reading each word.

Preview.

Read p. 6 with students.

Do you see any of the words we just learned on this page? Together with students, read the sentences on p. 6 describing each selection. Talk about how the vocabulary words might be used in the selections.

MORE PRACTICE

Deepen understanding of *diversity.*

Have students demonstrate understanding by answering questions. **How much** *diversity* **is there in what you eat? How about in the clothes that you wear? Give some examples. Why is** *diversity* **important?**

*Routine Cards are found at the back of this Teacher's Guide.

ACTIVITY **2**   Read a Passage

Develop Concepts "Diversity," pp. 8–11

10–15 minutes

	To Do	**To Say**
Practice strategic prereading.	See Routine Card 2. Think aloud.	**Discuss Genre** Read the title on p. 8 and have students look at the illustrations on pp. 8–11. Model determining genre. The photographs are a clue that this is nonfiction. They look like pictures of real people in real places. I think this article will tell me about different cultures and celebrations.
Scaffold instruction.	Review text structure.	**Ask Questions** To help you understand nonfiction, ask yourself the following questions: What did I learn? What is this mainly about? As you read this article, ask these questions and look for the answers.
Guide comprehension. **Develop language and concepts.**	Read pp. 8–11 aloud.	**Read** Read the article as students follow along. Then read it a second time, having students join in. If necessary, stop at the end of each paragraph to check comprehension. Ask questions to promote discussion and develop the concept. • What are some of the special occasions that other cultures celebrate? • What are some of the ways that people celebrate? • What can we learn from cultural celebrations? • What words on the concept web could help you describe different celebrations?

MORE PRACTICE

Have students reread "Diversity." As they read, have them make a list of the special events they read about and the significance of those events. Invite them to share their lists with family members tonight.

Reread for Fluency "Diversity," p. 11

5 minutes

	To Do	**To Say**
CORRECTIVE FEEDBACK	Monitor oral reading.	Read p. 11 aloud. Reread the page three or four times so your reading gets better each time. Give feedback on students' oral reading, using the *if . . . then* statements on Routine Card 4. Model fluent reading if necessary. You may want to have students read along with the DVD-ROM.

ACTIVITY **3**   Write

Response to Literature

5 minutes

	To Do	**To Say**
Prompt journal writing.	Write on the board or a transparency: *What brings different people together?*	Take out your journals. This week we are reading about diversity. Our question for this week is: *What brings different people together?* Write an answer to this question based on what you read today. Have students write about the topic, using what they read and their own experiences.

Homework	Practice Book, p. 1, Vocabulary

ACTIVITY 1 — Word Work

Phonics Closed Syllables with Short Vowels

	To Do	**To Say**	*5–10 minutes*
Teach closed syllables with short vowels.	Write on the board or a transparency: *He found a <u>fossil</u>.*	Remember, when you read a long word, look for meaningful parts. Look at the word *fossil*. What parts do you see in this word? *(fos sil)* Vowels usually have the short sound when they are followed by two consonants. What sound does the *o* in *fossil* have? (short *o*) Read the word together. Listen for the vowel sound in the accented syllable.	
Scaffold instruction.	Write *differ* and *button.*	If a word has two consonants in the middle, divide between them to make two syllables. Notice that the first syllables are closed—they end in consonants. Try the short vowel sound for these accented syllables.	
	Write *hundreds* and *husbands.*	What parts do you see in *hundreds* and *husbands?* (hun dreds, hus bands) What vowel sound is in each accented syllable? (short vowel)	
CORRECTIVE FEEDBACK	Write each practice word.	Have students practice reading closed-syllable words with short vowel sounds. Correct any words students miss and have them reread the list. bonnet gallons absent invent plaster puppet	
MORE PRACTICE	Write more practice words.	Have students practice reading these closed-syllable words with short vowel sounds. dollar ribbon customs velvet admit witness	

Amazing Words — Vocabulary

	To Do	**To Say**	*5 minutes*
Review vocabulary.	Review the homework. Deepen understanding of *culture.*	Ask students to go over answers and share their writing from Practice Book p. 1. See Routine Card 1 for the multisyllabic word routine. Remember, a person's *culture* includes his or her foods, celebrations, and languages. Celebrating Soyaluna is part of the Hopi *culture.* What foods and celebrations are important to your family's *culture?* Why?	

ACTIVITY 2 — Comprehension

Sequence

	To Do	**To Say**	*5 minutes*
Scaffold instruction.	Introduce sequence.	Today you will read about how to play a musical instrument. In both fiction and nonfiction, events usually take place in a certain order, or sequence. Directions describing how to do something usually follow a sequence as well. You can make more sense of what you are reading if you pay attention to the sequence. Words like *first, next,* and *then* give clues to the right sequence.	
	Model the skill.	For example, if I read that the *first* step in playing a flute is to keep my lips firm, I need to pay attention in order to understand the correct sequence of steps.	
	Distribute Graphic Organizer 6.	As you read "Beautiful Music," look for words that help you track the sequence of steps for learning to play the flute. Add these sequence words to your graphic organizer. See Routine Card 7.	

ACTIVITY 3 Read a Passage

Read for Comprehension "Beautiful Music," pp. 12–14

10–15 minutes

	To Do	To Say
Scaffold instruction.	Monitor student engagement.	**Read** Have students read pp. 12–14. Stop at the end of each page to ask questions. Students who can read on their own can do so without stopping. After reading, ask questions to promote discussion.
	See Routine Cards 2 and 3.	**Who invented the modern flute?** (a German musician) **When was it invented?** (1847)
		How do scientists know that the flute has been around for thousands of years? (They found a fossil of a bone flute.)
Model summarizing.	Think aloud.	**Summarize** What were the first three pages mainly about? What did you learn about the flute? Think aloud to model summarizing. **I learned a lot of details about the flute, such as the facts that flutes are important in German culture and they are played by different cultures all over the world. But the main thing I learned is that flutes have been around for thousands of years.**
Develop language and concepts.	Ask questions.	• Why is the flute such a popular instrument?
		• What does the fossil of the flute tell us about ancient cultures?
MORE PRACTICE	Have students reread p. 14.	**Reread** After they read, have students discuss other wind instruments they may know of that are similar to the flute.

Reread for Fluency "Beautiful Music," pp. 12–13

5 minutes

	To Do	To Say
MORE PRACTICE **CORRECTIVE FEEDBACK**	Pair students. Monitor paired reading.	Students read aloud pp. 12–13, switching readers at the end of the first page. Have partners reread; now the other partner begins. For optimal fluency, students should reread three or four times. Give feedback, using the *if . . . then* statements on Routine Card 4. You may want to have students read along with the DVD-ROM.

ACTIVITY 4 Write

Response to Literature

5 minutes

	To Do	To Say
Prompt writing.		The article says, "Many ethnic groups play instruments." Why do you think music is important to so many different cultures? How does music bring people of different backgrounds together? (Students should support their ideas and opinions.)
Homework		Practice Book, p. 2, Closed Syllables with Short Vowels

ACTIVITY **1** Word Work

Phonics Closed Syllables with Short Vowels

5 minutes

	To Do	**To Say**
Review closed syllables with short vowels. **Scaffold instruction.**	Review the homework. Discuss the word *weddings* on p. 16.	Ask students to share answers from Practice Book p. 2. Point out *weddings* on p. 16, paragraph 1. **What parts do you see in this word?** *(wed dings)* **What vowel sound do you hear in the accented syllable?** (short vowel sound) Then point to *messages* on p. 17, paragraph 1. **Use the same strategy to read this word. How is it like *weddings*?** (It is also plural; it has a double consonant in the middle; and it has a short vowel sound in the accented syllable.)
MORE PRACTICE	Model spelling words with closed syllables and short vowels.	**Spell and Write** You can spell words that have closed syllables with short vowel sounds by thinking about the syllables. What is the first syllable in *tennis*? (/ten/) What letters spell /ten/? Write *ten*. What is the second syllable? (/nis/) What letters spell /nis/? Write *nis*. Now spell *tennis*. Repeat with *invent, admit,* and *puppet*.

Amazing Words Vocabulary

5 minutes

	To Do	**To Say**
Build vocabulary.	Deepen understanding of *understanding* and *translated*.	Read aloud the first two sentences on p. 18, paragraph 2. **The author gives a clue about why Clarke was able to make a new kind of flute. What is the clue?** (He had an *understanding* of flutes.) **How would this help him?** (He *translated* what he knew about one kind of flute to invent another.) **Say a sentence using *understanding* and *translated*. How can thinking and experimenting lead to *understanding*?**

ACTIVITY **2** Comprehension

Sequence

5–10 minutes

	To Do	**To Say**
Scaffold instruction.	Review sequence.	**An author gives you clues to the sequence. Look for dates, phrases, or words such as *first, next, then*, and so on. As you read "Beautiful Music," look for the sequence of steps used to make an instrument.**
Guide practice.	Use Graphic Organizer 6.	**Listen as I read p. 18. I want you to notice that the author tells about the sequence of steps used to make a tin flute.** Read p. 18. Then ask: **What words help you understand the sequence?** *(first, next, then)* **Add these words to your graphic organizer. What did Clarke do first?** (drilled six holes into a tin tube). See Routine Card 7.
MORE PRACTICE	Have students preview pp. 15–19.	**Read the captions and look at the photographs on pp. 15–19. What do you think this section will be about?** (flute-playing in different cultures) **Why do you think so?** Think aloud to model using captions and illustrations to predict.
	Think aloud.	**The captions make me think the article will describe how different cultures have adapted and used the flute. From the pictures, I think we'll read about how different cultures make flutes and play flutes.**

ACTIVITY 3 Read a Passage

Read for Comprehension "Beautiful Music," pp. 15–19

10–15 minutes

	To Do	To Say
Scaffold instruction.	Monitor student engagement.	**Read** Have students read pp. 15–19. Stop at the end of each page to ask questions. Students who can read on their own can do so without stopping. After reading, ask questions to promote discussion.
	See Routine Cards 2 and 3.	**How is the kaval like other flutes?** (A player blows into it; it has holes.) **In what ways is it different?** (It's not made of metal; it is held in front instead of to the side.)
		How can music travel great distances? (People bring their music or instruments with them when they move to new places.)
		What are some materials people use to make flutes? (bone, wood, metal, tin, vines)
Review the multisyllabic word strategy.	Point out *entertainment* on p. 15.	Remind students to apply the multisyllabic word strategy to read this word. Guide them to chunk the word: *en ter tain ment,* or to recognize the word part *entertain.* Have students blend the parts to read the word. See Routine Card 1.
Assess comprehension.	Monitor understanding.	**After Reading** Have students discuss the What Do You Think? question. Prompt them to use sequence words in telling how to make an Irish tin whistle. Listen as they talk to assess comprehension.
	Summarize.	**What is this mainly about? What did you learn?** Work with students to summarize the selection.
MORE PRACTICE	Have students reread p. 18.	**Reread** As they read, tell students to note sequence words. *(first, next, then)* Have students add these words to their graphic organizers. After they read, have them use sequence words to retell how to make a tin whistle.

Reread for Fluency "Beautiful Music," p. 19

5 minutes

	To Do	To Say
CORRECTIVE FEEDBACK	Monitor oral reading.	**Read p. 19 aloud. Reread the page three or four times so your reading gets better each time.** Give feedback on students' oral reading, using the *if . . . then* statements on Routine Card 4. Model fluent reading if necessary. You may want to have students read along with the DVD-ROM.

ACTIVITY 4 Write

Response to Literature

5 minutes

	To Do	To Say
MORE PRACTICE	Prompt writing.	**The flutes in "Beautiful Music" were used for entertainment, but they had other purposes as well. What else were they used for? Write about some of the reasons that people play music today.** (Students should support their ideas.)
Homework		Practice Book, p. 3, Sequence

ACTIVITY 1 Word Work

Amazing Words Vocabulary

To Do	To Say	5–10 minutes

Extend word knowledge.

Write on the board or a transparency: *Have you ever felt homesick?*

Use the word *homesick* to extend word knowledge. **Remember, we read this word earlier this week. We looked for meaningful parts, and we noticed that this word is a compound word made of two smaller words: *home* and *sick*. Today we're going to look at other compound words that begin with *home*.**

Teach compound words.

Scaffold instruction.

Home can mean the place where you live, or it can mean the place where you were born or brought up. For example, you call the schoolwork that you bring home *homework*. You call the place where you are originally from your *homeland*. **How is the word *home* different in these two words?** (*Homework* refers to home as a place where you live; *homeland* refers to home as the place where you were born or brought up.) **What does *home* mean in *homemade*?**

Develop word meaning.

When do you feel *homesick*? When you feel *homesick*, what people or things do you miss? Can you think of other *home* words? (*homeroom, home page, home run, home town*) Write words as students name them and add some of your own.

MORE PRACTICE

Deepen understanding of *culture* and *backgrounds*.

Have individual students or partners use the words *culture* and *backgrounds* together in sentences. (For example: People from the same *culture* often have similar *backgrounds*.) Share sentences. Ask: **How do people's experiences or backgrounds influence their *culture*?**

ACTIVITY 2 Comprehension

Skill and Strategy Practice

To Do	To Say	5 minutes

Scaffold instruction.

Review sequence (homework).

Ask volunteers to read the passage and share answers from Practice Book p. 3. Remind students of the importance of following the sequence. **When you read a story or how-to article, the sequence of events is often important. There may be clue words to the order in which things happen. Look for these words. It may also help you to picture in your mind the steps as they are done.**

Practice strategic prereading.

See Routine Card 2.

Discuss Genre Read the title and the first paragraph on p. 20. Model determining genre.

Think aloud.

I first thought this might be fiction because of the illustrations. When I read the first paragraph, I knew it was fiction because the narrator is one of the kids in the class.

Teach story structure.

Ask Questions There are two questions you should ask yourself to help you understand a fictional story: What is the problem or goal? How is the problem solved or the goal reached? As you read this story, ask these questions and look for the answers.

ACTIVITY 3 · Read a Passage

Read for Comprehension "Paper Birds and Plantains," pp. 20–27

10–15 minutes

	To Do	To Say
Scaffold instruction.	Monitor student engagement. See Routine Card 3.	**Read** Have students read pp. 20–27 on their own and then discuss. For students who need more help, stop at the end of each page to discuss. After reading, ask questions. **Who is telling this story?** (Emi, a Japanese girl) **Who are the main characters?** (Emi and Miguel) **What are the settings?** (a school classroom, Emi's home, and Miguel's home) **What challenge does Emi face?** (She has just moved from Japan to the United States. She is worried that she can't speak English well enough to make friends.) **What do Miguel and Emi learn from each other?** (Emi teaches Miguel how to make paper birds; Miguel teaches Emi how to make *plantains con crema.* They both learn more about each other.)
Assess comprehension.	Monitor understanding.	**After Reading** Have students discuss the What Do You Think? question. Prompt them to use sequence words in retelling the story. Listen as they talk to assess comprehension.
MORE PRACTICE		**Reread** Have students reread p. 26 and then explain to a partner how to make the baked plantains.

Reread for Fluency "Paper Birds and Plantains," pp. 23–25

5–10 minutes

	To Do	To Say
CORRECTIVE FEEDBACK	Pair students. Monitor paired reading.	Students read aloud pp. 23–25, switching readers at the end of each page. Have partners reread; now the other partner begins. For optimal fluency, students should reread three or four times. Give feedback, using Routine Card 4. You may want to have students read along with the DVD-ROM.
MORE PRACTICE	**READERS' THEATER**	Work with a pair of students to adapt pp. 23–25 as a Readers' Theater scene. Have students rehearse reading the parts, with one student being Miguel, and one Emi. Discuss whether Emi should read all the transitional narration or whether it should be read by a narrator.

ACTIVITY 4 · Write

Response to Literature

5 minutes

	To Do	To Say
Prompt narrative writing.	Writing elements: organization	Describe the sequence of events that leads to the changes in Emi's life. Start with the sentence "First, Emi and Miguel meet to decide what to teach each other." Use other sequence words to show the order of events.

5

ACTIVITY 1 Read a Passage

Read Together "What's for Supper?" pp. 28–29

10 minutes

	To Do	**To Say**
Scaffold instruction.	Review sequence.	Have students preview pp. 28–29. **When you read a story or article, the sequence of events is often important. Sometimes there are clue words that help you follow the sequence of events or the steps in a process. Look for these words and picture in your mind events as they happen.**
	See Routine Card 3.	**Read** Read the article as students follow along. Then read it a second time, having students join in on the text. After reading, ask questions.
		How often do the residents of Metro Condos have their community dinner? (once a month)
		Why do the other families want to please the Garza family? (because the Garzas just moved to Metro Condos)
		How do you know that the families living at the Metro Condos are from different cultures? (Each family makes a different traditional dish, such as the Limerick ham or the Cambodian sweet and sour chicken wings.)
		Is sequence important in this selection? (No; it is rather like a list, in which items could be rearranged without changing the meaning much.)
Assess comprehension.	Monitor listening comprehension.	**Summarize** Have one student describe the monthly community dinner at the Metro Condos and what each family contributes.

ACTIVITY 2 Build Concepts

Amazing Words Vocabulary

5–10 minutes

	To Do	**To Say**
Review concept and vocabulary.	Display the concept web you began on Day 1.	**This week's question is *What brings different people together?* How do this week's words relate to the question?** (Have students answer the question, using some of the vocabulary they learned this week.)
		Ask students to add more words to the concept web. Have students explain how each word relates to diversity. Monitor students' understanding of vocabulary as they discuss the web. See Routine Card 5.
MORE PRACTICE	Write *ethnic* and *culture* on the board.	Have students relate *ethnic* and *culture*. **Give me an example of an *ethnic* food you like to eat. Do you know which *culture* it comes from? In what ways is it different from the foods you eat with your family?**

Name_____

Writing

Think about the foods you eat with your family and friends. Think about the things you do together. Which things would be fun to share with people from other countries? Write about them in the chart below.

Directions Fill in the chart with your ideas.

Food	Games	Holidays/Events

On another piece of paper, write a paragraph telling why you want to share each of these foods and activities. Make sure the names of the foods and holidays are spelled correctly.

© Pearson Education D

Home Activity This page helps your child write sentences about traditions he or she would like to share with people from another country. Work through the items with your child. Then ask your child what countries he or she would like to visit and why.

Write

Response to Literature "4 You 2 Do," p. 30

5–10 minutes

Guide response activities.

To Do	To Say
Discuss the directions on p. 30. Tell students to choose one activity to complete. See Routine Card 8.	**Word Play** Have students complete the first part on their own and then meet with a partner to share their coded words.

Making Connections Discuss the question in a group. (Answers will vary but may include names of the flutes, foods, and origami. Encourage students to give details or personal experiences to support their choices.)

On Paper Have students brainstorm some answers to the prompt before they write. Have them write on their own. Students can use Practice Book p. 4 to structure their written responses, or you can send the Practice Book page home for them to complete later.

MORE PRACTICE

If you have more time, direct students to complete all the activities.

Assessment Options

Passage Reading

10–15 minutes

To Do	To Say
See Routine Card 6. Take a two-minute timed sample of each student's oral reading.	While some students are doing Activity 3, determine which students you want to assess this week and choose from these options.

Check fluency.

Check comprehension.

Fluency Have a student read for two minutes from "Paper Birds and Plantains." Record the number of correct words read per minute. See p. 184 for monitoring fluency. Be sure each student is assessed at least every other week.

Have students graph their progress on the Fluency Progress Chart, p. 185.

Retelling Have students reread "Paper Birds and Plantains" and retell it. Prompt students if necessary. See p. 186 for monitoring retelling.

If you have time, assess every student.

Homework   Practice Book, p. 4, Writing

Unit 1 Week 2 *Exploration*

What can we learn by exploring new places?

Objectives *This week students will . . .*

Vocabulary
- build concepts and vocabulary: *area, confused, device, perspective, pioneers, territory, voyage*

Phonics
- read words with closed syllables (VC/CV) with long vowels (CVC*e*)
- apply knowledge of word structure to decode multisyllabic words when reading

Text Comprehension
- draw conclusions to improve comprehension
- write in response to literature
- make connections across text

Fluency
- practice fluency with oral rereading

Word Work *This week's phonics focus is . . .*

Closed Syllables with Long Vowels

Amazing Words Concept/Amazing Words *Tested Vocabulary*

The week's vocabulary is related to the concept of exploration.
The first appearance of each word in the Student Reader is noted below.

area	a place (p. 50)
confused	mixed up; not sure about something (p. 46)
device	something invented for use (p. 43)
perspective	the view of something from a distance (p. 49)
pioneers	those who go first, or do something first, and so prepare a way for other people (p. 38)
territory	land; one of the parts of a country (p. 38)
voyage	a journey by water; cruise (p. 38)

Student Reader Unit 1 *This week students will read the following selections.*

34	**Endless Discoveries**	Expository Nonfiction
38	**Look Inside Yourself!**	Expository Nonfiction
46	**Danger in the Meadow**	Animal Fantasy
54	**Aliens from Idaho!**	Humorous Fiction
56	**4 You 2 Do**	Activity Page

Daily Lesson Plan

	ACTIVITIES	MATERIALS
Day 1	**Build Concepts** Weekly Concept: Exploration Vocabulary: *area, confused, device, perspective, pioneers, territory, voyage* **Read a Passage** "Endless Discoveries," pp. 34–37 Comprehension: Use Strategies Reread for Fluency **Write** Response to Literature	Student Reader: Unit 1 Routine Cards 2, 4, 5 Tested Vocabulary Cards Student journals Practice Book, p. 5, Vocabulary Student Reader DVD-ROM
Day 2	**Word Work** Phonics: Closed Syllables with Long Vowels Vocabulary: Deepen word meaning **Comprehension** Draw Conclusions **Read a Passage** "Look Inside Yourself!" pp. 38–40 Reread for Fluency **Write** Response to Literature	Student Reader: Unit 1 Practice Book, p. 5, Vocabulary Graphic Organizer 2 Routine Cards 1, 2, 3, 4, 7 Practice Book, p. 6, Closed Syllables with Long Vowels Student Reader DVD-ROM
Day 3	**Word Work** Phonics: Closed Syllables with Long Vowels Vocabulary: Deepen word meaning **Comprehension** Draw Conclusions **Read a Passage** "Look Inside Yourself!" pp. 41–45 Reread for Fluency **Write** Response to Literature	Practice Book, p. 6, Closed Syllables with Long Vowels Tested Vocabulary Cards Student Reader: Unit 1 Graphic Organizer 2 Routine Cards 1, 2, 3, 4, 7 Practice Book, p. 7, Draw Conclusions Student Reader DVD-ROM
Day 4	**Word Work** Vocabulary: Extend word knowledge **Comprehension** Skill and Strategy Practice **Read a Passage** "Danger in the Meadow," pp. 46–53 Reread for Fluency **Write** Response to Literature	Practice Book, p. 7, Draw Conclusions Student Reader: Unit 1 Routine Cards 2, 3, 4 Student Reader DVD-ROM
Day 5	**Read a Passage** "Aliens from Idaho!" pp. 54–55 Comprehension: Draw Conclusions; Listening **Build Concepts** Vocabulary **Write** Response to Literature: "4 You 2 Do," p. 56 **Assessment Options** Fluency Comprehension	Student Reader: Unit 1 Routine Cards 3, 5, 6, 8 Fluency Progress Chart, p. 185 Practice Book, p. 8, Writing

See pp. xvi–xvii for how *My Sidewalks* integrates instructional practices for ELL.

Build Concepts

![Amazing Words] **Vocabulary**

	To Do	To Say
Develop oral vocabulary.	See Routine Card 6 and p. 199.	Introduce the Concept/Amazing Words with an oral routine prior to displaying them in print. Page 199 in this Teacher's Guide provides specific guidelines for introducing each word.
Develop word meaning.	See Routine Card 5. Discuss pp. 33–37.	Have students read p. 33 and then look at the pictures on pp. 34–37. **What do you notice?** (images of outer space and nature) **Can you use the word *exploration* to describe these pictures?** (Example: There is still a lot that we can discover through the *exploration* of things like outer space and nature.)
Scaffold instruction.	Create a concept web.	In the center of a web, write *Exploration.* **This week's concept is *exploration.* *Exploration* means traveling in unknown places in order to discover new things.** Provide an example to demonstrate meaning. **The *exploration* of space using powerful telescopes has taught us a lot about our solar system.**
	Add the other vocabulary words.	Discuss the meaning of each word as it relates to exploration, using the glossary as needed. (See p. 14 in this Teacher's Guide for definitions.)

Concept and Language Goals

territory

voyage
pioneers

area
Exploration
perspective

confused
device

		Use the Tested Vocabulary Cards. Follow this routine for each word:
Model the multisyllabic word strategy.	Display each word. Say it as you display it.	• **Look for Meaningful Parts** Do you recognize any parts of this word? What do these parts mean? Use the parts to read the word.
	Think aloud.	• **Model** I see *spect* in the middle of *perspective.* I know that *spect* means "to look." So I think *perspective* might have something to do with how you look at things. Discuss other words with this root. (*inspect, retrospective, introspective, spectacles, spectator*)
	Point to *voyage.*	• **Chunk Words with No Recognizable Parts** Model how to chunk the word *voyage.* I see a chunk at the beginning of the word: *voy.* I see a part at the end of the word: *age.* I say each chunk slowly: *voy age.* I say the chunks fast to make a whole word: *voyage.* Is it a real word? Yes, I know the word *voyage.*
		• Have students practice reading each word.
Preview.	Read p. 32 with students.	**Do you see any of the words we just learned on this page?** Together with students, read the sentences on p. 32 describing each selection. Talk about how the vocabulary words might be used in the selections.
MORE PRACTICE	Deepen understanding of *exploration.*	Have students demonstrate understanding by answering questions. **How has *exploration* changed over the years? How has technology given us more opportunities for *exploration?* Give an example.**

Closed Syllables with Long Vowels

Directions Write the two syllables that make up each word on the lines.

1. _____ + _____ = reptile

2. _____ + _____ = combine

3. _____ + _____ = mistake

4. _____ + _____ = capsize

5. _____ + _____ = confine

6. _____ + _____ = dispose

7. _____ + _____ = compete

8. _____ + _____ = tadpole

Directions Add the first syllable to the second syllable. Write the new word on the line.

9. es + cape = _____

10. in + vite = _____

11. ex + hale = _____

12. ad + vise = _____

13. ex + cuse = _____

14. in + vade = _____

15. en + gage = _____

Home Activity This page practices words with a long vowel sound in the second syllable, such as *inhale* and *trombone*. Work through the items with your child. Then have your child write the words from this page. Ask him or her to read each word and then tell the long vowel sound.

© Pearson Education D

Name_____

Closed Syllables with Long Vowels

Directions Write the two syllables that make up each word on the lines.

1. _____ + _____ = reptile

2. _____ + _____ = combine

3. _____ + _____ = mistake

4. _____ + _____ = capsize

5. _____ + _____ = confine

6. _____ + _____ = dispose

7. _____ + _____ = compete

8. _____ + _____ = tadpole

Directions Add the first syllable to the second syllable. Write the new word on the line.

9. es + cape = _____

10. in + vite = _____

11. ex + hale = _____

12. ad + vise = _____

13. ex + cuse = _____

14. in + vade = _____

15. en + gage = _____

© Pearson Education D

Home Activity This page practices words with a long vowel sound in the second syllable, such as *inhale* and *trombone*. Work through the items with your child. Then have your child write the words from this page. Ask him or her to read each word and then tell the long vowel sound.

Closed Syllables with Long Vowels

Directions Write the two syllables that make up each word on the lines.

1. _____ + _____ = reptile

2. _____ + _____ = combine

3. _____ + _____ = mistake

4. _____ + _____ = capsize

5. _____ + _____ = confine

6. _____ + _____ = dispose

7. _____ + _____ = compete

8. _____ + _____ = tadpole

Directions Add the first syllable to the second syllable. Write the new word on the line.

9. es + cape = _____

10. in + vite = _____

11. ex + hale = _____

12. ad + vise = _____

13. ex + cuse = _____

14. in + vade = _____

15. en + gage = _____

Home Activity This page practices words with a long vowel sound in the second syllable, such as *inhale* and *trombone*. Work through the items with your child. Then have your child write the words from this page. Ask him or her to read each word and then tell the long vowel sound.

© Pearson Education D

Closed Syllables with Long Vowels

Directions Write the two syllables that make up each word on the lines.

1. _____ + _____ = reptile

2. _____ + _____ = combine

3. _____ + _____ = mistake

4. _____ + _____ = capsize

5. _____ + _____ = confine

6. _____ + _____ = dispose

7. _____ + _____ = compete

8. _____ + _____ = tadpole

Directions Add the first syllable to the second syllable. Write the new word on the line.

9. es + cape = _____

10. in + vite = _____

11. ex + hale = _____

12. ad + vise = _____

13. ex + cuse = _____

14. in + vade = _____

15. en + gage = _____

Home Activity This page practices words with a long vowel sound in the second syllable, such as *inhale* and *trombone*. Work through the items with your child. Then have your child write the words from this page. Ask him or her to read each word and then tell the long vowel sound.

© Pearson Education D

Name_____

Closed Syllables with Long Vowels

Directions Write the two syllables that make up each word on the lines.

1. _____ + _____ = reptile

2. _____ + _____ = combine

3. _____ + _____ = mistake

4. _____ + _____ = capsize

5. _____ + _____ = confine

6. _____ + _____ = dispose

7. _____ + _____ = compete

8. _____ + _____ = tadpole

Directions Add the first syllable to the second syllable. Write the new word on the line.

9. es + cape = _____

10. in + vite = _____

11. ex + hale = _____

12. ad + vise = _____

13. ex + cuse = _____

14. in + vade = _____

15. en + gage = _____

Home Activity This page practices words with a long vowel sound in the second syllable, such as *inhale* and *trombone*. Work through the items with your child. Then have your child write the words from this page. Ask him or her to read each word and then tell the long vowel sound.

Name_____

Draw Conclusions

Directions Read the passage. Then answer the questions below.

Josh was bored. He was visiting his grandparents, but he didn't have much to do. "Why don't you explore the attic?" his grandma asked. Josh was thrilled. Who knew what he might find? Everything looked old and dusty. Josh found a huge trunk in the corner. In the trunk Josh found lots of pictures. He couldn't believe how different people looked and dressed! He even dug up an old army uniform. Many badges and ribbons were pinned to the front. Josh felt his chest swell with pride. He knew a real hero!

1. Why do you think Josh wanted to explore the attic?

_____

_____

2. What kinds of pictures do you think Josh found?

_____

_____

3. What details support this conclusion?

_____

_____

4. Draw a conclusion about whose uniform Josh found.

_____

5. What details support this conclusion?

_____

_____

Home Activity This page helps your child draw conclusions based on facts and details. Work through the items with your child. Then explore old photos, cards, clothes, or other family artifacts with your child. Talk about where each item came from.

ACTIVITY **2** Read a Passage

Develop Concepts "Endless Discoveries," pp. 34–37

10–15 minutes

	To Do	**To Say**
Practice strategic prereading.	See Routine Card 2.	**Discuss Genre** Read the title on p. 34 and have students look at the illustrations on pp. 34–37. Model determining genre.
	Think aloud.	The photographs are a clue that this is nonfiction. They look like real photos taken in space or in a science lab. I think this article will tell about discoveries that have come from exploration.
Scaffold instruction.	Teach text structure.	**Ask Questions** There are two questions you can ask yourself to help you understand nonfiction: What did I learn? What is this mainly about? As you read this article, ask yourself these questions and look for the answers.
Guide comprehension.	Read pp. 34–37 aloud.	**Read** Read the article as students follow along. Then read it a second time, having students join in. If necessary, stop at the end of each paragraph to check comprehension. Ask questions to promote discussion and develop the concept.
Develop language and concepts.		• What sorts of things are still left to discover? • How can curiosity lead to discovery? • In what ways are telescopes and microscopes alike and different? • What words on the concept web could help you describe discoveries that come from exploration?

MORE PRACTICE

Have students reread "Endless Discoveries." As they read, tell them to make a list of some places or things that they would like to explore using the tools mentioned in the article. Invite them to share their lists with family members tonight.

Reread for Fluency "Endless Discoveries," p. 37

5 minutes

	To Do	**To Say**
CORRECTIVE FEEDBACK	Monitor oral reading.	**Read p. 37 aloud. Reread the page three or four times so your reading gets better each time.** Give feedback on students' oral reading, using the *if... then* statements on Routine Card 4. Model fluent reading if necessary. You may want to have students read along with the DVD-ROM.

ACTIVITY **3** Write

Response to Literature

5 minutes

	To Do	**To Say**
Prompt journal writing.	Write on the board or a transparency: *What can we learn by exploring new places?*	**Take out your journals. This week we are reading about exploration. Our question for this week is: *What can we learn by exploring new places?* Write an answer to this question based on what you read today.** Have students write on the topic, using what they read and their own experiences.
Homework		Practice Book, p. 5, Vocabulary

ACTIVITY 1 — Word Work

Phonics Closed Syllables with Long Vowels

	To Do	To Say	
			5–10 minutes
Teach closed syllables with long vowels.	Write on the board or a transparency: *Is a <u>tadpole</u> a <u>reptile</u>?*	**Remember, when you read a long word, look for meaningful parts. If a word has two consonants in the middle, divide between them to make two syllables. Look at the word** *tadpole.* **What parts do you see in this word?** *(tad pole)* **If the second syllable of the word ends with a CVCe pattern, try the long vowel sound for that syllable. What sound does the** *o* **in** *tadpole* **have?** (long *o*) **What parts do you see in reptile?** *(rep tile)* **What sound does the** *i* **in** *reptile* **have?** (long *i*)	
Scaffold instruction.	Write *inhale.*	**Here is another word with the CVCe pattern. What parts do you see in this word?** *(in hale)* **What vowel sound do you hear in the second syllable?** (long *a*)	
	Develop word meaning.	Have students think and converse. **The word** *inhale* **begins with the prefix** *in-,* **which means "in," or "into." Sometimes the prefix** *in-* **can mean "not." What other words can you think of that begin with the prefix** *in-?* *(insane, income, indirect, input, inboard, inactive)* **Can you tell which meaning of the prefix each word uses?**	
CORRECTIVE FEEDBACK	Write each practice word.	Have students practice reading closed syllable words with long vowel sounds. Correct any words students miss and have them reread the list. **invite trombone escape mistake admire concede**	
MORE PRACTICE	Write more practice words.	Have students practice reading these closed syllable words with long vowel sounds. **compute subscribe confine inside outrage compete intone**	

Vocabulary

	To Do	To Say	
			5 minutes
Review vocabulary.	Review the homework.	Ask students to go over answers and share their writing from Practice Book p. 5. See Routine Card 1 for the multisyllabic word routine.	
	Deepen understanding of *territory.*	**Remember,** *territory* **means "land; one of the parts of a country." Most of the** *territory* **that is the United States has been explored. What territories or regions other than land regions are still unexplored?**	

ACTIVITY 2 — Comprehension

Draw Conclusions

	To Do	To Say	
			5 minutes
Scaffold instruction.	Introduce drawing conclusions.	**A conclusion is a decision you reach based on the details or facts that you read. When you draw a conclusion you must consider those facts and details, as well as your own experience and what you know to be true.**	
	Model the skill.	**For example, if I read that the explorers in a movie shrink their bodies in order to travel in a tiny submarine through the human body, I can draw the conclusion that the movie is a fantasy; not based on real-life events.**	
	Distribute Graphic Organizer 2.	**As you read "Look Inside Yourself!" look for facts and details that can help you draw logical conclusions. Add these facts and details to your graphic organizer.** See Routine Card 7.	

Name_____

Vocabulary

Directions Choose the word from the box that best completes each sentence. Write the word on the line.

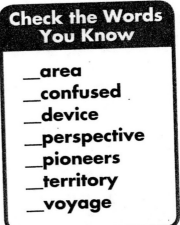

Check the Words You Know

__area
__confused
__device
__perspective
__pioneers
__territory
__voyage

1. The map out to the country _____ us.

2. What other _____ can we use to find our way?

3. For our next _____ , we can go by plane!

4. Our country home is in a remote _____ .

5. You can get a better _____ from the top of that hill.

6. Native Americans used to live in this _____ .

Directions Circle the word that has the same or nearly the same meaning as the first word in each group.

7. **pioneers**	bankers	settlers	teachers
8. **confused**	angry	brave	puzzled
9. **area**	home	address	district
10. **voyage**	school	trip	plane
11. **device**	gadget	signal	talent
12. **perspective**	call	sound	view

© Pearson Education D

School + Home **Home Activity** This page helps your child learn to read and write vocabulary words. Work through the items with your child. Then have your child use each word in an original sentence.

ACTIVITY 3 Read a Passage

Read for Comprehension "Look Inside Yourself!" pp. 38–40

10–15 minutes

	To Do	To Say
Scaffold instruction.	Monitor student engagement.	**Read** Have students read pp. 38–40. Stop at the end of each page to ask questions. Students who can read on their own can do so without stopping. After reading, ask questions to promote discussion.
	See Routine Cards 2, 3.	**On p. 38, into what "strange territory" do the explorers travel? How?** (They explore a human body by shrinking and traveling in a tiny submarine.)
		If you had a serious stomach problem forty years ago, how would doctors discover the cause? (They would X-ray your stomach.) **How would they discover the cause today?** (with a tiny camera and tools attached to a tube)
	Point out *discover* on p. 38.	Demonstrate using your finger to circle *dis-* at the beginning and then reading the base word *cover* that remains.
		What do you think the rest of the article will be about? (Answers will vary. The title suggests that it will describe different ways to look inside the human body.)
Model summarizing.	Think aloud.	**Summarize What were the first three pages mainly about? What did you learn about the tools that doctors use to help fix the human body?** Think aloud to model summarizing. **I learned about some different ways that doctors can look inside a human body, but the main thing I learned is that the techniques that doctors use for making people better are improving all the time.**
Develop language and concepts.	Ask questions.	• **Why is the camera tube an improvement over the X ray?**
		• **What techniques might future doctors use to diagnose stomach problems?**
MORE PRACTICE	Have students reread p. 40.	**Reread** Tell students to draw conclusions about whether or not the current technique that doctors use to diagnose stomach problems is an improvement over using X rays.

Reread for Fluency "Look Inside Yourself!" pp. 39–40

5 m[inutes]

	To Do	To Say
MORE PRACTICE **CORRECTIVE FEEDBACK**	Pair students. Monitor paired reading.	Students read aloud pp. 39–40, switching readers at the end of the first page. Have partners reread; now the other partner begins. For optimal fluency, student[s] should reread three or four times. Give feedback, using the *if... then* statements [on] Routine Card 4. You may want to have students follow along with the DVD-ROM.

[handwritten note:]
– read tog[ether]
– discuss
– what's for
– discuss
– writing p[...]

ACTIVITY 4 Write

Response to Literature

5 minutes

	To Do	To Say
Prompt writing.	Writing elements: support	**What have you learned so far about old and new ways of exploring the human body? Include details and examples.**

Homework	Practice Book, p. 6, Closed Syllables with Long Vowels

Word Work

Phonics Closed Syllables with Long Vowels

	To Do	To Say	*5 minutes*
Review closed syllables. **Scaffold instruction.**	Review the homework. Discuss the word *arrives* on p. 40.	Ask students to share answers from Practice Book p. 6. Point out *arrives* on p. 40, paragraph 1. **What parts do you see in this word?** *(ar rives)* **What vowel sound do you hear in the second syllable?** (long *i*) Then point to *mistakes* on p. 44, paragraph 2. **Use the same strategy to read this word. What parts do you see?** *(mis takes)* **How do you pronounce the second syllable?** (with the sound long *a*)	
MORE PRACTICE	Model spelling words with closed syllables and long vowels.	**Spell and Write** Write *inside*. **Which syllable has a long vowel sound?** (the second) **What letters spell *side?* ** Underline *side*. **Notice that the long vowel sound is spelled with the vowel letter and the final *e*.** Repeat with *mistake, arrive,* and *remote*.	

Amazing Words **Vocabulary**

	To Do	To Say	*5 minutes*
Build vocabulary. **Lead cumulative review.**	Deepen understanding of *pioneers* and *territory*.	**Hundreds of years ago, *pioneers* traveled west to explore unknown *territory* in the United States. In what ways are doctors today like *pioneers*, and the human body like unknown *territory*?** (Doctors explore the human body in order to learn how it works and how to fix it. We still have a lot to learn about the human body because we cannot see inside it.) **Say a sentence using *pioneers* and *territory*.** Use the Tested Vocabulary Cards to review words from previous weeks.	

Comprehension

Draw Conclusions

	To Do	To Say	*5–10 minutes*
Scaffold instruction.	Review drawing conclusions.	**An author may not draw conclusions for you. Some ideas are left for you to figure out from the facts and details you read and from your own experience. As you read "Look Inside Yourself!" look for evidence to support a conclusion.**	
Guide practice.	Use Graphic Organizer 2.	**Listen as I read p. 41. I want you to notice that the author describes a new method for seeing the inside of the human stomach.** Read p. 41. Then ask: **What conclusion can you draw about the camera pill? Is it better than the tube? What details from the article and from your own experience support your conclusion? Add them to your graphic organizer.** See Routine Card 7.	
MORE PRACTICE	Have students preview pp. 41–45.	**Read the captions and look at the photos on pp. 41–45. What do you think this section will be about?** (techniques for looking inside the human body) **Why do you think so?** Think aloud to model using captions and illustrations to predict.	
	Think aloud.	**The captions make me think the article will describe newer ways to look inside the body. The pictures show different medical tools and techniques.**	

ACTIVITY 3 Read a Passage

Read for Comprehension "Look Inside Yourself!" pp. 41–45

10–15 minutes

	To Do	To Say
Scaffold instruction.	Monitor student engagement.	**Read** Have students read pp. 41–45. Stop at the end of each page to ask questions. Students who can read on their own can do so without stopping. After reading, ask questions to promote discussion.
	See Routine Cards 2 and 3.	**What are some benefits of the camera pill?** (It can go where the tube cannot; the patient can't feel it; it can take lots of pictures.)
		How do scientists hope to improve the camera pill? (They want to put tiny tools on it; they want to make it smaller.)
		What is a catheter? (a very thin tube with cameras that goes into the blood vessels of the heart) **What does it do?** (It shows doctors what is wrong with the heart and helps them fix it.)
Review the multisyllabic word strategy.	Point out *jellybean*, p. 43.	Remind students to apply the multisyllabic word strategy to read this word. Demonstrate framing the smaller words *jelly* and *bean.* Have students blend the parts to read the compound word. See Routine Card 1.
Assess comprehension.	Monitor understanding.	**After Reading** Have students discuss the What Do You Think? question. Prompt them to use details from the article, as well as their own experience to draw conclusions about how cameras might be used in the future. Listen as they talk to assess comprehension.
	Summarize.	**What is this mainly about? What did you learn?** Work with students to summarize the selection.
MORE PRACTICE	Have students reread p. 44.	**Reread** As they read, tell students to draw a conclusion about whether or not the catheter is as valuable a tool as the camera pill. Have students add details that support their conclusion to the graphic organizer.

Reread for Fluency "Look Inside Yourself!" p. 45

5 minutes

	To Do	To Say
CORRECTIVE FEEDBACK	Monitor oral reading.	**Read p. 45 aloud. Reread the page three or four times so your reading gets better each time.** Give feedback on students' oral reading, using the *if... then* statements on Routine Card 4. Model fluent reading if necessary. You may want to have students read along with the DVD-ROM.

ACTIVITY 4 Write

Response to Literature

5 minutes

	To Do	To Say
MORE PRACTICE	Prompt writing.	**Which makes more sense to you: shrinking a team of doctors to travel inside a human body, or using tiny instruments to get to places inside the body? Explain your thinking.**
	Homework	Practice Book, p. 7, Draw Conclusions

ACTIVITY 1 Word Work

Amazing Words Vocabulary

	To Do	**To Say**	*5–10 minutes*
Extend word knowledge. **Teach Latin root words.**	Write on the board or a transparency: *The submarine travels into a strange* <u>territory</u>.	Use the word *territory* to extend word knowledge. **Remember, we read this word earlier this week. Today I want you to notice the Latin root word *terra*, which means "earth" or "land." Can you think of other words that relate to earth or land with this same root?** *(terrain, terrace, terra cotta, terrarium, subterranean, extraterrestrial)* Write words as students name them and add some of your own. Talk about the meanings of the words. Read and discuss these words and their meanings.	
Scaffold instruction.	Develop word meaning.	**Does the word *territory* refer only to land? What unexplored *territories* can you think of?** *(outer space, the human body, the natural world)* Point out that the word *territory* does not only refer to land, but also to regions in general.	
MORE PRACTICE	Deepen understanding of *territory* and *area*.	**Have individual students or partners use the two words *territory* and *area* together in a sentence.** (For example: The vast *territory* to the north of us covers an *area* of more than half a million square miles.) **What kind of connection might there be between a *territory* and the population?**	

ACTIVITY 2 Comprehension

Skill and Strategy Practice

	To Do	**To Say**	*5 minutes*
Scaffold instruction.	Review drawing conclusions (homework).	Ask volunteers to read the passage and share answers from Practice Book p. 7. Remind students how to draw conclusions. **When you read an article, remember that the author may not draw conclusions for you. Pay attention to facts and details and use your experience to help you make your own decisions about what you have read. Be prepared to adjust your conclusions as you gather new information.**	
Practice strategic prereading.	See Routine Card 2.	**Discuss Genre** Read the title and the first two paragraphs on p. 46. Model determining genre.	
	Think aloud.	**I first thought this might be fiction because of the illustrations. When I read the first two paragraphs, I knew it was fiction because it is told from the point of view of a ladybug named Belle.**	
	Teach story structure.	**Ask Questions** There are two important questions to ask yourself to help you understand a fictional story: What is the problem or goal? How is the problem solved or the goal reached? As you read this story, ask these questions and look for the answers.**	

ACTIVITY 3 · Read a Passage

Read for Comprehension "Danger in the Meadow," pp. 46–53

	To Do	To Say *10–15 minutes*
Scaffold instruction.	Monitor student engagement. See Routine Card 3.	**Read** Have students read pp. 46–53 on their own and then discuss. For students who need more help, stop at the end of each page to discuss. After reading, ask questions. **Who are the main characters?** (Belle the ladybug and Jack the bee) **What is the setting?** (a meadow) **What problem do the insects face?** (A tractor is plowing down the meadow and ruining their homes.) **What is the "yellow mountain" on p. 48?** (a large earth-moving machine on wheels) **How do Belle and Jack save one another?** (They look for new homes together; they alert each other to dangers.) **Why is the caterpillar confused at first?** (He thinks that ladybugs and bees can't be friends.)
Assess comprehension.	Monitor understanding.	**After Reading** Have students discuss the What Do You Think? question. Prompt them to use details from the story to help them draw conclusions. Listen as they talk to assess comprehension.
MORE PRACTICE		**Reread** Have students reread pp. 49–50 and then explain where Belle is and why she feels sick.

Reread for Fluency "Danger in the Meadow," pp. 51–53

	To Do	To Say *5–10 minutes*
CORRECTIVE FEEDBACK	Pair students. Monitor paired reading.	Students read aloud pp. 51–53, switching readers at the end of each page. Have partners reread; now the other partner begins. For optimal fluency, students should reread three or four times. Give feedback, using Routine Card 4. You may want to have students read along with the DVD-ROM.
MORE PRACTICE	**READERS' THEATER**	Work with a group of four students to adapt pp. 51–53 as a radio play. Have students rehearse reading the parts, with one student as the narrator, one as Belle, one as Jack, and one as the caterpillar.

ACTIVITY 4 · Write

Response to Literature

	To Do	To Say *5 minutes*
Prompt descriptive writing.	Review pp. 51–53. Writing elements: focus, support	**What conclusions can you draw about Jack and Belle's new home? Support your conclusions with details from the story and your own experience.**

ACTIVITY 1 — Read a Passage

Read Together "Aliens from Idaho!" pp. 54–55

	To Do	To Say	10 minutes
Scaffold instruction.	Review draw conclusions.	Have students preview pp. 54–55. **This fictitious newspaper article describes aliens who visit a place called Midia. The author gives a different perspective on exploration and discovery. As you read, think about the conclusions that the Midians draw in the article.**	
	See Routine Card 3.	**Read** Read the article as students follow along. Then read it a second time, having students join in on the text. After reading, ask questions.	
		Who are the aliens in this article? (humans)	
		What conclusion can you draw about Dr. Zweeb's knowledge of humans? (He claims to know a lot, but his facts are wrong.)	
	LOOK AT AUTHOR'S CRAFT	**The author adds a humorous tone to the article by making silly statements in a serious way.** Reread p. 55. **Why are Dr. Zweeb's findings so funny?** (He teaches with authority, but the readers know his facts are wrong.)	
Assess comprehension.	Monitor listening comprehension.	**Summarize** Have one student retell what happens when the family of humans arrives on Midia and what clues tell you that this meeting does not take place on Earth.	

ACTIVITY 2 — Build Concepts

 **Vocabulary**

	To Do	To Say	5–10 minutes
Review concept and vocabulary.	Display the concept web you began on Day 1.	**This week's question is *What can we learn by exploring new places?* How do this week's words relate to the question?** (Have students answer the question, using some of the vocabulary they learned this week.)	
		Ask students to add more words to the concept web. Have students explain how each word relates to exploration. Monitor students' understanding of vocabulary as they discuss the web. See Routine Card 5.	
MORE PRACTICE	Write *device* and *perspective* on the board.	Have students relate *device* and *perspective*. **Give me an example of a *device* that changes your *perspective*. When might you need a different *perspective* in order to solve a problem? How do doctors or scientists use different *devices* to change or improve their *perspectives?***	

ACTIVITY 3 | Write

Response to Literature "4 You 2 Do," p. 56

5–10 minutes

	To Do	**To Say**
Guide response activities.	Discuss the directions on p. 56. Tell students to choose one activity to complete. See Routine Card 8.	**Word Play** Have students complete the first part on their own and then meet with a partner to quiz each other with their own partial words.

Making Connections Discuss the question in a group. (Answers will vary, but should show that insects use their senses, but doctors use their senses as well as instruments and education.)

On Paper Have students brainstorm some answers to the prompt before they write. Have them write on their own. Students can use Practice Book p. 8 to structure their written responses, or you can send the Practice Book page home for them to complete later.

MORE PRACTICE

If you have more time, direct students to complete all the activities.

ACTIVITY 4 | Assessment Options

Passage Reading

10–15 minutes

	To Do	**To Say**
Check fluency.	See Routine Card 6. Take a two-minute timed sample of each student's oral reading.	While some students are doing Activity 3, determine which students you want to assess this week and choose from these options.

Fluency Have a student read for two minutes from "Danger in the Meadow." Record the number of correct words read per minute. See p. 184 for monitoring fluency. Be sure each student is assessed at least every other week.

Have students graph their progress on the Fluency Progress Chart, p. 185.

Check comprehension.

Retelling Have students reread "Danger in the Meadow" and retell it. Prompt students if necessary. See p. 186 for monitoring retelling.

If you have time, assess every student.

Homework   Practice Book, p. 8, Writing

Unit 1 Week 3 *Travel America*

(?) What can we learn about the United States as we travel?

Objectives *This week students will...*

Vocabulary
- build concepts and vocabulary: *itineraries, journey, miles, mode, route, transportation, views*

Phonics
- Read words with plurals and inflected endings *-s, -es, -ies*; spelling change: *y* to *i*
- apply knowledge of word structure to decode multisyllabic words when reading

Text Comprehension
- use sequence to improve comprehension
- write in response to literature
- make connections across text

Fluency
- practice fluency with oral rereading

Word Work *This week's phonics focus is . . .*

Plurals and Inflected Endings *-s, -es, -ies*

Amazing Words **Concept/Amazing Words** *Tested Vocabulary*

The week's vocabulary is related to the concept of traveling America.
The first appearance of each word in the Student Reader is noted below.

itineraries	routes of travel; plans of travel (p. 71)
journey	a long trip from one place to another (p. 71)
miles	units for measuring length or distance. (p. 64)
mode	the way or manner in which something is done; method (p. 71)
route	a way that you choose to get somewhere (p. 60)
transportation	a way to move people or things (p. 66)
views	what you can see from certain places (p. 74)

Student Reader Unit 1 *This week students will read the following selections.*

60	**Route 66**	Expository Nonfiction
62	**A Cause for Walking**	Expository Nonfiction
70	**The Longest Route**	Realistic Fiction
78	**Odd Places, U.S.A.**	Expository Nonfiction
82	**4 You 2 Do**	Activity Page

Daily Lesson Plan

	ACTIVITIES	MATERIALS
Day 1	**Build Concepts** Weekly Concept: Travel America Vocabulary: *itineraries, journey, miles, mode, route, transportation, views* **Read a Passage** "Route 66," pp. 60–61 Comprehension: Use Strategies Reread for Fluency **Write** Response to Literature	Student Reader: Unit 1 Routine Cards 2, 4, 5 Tested Vocabulary Cards Student journals Practice Book, p. 9, Vocabulary Student Reader DVD-ROM
Day 2	**Word Work** Phonics: Plurals and Inflected Endings *–s, -es, -ies;* Spelling Change: *y* to *i* Vocabulary: Deepen word meaning **Comprehension** Sequence **Read a Passage** "A Cause for Walking," pp. 62–66 Reread for Fluency **Write** Response to Literature	Student Reader: Unit 1 Practice Book, p. 9, Vocabulary Graphic Organizer 5 Routine Cards 1, 2, 3, 4, 7 Practice Book, p. 10, Inflected Endings *-s, -es, -ies* Student Reader DVD-ROM
Day 3	**Word Work** Phonics: Plurals and Inflected Endings *–s, -es, -ies;* Spelling Change: *y* to *i* Vocabulary: Deepen word meaning **Comprehension** Sequence **Read a Passage** "A Cause for Walking," pp. 67–69 Reread for Fluency **Write** Response to Literature	Practice Book, p. 10, Inflected Endings *-s, -es, -ies* Tested Vocabulary Cards Student Reader: Unit 1 Graphic Organizer 5 Routine Cards 1, 2, 3, 4, 7 Practice Book, p. 11, Sequence Student Reader DVD-ROM
Day 4	**Word Work** Vocabulary: Extend word knowledge **Comprehension** Skill and Strategy Practice **Read a Passage** "The Longest Route," pp. 70–77 Reread for Fluency **Write** Response to Literature	Practice Book, p. 11, Sequence Student Reader: Unit 1 Routine Cards 2, 3, 4 Student Reader DVD-ROM
Day 5	**Read a Passage** "Odd Places, U.S.A.," pp. 78–81 Comprehension: Sequence; Listening **Build Concepts** Vocabulary **Write** Response to Literature: "4 You 2 Do," p. 82 **Assessment Options** Fluency Comprehension	Student Reader: Unit 1 Routine Cards 3, 5, 6, 8 Fluency Progress Chart, p. 185 Practice Book, p. 12, Writing

See pp. xvi–xvii for how *My Sidewalks* integrates instructional practices for ELL.

Build Concepts

Amazing Words Vocabulary

| To Do | To Say | 10–15 minutes |

Develop oral vocabulary.

See Routine Card 6 and p. 200.

Introduce the Concept/Amazing Words with an oral routine prior to displaying them in print. Page 200 in this Teacher's Guide provides specific guidelines for introducing each word.

Develop word meaning.

See Routine Card 5. Discuss pp. 59–61.

Have students read p. 59 and then look at the pictures on pp. 60–61. **What do these images have in common?** (They all have to do with car travel on Route 66.) **Can you use the word *travel* to describe what you see?** (Example: The pictures show some of the things people might they see if they *travel* on Route 66.)

Scaffold instruction.

Create a concept web.

In the center of a web, write *Travel America*. **This week's concept is *Travel America*. To travel is to go from one place to another.** Provide an example to demonstrate meaning. **Different people enjoy different ways to *travel*, some people like to fly, while others like to drive cars or ride on trains.**

Add the other vocabulary words.

Discuss the meaning of each word as it relates to travel America, using the glossary as needed. (See p. 26 in this Teacher's Guide for definitions.)

Concept and Language Goals

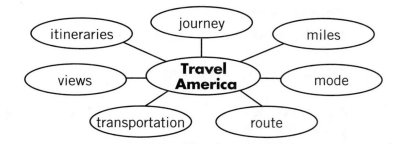

Model the multisyllabic word strategy.

Display each word. Say it as you display it.

Use the Tested Vocabulary Cards. Follow this routine for each word:

- **Look for Meaningful Parts** Do you recognize any parts of this word? What do these parts mean? Use the parts to read the word.

Think aloud.

- **Model** I see *trans-* at the beginning of *transportation*. I know the prefix *trans-* can mean "in or to a different place or condition." I also recognize the word *port*. I know the Latin root *port* can mean "to carry." So I think *transport* must have to do with carrying things from one place to another, and *transportation* is the act of doing that. List other words with these word parts. (*portable, porter, export, import, transfer, transform, transplant*).

Point to *journey*.

- **Chunk Words with No Recognizable Parts** Model how to chunk the word *journey*. I see a chunk at the beginning of the word: *jour*. I see a part at the end of the word: *ney*. I say each chunk slowly: *jour ney*. I say the chunks faster to make a whole word: *journey*. Is it a real word? Yes, I know the word *journey*.

- Have students practice reading each word.

Preview.

Read p. 58 with students.

Do you see any of the words we just learned on this page? Together with students, read the sentences on p. 58 describing each selection. Talk about how the vocabulary words might be used in the selections.

MORE PRACTICE

Deepen understanding of *travel*.

Have students demonstrate understanding by answering questions. **How is *travel* by car different from *travel* by airplane? Which do you prefer? Why?**

ACTIVITY 2 Read a Passage

Develop Concepts "Route 66," pp. 60–61

10–15 minutes

	To Do	To Say
Practice strategic prereading.	See Routine Card 2. Think aloud.	**Discuss Genre** Read the title on p. 60 and have students look at the illustrations on pp. 60–61. Model determining genre. The photographs are a clue that this is nonfiction. They look like photos of real places and things. I think this article will tell me about the history of Route 66.
Scaffold instruction.	Review text structure.	**Ask Questions** In order to understand nonfiction, ask yourself the following questions: What did I learn? What is this mainly about? As you read this article, ask yourself these questions and look for the answers.
Guide comprehension. **Develop language and concepts.**	Read pp. 60–61 aloud.	**Read** Read the article as students follow along. Then read it a second time, having students join in. If necessary, stop at the end of each paragraph to check comprehension. Ask questions to promote discussion and develop the concept. • **Why was Route 66 so famous?** • **What were some of the attractions along Route 66?** • **Why did people stop traveling on Route 66?** • **What words on the concept web could help you describe travel across America?**
MORE PRACTICE		Have students reread "Route 66." As they read, tell them to make a list of Route 66's roadside attractions to share with family members tonight.

Reread for Fluency "Route 66," p. 61

5 minutes

	To Do	To Say
CORRECTIVE FEEDBACK	Monitor oral reading.	**Read p. 61 aloud. Reread the page three or four times so your reading gets better each time.** Give feedback on students' oral reading, using the *if... then* statements on Routine Card 4. Model fluent reading if necessary. You may want to have students read along with the DVD-ROM.

ACTIVITY 3 Write

Response to Literature

5 minutes

	To Do	To Say
Prompt journal writing.	Write on the board or a transparency: *What can we learn about the United States as we travel?*	Take out your journals. This week we are reading about travel in America. Our question for this week is: *What can we learn about the United States as we travel?* Write an answer to this question based on what you read today. Have students write about the topic, using what they read and their own experiences.
Homework		Practice Book, p. 9, Vocabulary

ACTIVITY **1** Word Work

Phonics Plurals and Inflected Endings -s, -es, -ies; Spelling Change: *y* to *i*

5–10 minutes

	To Do	**To Say**
Teach plurals and inflected endings -s, -es, -ies; spelling change: *y* to *i*.	Write on the board or a transparency: *volunteer, pledge, coach, itinerary.*	**You can make words plural by adding the endings -s, -es, or -ies.** Add an -s to *volunteer.* **You can make most nouns plural by adding -s. How does adding an -s to volunteer change its meaning?** (*Volunteer* refers to one volunteer; *volunteers* refers to more than one volunteer.) **Nouns that end in a soft *ch*, *sh*, *s*, *ss*, *x*, *z*, or *zz* can be made plural by adding -es.** Add an -es to *coach.* **When a noun ends in *y*, change the *y* to *i* and add -es to form the plural.** Erase the *y* in *itinerary* and add -ies.
	Develop word meaning.	Have students think and converse. **Most people use an *itinerary* when they travel. How can an *itinerary* help you before you take a trip? What are some ways you might use an *itinerary* after your trip?**
Scaffold instruction.	Write *memory, crutch,* and *route*.	**Here are three more nouns, each with a different ending. How do you make each one plural?** (*memories, crutches, routes*) Guide students in adding the correct ending to each word.
CORRECTIVE FEEDBACK	Write each practice word.	Have students practice reading these words with plural endings. Correct any words students miss and have them reread the list.
		towers raises stations worries stories vehicles
MORE PRACTICE	Write more practice words.	Have students practice reading these words with plural endings.
		places families passengers bridges flurries destinations

Amazing Words Vocabulary

5 minutes

	To Do	**To Say**
Review vocabulary.	Review the homework.	Ask students to go over answers and share their writing from Practice Book p. 9. See Routine Card 1 for the multisyllabic word routine.
	Deepen understanding of *route*.	**Remember, a *route* is a way you choose to get somewhere. A city bus drives the same *route* every day. When might you pick a scenic *route* instead of a faster or more direct *route*? Why do some people like to have more than one *route*?**

ACTIVITY **2** Comprehension

Sequence

5 minutes

	To Do	**To Say**
Scaffold instruction.	Introduce sequence.	**Today you will read about people who walk long distances for different causes. As you read, try to keep track of the sequence of events in order to understand the information better. Look for words like *first, next, then,* and *finally* for clues to the sequence. Or look for steps in a list or in number order.**
	Model the skill.	**For example, if I read that a group of volunteers starts by asking friends and family members for pledges, I need to pay attention to the sequence to understand how people raise money by walking.**
	Distribute Graphic Organizer 5.	**As you read "A Cause for Walking," ask yourself, What comes next? Look for words that help you track the sequence of events involved in raising money for a good cause. Add these sequence words to your graphic organizer.** See Routine Card 7.

ACTIVITY **3** Read a Passage

Read for Comprehension "A Cause for Walking," pp. 62–66

10–15 minutes

	To Do	To Say
Scaffold instruction.	Monitor student engagement.	**Read** Have students read pp. 62–66. Stop at the end of each page to ask questions. Students who can read on their own can do so without stopping. After reading, ask questions to promote discussion.
	See Routine Cards 2 and 3.	**What are pledges?** (promises to give money for each mile walked)
		What do Eric Latham and Ron Reschke have in common? (They both walked in order to raise money for cancer research and treatment.)
	Model using context for word meaning.	Read aloud p. 62. Explain how sentence 5 provides clues to the meaning of *pledges* by giving a definition, and the last sentence gives an example.
		What do you think the rest of the article will be about? (Answers will vary. The title suggests it will be about more ways to raise money for charitable causes by walking.)
Model summarizing.	Think aloud.	**Summarize** What were the first five pages mainly about? What did you learn about walking for causes? Think aloud to model summarizing. **I learned a lot of details about people walking for different causes. But the main thing I learned is that there are charitable walks of different lengths all over the country.**
Develop language and concepts.	Ask questions.	• **Why is walking a good way to earn money for charity?**
		• **What are some of the reasons that people walk for charity?**
MORE PRACTICE	Have students reread p. 63.	**Reread** Have students use a map to locate the starting and ending points of Eric Latham's walk. Invite them to map the route that they would take to walk between the two points.

Reread for Fluency "A Cause for Walking," pp. 64–65

5 minutes

	To Do	To Say
MORE PRACTICE **CORRECTIVE FEEDBACK**	Pair students. Monitor paired reading.	Students read aloud pp. 64–65, switching readers at the end of the first page. Have partners reread; now the other partner begins. For optimal fluency, students should reread three or four times. Give feedback, using *if... then* statements on Routine Card 4. You may want to have students read along with the DVD-ROM.

ACTIVITY **4** Write

Response to Literature

5 minutes

	To Do	To Say
Prompt writing.	Writing elements: support	**On p. 65, you read that Ron Reschke's goal was to walk more than 1,000 miles. If you were going to walk 1,000 miles, what route would you choose? Why?** (Look for reasonable responses that include logical support.)
Homework		Practice Book, p. 10, Inflected Endings -s, -es, -ies

3

Word Work

Phonics Plurals and Inflected Endings -s, -es, -ies; Spelling Change: y to i

5 minutes

	To Do	**To Say**
Review plurals and inflected endings. **Scaffold instruction.**	Review the homework. Discuss the word *cities* on p. 66.	Ask students to share answers from Practice Book, p. 10. Point out *cities* on p. 66, paragraph 1. **Remember, when a noun ends in *y*, change the *y* to *i* and add *-es* to form the plural. What is the singular form of this plural word?** (city) Then point to *place* and *friend* on p. 66, paragraphs 2 and 3. **How would you form the plural of *place*? of *friend*?** (Add an -s to both.)
MORE PRACTICE	Model spelling words with endings that change *y* to *i*.	**Spell and Write** Write the word *city.* **How do we change the word to spell *cities*?** Write the word *cities.* **Who can tell me what changed to make the word *cities*?** Repeat with *company.*

Amazing Words Vocabulary

5 minutes

	To Do	**To Say**
Build vocabulary.	Deepen understanding of *transportation.*	**Most of the people in "A Cause for Walking" used their feet as a form of *transportation*. What other kinds of *transportation* can you name that don't require engines?** (Examples: bikes, skates, rowboats, kayaks, canoes, sleds, wagons, horses) **What powers these forms of *transportation*?**
Lead cumulative review.		Use the Tested Vocabulary Cards to review concept words from previous weeks.

Comprehension

Sequence

5–10 minutes

	To Do	**To Say**
Scaffold instruction.	Review sequence.	**An author may use numbered directions to show you the order in which things should happen. As you read the advice on pp. 67–68, pay attention to the order that the suggestions appear in, and think about how the outcome would change if the order were different.**
Guide practice.	Use Graphic Organizer 5.	**Listen as I read pp. 67–68. I want you to notice that the author lists several suggestions for planning for a long-distance walk.** Read pp. 67–68. Then ask: **Why does the author list "Start training" as the first step in preparing for the walk?** (Before you can attempt a long walk, the first thing you must do is train for it.) **Which of these activities should happen before the walk?** (numbers 1–3) **Which happen during the walk?** (numbers 4–6) See Routine Card 7.
MORE PRACTICE	Have students preview pp. 66–69.	**Read the captions and look at the map and photos on pp. 66–69. What do you think this section will be about?** (different long-distance walks and how to prepare for them)
	Think aloud.	**The captions and pictures make me think that this part of the article will describe how to prepare for and participate in a long-distance walking event.**

ACTIVITY 3 Read a Passage

Read for Comprehension "A Cause for Walking," pp. 67–69

10–15 minutes

	To Do	**To Say**
Scaffold instruction.	Monitor student engagement. See Routine Cards 2 and 3.	**Read** Have students read pp. 67–69. Stop at the end of each page to ask questions. Students who can read on their own can do so without stopping. After reading, ask questions to promote discussion. **What can you do to prepare for a long walk?** (exercise, choose the right equipment, get plenty of sleep and water) **Why does the author suggest keeping a journal?** (to keep track of what you saw and how you felt on different parts of the walk) **What should you do when you feel like giving up?** (focus on the goal; remember that your efforts will help others)
Review the multisyllabic word strategy.	Point out *landmarks,* p. 68.	Remind students to apply the multisyllabic word strategy to read this word. Guide them to find the meaningful parts *land* and *marks.* Have students blend the parts to read the whole word. **What are some *landmarks* you pass on your way to school?** See Routine Card 1.
Assess comprehension.	Monitor understanding. Summarize.	**After Reading** Have students discuss the What Do You Think? question. Prompt them to use sequence words when describing the three things they would do to prepare for a walk for a cause. Listen as they talk to assess comprehension. **What is this mainly about? What did you learn?** Work with students to summarize the selection.
MORE PRACTICE	Have students reread pp. 67–68.	**Reread** As they read, have students note the advice they think is most valuable and why. After they read, ask them to discuss the order in which they think each of the suggestions should appear.

Reread for Fluency "A Cause for Walking," p. 69

5 minutes

	To Do	**To Say**
CORRECTIVE FEEDBACK	Monitor oral reading.	**Read p. 69 aloud. Reread the page three or four times so your reading gets better each time.** Give feedback on students' oral reading, using the *if... then* statements on Routine Card 4. Model fluent reading if necessary. You may want to have students read along with the DVD-ROM.

ACTIVITY 4 Write

Response to Literature

5 minutes

	To Do	**To Say**
MORE PRACTICE	Prompt writing.	**This week's concept is *Travel America.* How does traveling on foot differ from traveling by car or plane or other modern forms of transportation? What could you learn about America by traveling on foot?** (All ideas should relate to the topic. Details should support ideas.)
Homework		Practice Book, p. 11, Sequence

ACTIVITY 1 Word Work

Amazing Words Vocabulary

	To Do	To Say	*5–10 minutes*

Extend word knowledge.

To Do: Write on the board or a transparency: *What form of* <u>transportation</u> *do you prefer?*

To Say: Use the word *transportation* to extend word knowledge. **Remember we read this word earlier this week. We looked for meaningful parts and we noticed *trans-* and *port*. The word *port* means "carry," and *trans-* means "in or to a different place or condition" or "across." When you *transport* something, you carry it from one place to another. Can you think of other words that use *trans-* or *port*?** *(transfer, transplant, transform, translate, export, import, portable, porter)* Write words as students name them and add some of your own. Talk about the meanings of the words.

Teach suffix -ation.

Scaffold instruction.

To Say: **The suffix *-ation* changes the verb *transport* into a noun that describes the act or means of carrying people or things from one place to another. Can you think of other words that end in the suffix *-ation*?** *(adaptation, formation, temptation, quotation, combination, identification)* Write words as students name them and add some of your own. Talk about the meanings of the words. Point out that *t* is pronounced /sh/ when followed by *-ion*.

To Do: Develop word meaning.

To Say: **How do we *transport* goods from one place to another? Do we use the same forms of *transportation* that we use to *transport* people?**

MORE PRACTICE

To Do: Deepen understanding of *transportation* and *journey*.

To Say: Have individual students or partners use the two words *transportation* and *journey* together in a sentence. (For example: During our *journey* across Europe we used several different forms of *transportation*, including trains and buses.) Share sentences. Ask: **Is choosing the right form of transportation important when planning a journey? Why?**

ACTIVITY 2 Comprehension

Skill and Strategy Practice

	To Do	To Say	*5 minutes*

Scaffold instruction.

To Do: Review sequence (homework).

To Say: Ask volunteers to read the passage and share answers from Practice Book p. 11. Remind students of the importance of following the sequence. **When you read a story, the sequence of events is often important. There might be clue words that help you figure out the order in which things happen. Look for these words. Other clues, such as times of day and dates, can also help you figure out the sequence. As you read the story, picture in your mind events as they happen.**

Practice strategic prereading.

To Do: See Routine Card 2.

Think aloud.

To Say: **Discuss Genre** Read the title and p. 70. Model determining genre.

I first thought this might be fiction because of the illustrations. When I read the first page, I knew it was realistic fiction because the cousins are at a family reunion.

To Do: Review story structure.

To Say: **Ask Questions** Remember to ask yourself two important questions to help you understand fiction: **What is the problem or goal? How is the problem solved or the goal reached? As you read this story, ask these questions and look for the answers.**

ACTIVITY **3** Read a Passage

Read for Comprehension "The Longest Route," pp. 70–77

10–15 minutes

	To Do	To Say
Scaffold instruction.	Monitor student engagement. See Routine Card 3.	**Read** Have students read pp. 70–77 on their own and then discuss. For students who need more help, stop at the end of each page to discuss. After reading, ask questions.
		Who are the main characters? (Kayla, Janet, and Sam)
		What is the setting? (a family reunion in Denver, Colorado)
		What are the three cousins trying to figure out? (who traveled the farthest to get to the reunion)
		What forms of transportation did the cousins use to get to the reunion? (plane, train, bus)
		Who had the longest travel time? (Sam) **Who traveled the farthest?** (Kayla)
Assess comprehension.	Monitor understanding.	**After Reading** Have students discuss the What Do You Think? question. Prompt them to use sequence words in telling the order in which the cousins arrived at the campsite. Listen as they talk to assess comprehension.
MORE PRACTICE		**Reread** Have students reread p. 70 and then explain why they think the cousins are up so late after so much traveling.

Reread for Fluency "The Longest Route," pp. 74–75

5–10 minutes

	To Do	To Say
CORRECTIVE FEEDBACK	Pair students. Monitor paired reading.	Students read aloud pp. 74–75, switching readers at the end of each page. Have partners reread; now the other partner begins. For optimal fluency, students should reread three or four times. Give feedback, using Routine Card 4. You may want to have students read along with the DVD-ROM.
MORE PRACTICE	**READERS' THEATER**	Work with a group of students to adapt pp. 71–76 as a radio play. Have students rehearse reading the parts of Kayla, Sam, Janet, and one or two narrators.

ACTIVITY **4** Write

Response to Literature

5 minutes

	To Do	To Say
Prompt expository writing.	Review pp. 70–77. Writing elements: organization, conventions.	**Explain the sequence of events on the first day of the Miller family reunion. List each event, beginning with the cousins' arrival at the campsite. Include sequence words. Use complete sentences to express your ideas.** (Responses should include sequence words such as *first, then,* and *finally.* Order of events should be clear and connected.)

ACTIVITY 1 | Read a Passage

Read Together "Odd Places, U.S.A.," pp. 78–81

10 minutes

	To Do	**To Say**
Scaffold instruction.	Review sequence.	Have students preview pp. 78–81. **This article describes some unusual travel destinations in the United States. As you read this selection, think about which destination you'd like to visit first, second, and so on. Imagine the itinerary you might plan.**
	See Routine Card 3.	**Read** Read the article as students follow along. Then read it a second time, having students join in on the text. After reading, ask questions.
		How big is Lucy the Elephant? (six stories high)
		What makes the newspaper house so unusual? (The walls and furniture are made of rolled newspapers.)
		Was the upside-down house really deposited there by a tornado? Explain. (No; it was built in 1998 in its upside-down condition, apparently to serve as a tourist attraction.)
		The introduction says, "These are not the usual places that tourists visit." Why? (Answers will vary. Example: These attractions are in small towns and out-of-the-way places.)
Assess comprehension.	Monitor listening comprehension.	**Summarize** Have one student explain what the Spoonbridge and Cherry is.

ACTIVITY 2 | Build Concepts

Amazing Words Vocabulary

5–10 minutes

	To Do	**To Say**
Review concept and vocabulary.	Display the concept web you began on Day 1.	**This week's question is *What can we learn about the United States as we travel?* How do this week's words relate to the question?** (Have students answer the question, using some of the vocabulary they learned this week.)
		Ask students to add more words to the concept web. Have students explain how each word relates to travel America. Monitor students' understanding of vocabulary as they discuss the web. See Routine Card 5.
MORE PRACTICE	Write *views, mode,* and *transportation* on the board.	Have students relate *views, mode,* and *transportation.* **How might the *views* that you see while traveling differ, depending on the *mode* of *transportation* that you use? Explain. What else helps you decide what *mode* of *transportation* you are going to use on a trip?**

ACTIVITY **3** Write

Response to Literature "4 You 2 Do," p. 82

To Do	To Say

5–10 minutes

Guide response activities.

Discuss the directions on p. 82. Tell students to choose one activity to complete. See Routine Card 8.

Word Play Have students complete the first part on their own and then meet with a partner to make up riddles with other concept words.

Making Connections Discuss the question in a group. (Answers will vary. Students may say that people talk about their lives or why they decided to do this walk. They may tell stories or sing songs.)

On Paper Have students brainstorm some answers to the prompt before they write. Have them write on their own. Students can use Practice Book p. 12 to structure their written responses, or you can send the Practice Book page home for them to complete later.

MORE PRACTICE

If you have more time, direct students to complete all the activities.

ACTIVITY **4** Assessment Options

Passage Reading

To Do	To Say

10–15 minutes

See Routine Card 6.

While some students are doing Activity 3, determine which students you want to assess this week and choose from these options.

Check fluency.

Take a two-minute timed sample of each student's oral reading.

Fluency Have a student read for two minutes from "A Cause for Walking." Record the number of correct words read per minute. See p. 184 for monitoring fluency. Be sure each student is assessed at least every other week.

Have students graph their progress on the Fluency Progress Chart, p. 185.

Check comprehension.

Retelling Have students reread "A Cause for Walking" and retell it. Prompt students if necessary. See p. 186 for monitoring retelling.

If you have time, assess every student.

Homework

Practice Book, p. 12, Writing

Unit 1 Week 4 *The Southwest*

What is special about the landscape of the Southwest?

Objectives *This week students will...*

Vocabulary
- build concepts and vocabulary: *arid, canyon, carved, cliffs, frontier, guide, hiking*

Phonics
- read words with verb endings
- apply knowledge of word structure to decode multisyllabic words when reading

Text Comprehension
- compare and contrast to improve comprehension
- write in response to literature
- make connections across text

Fluency
- practice fluency with oral rereading

Word Work *This week's phonics focus is . . .*

Verb Endings

Amazing Words Concept/Amazing Words *Tested Vocabulary*

The week's vocabulary is related to the concept of the Southwest.
The first appearance of each word in the Student Reader is noted below.

arid	having very little rainfall; dry (p. 86)
canyon	a narrow valley with high, steep sides, usually with a stream at the bottom (p. 86)
carved	cut something (p. 90)
cliffs	very steep, rocky slopes (p. 88)
frontier	the farthest edge of settled country, where the wilderness begins (p. 91)
guide	someone or something that shows the way (p. 102)
hiking	taking a long walk; marching (p. 99)

Student Reader Unit 1 *This week students will read the following selections.*

86	**Scenes from the Southwest**	Expository Nonfiction
90	**Wild, Wild Westerns**	Expository Nonfiction
98	**Searching for Sure Foot**	Realistic Fiction
106	**Poetry**	Poems
108	**4 You 2 Do**	Activity Page

Daily Lesson Plan

	ACTIVITIES	MATERIALS
Day 1	**Build Concepts** Weekly Concept: The Southwest Vocabulary: *arid, canyon, carved, cliffs, frontier, guide, hiking* **Read a Passage** "Scenes from the Southwest," pp. 86–89 Comprehension: Use Strategies Reread for Fluency **Write** Response to Literature	Student Reader: Unit 1 Routine Cards 2, 4, 5 Tested Vocabulary Cards Student journals Practice Book, p. 13, Vocabulary Student Reader DVD-ROM
Day 2	**Word Work** Phonics: Verb Endings Vocabulary: Deepen word meaning **Comprehension** Compare and Contrast **Read a Passage** "Wild, Wild Westerns," pp. 90–93 Reread for Fluency **Write** Response to Literature	Student Reader: Unit 1 Practice Book, p. 13, Vocabulary Graphic Organizer 3 Routine Cards 1, 2, 3, 4, 7 Practice Book, p. 14, Verb Endings With and Without Spelling Changes Student Reader DVD-ROM
Day 3	**Word Work** Phonics: Verb Endings Vocabulary: Deepen word meaning **Comprehension** Compare and Contrast **Read a Passage** "Wild, Wild Westerns," pp. 94–97 Reread for Fluency **Write** Response to Literature	Practice Book, p. 14, Verb Endings With and Without Spelling Changes Tested Vocabulary Cards Student Reader: Unit 1 Graphic Organizer 3 Routine Cards 1, 2, 3, 4, 7 Practice Book, p. 15, Compare and Contrast Student Reader DVD-ROM
Day 4	**Word Work** Vocabulary: Extend word knowledge **Comprehension** Skill and Strategy Practice **Read a Passage** "Searching for Sure Foot," pp. 98–105 Reread for Fluency **Write** Response to Literature	Practice Book, p. 15, Compare and Contrast Student Reader: Unit 1 Routine Cards 2, 3, 4 Student Reader DVD-ROM
Day 5	**Read a Passage** Poetry, pp. 106–107 Comprehension: Compare and Contrast; Listening **Build Concepts** Vocabulary **Write** Response to Literature: "4 You 2 Do," p. 108 **Assessment Options** Fluency Comprehension	Student Reader: Unit 1 Routine Cards 3, 5, 6, 8 Fluency Progress Chart, p. 185 Practice Book, p. 16, Writing

See pp. xvi–xvii for how *My Sidewalks* integrates instructional practices for ELL.

ACTIVITY **1** Build Concepts

Amazing Words Vocabulary

To Do	To Say	*10–15 minutes*

Develop oral vocabulary.

See Routine Card 6 and p. 201.

Introduce the Concept/Amazing Words with an oral routine prior to displaying them in print. Page 201 in this Teacher's Guide provides specific guidelines for introducing each word.

Develop word meaning.

Scaffold instruction.

See Routine Card 5. Discuss pp. 85–89.

Have students read p. 85 and then look at the pictures on pp. 86–89. **What do you see?** (different Southwestern scenes, such as cactus and cowboys and old buildings made of mud) **Can you use the word** *Southwest* **to describe what all of these pictures have in common?** (Example: Each of these pictures shows something you might see in the *Southwest*.)

Create a concept web.

In the center of a web, write *The Southwest.* **This week's concept is** *the Southwest.* *The Southwest* **is a region of the country that includes Texas, New Mexico, Oklahoma, and Arizona.** Provide an example to demonstrate meaning. **If you travel to** *the Southwest,* **you'll find a region rich in history and culture.**

Add the other vocabulary words.

Discuss the meaning of each word as it relates to the Southwest, using the glossary as needed. (See p. 38 in this Teacher's Guide for definitions.)

Concept and Language Goals

Concept web with "The Southwest" in the center, connected to: arid, canyon, carved, hiking, cliffs, guide, frontier.

Model the multisyllabic word strategy.

Display each word. Say it as you display it.

Use the Tested Vocabulary Cards. Follow this routine for each word:

- **Look for Meaningful Parts** Do you recognize any parts of this word? What do these parts mean? Use the parts to read the word.

- **Chunk Words with No Recognizable Parts** Model how to chunk the word *canyon.*

Think aloud.

- **Model** I see a chunk at the beginning of the word: *can.* I see a part at the end of the word: *yon.* I'll try saying them slowly: *can yon.* I say the chunks faster to make a whole word: *canyon.* Is it a real word? Yes, I know the word *canyon.*

- Have students practice reading each word.

Preview.

Read p. 84 with students.

Do you see any of the words we just learned on this page? Together with students, read the sentences on p. 84 describing each selection. Talk about how the vocabulary words might be used in the selections.

MORE PRACTICE

Deepen understanding of *the Southwest.*

Have students demonstrate understanding by answering questions. **What makes** *the Southwest* **such an interesting part of the country? What images do you associate with** *the Southwest?* **Give examples.**

ACTIVITY **2** Read a Passage

Develop Concepts "Scenes from the Southwest," pp. 86–89

10–15 minutes

	To Do	**To Say**
Practice strategic prereading.	See Routine Card 2. Think aloud.	**Discuss Genre** Read the title on p. 86 and have students look at the illustrations on pp. 86–89. Model determining genre. The photographs are a clue that this is nonfiction. They look like pictures of real places. I think this article will tell why the Southwest is such an interesting region of the country.
Scaffold instruction.	Review text structure.	**Ask Questions** There are two questions you can ask yourself to help you understand nonfiction: What did I learn? What is this mainly about? As you read this article, ask yourself these questions and look for the answers.
Guide comprehension. **Develop language and concepts.**	Read pp. 86–89 aloud.	**Read** Read the article as students follow along. Then read it a second time, having students join in. If necessary, stop at the end of each paragraph to check comprehension. Ask questions to promote discussion and develop the concept. • What are some of the different things you can do in the Southwest? • Where did Native Americans live long ago? • What jobs helped Southwestern towns to grow? • What words on the concept web could help you describe the Southwest?
MORE PRACTICE		Have students reread "Scenes from the Southwest." As they read, they should list the unique landforms and features of the area. Invite them to share the list with family members tonight.

Reread for Fluency "Scenes from the Southwest," p. 88

5 minutes

	To Do	**To Say**
CORRECTIVE FEEDBACK	Monitor oral reading.	**Read p. 88 aloud. Reread the page three or four times so your reading gets better each time.** Give feedback on students' oral reading, using the *if... then* statements on Routine Card 4. Model fluent reading if necessary. You may want to have students read along with the DVD-ROM.

ACTIVITY **3** Write

Response to Literature

5 minutes

	To Do	**To Say**
Prompt journal writing.	Write on the board or a transparency: *What is special about the landscape of the Southwest?*	**Take out your journals. This week we are reading about the Southwest. Our question for this week is: *What is special about the landscape of the Southwest?* Write an answer to this question based on what you read today.** Have students write about the topic, using what they read and their own experiences.
Homework		Practice Book, p. 13, Vocabulary

ACTIVITY **1** # Word Work

Phonics Verb Endings

To Do	To Say	5–10 minutes

Teach verb endings with and without spelling changes.

Write on the board or a transparency: *In order to stop <u>slipping</u>, I <u>grabbed</u> a tree branch.*

This week we will look at verb endings with and without spelling changes. For some base words, simply add *-ed* or *-ing* to the end of the word. (Examples: *looking, painting, hiked, herded*) **Other base words change when you add *-ed* and *-ing*. Look at the sentence. Let's circle the base word in each underlined word.** Read the sentence aloud with students. Circle *slip* and *grab*. **When a one-syllable word ends in a single vowel plus a single consonant (VC), the consonant is usually doubled when you add the ending.**

Scaffold instruction.

Write the words *hiking, hoping, baking,* and *saluting.*

How does the base word *hike* change when you add *-ing*? (You drop the silent *e*.) **What are the other base words?** *(hope, bake, salute)* **Listen to the vowel sound in each of those words. What do you notice?** (All have long vowels.) **To add *-ing* to words with a long vowel sound formed with a final *e*, drop the silent *e* before adding *-ing*.**

CORRECTIVE FEEDBACK

Write each practice word.

Have students practice reading these words ending with *-ed* or *-ing*. Correct any words students miss and have them reread the list.

shopping	standing	running	blamed	pinned	sobbed

MORE PRACTICE

Write more practice words.

Have students practice reading these words ending with *-ed* or *-ing*:

filming	biting	swimming	driving	chatted	striped

Amazing Words ## Vocabulary

To Do	To Say	5 minutes

Review vocabulary.

Review the homework.

Ask students to go over answers and share their writing from Practice Book p. 13. See Routine Card 1 for the multisyllabic word routine.

Deepen understanding of *arid.*

Remember, *arid* means "very dry." Regions of the country that get very little rainfall are usually *arid*. What do you think the landscape and vegetation look like in *arid* regions? Why might it be more difficult for people, plants, and animals to survive there?

ACTIVITY **2** # Comprehension

Compare and Contrast

To Do	To Say	5 minutes

Scaffold instruction.

Introduce compare and contrast.

Today you will read about western movies. You'll read how early westerns were different from those filmed many years later. When you compare and contrast two or more things, pay attention to details that tell you how those things are alike and how they are different.

Model the skill.

For example, if I read that early westerns were filmed in a studio and later westerns were filmed outdoors, I need to recognize that the author is describing one way that early westerns were different from later westerns.

Distribute Graphic Organizer 3.

As you read "Wild, Wild Westerns," compare and contrast the ways that early westerns were different from those that were made in later years. Add the similarities and differences you find to your graphic organizer. See Routine Card 7.

ACTIVITY **3** Read a Passage

Read for Comprehension "Wild, Wild Westerns," pp. 90–93

10–15 minutes

	To Do	To Say
Scaffold instruction.	Monitor student engagement. See Routine Cards 2 and 3. Point to *painted* on p. 91.	**Read** Have students read pp. 90–93. Stop at the end of each page to ask questions. Students who can read on their own can do so without stopping. After reading, ask questions to promote discussion. **Where were the early westerns filmed?** (inside studios) **Why did westerns start looking more realistic in the 1930s?** (The cameras improved; they spent more money; they filmed the scenes outdoors.) **How did Monument Valley become one of the world's most famous landscapes?** (John Ford filmed many movies there.) Demonstrate using your finger to circle *-ed* in the end of the word and then reading the base word *paint* that remains. **What do you think the rest of the article will be about?** (Answers will vary. The title suggests it will tell more about westerns.)
Model summarizing. **Develop language and concepts.**	Think aloud. Ask questions.	**Summarize** What were the first four pages mainly about? What did you learn about filming westerns and why the Southwest was a popular place to shoot? Think aloud to model summarizing. **I learned some details about how westerns were made, such as the fact that they used to be filmed indoors. But the main thing I learned was that westerns helped make the landscape of the Southwest famous.** • **Why is there a spot in Monument Valley called John Ford Point?** • **Why was the Southwest a good background for westerns?**
MORE PRACTICE	Have students reread p. 90.	**Reread** Have students draw a picture of one or more of the Southwestern landforms described on p. 90.

Reread for Fluency "Wild, Wild Westerns," pp. 91–92

5 minutes

	To Do	To Say
MORE PRACTICE **CORRECTIVE FEEDBACK**	Pair students. Monitor paired reading.	Students read aloud pp. 91–92, switching readers at the end of each paragraph. Have partners reread; now the other partner begins. For optimal fluency, students should reread three or four times. Give feedback, using the *if... then* statements on Routine Card 4. You may want to have students read along with the DVD-ROM.

ACTIVITY **4** Write

Response to Literature

5 minutes

	To Do	To Say
Prompt descriptive writing.	Writing elements: support	The article says that the landscape of the Southwest "made a stunning background" for the many westerns filmed there. What are some reasons that the Southwest was such a good place to film westerns? Support your ideas with descriptive language.
Homework		Practice Book, p. 14, Verb Endings With and Without Spelling Changes.

3

Word Work

Phonics Verb Endings

	To Do	To Say	*5 minutes*
Review verb endings. **Scaffold instruction.**	Review the homework. Discuss the word *starred* on p. 93 in the Student Reader.	Ask students to share answers from Practice Book p. 14. Point out *starred* on p. 93, paragraph 2. **What ending do you see in this word?** *(-ed)* **What is the base word?** *(star)* **What do you need to do to the base word before adding the ending?** (double the *r* before adding *-ed*) Then point to *loved* and *watched* on p. 91, paragraph 1. **What is the base word for each of these words?** *(love, watch)* **How are the endings added?** Simply add *-ed* to watch. You have to drop the final *e* in *love* before adding *-ed*.	
MORE PRACTICE	Model spelling words with verb endings.	**Spell and Write** Write *starred, strumming, carved, loved, watched,* and *painted.* Point to the first word. **How do we change *star* to spell *starred?*** Continue with the other words and review how to add the ending to each pair of words.	

Amazing Words **Vocabulary**

	To Do	To Say	*5 minutes*
Build vocabulary. **Lead cumulative review.**	Deepen understanding of *carved.*	Read aloud the first paragraph on p. 90. **What does the author mean when he says that wind and water *carved* the mesas and buttes over time?** Say a sentence using *carved.* **What are some other ways that the elements can alter a landscape?** Use the Tested Vocabulary Cards to review words from previous weeks.	

Comprehension

Compare and Contrast

	To Do	To Say	*5–10 minutes*
Scaffold instruction.	Review compare and contrast.	**An author helps you understand new ideas by comparing them with things you already know. As you read the second part of "Wild, Wild Westerns," look for similarities and differences between the western settings, and compare the information with what you already know.**	
Guide practice.	Use Graphic Organizer 3.	**Listen as I read p. 94. I want you to notice that the author tells about a movie set.** Read p. 94. Then ask: **What similarities between John Ford and other filmmakers does the author describe?** (Other filmmakers wanted to film in the Southwest as well.) **Add that detail to your graphic organizer. How is Old Tucson similar to the sets of the early westerns?** (Old Tucson was also built by the studios.) See Routine Card 7.	
MORE PRACTICE	Have students preview pp. 94–97.	**Read the captions and look at the photos on pp. 94–97. What do you think this section will be about?** (Old Tucson) **Why do you think so?** Think aloud to model using captions and illustrations to predict.	
	Think aloud.	**The captions make me think that this section will describe a movie set called Old Tucson. From the pictures I can tell that some well-known movies and shows were filmed there.**	

Read a Passage

Read for Comprehension "Wild, Wild Westerns," pp. 94–97

10–15 minutes

	To Do	**To Say**
Scaffold instruction.	Monitor student engagement.	**Read** Have students read pp. 94–97. Stop at the end of each page to ask questions. Students who can read on their own can do so without stopping. After reading, ask questions to promote discussion.
	See Routine Cards 2 and 3.	**Who built Old Tucson?** (a movie studio) **Why?** (Filmmakers wanted a realistic-looking frontier town to use in their movies.)
		Why did Old Tucson keep growing? (Each new movie needed a new setting.)
		What happened to Old Tucson in 1960? (It opened to the public.)
		Why is Old Tucson known as "Hollywood in the Desert"? (because so many movies and television shows were filmed there)
Review the multisyllabic word strategy.	Point out *destroyed* on p. 96.	Remind students to apply the multisyllabic word strategy to read this word. Demonstrate framing the meaningful parts *destroy* and *-ed.* Have students blend the parts to read the whole word. See Routine Card 1.
Assess comprehension.	Monitor understanding.	**After Reading** Have students discuss the What Do You Think? question. Prompt them to find similarities and differences between early westerns and later westerns. Listen as they talk to assess comprehension.
	Summarize.	**What is this mainly about? What did you learn?** Work with students to summarize the selection.
MORE PRACTICE	Have students reread pp. 95–96.	**Reread** As they read, invite students to compare and contrast Old Tucson when it was first built to Old Tucson in the 1970s. Have students add these details to their graphic organizers. How did Old Tucson change after the 1970s?

Reread for Fluency "Wild, Wild Westerns," p. 97

5 minutes

	To Do	**To Say**
CORRECTIVE FEEDBACK	Monitor oral reading.	**Read p. 97 aloud. Reread the page three or four times so your reading gets better each time.** Give feedback on students' oral reading, using the *if... then* statements on Routine Card 4. Model fluent reading if necessary. You may want to have students read along with the DVD-ROM.

Write

Response to Literature

5 minutes

	To Do	**To Say**
MORE PRACTICE	Prompt writing.	**This article describes both the real landscape of the Southwest and the fake frontier town that was built by a movie studio. Which would you prefer to see: the actual landscape or the studio town? Use details to explain your opinion.**
Homework		Practice Book, p. 15, Compare and Contrast

Word Work

Amazing Words Vocabulary

To Do	To Say	5–10 minutes

Extend word knowledge.

Scaffold instruction.

Write on the board or a transparency:
The tour guide led us down the trail.

Use the word *guide* to extend word knowledge. **Remember, we read this word earlier this week. A *guide* is someone or something that shows the way. Why do people often need a *guide* when they travel? What skills should a *guide* have?** Talk about the skills a guide should have, such as knowledge of a specific area. Point out that *ui* is pronounced /ī/ in *guide*. **Not all *guides* are people. Sometimes we use other types of *guides*,** such as books, to show us how to get around a place. **What other types of *guides* can you think of?** (audio guides in museums, maps, video or television travel guides)

Develop word meaning.

How would the skills of a tour *guide* in a city differ from those of a tour *guide* in a wilderness area?

MORE PRACTICE

Deepen understanding of *canyon* and *cliffs*.

Have individuals or partners use the two words *canyon* and *cliffs* together in a sentence. (For example, From the bottom of the *canyon,* the steep *cliffs* rose above us on all sides.) Share sentences. Ask: **Is a canyon surrounded by cliffs? Why?**

Comprehension

Skill and Strategy Practice

To Do	To Say	5 minutes

Scaffold instruction.

Review compare and contrast (homework).

Ask volunteers to read the passage and share answers from Practice Book p. 15. Remind students of the importance of looking for similarities and differences between things as they read. **When you read a story, you can compare and contrast characters, settings, outcomes, or other story elements. You can also compare one story to another. Look for ways that things are alike and different. This will help you better understand the story.**

Practice strategic prereading.

See Routine Card 2.

Discuss Genre Read the title and the first paragraph on p. 98. Model determining genre.

Think aloud.

I first thought this might be fiction because of the illustrations. When I read the first paragraph, I knew it was fiction because of the description of Sarah.

Review story structure.

Ask Questions Remember to ask yourself two important questions to help you understand fictional stories: What is the problem or goal? How is the problem solved or the goal reached? As you read this story, ask these questions and look for the answers.

ACTIVITY 3 Read a Passage

Read for Comprehension "Searching for Sure Foot," pp. 98–105

To Do | **To Say** | *10–15 minutes*

Scaffold instruction.

To Do: Monitor student engagement.

See Routine Card 3.

To Say: **Read** Have students read pp. 98–105 on their own and then discuss. For students who need more help, stop at the end of each page to discuss. After reading, ask questions.

Who are the main characters? (Sarah, Sarah's parents, Mr. Manakaja)

What is the setting? (the village of Supai)

Who was Sure Foot? (Sarah's great-grandmother) **How did she get her name?** (She could go anywhere in the canyon without falling.)

Why does Mr. Manakaja suggest that the family visit Mooney Falls? (so that Sarah can learn how her great-grandmother got her name)

Why does Mr. Manakaja call Sarah Little Sure Foot at the end of the story? (because she was brave enough to hike down to the falls)

Assess comprehension.

To Do: Monitor understanding.

To Say: **After Reading** Have students discuss the What Do You Think? question. Guide them to use details from the story to compare and contrast Sarah and her great-grandmother. Listen as they talk to assess comprehension.

MORE PRACTICE

Reread Have students reread p. 103 and then explain why the hike is so difficult.

Reread for Fluency "Searching for Sure Foot," pp. 101–102

To Do | **To Say** | *5–10 minutes*

CORRECTIVE FEEDBACK

To Do: Pair students. Monitor paired reading.

To Say: Students read aloud pp. 101–102, switching readers at the end of each page. Have partners reread; now the other partner begins. For optimal fluency, students should reread three or four times. Give feedback, using Routine Card 4. You may want to have students read along with the DVD-ROM.

MORE PRACTICE

READERS' THEATER

Work with a group of four students to adapt pp. 100–102 as a radio play. Have students rehearse reading the parts, with one student narrating, one student playing the woman in the store, one playing Sarah, and one playing Mr. Manakaja.

ACTIVITY 4 Write

Response to Literature

To Do | **To Say** | *5 minutes*

Prompt descriptive writing.

To Do: Review p. 100.

Writing elements: organization

To Say: **Tell how the village of Supai is different from or similar to the town where you live. Include details from the story as you compare and contrast the two places.** (Students should use words that compare and contrast, such as *both* and *however*.)

ACTIVITY 1 | Read a Passage

Read Together Poetry, pp. 106–107

10 minutes

	To Do	**To Say**
Scaffold instruction.	Review compare and contrast.	Have students preview pp. 106–107. **These poems describe different scenes or qualities that are unique to the Southwest. When you read different poems that deal with the same setting, comparing and contrasting the poems can help you understand them better. As you read each poem, think about the similarities and differences in the images they describe.**
	See Routine Card 3.	**Read** Read the poems as students follow along. Then read them a second time, having students join in on the text. After reading, ask questions.
		What is the "snow" in the poem "Desert Snow"? (the stars)
		Who is Coyote serenading? (Moon)
		On p. 107, what is special about the windy cave in the Painted Rock Mountains? (It was a place where any wish was granted.)
		Who is the "They" that the author refers to in the first line of "How the Maricopas Made Wishes Come True"? (the Maricopa people)
Assess comprehension.	Monitor listening comprehension.	**Summarize** Choose two students to describe for the class what each poem is about.

ACTIVITY 2 | Build Concepts

Amazing Words Vocabulary

5–10 minutes

	To Do	**To Say**
Review concept and vocabulary.	Display the concept web you began on Day 1.	**This week's question is *What is special about the landscape of the Southwest?* How do this week's words relate to the question?** (Have students answer the question, using some of the vocabulary they learned this week.)
		Ask students to add more words to the concept web. Have students explain how each word relates to the Southwest. Monitor students' understanding of vocabulary as they discuss the web. See Routine Card 5.
MORE PRACTICE	Write *arid* and *Southwest* on the board.	Have students relate *arid* and *Southwest*. **Why are so many parts of the *Southwest* *arid?* How has this affected the history and culture of the region? How has it affected the lifestyles of people living there?**

ACTIVITY **3**   Write

Response to Literature "4 You 2 Do," p. 108

To Do	To Say	5–10 minutes

Guide response activities.

Discuss the directions on p. 108. Tell students to choose one activity to complete. See Routine Card 8.

Word Play Have students work in pairs or small groups to play the guessing game.

Making Connections Discuss the question in a group. (Answers will vary. Students may say that some people wrote poems about it; people watched westerns made in the Southwest; a girl learned about an ancestor from that region and climbed the same canyon she did.)

On Paper Have students brainstorm some answers to the prompt before they write. Have them write on their own. Students can use Practice Book p. 16 to structure their written responses, or you can send the Practice Book page home for them to complete later.

MORE PRACTICE

If you have more time, direct students to complete all the activities.

ACTIVITY **4**   Assessment Options

Passage Reading

To Do	To Say	10–15 minutes

See Routine Card 6.

While some students are doing Activity 3, determine which students you want to assess this week and choose from these options.

Check fluency.

Take a two-minute timed sample of each student's oral reading.

Fluency Have a student read for two minutes from "Searching for Sure Foot." Record the number of correct words read per minute. See p. 184 for monitoring fluency. Be sure each student is assessed at least every other week.

Have students graph their progress on the Fluency Progress Chart, p. 185.

Check comprehension.

Retelling Have students reread "Searching for Sure Foot" and retell it. Prompt students if necessary. See p. 186 for monitoring retelling.

If you have time, assess every student.

Homework   Practice Book, p. 16, Writing

Unit 1 Week 5 *The West*

? What is special about the West?

Objectives *This week students will...*

Vocabulary
- build concepts and vocabulary: *astonishing, eruptions, formed, gigantic, naturally, unbelievable*

Phonics
- read words with prefixes *un-, re-, in-, dis-*
- apply knowledge of word structure to decode multisyllabic words when reading

Text Comprehension
- use main idea to improve comprehension
- write in response to literature
- make connections across text

Fluency
- practice fluency with oral rereading

Word Work *This week's phonics focus is . . .*

Prefixes *un-, re-, in-, dis-*

Amazing Words Concept/Amazing Words *Tested Vocabulary*

The week's vocabulary is related to the concept of the West.
The first appearance of each word in the Student Reader is noted below.

astonishing	surprising greatly; amazing (p. 115)
eruptions	explosions of lava and steam from a volcano (p. 125)
formed	took shape (p. 125)
gigantic	like a giant; very large or powerful; huge (p. 122)
naturally	not made by humans or one's own talent (p. 116)
unbelievable	thinking something is not true (p. 116)

Student Reader Unit 1 *This week students will read the following selections.*

Daily Lesson Plan

	ACTIVITIES	MATERIALS
Day 1	**Build Concepts** Weekly Concept: The West Vocabulary: *astonishing, eruptions, formed, gigantic, naturally, unbelievable* **Read a Passage** "California," pp. 112–113 Comprehension: Use Strategies Reread for Fluency **Write** Response to Literature	Student Reader: Unit 1 Routine Cards 2, 4, 5 Tested Vocabulary Cards Student journals Practice Book, p. 17, Vocabulary Student Reader DVD-ROM
Day 2	**Word Work** Phonics: Prefixes *un-, re-, in-, dis-* Vocabulary: Deepen word meaning **Comprehension** Main Idea **Read a Passage** "Surf's Up!" pp. 114–117 Reread for Fluency **Write** Response to Literature	Student Reader: Unit 1 Practice Book, p. 17, Vocabulary Graphic Organizer 1 Routine Cards 1, 2, 3, 4, 7 Practice Book, p. 18, Prefixes *un-, re-,* *in-, dis-* Student Reader DVD-ROM
Day 3	**Word Work** Phonics: Prefixes *un-, re-, in-, dis-* Vocabulary: Deepen word meaning **Comprehension** Main Idea **Read a Passage** "Surf's Up!" pp. 118–121 Reread for Fluency **Write** Response to Literature	Practice Book, p. 18, Prefixes *un-, re-,* *in-, dis-* Tested Vocabulary Cards Student Reader: Unit 1 Graphic Organizer 1 Routine Cards 1, 2, 3, 4, 7 Practice Book, p. 19, Main Idea and Details Student Reader DVD-ROM
Day 4	**Word Work** Vocabulary: Extend word knowledge **Comprehension** Skill and Strategy Practice **Read a Passage** "Natural Treasures," pp. 122–129 Reread for Fluency **Write** Response to Literature	Practice Book, p. 19, Main Idea and Details Student Reader: Unit 1 Routine Cards 2, 3, 4 Student Reader DVD-ROM
Day 5	**Read a Passage** "All Steamed Up," pp. 130–133 Comprehension: Main Idea; Listening **Build Concepts** Vocabulary **Write** Response to Literature: "4 You 2 Do," p. 134 **Assessment Options** Fluency, Comprehension End-of-Unit Test	Student Reader: Unit 1 Routine Cards 3, 5, 8 Practice Book, p. 20, Writing Assessment Book, p. 24

See pp. xvi–xvii for how *My Sidewalks* integrates instructional practices for ELL.

ACTIVITY 1 Build Concepts

Amazing Words Vocabulary

	To Do	**To Say**	*10–15 minutes*

Develop oral vocabulary.

See Routine Card 6 and p. 202.

Introduce the Concept/Amazing Words with an oral routine prior to displaying them in print. Page 202 in this Teacher's Guide provides specific guidelines for introducing each word.

Develop word meaning.

See Routine Card 5. Discuss pp. 111–113.

Have students read p. 111 and then look at the pictures on pp. 112–113. **What do you see?** (photographs of unusual attractions) **Can you use the word *astonishing* to talk about these images?** (Example: The pictures show some *astonishing* sights, such as a gift shop inside a tree.)

Scaffold instruction.

Create a concept web.

In the center of a web, write *The West.* **This week's concept is *the West.* This region includes the states of California, Oregon, and Washington, as well as Alaska and Hawaii.** Provide an example to demonstrate meaning. **There are many attractions in *the West,* including sandy beaches, giant redwood trees, and snow-capped mountains.**

Add the other vocabulary words.

Concept and Language Goals

Discuss the meaning of each word as it relates to the West, using the glossary as needed. (See p. 50 in this Teacher's Guide for definitions.)

astonishing · eruptions · unbelievable · **The West** · formed · naturally · gigantic

Model the multisyllabic word strategy.

Display each word. Say it as you display it.

Use the Tested Vocabulary Cards. Follow this routine for each word:

- **Look for Meaningful Parts** Do you recognize any parts of this word? What do these parts mean? Use the parts to read the word. As you introduce the words, be sure students notice the following: the prefix *un-, erupt, believe, natural.*

Think aloud.

- **Model** I see *un-* at the beginning of *unbelievable.* I know that the prefix *un-* can mean "not." I also recognize the word *believe.* I know *believe* means "to think something is true or real." Then I see the suffix *-able,* which makes the word an adjective. I think something that is *unbelievable* must be something that you can't think is true or real.

Point to *gigantic.*

- **Chunk Words with No Recognizable Parts** Model how to chunk the word *gigantic.* I see a chunk at the beginning of the word: *gi.* I see a part in the middle: *gan,* and a part at the end: *tic.* I say each chunk slowly: *gi gan tic.* I say the chunks fast to make a whole word: *gigantic.* Is it a real word? Yes, I know the word *gigantic.*

- Have students practice reading each word.

Preview.

Read p. 110 with students.

Do you see any of the words we just learned on this page? Together with students, read the sentences on p. 110 describing each selection. Talk about how the vocabulary words might be used in the selections.

MORE PRACTICE

Deepen understanding of *the West.*

Have students demonstrate understanding by answering questions. **What do you think the different states in *the West* have in common? How might the climate and landscape there differ from other regions of the country?**

ACTIVITY 2 Read a Passage

Develop Concepts "California," pp. 112–113

	To Do	**To Say**	*10–15 minutes*

Practice strategic prereading.

See Routine Card 2.

Think aloud.

Discuss Genre Read the title and have students look at the photographs on pp. 112–113. Model determining genre.

The photographs are a clue that this is nonfiction. They look like photos of real places. I think this article will tell me about interesting attractions in the state of California.

Scaffold instruction.

Review text structure.

Ask Questions There are two basic questions you can ask yourself in order to understand nonfiction better: What did I learn? What is this mainly about? As you read this article, ask yourself these questions and look for the answers.

Guide comprehension.

Read pp. 112–113 aloud.

Read Read the article as students follow along. Then read it a second time, having students join in. If necessary, stop at the end of each paragraph to check comprehension. Ask questions to promote discussion and develop the concept.

Develop language and concepts.

- Why do people use the word *big* to describe California's attractions?
- What is special about California's attractions?
- What is unusual about the attractions the author describes?
- What words on the concept web could help you describe some of the sights in California?

MORE PRACTICE

Have students reread "California." As they read, tell them to make a list of all the attractions they read about to share with family members tonight.

Reread for Fluency "California," p. 112

	To Do	**To Say**	*5 minutes*

CORRECTIVE FEEDBACK

Monitor oral reading.

Read p. 112 aloud. Reread the page three or four times so your reading gets better each time. Give feedback on students' oral reading, using the *if... then* statements on Routine Card 4. Model fluent reading if necessary. You may want to have students read along with the DVD-ROM.

ACTIVITY 3 Write

Response to Literature

	To Do	**To Say**	*5 minutes*

Prompt journal writing.

Write on the board or a transparency: *What is special about the West?*

Take out your journals. This week we are reading about the West. Our question for this week is: *What is special about the West?* Write an answer to this question based on what you read today. Have students write about the topic, using what they read and their own experiences.

Homework   Practice Book, p. 17, Vocabulary

ACTIVITY 1 Word Work

Phonics Prefixes *un-, re-, in-, dis-*

	To Do	To Say	5–10 minutes

Teach prefixes *un-, re-, in-, dis-*.

To Do: Write on the board or a transparency: I <u>reread</u> the letter because it was <u>unclear</u>.

To Say: **Remember, when you read a long word, look for meaningful parts. What parts do you see in the word *reread*?** Frame *re* and *read*. **The word part *re*- is a prefix. Prefixes usually form separate syllables from the base words. What parts do you see in *unclear*?** Frame *un* and *clear*. **What is the base word?** *(clear)* **What is the prefix?** *(un-)*

The prefix *re*- means "again." The prefix *un*- means "not." What other words can you think of that use the prefixes *re*- or *un-*? Write students' suggestions on the board.

Scaffold instruction.

To Do: Write *disagree* and *indirect*.

To Say: **The prefix *in*- and the prefix *dis*- both mean "not." What parts do you see in the word *disagree*?** *(dis* and *agree)* **What does it mean if you *disagree* with someone?** (You don't agree with that person.) **What is the base word in *indirect*?** *(direct)* **What is the prefix?** *(in-)*

To Do: Develop word meaning.

To Say: Have students think and converse. **When might you take an *indirect* route to get somewhere? Why?**

CORRECTIVE FEEDBACK

To Do: Write each practice word.

To Say: Have students practice reading these words that start with prefixes. Correct any words students miss and have them reread the list.

unspoiled	reappear	injustice	insincere	dishonest	disapprove

MORE PRACTICE

To Do: Write more practice words.

To Say: Have students practice reading these words that start with prefixes:

uncertain	unspoken	redirect	rerecord	indefinite	disconnect

Amazing Words Vocabulary

	To Do	To Say	5 minutes

Review vocabulary.

To Do: Review the homework.

To Say: Ask students to go over answers and share their writing from Practice Book p. 17. See Routine Card 1 for the multisyllabic word routine.

To Do: Deepen understanding of *astonishing*.

To Say: **Remember, *astonishing* means "very surprising; amazing." When you see an athlete perform a difficult feat, it can be *astonishing*. Why? What sights are *astonishing* to you? Explain why.**

ACTIVITY 2 Comprehension

Main Idea

	To Do	To Say	5 minutes

Scaffold instruction.

To Do: Introduce main idea.

To Say: **When you read an article, the main idea is usually the most important thing the author has to say about the subject. Today you will read about surfing, a popular sport in California. As you read, look for supporting details that help tell what the most important idea about surfing is.**

To Do: Model the skill.

To Say: **For example, if I read that people can surf all year long in California, and that California has many great beaches, I think that the main idea of the article may have something to do with why California is considered such a great place to surf.**

To Do: Distribute Graphic Organizer 1.

To Say: **As you read "Surf's Up!" look for details that help tell you what the most important idea is about surfing. Add these details to your graphic organizer.** See Routine Card 7.

ACTIVITY 3 Read a Passage

Read for Comprehension "Surf's Up!" pp. 114–117

10–15 minutes

	To Do	**To Say**
Scaffold instruction.	Monitor student engagement.	**Read** Have students read pp. 114–117. Stop at the end of each page to ask questions. Students who can read on their own can do so without stopping. After reading, ask questions to promote discussion.
	See Routine Cards 2 and 3.	**What makes California ideal for surfing?** (It has more than 1,000 miles of shoreline, with beaches that are great for surfing.)
		Where did surfing begin? (Hawaii) **Who introduced surfing to California?** (George Freeth)
		Why is Huntington Beach known as "Surf City"? (It has a long beach, and the waves are always good.)
	Point out *astonishing* on p. 115.	Demonstrate by using your finger to circle *-ing* at the end of the word and then reading the base word *astonish* that remains.
		What do you think the rest of the article will be about? (Answers will vary. The title suggests that it will tell more about surfing.)
Model summarizing.	Think aloud.	**Summarize** What were the first four pages mainly about? What did you learn about surfing? Think aloud to model summarizing. **I learned a lot of details about surfing, such as that the sport began in Hawaii and that it's popular all over the world now. But the main thing I learned is that California is an ideal place to surf because of its many beaches and mild climate.**
Develop language and concepts.	Ask questions.	• **Why are people attracted to the sport of surfing?** • **Why was George Freeth known as the man who could "walk on water"?**
MORE PRACTICE	Have students reread p. 117.	**Reread** Have students draw pictures that show what surfers on Huntington Beach might look like during a surfing competition.

Reread for Fluency "Surf's Up!" pp. 114–115

5 minutes

	To Do	**To Say**
MORE PRACTICE **CORRECTIVE FEEDBACK**	Pair students. Monitor paired reading.	Students read aloud pp. 114–115, switching readers at the end of each paragraph. Have partners reread; now the other partner begins. For optimal fluency, students should reread three or four times. Give feedback, using the *if...then* statements on Routine Card 4. You may want to have students read along with the DVD-ROM.

ACTIVITY 4 Write

Response to Literature

5 minutes

	To Do	**To Say**
Prompt writing.	Writing elements: focus, support	**Identify the main idea of pp. 114–117 in "Surf's Up!" Include the details from the article that support your answer.**
	Homework	Practice Book, p. 18, Prefixes *un-, re-, in-, dis-*

3

ACTIVITY 1 | Word Work

Phonics Prefixes *un-, re-, in-, dis-*

	To Do	To Say	5 minutes
Review prefixes *un-, re-, in-, dis-*. **Scaffold instruction.**	Review the homework. Discuss the word *unbelievable* on p. 116.	Ask students to share answers from Practice Book p. 18. Point out *unbelievable* on p. 116. **Remember, look for meaningful parts when reading a long word. What parts do you see in this word?** *(un believe able)* **What is the base word?** *(believe)* **What is the prefix?** *(un-)* **What does *unbelievable* mean?** (not believable) Then point to *unbroken* on p. 117. **What parts do you see in this word?** *(un broke en)* **Use the parts to read the word. How is it like *unbelievable*?** (Both words use the prefix *un-*.) **What does *unbroken* mean?** (not broken)	
MORE PRACTICE	Model spelling words with prefixes.	**Spell and Write** Write the word *unbroken*. **What prefix has been added to the word *broken*? Does the spelling of the base word change when the prefix is added? Do you know other words that have a prefix?** List responses on the board.	

Amazing Words Vocabulary

	To Do	To Say	5 minutes
Build vocabulary.	Deepen understanding of *unbelievable* and *astonishing*.	**Can you find a synonym for *unbelievable*?** *(amazing, incredible)* **We learned another word this week that is related to *unbelievable*.** Write *unbelievable* and *astonishing*. **How are these two words similar? Say a sentence using *unbelievable* and *astonishing*. Have you ever seen anything you would use these words to describe? What was it?**	
Lead cumulative review.		Use the Tested Vocabulary Cards to review words from previous weeks.	

ACTIVITY 2 | Comprehension

Main Idea

	To Do	To Say	5–10 minutes
Scaffold instruction.	Review main idea.	**The main idea is the most important statement about the topic. As you read the rest of "Surf's Up!" look for details that tell you what the main idea is.**	
Guide practice.	Use Graphic Organizer 1.	**Listen as I read p. 118. I want you to notice that on this page, the author is describing the unique language that surfers use.** Read p. 118. Then ask: **What is this page mainly about?** (the special language that surfers use) **As you read the rest of the article, think about how this detail helps support the main idea.** See Routine Card 7.	
MORE PRACTICE	Have students preview pp. 118–121.	**Read the captions and look at the photos on pp. 118–121. What do you think this section will be about?** (more about surfing) **Why do you think so?** Think aloud to model using captions and illustrations to predict.	
	Think aloud.	**The captions make me think this section of the article will tell about different kinds of waves and some of the dangers of surfing. Looking at the pictures, I think that surfing must be challenging but fun.**	

ACTIVITY 3 Read a Passage

Read for Comprehension "Surf's Up!" pp. 118–121

10–15 minutes

	To Do	**To Say**
Scaffold instruction.	Monitor student engagement.	**Read** Have students read pp. 118–121. Stop at the end of each page to ask questions. Students who can read on their own can do so without stopping. After reading, ask questions to promote discussion.
	See Routine Cards 2 and 3.	**If surfers say, "We're stoked about these swells!" what do they mean?** (We're excited about the waves.)
		What does the SAS want to prevent? (sewage in the ocean)
		On p. 120, what qualities do you need in order to surf? (skill, focus, good physical shape)
		What rules do surfers follow to stay safe? (lead with your hands; pay attention.)
Review the multisyllabic word strategy.	Point out *pipeline*, p. 118, paragraph 2.	Remind students to look for meaningful parts. Demonstrate framing the smaller words *pipe* and *line*. Have students blend the parts to read the compound word. See Routine Card 1.
Assess comprehension.	Monitor understanding.	**After Reading** Have students discuss the What Do You Think? question. Prompt them to think about the details in the article that help them answer the question. Listen as they talk to assess comprehension.
	Summarize.	**What is this mainly about? What did you learn?** Work with students to summarize the selection.
MORE PRACTICE	Have students reread p. 119.	**Reread** After they read, ask students to explain the purpose of the group SAS and how it helps people other than surfers.

Reread for Fluency "Surf's Up!" pp. 120–121

5 minutes

	To Do	**To Say**
CORRECTIVE FEEDBACK	Monitor oral reading.	**Read pp. 120–121 aloud. Reread the page three or four times so your reading gets better each time.** Give feedback on students' oral reading, using the *if... then* statements on Routine Card 4. Model fluent reading if necessary. You may want to have students read along with the DVD-ROM.

ACTIVITY 4 Write

Response to Literature

5 minutes

	To Do	**To Say**
MORE PRACTICE	Prompt writing.	**On p. 118, the author gives examples of special words surfers use. Why do you think surfers chose these particular words to describe things such as waves and surfboards? Are they more effective than more common words? Why?** (Students should support their ideas and opinions.)
Homework		Practice Book, p. 19, Main Idea and Details

ACTIVITY 1 Word Work

Amazing Words Vocabulary

To Do	To Say	*5–10 minutes*

Extend word knowledge.

Explore words with the root word *rupt*.

Scaffold instruction.

Write on the board or a transparency: *There were several eruptions from the volcano.*

Use the word *eruptions* to extend word knowledge. **Remember, we read this word earlier this week.** Frame the word part *rupt*. **We can use the word part, *rupt*, to help us read other words.**

The root word *rupt* comes from a Latin word that means "break." Can you think of other words that contain the word *rupt*? *(interrupt, abrupt, corrupt, disrupt, bankrupt, rupture)* Write words as students name them and add some of your own. Talk about the meanings of the words and point out how each relates to a break of some sort.

Develop word meaning.

Why might you *interrupt* a conversation that other people are having?

MORE PRACTICE

Deepen understanding of *eruptions*.

Have individual students or partners use the word *eruptions* in their own sentences. (For example: Volcanic *eruptions* can change the landscape of a place over time.) Share sentences. Ask: **What else might have *eruptions*, like a volcano? Why?**

ACTIVITY 2 Comprehension

Skill and Strategy Practice

To Do	To Say	*5 minutes*

Scaffold instruction.

Review main idea (homework).

Ask volunteers to read the passage and share answers from Practice Book p. 19. Remind students of the importance of finding the main idea and supporting details as they read. **When you read, finding the main idea and supporting details can help you better understand the topic.**

Practice strategic prereading.

See Routine Card 2.

Discuss Genre Read the title and the first paragraph on p. 122. Model determining genre.

Think aloud.

I first thought this might be nonfiction because of the photographs. When I read the first paragraph, I knew it was nonfiction because of the information about Denali National Park.

Review text structure.

Ask Questions Remember to ask yourself two important questions to help you understand nonfiction: What did I learn? What is this mainly about? As you read this article, ask these questions and look for the answers.

ACTIVITY **3** | Read a Passage

Read for Comprehension "Natural Treasures," pp. 122–129

10–15 minutes

	To Do	**To Say**
Scaffold instruction.	Monitor student engagement. See Routine Card 3.	**Read** Have students read pp. 122–129 on their own and then discuss. For students who need more help, stop at the end of each page to discuss. After reading, ask questions.
		Where can you find the tallest mountain in North America? (in Denali National Park in Alaska)
		What is special about Death Valley? (It is the lowest point in North America and one of the hottest places on Earth.)
		How was Crater Lake formed? (from a volcanic eruption)
		Where can you experience three climates in one park? (Washington state's Olympic National Park)
	Model using context for word meaning.	Read aloud p. 125, paragraph 1. Explain how the second sentence gives a synonym *(shaped)* for the vocabulary word *formed,* and the rest of the paragraph provides further clues to the definition.
Assess comprehension.	Monitor understanding.	**After Reading** Have students discuss the What Do You Think? question. Guide them to use details from the story to support their answers. Listen as they explain to assess comprehension.
MORE PRACTICE		**Reread** Have students reread p. 128 and then explain what is unusual about the rock formations in this part of Utah.

Reread for Fluency "Natural Treasures," pp. 124–125

5–10 minutes

	To Do	**To Say**
CORRECTIVE FEEDBACK	Pair students. Monitor paired reading.	Students read aloud pp. 124–125, switching readers at the end of each page. Have partners reread; now the other partner begins. For optimal fluency, students should reread three or four times. Give feedback, using Routine Card 4. You may want to have students read along with the DVD-ROM.
MORE PRACTICE	**READERS' THEATER**	Work with a group of students to adapt pp. 122–129 as a radio advertisement. Have students rehearse reading the text as ads, with one student describing each park. They may want to add some "sell" lines such as "Visit _____ Park!"

ACTIVITY **4** | Write

Response to Literature

5 minutes

	To Do	**To Say**
Prompt expository writing.	Review pp. 122–129. Writing elements: support	**What do you think makes the attractions featured in "Natural Treasures" so amazing? Use details from the article to support your answer.**

ACTIVITY 1 Read a Passage

Read Together "All Steamed Up," pp. 130–133

	To Do	To Say	10 minutes
Scaffold instruction.	Review main idea.	Have students preview pp. 130–133. **This article tells about a famous attraction at Yellowstone National Park. As you read, try to find the main idea of the article and the details that support it.**	
	See Routine Card 3.	**Read** Read the article as students follow along. Then read it a second time, having students join in on the text. After reading, ask questions.	
		How did Old Faithful get its name? (It erupts faithfully, or regularly, at least once every few hours.)	
		What happens when Old Faithful erupts? (Boiling water sprays high into the sky, and a huge steam cloud fills the air.)	
		What once stood where Yellowstone National Park is today? (a volcano)	
Assess comprehension.	Monitor listening comprehension.	**Summarize** Have one student retell the sequence of events that leads to an eruption of the Old Faithful geyser.	

ACTIVITY 2 Build Concepts

Amazing Words Vocabulary

	To Do	To Say	5–10 minutes
Review concept and vocabulary.	Display the concept web you began on Day 1.	**This week's question is *What is special about the West?* How do this week's words relate to the question?** (Have students answer the question, using some of the vocabulary they learned this week.)	
		Ask students to add more words to the concept web. Have students explain how each word relates to the West. Monitor students' understanding of vocabulary as they discuss the web. See Routine Card 5.	
MORE PRACTICE	Write *astonishing* and *unbelievable* on the board.	Have students relate *astonishing* and *unbelievable* to the week's theme of the West. **Give me an example of places or things in the West that are *astonishing* and *unbelievable*. What other words could you use to describe these places or things?**	

ACTIVITY 3 Write

Response to Literature "4 You 2 Do," p. 134

5–10 minutes

	To Do	To Say
Guide response activities.	Discuss the directions on p. 134. Tell students to choose one activity to complete. See Routine Card 8.	**Word Play** Have students work independently to describe their places of choice. Invite volunteers to share their writings. **Making Connections** Discuss the question in a group. (Answers will vary but may reflect an understanding that national parks are home to many different plants and animals. Students may help protect the natural environment in their communities by picking up litter, getting involved with local parks, or participating in local Earth Day or environment awareness activities.) **On Paper** Have students brainstorm some answers to the prompt before they write. Have them write on their own. Students can use Practice Book p. 20 to structure their written responses, or you can send the Practice Book page home for them to complete later.
MORE PRACTICE		If you have more time, direct students to complete all the activities.

ACTIVITY 4 Assessment Options

End-of-Unit Test

10–15 minutes

	To Do	To Say
Assess fluency and comprehension.	Use Assessment Book, p. 24.	Options for end-of-unit assessment are available in the Assessment Book, p. 24.

Homework   Practice Book, p. 20, Writing

Unit 2 Week 1 *New Ideas*

What can we learn from the talents of others?

Objectives *This week students will...*

Vocabulary
- build concepts and vocabulary: *awareness, comprehend, exhibit, experience, horizons, interactive*

Phonics
- read multisyllabic words with *r*-controlled *ar, or, ore*
- apply knowledge of word structure to decode multisyllabic words when reading

Text Comprehension
- compare and contrast to improve comprehension
- write in response to literature
- make connections across text

Fluency
- practice fluency with oral rereading

Word Work *This week's phonics focus is . . .*

r-Controlled Syllables *ar, or, ore*

Amazing Words Concept/Amazing Words *Tested Vocabulary*

The week's vocabulary is related to the concept of new ideas, or developing new understandings. The first appearance of each word in the Student Reader is noted below.

awareness	knowledge (p. 22)
comprehend	to understand something (p. 19)
exhibit	public showing or display (p. 12)
experience	events that are seen, done, or lived through (p. 12)
horizons	ranges of one's thinking, experience, interest, or outlook (p. 21)
interactive	allowing a person to use more than one sense to learn something (p. 12)

Student Reader Unit 2 *This week students will read the following selections.*

8	**Other Ways of Learning**	Expository Nonfiction
12	**Amazing Exhibits**	Expository Nonfiction
20	**The Beast in Grandpa's House**	Realistic Fiction
28	**Japanese Cartoons**	Expository Nonfiction
30	**4 You 2 Do**	Activity Page

Daily Lesson Plan

	ACTIVITIES	MATERIALS
Day 1	**Build Concepts** Weekly Concept: New Ideas Vocabulary: *awareness, comprehend, exhibit, experience, horizons, interactive* **Read a Passage** "Other Ways of Learning," pp. 8–11 Comprehension: Use Strategies Reread for Fluency **Write** Response to Literature	Student Reader: Unit 2 Routine Cards 2, 4, 5 Tested Vocabulary Cards Student journals Practice Book, p. 21, Vocabulary Student Reader DVD-ROM
Day 2	**Word Work** Phonics: Syllables with *r*-Controlled *ar, or, ore* Vocabulary: Deepen word meaning **Comprehension** Compare and Contrast **Read a Passage** "Amazing Exhibits," pp. 12–15 Reread for Fluency **Write** Response to Literature	Student Reader: Unit 2 Practice Book, p. 21, Vocabulary Graphic Organizer 3 Routine Cards 1, 2, 3, 4, 7 Practice Book, p. 22, Words with *r*-Controlled Syllables *ar, or, ore* Student Reader DVD-ROM

Day 3	**Word Work** Phonics: Syllables with *r*-Controlled *ar, or, ore*
	Vocabulary: Deepen word meaning
	
	Comprehension Compare and Contrast
	
	Read a Passage "Amazing Exhibits," pp. 16–19
	Reread for Fluency
	
	Write Response to Literature
		Practice Book, p. 22, Words with
		   r-Controlled Syllables *ar, or, ore*
		Tested Vocabulary Cards
		Student Reader: Unit 2
		Graphic Organizer 3
		Routine Cards 1, 2, 3, 4, 7
		Practice Book, p. 23, Compare and
		   Contrast
		Student Reader DVD-ROM

Day 4	**Word Work** Vocabulary: Extend word knowledge **Comprehension** Skill and Strategy Practice **Read a Passage** "The Beast in Grandpa's House," pp. 20–27 Reread for Fluency **Write** Response to Literature	Practice Book, p. 23, Compare and Contrast Student Reader: Unit 2 Routine Cards 2, 3, 4 Student Reader DVD-ROM
Day 5	**Read a Passage** "Japanese Cartoons," pp. 28–29 Comprehension: Compare and Contrast; Listening **Build Concepts** Vocabulary **Write** Response to Literature: "4 You 2 Do," p. 30 **Assessment Options** Fluency Comprehension	Student Reader: Unit 2 Routine Cards 3, 5, 6, 8 Fluency Progress Chart, p. 185 Practice Book, p. 24, Writing

See pp. xvi–xvii for how *My Sidewalks* integrates instructional practices for **ELL.**

ACTIVITY 1 Build Concepts

Amazing Words **Vocabulary**

| To Do | To Say | 10–15 minutes |

Develop oral vocabulary.

See Routine Card 6 and p. 203.

Introduce the Concept/Amazing Words with an oral routine prior to displaying them in print. Page 203 in this Teacher's Guide provides specific guidelines for introducing each word.

Develop word meaning.

See Routine Card 5. Discuss pp. 7–11.

Have students read p. 7 and then look at the pictures on pp. 8–11. **What do you notice about the children?** (They are playing sports, chess, and musical instruments; they are using computers.) **Can you use the word** *experience* **to describe what's happening?** (Example: The children are learning from their experience of playing a musical instrument.)

Scaffold instruction.

Create a concept web.

In the center of a web, write *New Ideas*. **This week's concept is** *new ideas*. **When people learn new things they can develop** *new ideas* **or new ways of thinking about things.** Provide an example to demonstrate meaning. **If you see live lizards in a museum, you may develop** *new ideas* **about them that you didn't learn from reading about them in a book.**

Add the other vocabulary words.

Concept and Language Goals

Discuss the meaning of each word as it relates to learning new ideas, using the glossary as needed. (See p. 62 in this Teacher's Guide for definitions.)

```
        awareness        comprehend

interactive      New Ideas           exhibit

        horizons         experience
```

Model the multisyllabic word strategy.

Display each word. Say it as you display it.

Use the Tested Vocabulary Cards. Follow this routine for each multisyllabic word.

- **Look for Meaningful Parts** **Do you recognize any parts of this word? What do these parts mean? Use the parts to read the word.** Be sure students notice the following: *aware* and *active*.

Point to *exhibit*.

Think aloud.

- **Chunk Words with No Recognizable Parts** Model how to chunk the word *exhibit* to read it.

- **Model** **I see a chunk at the beginning of the word:** *ex*. **I see a part in the middle:** *hib*. **I see a part at the end of the word:** *it*. **I say each chunk slowly:** *ex hib it*. **I say the chunks fast to make a whole word:** *exhibit*. **Is it a real word? Yes, I know the word** *exhibit*.

- Have students practice reading each word.

Preview.

Read p. 6 with students.

Do you see any of the words we just learned on this page? Together with students, read the sentences on p. 6 describing each selection. Talk about how the vocabulary words might be used in the selections.

MORE PRACTICE

Deepen understanding of *experience*.

Have students demonstrate understanding by answering questions. **If you want to have the** *experience* **of playing a sport, what can you do? How can you help another kid have a good** *experience* **in learning something new, like playing a game?**

ACTIVITY 2 Read a Passage

Develop Concepts "Other Ways of Learning," pp. 8–11

10–15 minutes

	To Do	**To Say**
Practice strategic prereading.	See Routine Card 2. Think aloud.	**Discuss Genre** Read the title on p. 8 and have students revisit the illustrations on pp. 8–11. Model determining genre. The photographs are a clue that this is nonfiction. They look like photos of real people and real places. I think this article will tell me about different ways to learn.
Scaffold instruction.	Review text structure.	**Ask Questions** What questions do you ask yourself to help you understand nonfiction? (What did I learn? What is this mainly about?) As you read this article, ask these questions and look for the answers.
Guide comprehension. **Develop language and concepts.**	Read pp. 8–11 aloud.	**Read** Read the article as students follow along. Then read it a second time, having students join in. If necessary, stop at the end of each paragraph to check comprehension. Ask questions to promote discussion and develop the concept. • What happens when you share your skills, talent, or knowledge with someone else? • How can you learn with music? • What words on the concept web could help you describe new ways of learning?
MORE PRACTICE		Have students reread "Other Ways of Learning." As they read, tell them to make a list of the benefits of teaching others. They can share their lists with family members tonight.

Reread for Fluency "Other Ways of Learning," p. 9

5 minutes

	To Do	**To Say**
CORRECTIVE FEEDBACK	Monitor oral reading.	Read p. 9 aloud. Reread the page three or four times so your reading gets better each time. Give feedback on students' oral reading, using the *if . . . then* statements on Routine Card 4. Model fluent reading if necessary. You may want to have students read along with the DVD-ROM.

ACTIVITY 3 Write

Response to Literature

5 minutes

	To Do	**To Say**
Prompt journal writing.	Write on the board or a transparency: *What can we learn from the talents of others?*	Take out your journals. This week we are reading about new ideas. Our question for this week is: *What can we learn from the talents of others?* Write an answer to this question based on what you read today. Have students write about the topic, using what they read and their own experiences.
Homework		Practice Book, p. 21, Vocabulary

ACTIVITY **1** # Word Work

Phonics Syllables with *r*-Controlled *ar, or, ore* (2- and 3-syllable VC/CV words)

5–10 minutes

	To Do	To Say
Teach syllables with *r*-Controlled *ar, or, ore*.	Write on the board or a transparency: *We bought a new carpet for the floor.*	If a word has two consonants in the middle, divide between the consonants. Frame *car* and *pet*. **Look at the first syllable in *carpet*. If a syllable has a vowel followed by an *r*, it's called an *r*-controlled vowel. Now try the short vowel sound for the second syllable.**
	Write *ignore*.	**Here is another word with two consonants in the middle. How would you divide this word?** (between the *g* and the *n*) **What vowel sound do you hear in the first syllable?** (short *i*) **What vowel sound do you hear in the second syllable?** (*r*-controlled vowel sound *ore*)
Scaffold instruction.	Develop word meaning.	Have students think and converse. **If you're learning something new, it's important not to *ignore* your teacher. Why?**
CORRECTIVE FEEDBACK	Write each practice word.	Have students practice reading these words with *r*-controlled *ar, or,* or *ore*. Correct any words students miss and have them reread the list.
		carton darling order inform fortune popcorn morning
MORE PRACTICE	Write more practice words.	Have students practice reading these words with *r*-controlled *ar, or,* or *ore*.
		bombard harbor tarnish garlic forgery corner organize

Amazing Words ## **Vocabulary**

5 minutes

	To Do	To Say
Review vocabulary.	Review the homework.	Ask students to go over answers and share their writing from Practice Book p. 21. See Routine Card 1 for the multisyllabic word routine.
	Deepen understanding of *horizons*.	*Horizon* **also means a line where the sky and earth meet.** Explain to students that because the horizon appears as a distant line, the word *horizons* can also refer to borders or boundary lines in your mind. **When we use the expression "expand your horizons," we mean "stretch your mind by learning new things." How does learning new things help you expand your *horizons*?**

ACTIVITY **2** # Comprehension

Compare and Contrast

5 minutes

	To Do	To Say
Scaffold instruction.	Introduce compare and contrast.	**Today you will read about different field trip destinations. When you read, it's important to compare and contrast in order to understand better what you're reading. Compare and contrast by finding ways in which things are alike and ways in which things are different.**
	Model the skill.	**For example, if I read that one museum exhibit teaches about outer space and another teaches about plants, I've found one way that the two exhibits are different. If I read that both exhibits use computers to display information, then I've found one way that they are alike.**
	Distribute Graphic Organizer 3.	**As you read "Amazing Exhibits," compare and contrast the different kinds of field trips the author describes. Add these details to your graphic organizer.** See Routine Card 7.

ACTIVITY 3 Read a Passage

Read for Comprehension "Amazing Exhibits," pp. 12–15

10–15 minutes

	To Do	**To Say**
Scaffold instruction.	Monitor student engagement. See Routine Cards 2 and 3.	**Read** Have students read pp. 12–15. Stop at the end of each page to ask questions. Students who can read on their own can do so without stopping. After reading, ask questions to promote discussion. **What does it mean if a museum exhibit is *interactive*?** (You can touch it, smell it, hear it, or see it up close.) **What are some of the things we can learn about at museums?** (space, stars, weather, insects) **What do you think the rest of the article will be about?** (Answers will vary. The title suggests that it will tell about interesting exhibits.)
Model summarizing.	Think aloud.	**Summarize** **What were the first four pages mainly about? What did you learn?** Think aloud to model summarizing. **I learned a lot of details about museums. Some museums have exhibits about butterflies, while others have exhibits about the solar system. But the main thing I learned is that museum exhibits can teach us a lot about the world around us.**
Develop language and concepts.	Ask questions.	• **What methods do museums use to teach visitors?** • **How do the museum exhibits in this article differ?**
MORE PRACTICE	Have students reread p. 15.	**Reread** Have students describe how it might look and feel to walk among the living butterflies at the Museum of Natural Science in Houston.

Reread for Fluency "Amazing Exhibits," pp. 13–14

5 minutes

	To Do	**To Say**
MORE PRACTICE **CORRECTIVE FEEDBACK**	Pair students. Monitor paired reading.	Students read aloud pp. 13–14, switching readers at each new paragraph. Have partners reread; now the other partner begins. For optimal fluency, students should reread three or four times. Give feedback, using the *if . . . then* statements on Routine Card 4. You may want to have students read along with the DVD-ROM.

ACTIVITY 4 Write

Response to Literature

5 minutes

	To Do	**To Say**
Prompt writing.	Writing elements: support	**This week we're learning about new ideas. How do museums share information with the public? How does this help people develop new ideas? Use details to support your ideas.**
	Homework	Practice Book, p. 22, Syllables with *r*-Controlled *ar, or, ore*

ACTIVITY 1 Word Work

Phonics Syllables with *r*-Controlled *ar, or, ore* (2- and 3-syllable VC/CV words)

5 minutes

	To Do	**To Say**
Review syllables with *r*-controlled *ar, or, ore.* **Scaffold instruction.**	Review the homework. Discuss *tornado* on p. 14 in the Student Reader.	Ask students to share answers from Practice Book p. 22. Point out *tornado* on p. 14, paragraph 2. **Remember, if a word has two consonants in the middle, divide between the consonants. What parts do you see in this word?** *(tor na do)* **Look at the first syllable in *tornado*. It has a vowel followed by an *r*, so the *r* controls the vowel sound in that syllable.** **What vowel sound do you hear in the first syllable?** (*r*-controlled vowel sound in *or*) **What vowel sound do you hear in the second syllable?** (long *a*) **What vowel sound do you hear in the third syllable?** (long *o*) Have students compare the vowel sound in the first syllable to that in the last syllable.
MORE PRACTICE	Model words with *r*-controlled *ar, or, ore.*	**Spell and Write** Write *north, explore,* and *stars.* Say *north.* **What vowel sound do you hear in this word? What letters spell that vowel sound?** Underline *or*. Continue with *explore (ore)* and *stars (ar)*. **Look for words in the selections that have these vowel sounds.**

Amazing Words Vocabulary

5 minutes

	To Do	**To Say**
Build vocabulary. **Lead cumulative review.**	Deepen understanding of *comprehend* and *exhibit.*	Read aloud p. 19. **What is a synonym for *comprehend* as it is used on this page?** (understand) **How can educators make an *exhibit* that people will *comprehend*?** (They can use a movie or things that people can touch.) Use the Tested Vocabulary Cards to review words from previous weeks.

ACTIVITY 2 Comprehension

Compare and Contrast

5–10 minutes

	To Do	**To Say**
Scaffold instruction. **Guide practice.**	Review compare and contrast. Use Graphic Organizer 3.	**When you compare and contrast, you look for ways that things are similar and different. Organizing information this way can help you better understand what you read.** **Listen as I read p. 16. I want you to notice that the author describes a special museum in Seattle, Washington.** Read p. 16. Then ask: **How is this museum different from some of the other museums you've read about?** (This museum is all about music.) **How is it similar to other museums you've read about?** (It has interactive exhibits.) **Add these details to your graphic organizer.** See Routine Card 7.
MORE PRACTICE	Have students preview pp. 16–19.	**Read the captions and look at the photos on pp. 16–19. What do you think this section will be about?** (more about interesting, interactive museum exhibits; how exhibits are created). **Why do you think so?** Think aloud to model using illustrations and captions to predict.
	Think aloud.	**The pictures make me think that the article will describe more interesting museums and exhibits from all over the world and how exhibits are made. From the captions, I think that the article will tell some of the things you can learn at these museums and what kinds of people help create exhibits.**

ACTIVITY 3 Read a Passage

Read for Comprehension "Amazing Exhibits," pp. 16–19

10–15 minutes

	To Do	To Say
Scaffold instruction.	Monitor student engagement. See Routine Cards 2 and 3.	**Read** Have students read pp. 16–19. Stop at the end of each page to ask questions. Students who can read on their own can do so without stopping. After reading, ask questions to promote discussion. **What is interactive about the Experience Music Project?** (You can play instruments.) **Why does an exhibit sometimes move from one museum to another?** (to allow more people to see it; to share ideas) **How are curators and content experts similar? How are they different?** (Both work as a team to make an exhibit. The curator has the idea for the exhibit, while the content experts choose the information to use in it.)
Review the multisyllabic word strategy.	Point out *curator* on p. 18, paragraph 2.	Analyze *curator* by chunking the whole word into smaller parts, saying each part slowly: *cu ra tor*. Then blend the parts, saying each part more quickly to make a whole word: *curator*. See Routine Card 1.
Assess comprehension.	Monitor understanding. Summarize.	**After Reading** Have students discuss the What Do You Think? question. Prompt them to think of similarities and differences between museum learning and classroom learning. Listen as they talk to assess comprehension. **What is this mainly about? What did you learn?** Work with students to summarize the selection.
MORE PRACTICE	Have students reread p. 19.	**Reread** As they read, tell students to note the ways that the job of the designer is similar to and different from the job of the educator.

Reread for Fluency "Amazing Exhibits," p. 16

5 minutes

	To Do	To Say
CORRECTIVE FEEDBACK	Monitor oral reading.	**Read p. 16 aloud. Reread the page three or four times so your reading gets better each time.** Give feedback on students' oral reading, using the *if . . . then* statements on Routine Card 4. Model fluent reading if necessary. You may want to have students read along with the DVD-ROM.

ACTIVITY 4 Write

Response to Literature

5 minutes

	To Do	To Say
MORE PRACTICE	Prompt writing.	**How is learning in a classroom environment different from learning in an interactive museum environment? How is it the same? Use supporting information as you explain your thoughts.**
Homework		Practice Book, p. 23, Compare and Contrast

ACTIVITY 1 | Word Work

Amazing Words Vocabulary

	To Do	**To Say**	5–10 minutes
Extend word knowledge.	Write on the board or a transparency: *I have an <u>awareness</u> that some math is hard for me.*	Use the word *awareness* to extend word knowledge. **Remember, we read this word earlier this week and learned its meaning. We looked for meaningful parts and we noticed the word *aware*. If you are *aware* of something, you have knowledge of it. Today I want you to notice the suffix -*ness*. We can use this suffix to read other words.**	
Teach suffix -ness.		**The suffix -*ness* refers to a quality or a state of being. So *awareness* is the state of being aware. Can you think of other words ending in -*ness*?** *(kindness, happiness, sadness, shyness, laziness)* Write words as students name them and add some of your own. Talk about the meanings of the words.	
Scaffold instruction.	Develop word meaning.	**If someone is afraid of learning a new skill, how can an *awareness* of that person's fear help us to teach him or her?**	
MORE PRACTICE	Deepen understanding of *awareness*.	Have students think about how people develop *awareness* as they get older and gain more experience. **What does a baby have *awareness* of? How does *awareness* grow as you get older? Explain.**	

ACTIVITY 2 | Comprehension

Skill and Strategy Practice

	To Do	**To Say**	5 minutes
Scaffold instruction.	Review compare and contrast (homework).	Ask volunteers to read the passage and share answers from Practice Book p. 23. Remind students of the importance of comparing and contrasting. **When you read, pay attention to the ways that an author compares and contrasts information. You can also compare and contrast what you read with what you already know.**	
Practice strategic prereading.	See Routine Card 2.	**Discuss Genre** Read the title and the beginning of the story on p. 20 in the Student Reader. Model determining genre.	
	Think aloud.	**I first thought this might be fiction because of the illustrations. When I read the first page, I knew it was fiction because of the way Grandpa Alex talks to Maria and the fact that she is narrating her own story.**	
	Review story structure.	**Ask Questions** What questions do you ask yourself to help you understand a fictional story? (What is the problem or goal? How is the problem solved or the goal reached?) As you read this story, ask these questions and look for the answers.	

ACTIVITY 3 Read a Passage

Read for Comprehension "The Beast in Grandpa's House," pp. 20–27

10–15 minutes

	To Do	**To Say**
Scaffold instruction.	Monitor student engagement. See Routine Card 3.	**Read** Have students read pp. 20–27 on their own and then discuss. For students who need more help, stop at the end of each page to discuss. After reading, ask questions. **Who is telling this story?** (Maria, a young girl) **Who are the main characters?** (Maria and her Grandpa Alex) **What is the beast?** (Grandpa Alex's computer) **What problem does Maria need to solve?** (She needs to help Grandpa Alex learn how to conquer his fear and use his computer.) **What idea does Maria use to help Grandpa overcome his fear?** (She shows him that he can play chess on the computer.)
	LOOK AT POINT OF VIEW	**Explain how the story would have been different if it were told from Grandpa Alex's point of view.** (The story might have told more about Grandpa Alex's fear of computers and focused on how he overcame his fear rather than on Maria's challenge in having to teach Grandpa Alex.)
Assess comprehension.	Monitor understanding.	**After Reading** Have students discuss the What Do You Think? question. Prompt them to compare Grandpa's changing feelings toward computers. Listen as they talk to assess comprehension.
MORE PRACTICE		**Reread** Have students reread pp. 23–24 and then explain why Grandpa Alex makes so many jokes.

Reread for Fluency "The Beast in Grandpa's House," pp. 20–22

5–10 minutes

	To Do	**To Say**
CORRECTIVE FEEDBACK	Pair students. Monitor paired reading.	Students read aloud pp. 20–22, switching readers at the end of each paragraph. Have partners reread; now the other partner begins. For optimal fluency, students should reread three or four times. Give feedback, using Routine Card 4. You may want to have students read along with the DVD-ROM.
MORE PRACTICE	**READERS' THEATER**	Work with a group of three students to adapt pp. 20–22 as a radio play. Have students rehearse reading the parts: Narrator, Grandpa Alex, and Maria. Discuss the tone of voice Grandpa Alex should use when talking about his computer.

ACTIVITY 4 Write

Response to Literature

5 minutes

	To Do	**To Say**
Prompt descriptive writing.	Review pp. 20–27. Writing elements: support, conventions	**In "The Beast in Grandpa's House," Maria is the teacher, and Grandpa Alex is the student. Include details from the story to compare and contrast Maria's attitude toward computers with Grandpa Alex's attitude. Use complete sentences to express your ideas.** (Students should use words that compare and contrast, such as *both, however,* and *also.*)

ACTIVITY 1 Read a Passage

Read Together "Japanese Cartoons," pp. 28–29

	To Do	To Say	
			10 minutes

Scaffold instruction.

Review compare and contrast.

Have students preview pp. 28–29. **This article is about the process of creating Japanese cartoons. When you read something, look for the similarities and differences that the author describes, or make comparisons on your own. Comparing and contrasting can help you better understand what you read.**

See Routine Card 3.

Read Read the article as students follow along. Then read it a second time, having students join in on the text. After reading, ask questions.

What is the first step in creating a cartoon? (writing a story) **What is the last step in the *anime* process?** (putting all of the pieces together)

Why does it take so many people to create one cartoon? (Everyone does a different job, including drawing pictures, recording voices, and adding sound effects.)

Assess comprehension.

Monitor listening comprehension.

Summarize Have students describe some of the steps needed to create Japanese cartoons.

ACTIVITY 2 Build Concepts

Amazing Words Vocabulary

	To Do	To Say	
			5–10 minutes

Review concept and vocabulary.

Concept and Language Goals

Display the concept web you began on Day 1.

This week's question is *What can we learn from the talents of others?* How do this week's words relate to the question? (Have students answer the question, using some of the vocabulary they learned this week.)

Ask students to add more words to the concept web. Have students explain how each word relates to new ideas. Monitor students' understanding of vocabulary as they discuss the web. See Routine Card 5.

MORE PRACTICE

Write *awareness* and *horizons* on the board.

Have students relate *awareness* and *horizons*. **Can an *awareness* of a new skill widen your *horizons*? Give an example of an *awareness* of something widening a person's *horizons*.**

ACTIVITY 3 | Write

Response to Literature "4 You 2 Do," p. 30

5–10 minutes

	To Do	To Say
Guide response activities.	Discuss the directions on p. 30. Tell students to choose one activity to complete. See Routine Card 8.	**Word Play** Have students complete the activity on their own and then meet with a partner to share and compare responses. **Making Connections** Discuss the question in a group. (Answers will vary, but should include that museum exhibits teach about many subjects and allow many people to learn about the talents of others; Grandpa Alex might visit a chess exhibit.) **On Paper** Have students brainstorm some answers to the prompt before they write. Have them write on their own. Students can use Practice Book p. 24 to structure their written responses, or you can send the Practice Book page home for them to complete later.
MORE PRACTICE		If you have more time, direct students to complete all the activities.

ACTIVITY 4 | Assessment Options

Passage Reading

10–15 minutes

	To Do	To Say
Check fluency. **Check comprehension.**	See Routine Card 6. Take a two-minute timed sample of each student's oral reading.	While some students are doing Activity 3, determine which students you want to assess this week and choose from these options. **Fluency** Have a student read for two minutes from "The Beast in Grandpa's House." Record the number of correct words read per minute. See p. 184 for monitoring fluency. Be sure each student is assessed at least every other week. Have students graph their progress on the Fluency Progress Chart, p. 185. **Retelling** Have students reread "The Beast in Grandpa's House" and retell it. Prompt students if necessary. See p. 186 for monitoring retelling.
		If you have time, assess every student.

Homework	Practice Book, p. 24, Writing	

Unit 2 Week 2 *Working Together*

How can we work together to achieve a goal?

Objectives *This week students will...*

Vocabulary
- build concepts and vocabulary: *accomplished, collaboration, cooperate, members, orchestra, teamwork*

Phonics
- read words that contain syllables with *r*-controlled *er, ir, ur*
- apply knowledge of word structure to decode multisyllabic words when reading

Text Comprehension
- draw conclusions to improve comprehension
- write in response to literature
- make connections across text

Fluency
- practice fluency with oral rereading

Word Work *This week's phonics focus is . . .*

r-Controlled Syllables *er, ir, ur*

Amazing Words Concept/Amazing Words *Tested Vocabulary*

The week's vocabulary is related to the concept of working together.
The first appearance of each word in the Student Reader is noted below.

accomplished	completed; carried out (p. 45)
collaboration	working together to get something done (p. 37)
cooperate	to work together (p. 49)
members	people, animals, or things belonging to a group (p. 40)
orchestra	a group of musicians playing strings, brass, woodwinds, and percussion instruments (p. 37)
teamwork	the combined action of a number of people that makes the work of the group successful and effective (p. 35)

Student Reader Unit 2 *This week students will read the following selections.*

34	**Teamwork**	Expository Nonfiction
36	**All Together Now**	Expository Nonfiction
44	**Molly's New Role**	Realistic Fiction
52	**Winning Teams**	Expository Nonfiction
56	**4 You 2 Do**	Activity Page

Daily Lesson Plan

	ACTIVITIES	MATERIALS
Day 1	**Build Concepts** Weekly Concept: Working Together Vocabulary: *accomplished, collaboration, cooperate, members, orchestra, teamwork* **Read a Passage** "Teamwork," pp. 34–35 Comprehension: Use Strategies Reread for Fluency **Write** Response to Literature	Student Reader: Unit 2 Routine Cards 2, 4, 5 Tested Vocabulary Cards Student journals Practice Book, p. 25, Vocabulary Student Reader DVD-ROM
Day 2	**Word Work** Phonics: Syllables with *r*-Controlled *er, ir, ur* Vocabulary: Deepen word meaning **Comprehension** Draw Conclusions **Read a Passage** "All Together Now!" pp. 36–39 Reread for Fluency **Write** Response to Literature	Student Reader: Unit 2 Practice Book, p. 25, Vocabulary Graphic Organizer 2 Routine Cards 1, 2, 3, 4, 7 Practice Book, p. 26, Syllables with *r*-Controlled *er, ir, ur* Student Reader DVD-ROM
Day 3	**Word Work** Phonics: Syllables with *r*-Controlled *er, ir, ur* Vocabulary: Deepen word meaning **Comprehension** Draw Conclusions **Read a Passage** "All Together Now," pp. 40–43 Reread for Fluency **Write** Response to Literature	Practice Book, p. 26, Syllables with *r*-Controlled *er, ir, ur* Tested Vocabulary Cards Student Reader: Unit 2 Graphic Organizer 2 Routine Cards 1, 2, 3, 4, 7 Practice Book, p. 27, Draw Conclusions Student Reader DVD-ROM
Day 4	**Word Work** Vocabulary: Extend word knowledge **Comprehension** Skill and Strategy Practice **Read a Passage** "Molly's New Role," pp. 44–51 Reread for Fluency **Write** Response to Literature	Practice Book, p. 27, Draw Conclusions Student Reader: Unit 2 Routine Cards 2, 3, 4 Student Reader DVD-ROM
Day 5	**Read a Passage** "Winning Teams," pp. 52–55 Comprehension: Draw Conclusions; Listening **Build Concepts** Vocabulary **Write** Response to Literature: "4 You 2 Do," p. 56 **Assessment Options** Fluency Comprehension	Student Reader: Unit 2 Routine Cards 3, 5, 6, 8 Fluency Progress Chart, p. 185 Practice Book, p. 28, Writing

See pp. xvi–xvii for how *My Sidewalks* integrates instructional practices for ELL.

ACTIVITY **1** Build Concepts

Amazing Words **Vocabulary**

	To Do	**To Say**	*10–15 minutes*

Develop oral vocabulary.

See Routine Card 6 and p. 204.

Introduce the Concept/Amazing Words with an oral routine prior to displaying them in print. Page 204 in this Teacher's Guide provides specific guidelines for introducing each word.

Develop word meaning.

See Routine Card 5. Discuss pp. 33–35.

Have students read p. 33 and then look at the pictures on pp. 34–35. **What do you notice?** (people working on a construction site, a football team huddled together) **Can you use the word** *teamwork* **to describe any of these pictures?** (Example: The football players are using *teamwork* to win the game.)

Scaffold instruction.

Create a concept web.

In the center of a web, write *Working Together*. **This week's concept is** *working together.* **People** *working together* **can achieve more than someone acting alone.** Provide an example to demonstrate meaning. **Moving an object that is too heavy to lift alone requires** *working together.*

Add the other vocabulary words.

Concept and Language Goals

Discuss the meaning of each word as it relates to working together, using the glossary as needed. (See p. 74 in this Teacher's Guide for definitions.)

accomplished — collaboration — teamwork — **Working Together** — cooperate — orchestra — members

Model the multisyllabic word strategy.

Display each word. Say it as you display it.

Use the Tested Vocabulary Cards. Follow this routine for each word:

- **Look for Meaningful Parts** Remind students to look for meaningful parts. **As you say each word, ask yourself: Do I see any parts I know?** As you introduce the words, have students notice the base words *accomplish, operate,* and *collaborate,* and the compound word *teamwork.*

Think aloud.

- **Model** I see *team* at the beginning of *teamwork,* and *work* at the end of the word. I know that *team* means "people working or acting together," and *work* is "the effort in making or doing something." So I think *teamwork* means "people working or acting together to be successful at something."

Point to *members.*

- **Chunk Words with No Recognizable Parts** Model how to chunk the word *members* to read it. I see a chunk at the beginning of the word: *mem.* I see a part at the end of the word: *bers.* I say each chunk slowly: *mem bers.* I say the chunks fast to make a whole word: *members.* Is it a real word? Yes, I know the word *members.*

- Have students practice reading each word.

Preview.

Read p. 32 with students.

Do you see any of the words we just learned on this page? Together with students, read the sentences on p. 32 describing each selection. Talk about how the concept words might be used in the selections.

MORE PRACTICE

Deepen understanding of *teamwork.*

Have students demonstrate understanding by answering questions. **Which one requires** *teamwork:* **writing a letter to a friend or organizing a talent show? Why? Why is** *teamwork* **so important when you have a big challenge or task to complete?**

ACTIVITY 2 Read a Passage

Develop Concepts "Teamwork," pp. 34–35

10–15 minutes

	To Do	**To Say**
Practice strategic prereading.	See Routine Card 2. Think aloud.	**Discuss Genre** Read the title on p. 34 and have students look at the illustrations on pp. 34–35. Model determining genre. The photographs are a clue that this is nonfiction. They look like pictures of real people and real activities. I think this article will tell me about different ways that people work together to get things done.
Scaffold instruction.	Review text structure.	**Ask Questions** What questions do you ask yourself to help you understand nonfiction? (What did I learn? What is this mainly about?) As you read this article, ask these questions and look for the answers.
Guide comprehension. **Develop language and concepts.**	Read pp. 34–35 aloud.	**Read** Read the article as students follow along. Then read it a second time, having students join in. If necessary, stop at the end of each paragraph to check comprehension. Ask questions to promote discussion and develop the concept. • What are some jobs where working together is needed? • Why is the process of putting together a newspaper a good example of teamwork? • What words on the concept web could help you describe working together?
MORE PRACTICE		Have students reread "Teamwork." As they read, tell them to make a list of all the examples of teamwork the article describes to share with family members tonight.

Reread for Fluency "Teamwork," p. 35

5 minutes

	To Do	**To Say**
CORRECTIVE FEEDBACK	Monitor oral reading.	**Read p. 35 aloud. Reread the page three or four times so your reading gets better each time.** Give feedback on students' oral reading, using the *if . . . then* statements on Routine Card 4. Model fluent reading if necessary. You may want to have students read along with the DVD-ROM.

ACTIVITY 3 Write

Response to Literature

5 minutes

	To Do	**To Say**
Prompt journal writing.	Write on the board or a transparency: *How can we work together to achieve a goal?*	**Take out your journals. This week we are reading about working together. Our question for this week is:** *How can we work together to achieve a goal?* **Write an answer to this question based on what you read today.** Have students write about the topic, using what they read and their own experiences.
Homework		Practice Book, p. 25, Vocabulary

ACTIVITY 1 # Word Work

Phonics Syllables with *r*-Controlled *er, ir, ur*

	To Do	**To Say**	*5–10 minutes*

Teach syllables with *r*-controlled *er, ir, ur*.

Scaffold instruction.

CORRECTIVE FEEDBACK

Write on the board or a transparency: *The tigers came out from behind the* <u>curtain</u> *at the* <u>circus</u>.

Write *person*.

Write each practice word.

If a word has two consonants in the middle, divide between the consonants. Frame *cur* and *tain*. **Look at the first syllable in *curtain*. If a syllable has a vowel followed by an *r*, it's called an *r*-controlled vowel. The *r*-controlled *er, ir,* and *ur* vowels all make the same sound: /ėr/. How would you divide the word *circus*?** (between the *r* and the *c*) **What vowel sound do you hear in the first syllable?** (/ėr/)

Here is another word with two consonants in the middle. How would you divide this word? (per son) **What vowel sound do you hear in the first syllable?** (/ėr/)

Have students practice reading these words with *r*-controlled vowel sounds. Correct any words students miss and have them reread the list.

circle   thirty   turtle   perfume   nursery

MORE PRACTICE

Write more practice words.

Have students practice reading these words with *r*-controlled sounds.

servant   certainly   virtue   turkey   pursue

Amazing Words Vocabulary

	To Do	**To Say**	*5 minutes*

Review vocabulary.

Review the homework.

Deepen understanding of *collaboration*.

Ask students to go over answers and share their writing from Practice Book p. 25. See Routine Card 1 for the multisyllabic word routine.

Remember, *collaboration* is working together to get something done. It took the skills of many different people to help rebuild the school after the tornado. Why is this an example of *collaboration*? What else is an example of *collaboration*? Why?

ACTIVITY 2 # Comprehension

Draw Conclusions

	To Do	**To Say**	*5 minutes*

Scaffold instruction.

Introduce drawing conclusions.

Model the skill.

Distribute Graphic Organizer 2.

Today you will read about how an orchestra works. It's important to draw conclusions as you read. When you draw conclusions, you use the information that you get from a story or article, along with what you already know, to make decisions about what you have read.

For example, if I read that a person practices playing the piano every day for several hours, and that he or she also hopes to play in a band one day, I can draw the conclusion that music is an important part of his or her life.

As you read "All Together Now," use details from the article and what you already know to draw conclusions about what you read. Add these details to your graphic organizer. See Routine Card 7.

ACTIVITY 3 | Read a Passage

Read for Comprehension "All Together Now," pp. 36–39

10–15 minutes

	To Do	To Say
Scaffold instruction.	Monitor student engagement.	**Read** Have students read pp. 36–39. Stop at the end of each page to ask questions. Students who can read on their own can do so without stopping. After reading, ask questions to promote discussion.
	See Routine Cards 2 and 3.	**How does a conductor lead without speaking?** (by gesturing with his arms and hands)
		What is an orchestra? (a large group of musicians playing instruments)
		What are the four sections of an orchestra? (strings, woodwinds, brass, percussion)
	Point out *closely* on p. 36.	Demonstrate using your finger to circle -*ly* at the end of the word, and then read the base word *close* that remains.
		What do you think the rest of the article will be about? (Answers will vary. The title suggests it will tell more about the ways members of an orchestra work together.)
Model summarizing.	Think aloud.	**Summarize** **What were the first four pages mainly about? What did you learn about orchestras?** Think aloud to model summarizing. **I learned many details about orchestras, such as that a conductor uses gestures to tell the musicians how to play. But the main thing I learned is that every section of an orchestra is important, and they must all work together to make music.**
Develop language and concepts.	Ask questions.	• **Why is it important for the musicians and conductor to collaborate?**
		• **In what way is each section of an orchestra important?**
MORE PRACTICE	Have students reread pp. 37–39.	**Reread** Tell students to draw a picture showing the four sections of an orchestra and the conductor.

Reread for Fluency "All Together Now," pp. 38–39

5 minutes

	To Do	To Say
MORE PRACTICE **CORRECTIVE FEEDBACK**	Pair students. Monitor paired reading.	Students read aloud pp. 38–39, switching readers at each new paragraph. Have partners reread; now the other partner begins. For optimal fluency, students should reread three or four times. Give feedback, using the *if . . . then* statements on Routine Card 4. You may want to have students read along with the DVD-ROM.

ACTIVITY 4 | Write

Response to Literature

5 minutes

	To Do	To Say
Prompt writing.	Writing elements: support	**What conclusion can you draw about musicians who play in an orchestra? Use details from the article to support your conclusion.**
	Homework	Practice Book, p. 26, Syllables with *r*-Controlled *er, ir, ur*

ACTIVITY 1 — Word Work

Phonics Syllables with r-Controlled er, ir, ur

	To Do	**To Say**	5 minutes

Review syllables with r-Controlled er, ir, ur.

Scaffold instruction.

Review the homework. Discuss *certain* on p. 40 in the Student Reader.

Ask students to share answers from Practice Book p. 26.

Point out *certain* on p. 40, paragraph 1. **Remember, if a syllable has a vowel followed by an *r*, it's called an *r*-controlled vowel. What parts do you see in this word?** (*cer tain*) **What vowel sound do you hear in the first syllable?** (/ėr/) Guide students in identifying the vowel sound in each syllable and in blending the word parts into the word.

Then point to *perfect* on p. 49, paragraph 5. **What parts do you see in this word?** (*per fect*) **What vowel sound do you hear in the first syllable?** (/ėr/) Ask students to look for other *r*-controlled syllables as they read.

MORE PRACTICE

Model spelling words with syllables with *r*-controlled *er, ir, ur.*

Spell and Write Write *perfect, third,* and *curtain.* Say perfect. **What vowel sound do you hear in this word? What letters spell that vowel sound?** Underline er. Continue with *third* (ir) and *curtain* (ur). Point out that different letters spell the same vowel sound. Have students look for other words in the selections that have this vowel sound.

Amazing Words Vocabulary

	To Do	**To Say**	5 minutes

Build vocabulary.

Lead cumulative review.

Deepen understanding of *members* and *teamwork.*

Read aloud the first paragraphs on pp. 40–41. **What group are the musicians described on p. 40 *members* of?** (the orchestra) **What groups are the musicians described on p. 41 *members* of?** (woodwinds, brass, and percussion) **Say a sentence using *teamwork* and *members.* Why is *teamwork* important for all *members* of a group?**

Use the Tested Vocabulary Cards to review words from previous weeks.

ACTIVITY 2 — Comprehension

Draw Conclusions

	To Do	**To Say**	5–10 minutes

Scaffold instruction.

Review drawing conclusions.

Sometimes, an author draws conclusions for you. Other times, you must use details from a story or article, along with what you know, to draw your own conclusions. As you read "All Together Now," look for information that helps you draw conclusions, and ask yourself whether your conclusions make sense.

Guide practice.

Use Graphic Organizer 2.

Listen as I read the first paragraph on p. 40. The author tells that the loudness of their instruments determines where the musicians sit. Read the first paragraph of p. 40. Then ask: What conclusion can you draw about where musicians who play quiet instruments would sit? (They would sit up front.) **What information did you use to draw this conclusion?** (It would be hard to hear the quiet instruments if they were in the back of the orchestra.) **Add this information to your graphic organizer.** See Routine Card 7.

MORE PRACTICE

Have students preview pp. 40–43.

Read the captions and look at the photos on pp. 40–43. What do you think this section will be about? (what it's like to be a musician in an orchestra) **Why do you think so?** Think aloud to model using captions and illustrations to predict.

Think aloud.

The captions make me think the article will tell more about what it's like to play an instrument in an orchestra. From the pictures I think the article will talk about adult musicians and child musicians.

ACTIVITY 3 Read a Passage

Read for Comprehension "All Together Now," pp. 40–43

10–15 minutes

	To Do	**To Say**
Scaffold instruction.	Monitor student engagement. See Routine Cards 2 and 3.	**Read** Have students read pp. 40–43. Stop at the end of each page to ask questions. Students who can read on their own can do so without stopping. After reading, ask questions to promote discussion. **Why is the strings section such an important part of the orchestra?** (They lead the orchestra's sound; they are the largest section in the orchestra.) **Why don't members of the woodwinds, brass, and percussion sections share music stands?** (They play different parts.) **What is the key to a successful orchestra?** (collaboration)
Review the phonics skill.	Point out *member* on p. 41, paragraph 2.	Remind students of how to read *r*-controlled syllables. Frame the parts *mem ber* and guide students to identify the vowel sound in each part. Then blend the word parts to read the word. See Routine Card 1.
Assess comprehension.	Monitor understanding.	**After Reading** Have students discuss the What Do You Think? question. Prompt them to use details from the article, along with what they know to draw conclusions about the strings section. Listen as they talk to assess comprehension.
	Summarize.	**What is this mainly about? What did you learn?** Work with students to summarize the selection.
MORE PRACTICE	Have students reread p. 42.	**Reread** As they read, ask students to draw a conclusion about why child musicians use smaller instruments. Have students add this information to their graphic organizers. After they read, have them tell what information they used to draw their conclusions.

Reread for Fluency "All Together Now," p. 43

5 minutes

	To Do	**To Say**
CORRECTIVE FEEDBACK	Monitor oral reading.	**Read p. 43 aloud. Reread the page three or four times so your reading gets better each time.** Give feedback on students' oral reading, using the *if . . . then* statements on Routine Card 4. Model fluent reading if necessary. You may want to have students read along with the DVD-ROM.

ACTIVITY 4 Write

Response to Literature

5 minutes

	To Do	**To Say**
MORE PRACTICE	Prompt writing.	**Why is the title "All Together Now" a good title for this article? Support your opinion with details and exact words.**
Homework		Practice Book, p. 27, Draw Conclusions

Word Work

Vocabulary

	To Do	To Say	*5–10 minutes*
Extend word knowledge.	Write on the board or a transparency: *We'll have to <u>cooperate</u> to finish on time.*	Use the word *cooperate* to extend word knowledge. **Remember we read this word earlier this week. We looked for meaningful parts, and we noticed the word** *operate,* **which can mean "to work or act." Today I want you to notice the prefix** *co-.* **We can use this prefix to read other words.**	
Teach prefix co-.		**The prefix** *co-* **means "with or together." So** *cooperate* **means "to work together." Can you think of other words that begin with the prefix** *co-?* *(coworker, coordinate, copilot)* Write words as students name them and add some of your own. If students suggest words that begin in *co* but not the prefix, explain the difference in meaning.	
Scaffold instruction.	Develop word meaning.	**How do people** *cooperate* **to make plays, movies, or television shows? What else is an example of** *cooperation?*	
MORE PRACTICE	Deepen understanding of *cooperation.*	Have individual students or partners use the word *cooperate* in a sentence. (For example: We will *cooperate* to build the set for the school play.) Share sentences. Ask: **Why is** *cooperation* **an important part of a play? How does** *cooperating* **help you accomplish a task? Explain.**	

Comprehension

Skill and Strategy Practice

	To Do	To Say	*5 minutes*
Scaffold instruction.	Review drawing conclusions (homework).	Ask volunteers to read the passage and share answers from Practice Book p. 27. Remind students of the importance of drawing conclusions. **Drawing conclusions about information, characters, and events can help you better understand what you read. Remember to use what you read and your own experience to draw conclusions, and ask yourself whether your conclusions make sense.**	
Practice strategic prereading.	See Routine Card 2.	**Discuss Genre** Read the title and the first paragraph on p. 44. Model determining genre.	
	Think aloud.	**I first thought this might be fiction because of the illustrations. When I read the first paragraph, I knew it was fiction because of the description of Molly's big day.**	
	Review story structure.	**Ask Questions** What questions do you ask yourself to help you understand a fictional story? (What is the problem or goal? How is the problem solved or the goal reached?) As you read this story, ask these questions and look for the answers.	

ACTIVITY **3** Read a Passage

Read for Comprehension "Molly's New Role," pp. 44–51

10–15 minutes

	To Do	**To Say**
Scaffold instruction.	Monitor student engagement. See Routine Card 3.	**Read** Have students read pp. 44–51 on their own and then discuss. For students who need more help, stop at the end of each page to discuss. After reading, ask questions. **Who is the main character in this story?** (Molly) **Why is Molly upset in the beginning of the story?** (She doesn't get a role in the play.) **How does she help her friend Jessica?** (She finds a real merry-go-round horse to use in the play.) **What does Molly learn by the end of the story?** (She enjoys working on props; putting a play on takes teamwork and she likes being part of the team.)
	LOOK AT AUTHOR'S CRAFT	**Explain why the title of the story is a good one.** (Molly learns to play a new role in putting on a play; rather than acting in the play, her new role is to work behind the scenes.)
Assess comprehension.	Monitor understanding.	**After Reading** Have students discuss the What Do You Think? question. Prompt them to draw conclusions about what Molly has learned. Listen as they talk to assess comprehension.
MORE PRACTICE		**Reread** Have students reread p. 45 and then explain why Mr. Andrews decided not to give Molly an acting role in the play.

Reread for Fluency "Molly's New Role," pp. 48–49

5–10 minutes

	To Do	**To Say**
CORRECTIVE FEEDBACK	Pair students. Monitor paired reading.	Students read aloud pp. 48–49, switching readers at the end of each page. Have partners reread; now the other partner begins. For optimal fluency, students should reread three or four times. Give feedback, using Routine Card 4. You may want to have students read along with the DVD-ROM.
MORE PRACTICE	**READERS' THEATER**	Work with a group of four students to adapt pp. 48–49 as a radio play. Have students rehearse reading the parts, with one student as the narrator, one as Molly, one as Jessica, one as Grandma, and one as Mr. Cohen.

ACTIVITY **4** Write

Response to Literature

5 minutes

	To Do	**To Say**
Prompt descriptive writing.	Review pp. 40–41, 47–48, 50–51. Writing elements: organization, support.	**In what ways is the teamwork of Molly and the other students organizing the play similar to the collaboration of the musicians in an orchestra? Use details to describe the teamwork.** (Students should include supporting details and transitional words and phrases to connect their ideas.)

ACTIVITY 1 — Read a Passage

Read Together "Winning Teams," pp. 52–55

10 minutes

	To Do	To Say
Scaffold instruction.	Review drawing conclusions.	Have students preview pp. 52–55. **This article is about the ways that different groups of people have worked together to overcome challenges. As you read, use details from the article and what you know to draw conclusions about how you can use teamwork to achieve a goal.**
	See Routine Card 3.	**Read** Read the article as students follow along. Then read it a second time, having students join in on the text. After reading, ask questions.
		What two things did the Apollo 13 crew do that helped them? (They stayed calm and used their training.)
		What did the Chicago White Sox have that helped them win? (determined players who played hard and smart)
		What was the result of the U.S. Women's Soccer Team's teamwork? (two Olympic gold medals)
		What event helped to unite the thirteen American colonies? (fighting for independence from Britain in 1776)
Assess comprehension.	Monitor listening comprehension.	**Summarize** Have one student explain how each of these groups was similar in their response to challenges.

ACTIVITY 2 — Build Concepts

Amazing Words Vocabulary

5–10 minutes

	To Do	To Say
Review concept and vocabulary.	Display the concept web you began on Day 1.	**This week's question is *How can we work together to achieve a goal?* How do this week's words relate to the question?** (Have students answer the question, using some of the vocabulary they learned this week.)
		Ask students to add more words to the concept web. Have students explain how each word relates to working together. Monitor students' understanding of vocabulary as they discuss the web. See Routine Card 5.
MORE PRACTICE	Write *accomplished* and *teamwork* on the board.	Have students relate *teamwork* and *accomplished*. **Give an example of a situation in which *teamwork* helped people *accomplish* something. Is *teamwork* always necessary for group *accomplishment*? Why? Why is it often a greater challenge for a group to *accomplish* something than an individual to *accomplish* something?**

ACTIVITY 3 | Write

Response to Literature "4 You 2 Do," p. 56

	To Do	To Say	
			5–10 minutes

Guide response activities.

Discuss the directions on p. 56. Tell students to choose one activity to complete. See Routine Card 8.

Word Play Have students complete the replacements on their own and then meet with a partner to share and compare responses.

Making Connections Discuss the question in a group. (Answers will vary, but should show an understanding that individuals involved behind the scenes of a performance contribute to its overall success.)

On Paper Have students brainstorm some answers to the prompt before they write. Have them write on their own. Students can use Practice Book p. 28 to structure their written responses, or you can send the Practice Book page home for them to complete later.

MORE PRACTICE

If you have more time, direct students to complete all the activities.

ACTIVITY 4 | Assessment Options

Passage Reading

	To Do	To Say	
			10–15 minutes

See Routine Card 6.

While some students are doing Activity 3, determine which students you want to assess this week and choose from these options.

Check fluency.

Take a two-minute timed sample of each student's oral reading.

Fluency Have a student read for two minutes from "Molly's New Role." Record the number of correct words read per minute. See p. 184 for monitoring fluency. Be sure each student is assessed at least every other week.

Have students graph their progress on the Fluency Progress Chart, p. 185.

Check comprehension.

Retelling Have students reread "Molly's New Role" and retell it. Prompt students if necessary. See p. 186 for monitoring retelling.

If you have time, assess every student.

Homework

Practice Book, p. 28, Writing

Unit 2 Week 3 *Team Effort*

? What can teams accomplish?

Objectives *This week students will...*

Vocabulary
- build concepts and vocabulary: *extraordinary, fantastic, inspiration, sculptures, skillful*

Phonics
- read multisyllabic words with comparative endings *-er, -est*
- apply knowledge of word structure to decode multisyllabic words when reading

Text Comprehension
- draw conclusions to improve comprehension
- write in response to literature
- make connections across text

Fluency
- practice fluency with oral rereading

Word Work *This week's phonics focus is . . .*

Comparative Endings *-er, -est*

Amazing Words Concept/Amazing Words *Tested Vocabulary*

The week's vocabulary is related to the concept of team effort.
The first appearance of each word in the Student Reader is noted below.

extraordinary	very unusual; remarkable; special (p. 61)
fantastic	causing wonder or surprise (p. 60)
inspiration	something that has a strong effect on what you feel or do, especially something good (p. 61)
sculptures	pieces of art made from stone, wood, clay, or other things (p. 63)
skillful	having ability, knowledge, or experience (p. 61)

Student Reader Unit 2 *This week students will read the following selections.*

60	**Team Effort**	Expository Nonfiction
62	**Racing Art**	Expository Nonfiction
70	**Sam and the Incredible Smash**	Humorous Fiction
78	**Sculptures in Sand**	Photo Essay
82	**4 You 2 Do**	Activity Page

Daily Lesson Plan

	ACTIVITIES	MATERIALS
Day 1	**Build Concepts** Weekly Concept: Team Effort Vocabulary: *extraordinary, fantastic, inspiration, sculptures, skillful* **Read a Passage** "Team Effort," pp. 60–61 Comprehension: Use Strategies Reread for Fluency **Write** Response to Literature	Student Reader: Unit 2 Routine Cards 2, 4, 5 Tested Vocabulary Cards Student journals Practice Book, p. 29, Vocabulary Student Reader DVD-ROM
Day 2	**Word Work** Phonics: Comparative Endings *-er, -est* Vocabulary: Deepen word meaning **Comprehension** Draw Conclusions **Read a Passage** "Racing Art," pp. 62–65 Reread for Fluency **Write** Response to Literature	Student Reader: Unit 2 Practice Book, p. 29, Vocabulary Graphic Organizer 2 Routine Cards 1, 2, 3, 4, 7 Practice Book, p. 30, Endings *-er, -est* Student Reader DVD-ROM
Day 3	**Word Work** Phonics: Comparative Endings *-er, -est* Vocabulary: Deepen word meaning **Comprehension** Draw Conclusions **Read a Passage** "Racing Art," pp. 66–69 Reread for Fluency **Write** Response to Literature	Practice Book, p. 30, Endings *-er, -est*, Tested Vocabulary Cards Student Reader: Unit 2 Graphic Organizer 2 Routine Cards 2, 3, 4, 7 Practice Book, p. 31, Draw Conclusions Student Reader DVD-ROM
Day 4	**Word Work** Vocabulary: Extend word knowledge **Comprehension** Skill and Strategy Practice **Read a Passage** "Sam and the Incredible Smash," pp. 70–77 Reread for Fluency **Write** Response to Literature	Practice Book, p. 31, Draw Conclusions Student Reader: Unit 2 Routine Cards 2, 3, 4 Student Reader DVD-ROM
Day 5	**Read a Passage** "Sculptures in Sand," pp. 78–81 Comprehension: Draw Conclusions; Listening **Build Concepts** Vocabulary **Write** Response to Literature: "4 You 2 Do," p. 82 **Assessment Options** Fluency Comprehension	Student Reader: Unit 2 Routine Cards 3, 5, 6, 8 Fluency Progress Chart, p. 185 Practice Book, p. 32, Writing

See pp. xvi–xvii for how *My Sidewalks* integrates instructional practices for ELL.

ACTIVITY 1 Build Concepts

Amazing Words Vocabulary

	To Do	**To Say**
Develop oral vocabulary.	See Routine Card 6 and p. 205.	Introduce the Concept/Amazing Words with an oral routine prior to displaying them in print. Page 205 in this Teacher's Guide provides specific guidelines for introducing each word.
Develop word meaning.	See Routine Card 5. Discuss pp. 59–61.	Have students read p. 59 and then look at the pictures on pp. 60–61. **What do you notice?** (people swimming, men with medals, a gold medal) **Can you use the words** *team effort* **to describe what's happening?** (Example: It took a *team effort* for the members of the swim team to win gold medals.)
Scaffold instruction.	Create a concept web.	In the center of a web, write *Team Effort*. **This week's concept is** *team effort*. **A** *team* **is a group of people who work or play together.** *Effort* **is trying hard.** *Team effort* **is the hard work the people on a team do to reach a goal.** Provide an example to demonstrate meaning. **All of the players on the soccer team worked hard. The** *team effort* **helped them win the championship.**
	Add the other vocabulary words.	Discuss the meaning of each word as it relates to team effort, using the glossary as needed. (See p. 86 in this Teacher's Guide for definitions.)
	Concept and Language Goals	

Concept web: **Team Effort** (center) connected to *fantastic*, *extraordinary*, *inspiration*, *skillful*, *sculptures*.

	To Do	**To Say**
Model the multisyllabic word strategy.	Display each word. Say it as you display it.	Use the Tested Vocabulary Cards. Follow this routine for each multisyllabic word.
		• **Look for Meaningful Parts** Do you recognize any parts of this word? What do these parts mean? Use the parts to read the word. Be sure students notice the following: *extra, ordinary, inspire, skill,* and the suffix *-ful.*
	Think aloud.	• **Model** I see the suffix *-ful* at the end of the word *skillful*. I know *-ful* means "having, showing, or being full of something." I also recognize the word *skill*. I know *skill* means "an ability to do something well." So I think *skillful* means "having ability to do things well." Discuss other words with the suffix *-ful*: *thoughtful, thankful, prideful.*
	Point to *fantastic.*	• **Chunk Words with No Recognizable Parts** Model how to chunk the word *fantastic*. I see a chunk at the beginning of the word: *fan*. I see a chunk in the middle: *tas*. I see a part at the end of the word: *tic*. I say each chunk slowly: *fan tas tic*. I say the chunks fast to make a whole word: *fantastic*. Is it a real word? Yes, I know the word *fantastic.*
		• Have students practice reading each word.
Preview.	Read p. 58 with students.	**Do you see any of the words we just learned on this page?** Together with students, read the sentences on p. 58 describing each selection. Talk about how the vocabulary words might be used in the selections.
MORE PRACTICE	Deepen understanding of *effort.*	Have students demonstrate understanding by answering questions. **Why is it important for each member of a team to make an** *effort?* **How does an individual person's** *effort* **affect a team as a whole? Give examples.**

ACTIVITY 2 Read a Passage

Develop Concepts "Team Effort," pp. 60–61

10–15 minutes

	To Do	**To Say**
Practice strategic prereading.	See Routine Card 2. Think aloud.	**Discuss Genre** Read the title on p. 60 and look at the pictures on pp. 60–61. Model determining genre. The photographs are a clue that this is nonfiction. They show real people swimming in a race. I think this article will tell me about how people on a swim team worked together to win a race.
Scaffold instruction.	Review text structure.	**Ask Questions** What questions do you ask yourself to help you understand nonfiction? (What did I learn? What is this mainly about?) **As you read this article, ask these questions and look for the answers.**
Guide comprehension. **Develop language and concepts.**	Read pp. 60–61 aloud.	**Read** Read the article as students follow along. Then read it a second time, having students join in. If necessary, stop at the end of each paragraph to check comprehension. Ask questions to promote discussion and develop the concept. • **What is a relay race and why is *team effort* important to win it?** • **How is racing as a *team* different from racing alone?** • **How did the *efforts* of the last swimmer help the *team* to win?** • **What words on the concept web could help you describe *team effort*?**

MORE PRACTICE

Have students reread "Team Effort." As they read, tell them to make a list of things Jason Lezak and the other three swimmers did that helped the team win. Have them share their list with family members tonight.

Reread for Fluency "Team Effort," p. 61

5 minutes

	To Do	**To Say**
CORRECTIVE FEEDBACK	Monitor oral reading.	**Read p. 61 aloud. Reread the page three or four times so your reading gets better each time.** Give feedback on students' oral reading, using the *if . . . then* statements on Routine Card 4. Model fluent reading if necessary. You may want to have students read along with the DVD-ROM.

ACTIVITY 3 Write

Response to Literature

5 minutes

	To Do	**To Say**
Prompt journal writing.	Write on the board or a transparency: *What can teams accomplish?*	**Take out your journals. This week we are reading about team effort. Our question for this week is: *What can teams accomplish?* Write an answer to this question based on what you read today.** Have students write about the topic, using what they read and their own experiences.
Homework	Practice Book, p. 29, Vocabulary	

ACTIVITY 1 Word Work

Phonics Comparative Endings -er, -est

	To Do	**To Say**	5–10 minutes
Teach comparative endings -er, -est.	Write on the board or a transparency: *The river is* <u>wide</u>.	When you compare things, you might use the endings *-er* and *-est* to show how many or how much. For example, if a river appears to be growing more and more wide, you might describe it as *wide*, then *wider*, and finally, *widest*. Write *wide, wider,* and *widest*. Notice that the spelling of *wide* changes when I add *-er* and *-est*. If a describing word ends in *e*, like *wide*, drop the *e* before adding *-er* and *-est*. When a word ends in *-er* or *-est*, the *-er* or *-est* adds another syllable to the word.	
Scaffold instruction.	Write *early*.	If a word ends in *y*, change the *y* to *i* before adding *-er* and *-est*. If you arrive at the movie theater before your friend, you arrive *earlier* than she does. If you arrive there before anyone else, you arrive the *earliest*.	
CORRECTIVE FEEDBACK	Write each practice word.	Have students practice reading these words with endings *-er* and *-est*. Correct any words students miss and have them reread the list. hardest higher bluer largest silliest fancier	
MORE PRACTICE	Write more practice words.	Have students practice reading these words with endings *-er* and *-est*. stronger greatest louder simplest angrier scariest	

Amazing Words Vocabulary

	To Do	**To Say**	5 minutes
Review vocabulary.	Review the homework.	Ask students to go over answers and share their writing from Practice Book p. 29. See Routine Card 1 for the multisyllabic word routine.	
	Deepen understanding of *inspiration*.	Remember, *inspiration* is something that has a strong effect on what you feel or do. When a painter sees colorful flowers, he might decide to paint a picture of them. Why are the flowers an example of *inspiration*? What else is an example of *inspiration*? Why?	

ACTIVITY 2 Comprehension

Draw Conclusions

	To Do	**To Say**	5 minutes
Scaffold instruction.	Introduce drawing conclusions.	Today you will read about a unique event that mixes racing with art. It's important to draw conclusions as you read. When you draw conclusions, you use the information that you get from a story or article, along with what you already know, to make decisions about what you have read.	
	Model the skill.	For example, if I read that people come from all over the country to participate in a race, I can draw the conclusion that the race is very popular.	
	Distribute Graphic Organizer 2.	As you read "Racing Art," use the information that the author gives you, as well as your own knowledge and experience, to draw conclusions about this unique race. Add your conclusions and the details that support them to your graphic organizer. See Routine Card 7.	

ACTIVITY 3 Read a Passage

Read for Comprehension "Racing Art," pp. 62–65

10–15 minutes

	To Do	To Say
Scaffold instruction.	Monitor student engagement.	**Read** Have students read pp. 62–65. Stop at the end of each page to ask questions. Students who can read on their own can do so without stopping. After reading, ask questions to promote discussion.
	See Routine Cards 2, 3.	**Why is the race called the Kinetic Sculpture Race?** (because it involves different sculptures in motion)
		How was the race invented? (Hobart Brown and his friend each made unusual moving sculptures, and then challenged each other to a race.)
		What do racers use to create their sculptures? (spare parts, lawn mowers, bicycles, car parts, tinfoil, feathers, paper)
	Model using context for word meaning.	Read aloud the paragraph with *fantastic* on p. 63. Explain how both sentences in the paragraph provide clues to the meaning of *fantastic*.
		What do you think the rest of the article will be about? (Answers will vary. The title suggests it will tell more about racing art.)
Model summarizing.	Think aloud.	**Summarize** What were the first four pages mainly about? What did you learn about racing art? Think aloud to model summarizing. **I learned many details about the Kinetic Sculpture Race, such as that people come from all over the country to participate. But the main thing I learned is that team effort can lead to exciting new things.**
Develop language and concepts.	Ask questions.	• **How did Hobart Brown's invention inspire others?**
		• **Why is the Kinetic Sculpture Race so popular?**
MORE PRACTICE	Have students reread p. 62.	**Reread** Tell students to imagine and then draw a picture of their own Kinetic Sculpture Race sculptures.

Reread for Fluency "Racing Art," pp. 64–65

5 minutes

	To Do	To Say
MORE PRACTICE **CORRECTIVE FEEDBACK**	Pair students. Monitor paired reading.	Students read aloud pp. 64–65, switching readers at the end of the first page. Have partners reread; now the other partner begins. For optimal fluency, students should reread three or four times. Give feedback, using the *if . . . then* statements on Routine Card 4. You may want to have students read along with the DVD-ROM.

ACTIVITY 4 Write

Response to Literature

5 minutes

	To Do	To Say
Prompt writing.	Writing elements: conventions	**Describe the ways that the racers in "Racing Art" use their imaginations to create racing sculptures. Use correct spelling and punctuation to express your ideas clearly.**
	Homework	Practice Book, p. 30, Endings *-er, -est*

ACTIVITY **1** Word Work

Phonics Comparative Endings -er, -est

	To Do	To Say	5 minutes
Review comparative endings -er, -est. **Scaffold instruction.**	Review the homework. Discuss the words *craziest* on p. 63 and *silliest* on p. 64 in the Student Reader.	Ask students to share answers from Practice Book p. 30. **Remember, you can add the endings -er and -est to most describing words. If the describing word ends in y, change the y to i before adding -er and -est. What describing word do you see in craziest?** (crazy) **What describing word do you see in silliest?** (silly) Then point to *wild* on p. 64, paragraph 3. **How would you describe a dragster that was more wild?** (wilder) **that was the most wild?** (wildest)	
MORE PRACTICE	Model spelling words with -er and -est.	**Spell and Write** Have students practice spelling these words with the endings -er and -est. longer fanciest sillier lightest safest sturdier	

Amazing Words **Vocabulary**

	To Do	To Say	5 minutes
Build vocabulary. **Lead cumulative review.**	Deepen understanding of *fantastic* and *extraordinary*.	Read aloud rule 5 on p. 66. **The author gives a clue to the meaning of fantastic when he writes "they can be any length." If something is fantastic, it causes great wonder or surprise. Why would a racing sculpture built as long as you want be described as fantastic? Can you find another word we learned this week that is a synonym for fantastic?** (extraordinary) Use the Tested Vocabulary Cards to review words from previous weeks.	

ACTIVITY **2** Comprehension

Draw Conclusions

	To Do	To Say	5–10 minutes
Scaffold instruction.	Review drawing conclusions.	**Sometimes, an author draws conclusions for you. Other times, you must use details from a story or article, along with what you know, to draw your own conclusions. As you read "Racing Art," look for information that helps you draw conclusions, and ask yourself whether your conclusions make sense.**	
Guide practice.	Use Graphic Organizer 2.	**Listen as I read p. 66. I want you to notice that the author lists some of the basic rules of sculpture racing, but he does not draw any conclusions about the rules.** Read p. 66. Then ask: **What conclusion can you draw from rule 4?** (Safety is important to the race organizers.) **How do you know?** (The rule says that sculptures must pass a safety test and have working brakes and lights.) **Add your conclusion and the details that support it to your graphic organizer.** See Routine Card 7.	
MORE PRACTICE	Have students preview pp. 66–69.	**Read the captions and look at the photos on pp. 66–69. What do you think this section will be about?** (more on the race and what some of the different sculptures look like) **Why do you think so?** Think aloud to model using illustrations and captions to predict.	
	Think aloud.	**The captions and pictures make me think that the article will describe some of the unusual sculptures that take part in the race and will also talk about the race course.**	

ACTIVITY 3 Read a Passage

Read for Comprehension "Racing Art," pp. 66–69

10–15 minutes

	To Do	To Say
Scaffold instruction.	Monitor student engagement. See Routine Cards 2 and 3.	**Read** Have students read pp. 66–69. Stop at the end of each page to ask questions. Students who can read on their own can do so without stopping. After reading, ask questions to promote discussion. **What is the silliest rule of the race?** (the rule that says every racer must carry a teddy bear) **What conclusion can you draw from the teddy bear rule?** (The race organizers want to keep the race fun.) **Why do drivers need to be strong?** (They have to power their machines for many miles.) **Do most racers care about winning?** (no) **What do they care about?** (finishing without pushing their sculpture and having fun)
Review the phonics skill.	Point out *funniest* and *craziest* on p. 68, paragraph 1.	Remind students they learned about describing words with the endings *-er* and *-est*. Both of these words end in *y*; remind students to change the *y* to *i* before adding *-est*.
Assess compre-hension.	Monitor understanding.	**After Reading** Have students discuss the What Do You Think? question. Prompt them to draw conclusions about how teamwork makes the sculptures better. Listen as they talk to assess comprehension.
	Summarize.	**What is this mainly about? What did you learn?** Work with students to summarize the selection.
MORE PRACTICE	Have students reread p. 69.	**Reread** As they read, ask students to draw a conclusion about why the Kinetic Sculpture Race offers different kinds of prizes. Have students add the details that helped them to draw a conclusion to their graphic organizers.

Reread for Fluency "Racing Art," p. 68

5 minutes

	To Do	To Say
CORRECTIVE FEEDBACK	Monitor oral reading.	**Read p. 68 aloud. Reread the page three or four times so your reading gets better each time.** Give feedback on students' oral reading, using the *if . . . then* statements on Routine Card 4. Model fluent reading if necessary. You may want to have students read along with the DVD-ROM.

ACTIVITY 4 Write

Response to Literature

5 minutes

	To Do	To Say
MORE PRACTICE	Prompt writing.	**How do the rules and awards at the Kinetic Sculpture Race encourage participants to use their imaginations? Use specific examples and details to support your ideas.**
Homework		Practice Book, p. 31, Draw Conclusions

ACTIVITY 1 | Word Work

Amazing Words Vocabulary

	To Do	To Say	5–10 minutes
Extend word knowledge.	Write on the board or a transparency: *She has an extraordinary imagination.*	Use the word *extraordinary* to extend word knowledge. **Remember, we read this word earlier this week and learned its meaning. Today I want you to notice the prefix extra-. We can use this prefix to read other words.**	
Teach prefix extra-.		**The prefix extra- means "outside or beyond." So extraordinary means something that is beyond ordinary. Can you think of other words beginning with extra-?** (*extrasensory, extraterrestrial, extravehicular, extracurricular*) Write words as students name them and add some of your own. Talk about the meanings of the words. Remind students that not every word that contains the letters *extra* actually uses those letters as a prefix. (In words such as *extract,* the prefix *ex-* is combined with a Latin root.)	
Scaffold instruction.	Develop word meaning.	**What makes something extraordinary?**	
MORE PRACTICE	Deepen understanding of *extraordinary* and *skillful.*	Have individual students or partners use the two words *extraordinary* and *skillful* in a sentence. (For example: It takes a *skillful* artist to create an *extraordinary* painting.) Share sentences. Ask: **How does a skillful artist create extraordinary art?**	

ACTIVITY 2 | Comprehension

Skill and Strategy Practice

	To Do	To Say	5 minutes
Scaffold instruction.	Review drawing conclusions (homework).	Ask volunteers to read the passage and share answers from Practice Book p. 31. Remind students of the importance of drawing conclusions. **Drawing conclusions about information, characters, and events can help you better understand what you read. Remember to use what you read and your own experience to draw conclusions, and then ask yourself whether your conclusions make sense.**	
Practice strategic prereading.	See Routine Card 2.	**Discuss Genre** Read the title and the first paragraph on p. 70 in the Student Reader. Model determining genre.	
	Think aloud.	**I first thought this might be fiction because of the illustrations. When I read the first paragraph, I knew it was fiction because of the name of the character.**	
	Review story structure.	**Ask Questions** What questions do you ask yourself to help you understand a fictional story? (What is the problem or goal? How is the problem solved or the goal reached?) **As you read this story, ask these questions and look for the answers.**	

ACTIVITY 3 Read a Passage

Read for Comprehension "Sam and the Incredible Smash," pp. 70–77

10–15 minutes

	To Do	**To Say**
Scaffold instruction.	Monitor student engagement. See Routine Card 3.	**Read** Have students read pp. 70–77 on their own and then discuss. For students who need more help, stop at the end of each page to discuss. After reading, ask questions. **Who is the main character in this story?** (Sam) **Who is Captain X-TRA?** (a character in Sam's imagination) **Where does the story really take place?** (at a soccer game) **What challenge is Sam faced with?** (staying focused to help his team) **How does Sam's imagination interfere with his playing?** (He gets distracted.) **How does Sam use his imagination to help his soccer team?** (He uses his imagination to picture scoring a goal and he scores.)
	LOOK AT GENRE	**How does the story mix fantasy and reality?** (The fantasy is Sam's daydreams of Captain X-TRA; the reality is the soccer game.)
Assess comprehension.	Monitor understanding.	**After Reading** Have students discuss the What Do You Think? question. Prompt them to draw conclusions based on details in the story. Listen as they talk to assess comprehension.
MORE PRACTICE		**Reread** Have students reread pp. 74–75 and then explain how Sam and Captain X-TRA are related.

Reread for Fluency "Sam and the Incredible Smash," pp. 76–77

5–10 minutes

	To Do	**To Say**
CORRECTIVE FEEDBACK	Pair students. Monitor paired reading.	Students read aloud pp. 76–77, switching readers at the end of each paragraph. Have partners reread; now the other partner begins. For optimal fluency, students should reread three or four times. Give feedback, using Routine Card 4. You may want to have students read along with the DVD-ROM.
MORE PRACTICE	**READERS' THEATER**	Work with a group of three students to adapt pp. 76–77 as a radio play. Have students rehearse reading the parts, with one student being the narrator, one Sam, and one Coach. Then have them perform for the class.

ACTIVITY 4 Write

Response to Literature

5 minutes

	To Do	**To Say**
Prompt expository writing.	Review pp. 76–77. Writing elements: support	In "Sam and the Incredible Smash," Sam learns how to use his imagination in a different way. What conclusion can you draw about how Sam might behave at his next soccer game? Provide details from the story to support your ideas.

ACTIVITY 1 | Read a Passage

Read Together "Sculptures in Sand," pp. 78–81

	To Do	**To Say**	*10 minutes*
Scaffold instruction.	Review drawing conclusions. See Routine Card 3.	Have students preview pp. 78–81. **This article is about a sand sculpture contest. As you read, use details from the article and what you know to draw conclusions about what makes sand sculptures so much fun to build.** **Read** Read the article as students follow along. Then read it a second time, having students join in on the text. After reading, ask questions. **What do the Sand Sculpture Contest judges look for?** (effort and imagination) **What are some ways that the sand sculpture artists show their imagination?** (They make unusual things and give their sculptures funny names.) **Why is it fun to build sand sculptures with a team?** (You can share ideas, imagination, and effort.)
Assess comprehension.	Monitor listening comprehension.	**Summarize** Have students describe some of the sand sculptures mentioned in the article.

ACTIVITY 2 | Build Concepts

Amazing Words Vocabulary

	To Do	**To Say**	*5–10 minutes*
Review concept and vocabulary.	**Concept and Language Goals** Display the concept web you began on Day 1.	This week's question is *What can teams accomplish?* **How do this week's words relate to the question?** (Have students answer the question, using some of the vocabulary they learned this week.) Ask students to add more words to the concept web. Have students explain how each word relates to team effort. Monitor students' understanding of vocabulary as they discuss the web. See Routine Card 5.
MORE PRACTICE	Write *inspiration* and *fantastic* on the board.	Have students relate *inspiration* and *fantastic*. **Give an example of a situation in which *inspiration* can lead to a *fantastic* outcome for a team. What people or things do you look to for *inspiration?* Why?**

ACTIVITY **3** Write

Response to Literature "4 You 2 Do," p. 82

5–10 minutes

	To Do	**To Say**
Guide response activities.	Discuss the directions on p. 82. Tell students to choose one activity to complete. See Routine Card 8.	**Word Play** Have students complete the word search on their own and then meet with a partner to share and compare responses. It may help students to manipulate letter tiles as an aid to help them find words. **Making Connections** Discuss the question in a group. (Answers will vary but should mention examples of ways teamwork helped the Olympic swim team to achieve their goals, and tell how sharing artistic skills helped participants in the Kinetic Sculpture Race and the Sand Sculpture Contest be creative and have fun.) **On Paper** Have students brainstorm some answers to the prompt before they write. Have them write on their own. Students can use Practice Book p. 32 to structure their written responses, or you can send the Practice Book page home for them to complete later.
MORE PRACTICE		If you have more time, direct students to complete all of the activities.

ACTIVITY **4** Assessment Options

Passage Reading

10–15 minutes

	To Do	**To Say**
	See Routine Card 6.	While some students are doing Activity 3, determine which students you want to assess this week and choose from these options.
Check fluency. **Check comprehension.**	Take a two-minute timed sample of each student's oral reading.	**Fluency** Have a student read for two minutes from "Racing Art." Record the number of correct words read per minute. See p. 184 for monitoring fluency. Be sure each student is assessed at least every other week. Have students graph their progress on the Fluency Progress Chart, p. 185. **Retelling** Have students reread "Racing Art" and retell it. Prompt students if necessary. See p. 186 for monitoring retelling.
		If you have time, assess every student.
Homework		Practice Book, p. 32, Writing

Unit 2 Week 4 *A Job Well Done*

How does working together get the job done?

Objectives *This week students will...*

Vocabulary
- build concepts and vocabulary: *career, contribution, energy, gear, option, workers*

Phonics
- read words with open (V/CV) and closed (VC/V) syllables
- apply knowledge of word structure to decode multisyllabic words when reading

Text Comprehension
- use sequence to improve comprehension
- write in response to literature
- make connections across text

Fluency
- practice fluency with oral rereading

Word Work *This week's phonics focus is . . .*

Open and Closed Syllables

Amazing Words Concept/Amazing Words *Tested Vocabulary*

The week's vocabulary is related to the concept of a job well done.
The first appearance of each word in the Student Reader is noted below.

career	a job that someone has (p. 91)
contribution	money, help, advice, that is given; gift (p. 103)
energy	strength; the power to work, move, or play (p. 101)
gear	the equipment needed for some purpose (p. 98)
option	something that can be chosen; a choice (p. 92)
workers	people who do a job (p. 91)

Student Reader Unit 2 *This week students will read the following selections.*

86	**Everyday Jobs**	Expository Nonfiction
90	**The Big Dig of Boston**	Expository Nonfiction
98	**All the Right Moves**	Realistic Fiction
106	**Why Do We Work?**	Expository Nonfiction
108	**4 You 2 Do**	Activity Page

Daily Lesson Plan

	ACTIVITIES	MATERIALS

Day 1	**Build Concepts** Weekly Concept: A Job Well Done
	    Vocabulary: *career, contribution, energy, gear, option, workers*
	Read a Passage "Everyday Jobs," pp. 86–89
	    Comprehension: Use Strategies
	    Reread for Fluency
	Write Response to Literature
		Student Reader: Unit 2
		Routine Cards 2, 4, 5
		Tested Vocabulary Cards
		Student journals
		Practice Book, p. 33, Vocabulary
		Student Reader DVD-ROM

Day 2	**Word Work** Phonics: Open (V/CV) and Closed (VC/V) Syllables
	    Vocabulary: Deepen word meaning
	Comprehension Sequence
	Read a Passage "The Big Dig of Boston," pp. 90–93
	    Reread for Fluency
	Write Response to Literature
		Student Reader: Unit 2
		Practice Book, p. 33, Vocabulary
		Graphic Organizer 6
		Routine Cards 1, 2, 3, 4, 7
		Practice Book, p. 34, Open and Closed
		    Syllables: V/CV, VC/V
		Student Reader DVD-ROM

Day 3	**Word Work** Phonics: Open (V/CV) and Closed (VC/V) Syllables
	    Vocabulary: Deepen word meaning
	Comprehension Sequence
	Read a Passage "The Big Dig of Boston," pp. 94–97
	    Reread for Fluency
	Write Response to Literature
		Practice Book, p. 34, Open and Closed
		    Syllables: V/CV, VC/V
		Tested Vocabulary Cards
		Student Reader: Unit 2
		Graphic Organizer 6
		Routine Cards 1, 2, 3, 4, 7
		Practice Book, p. 35, Sequence
		Student Reader DVD-ROM

Day 4	**Word Work** Vocabulary: Extend word knowledge **Comprehension** Skill and Strategy Practice **Read a Passage** "All the Right Moves," pp. 98–105 Reread for Fluency **Write** Response to Literature	Practice Book, p. 35, Sequence Student Reader: Unit 2 Routine Cards 2, 3, 4 Student Reader DVD-ROM

Day 5	**Read a Passage** "Why Do We Work?" pp. 106–107
	    Comprehension: Sequence; Listening
	Build Concepts Vocabulary
	Write Response to Literature: "4 You 2 Do," p. 108
	Assessment Options Fluency
	    Comprehension
		Student Reader: Unit 2
		Routine Cards 3, 5, 6, 8
		Fluency Progress Chart, p. 185
		Practice Book, p. 36, Writing

See pp. xvi–xvii for how *My Sidewalks* integrates instructional practices for ELL.

ACTIVITY 1 Build Concepts

Amazing Words Vocabulary

| To Do | To Say | 10–15 minutes |

Develop oral vocabulary.

See Routine Card 6 and p. 206.

Introduce the Concept/Amazing Words with an oral routine prior to displaying them in print. Page 206 in this Teacher's Guide provides specific guidelines for introducing each word.

Develop word meaning.

See Routine Card 5. Discuss pp. 85–89.

Have students read p. 85 and then look at the pictures on pp. 86–89. **What do you notice?** (people doing different jobs) **Can you use the words *worker* and *job* to describe any of these pictures?** (Example: The *workers* in these pictures are doing important *jobs*.)

Scaffold instruction.

Create a concept web.

In the center of a web, write *Jobs*. **This week's concept is *a job well done*. A *job* is the work that a person does.** Provide an example to demonstrate meaning. **Many high-school students work at summer *jobs* when they're not in school.**

Add the other vocabulary words.

Concept and Language Goals

Discuss the meaning of each word as it relates to jobs, using the glossary as needed. (See p. 98 in this Teacher's Guide for definitions.)

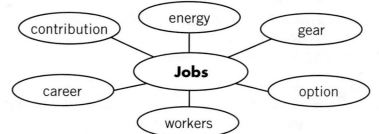

Model the multisyllabic word strategy.

Display each word. Say it as you display it.

Use the Tested Vocabulary Cards. Follow this routine for each word:

- **Look for Meaningful Parts** Remind students to look for meaningful parts. **As you say each word, ask yourself: Do I see any parts I know?** As you introduce the words, be sure students notice *work* in *workers* and *contribut(e)* in *contribution.* You may want to explain that in this word *contribution,* the suffix causes the primary accent to shift to the syllable *bu.*

- **Chunk Words with No Recognizable Parts** Model how to chunk the word *energy* to read it.

Think aloud.

- **Model** I see a chunk at the beginning of the word: *en.* I see a part in the middle: *er.* I see a part at the end of the word: *gy.* I say each chunk slowly: *en er gy.* I say the chunks fast to make a whole word: *energy.* Is it a real word? Yes, I know the word *energy.*

- Have students practice reading each word.

Preview.

Read p. 84 with students.

Do you see any of the words we just learned on this page? Together with students, read the sentences on p. 84 describing each selection. Talk about how the concept words might be used in the selections.

MORE PRACTICE

Deepen understanding of *workers.*

Have students demonstrate understanding by answering questions. **Which one is a *worker,* someone who goes to school or someone who performs at a job? Why are the *workers* who do everyday jobs so important?**

ACTIVITY 2 Read a Passage

Develop Concepts "Everyday Jobs," pp. 86–89

10–15 minutes

	To Do	**To Say**
Practice strategic prereading.	See Routine Card 2. Think aloud.	**Discuss Genre** Read the title on p. 86, and have students look at the illustrations on pp. 86–89. Model determining genre. The photographs are a clue that this is nonfiction. They look like photos of real people and real places. I think this article will tell me about everyday jobs.
Scaffold instruction.	Review text structure.	**Ask Questions** What questions do you ask yourself to help you understand nonfiction? (What did I learn? What is this mainly about?) As you read this article, ask these questions and look for the answers.
Guide comprehension. **Develop language and concepts.**	Read pp. 86–89 aloud.	**Read** Read the article as students follow along. Then read it a second time, having students join in. If necessary, stop at the end of each paragraph to check comprehension. Ask questions to promote discussion and develop the concept. • What are everyday jobs? • How do the people who do everyday jobs make our lives easier and better? • What words on the concept web could help you describe jobs?
MORE PRACTICE		Have students reread "Everyday Jobs." As they read, tell them to make a list of all the everyday jobs mentioned in the article to share with family members tonight.

Reread for Fluency "Everyday Jobs," p. 88

5 minutes

	To Do	**To Say**
CORRECTIVE FEEDBACK	Monitor oral reading.	Read p. 88 aloud. Reread the page three or four times so your reading gets better each time. Give feedback on students' oral reading, using the *if . . . then* statements on Routine Card 4. Model fluent reading if necessary. You may want to have students read along with the DVD-ROM.

ACTIVITY 3 Write

Response to Literature

5 minutes

	To Do	**To Say**
Prompt journal writing.	Write on the board or a transparency: *How does working together get the job done?*	Take out your journals. This week we are reading about jobs. Our question for this week is: *How does working together get the job done?* Write an answer to this question based on what you have read today. Have students write about the topic, using what they have read and their own experiences.
Homework	Practice Book, p. 33, Vocabulary	

ACTIVITY 1 Word Work

Phonics Open (V/CV) and Closed (VC/V) Syllables

5–10 minutes

	To Do	**To Say**
Teach open (V/CV) and closed (VC/V) syllables.	Write on the board or a transparency: *They didn't <u>notice</u> the supplies in the <u>closet</u>.*	If a word has one consonant following the first vowel, usually divide the word before the consonant. Where should you divide *notice? (no tice)* What vowel sound do you hear in the first syllable? (long *o*) Now look at the word *closet.* If you don't recognize the word when pronounced with a long vowel sound, divide after the consonant, and say the first syllable with a short vowel sound. Where should you divide *closet? (clos et)* What vowel sound do you hear in the first syllable? (short *o*)
Scaffold instruction.	Develop word meaning.	Have students think and converse. Sometimes, people don't *notice* things that they see every day. Why?
	Write *fever* and *second.*	Here are two more words. Where should you divide *fever? (fe ver)* What vowel sound do you hear in the first syllable? (long *e*) Where should you divide *second? (sec ond)* What vowel sound do you hear in the first syllable? (short *e*)
CORRECTIVE FEEDBACK	Write each practice word.	Have students practice reading these words with open and closed syllables. Correct any words students miss and have them reread the list.

paper   planet   female   lemon   pilot   linen   locate   humor

	To Do	**To Say**
MORE PRACTICE	Write more practice words.	Have students practice reading these words with open and closed syllables.

nature   camel   legal   finish   notice   body   music   study

Amazing Words Vocabulary

5 minutes

	To Do	**To Say**
Review vocabulary.	Review the homework.	Ask students to go over answers and share their writing from Practice Book p. 33. See Routine Card 1 for the multisyllabic word routine.
	Deepen understanding of *career.*	Remember, *career* means "an occupation or profession." You might know someone who works as a teacher, a doctor, or a veterinarian. Why are these jobs called *careers?* What else is an example of a *career?* Why?

ACTIVITY 2 Comprehension

Sequence

5 minutes

	To Do	**To Say**
Scaffold instruction.	Introduce sequence.	Today you will read about a real event that took place in the city of Boston, Massachusetts. When you read about real events, it's important to keep track of the sequence, or order, of events because it may help you understand what happened. Dates and words such as *first, then,* and *at last* give you clues to the sequence.
	Model the skill.	For example, if I read that a project *started* with a new road and *ended* with a new bridge, I need to pay attention to the sequence to understand how the project developed.
	Distribute Graphic Organizer 6.	As you read "The Big Dig of Boston," look for words that help you track the sequence of events during the project. Add these sequence words to your graphic organizer. See Routine Card 7.

ACTIVITY **3** | Read a Passage

Read for Comprehension "The Big Dig of Boston," pp. 90–93

10–15 minutes

	To Do	**To Say**
Scaffold instruction.	Monitor student engagement.	**Read** Have students read pp. 90–93. Stop at the end of each page to ask questions. Students who can read on their own can do so without stopping. After reading, ask questions to promote discussion.
	See Routine Cards 2 and 3.	**Why did Boston have such terrible traffic problems?** (The old highway wasn't wide enough, and it was falling apart.)
		What were city planners worried might happen if they didn't replace the old highway? (People wouldn't want to work in Boston or spend time there.)
		What is the Super Scoop? (a machine that was used to dig an underwater tunnel)
		What do you think the rest of the article will be about? (Answers will vary. The title suggests it will tell more about the Big Dig.)
Model summarizing.	Think aloud.	**Summarize** What were the first four pages mainly about? What did you learn about the Big Dig? Think aloud to model summarizing. **I learned a lot of details about the Big Dig, such as that it included digging a tunnel 50 feet under Boston Harbor. But the main thing I learned was that the city had to do something to solve their traffic problems.**
Develop language and concepts.	Ask questions.	• **What might have happened to the city of Boston if the old highway was not replaced?**
		• **Why did the old highway, train tracks, and subways have to stay open during the Big Dig?**
MORE PRACTICE	Have students reread p. 93.	**Reread** Tell students to draw a picture that shows the Super Scoop digging the tunnel.

Reread for Fluency "The Big Dig of Boston," pp. 90–91

5 minutes

	To Do	**To Say**
MORE PRACTICE **CORRECTIVE FEEDBACK**	Pair students. Monitor paired reading.	Students read aloud pp. 90–91, switching readers at each new paragraph. Have partners reread; now the other partner begins. For optimal fluency, students should reread three or four times. Give feedback, using the *if . . . then* statements on Routine Card 4. You may want to have students read along with the DVD-ROM.

ACTIVITY **4** | Write

Response to Literature

5 minutes

	To Do	**To Say**
Prompt writing.	Writing elements: conventions	**Think of all of the people who worked on the Big Dig. Why was the job they did so important to the people who live and work in Boston as well as those who visit the city? Use complete sentences to express your ideas.**
	Homework	Practice Book, p. 34, Open and Closed Syllables: V/CV, VC/V

3

Word Work

Phonics Open (V/CV) and Closed (VC/V) Syllables

	To Do	**To Say**	*5 minutes*
Review open (V/CV) and closed (VC/V) syllables. **Scaffold instruction.**	Review the homework. Point to *famous* on p. 86 in the Student Reader.	Ask students to share answers from Practice Book p. 34. Point out *famous* on p. 86, paragraph 1. **Remember, if a word has one consonant following the first vowel, usually divide the word before the consonant. Where should you divide *famous*?** *(fa mous)* **What vowel sound do you hear in the first syllable?** (long *a*) Guide students in blending the word parts into the word. Then point to *second* on p. 94, paragraph 1. **What vowel sound do you hear in the first syllable of *second*?** (short *e*) **Where should you divide the word?** *(sec ond)*	
MORE PRACTICE	Model spelling words with open and closed syllables.	**Spell and Write** Write *city*. **What vowel sound do you hear in the first syllable?** (short *i*) **What letter spells that sound?** *(i)* Continue with *notice, option, famous,* and *second.*	

Amazing Words Vocabulary

	To Do	**To Say**	*5 minutes*
Build vocabulary. **Lead cumulative review.**	Deepen understanding of *option.*	**Remember, *option* means "something that can be chosen." Can you think of a word that is a synonym for *option*?** *(choice)* **If something is not an *option*, does that mean that you can do it or that you can't do it? Give an example of something that is not an *option* for you at home. Why?** Use the Tested Vocabulary Cards to review words from previous weeks.	

Comprehension

Sequence

	To Do	**To Say**	*5–10 minutes*
Scaffold instruction. **Guide practice.**	Review sequence. Use Graphic Organizer 6.	**An author gives you clues to the sequence. Look for dates and words such as *today, first, then, next,* and so on to help you follow the sequence of events.** **Listen as I reread p. 93. I want you to notice that the author tells about the end of the first part of the Big Dig project.** Read p. 93. Then ask: **What words help you understand the sequence?** *(1995, first)* **Add these words to your graphic organizer. What happened in 1995?** (The first tunnel was finished.) **What happened next?** (Work began on a second tunnel.) See Routine Card 7.	
MORE PRACTICE	Have students preview pp. 94–97. Think aloud.	**Read the captions and look at the photos on pp. 94–97. What do you think this section will be about?** (work on the Big Dig) **Why do you think so?** Think aloud to model using illustrations and captions to predict. **The captions and pictures make me think the article will describe the special tunneling machines that worked on the Big Dig and the new bridges and highways that they built.**	

ACTIVITY 3 Read a Passage

Read for Comprehension "The Big Dig of Boston," pp. 94–97

	To Do	To Say	
			10–15 minutes

Scaffold instruction.

Monitor student engagement.

See Routine Cards 2 and 3.

Read Have students read pp. 94–97. Stop at the end of each page to ask questions. Students who can read on their own can do so without stopping. After reading, ask questions to promote discussion.

Why was it necessary to build a tunnel on legs? (so it wouldn't crush the tunnel already in place underneath it)

What was the "worm" and how did it work? (The worm was a giant tunnel box. Machines shoved it forward to make a path.)

When did the Big Dig project end? (2004)

Review the phonics skill.

Point out *columns*, p. 95, paragraph 1.

Remind students that if they don't recognize a word when pronounced with a long vowel sound, divide after the consonant, and say the first syllable with a short vowel sound. Demonstrate framing the parts *col umns*. Have students blend the parts to read the word. See Routine Card 1.

Assess comprehension.

Monitor understanding.

After Reading Have students discuss the What Do You Think? question. Prompt them to use sequence words in telling the order in which the bridges were built. Listen as they talk to assess comprehension.

Summarize.

What is this mainly about? What did you learn? Work with students to summarize the selection.

MORE PRACTICE

Have students reread p. 95.

Reread As they read about how the workers built the new tunnel, tell students to note sequence words. *(then, today)* Have students add these words to their graphic organizers. After they read, have them use sequence words to retell how the tunnel was built.

Reread for Fluency "The Big Dig of Boston," p. 96

	To Do	To Say	
			5 minutes

CORRECTIVE FEEDBACK

Monitor oral reading.

Read p. 96 aloud. Reread the page three or four times so your reading gets better each time. Give feedback on students' oral reading, using the *if . . . then* statements on Routine Card 4. Model fluent reading if necessary. You may want to have students read along with the DVD-ROM.

ACTIVITY 4 Write

Response to Literature

	To Do	To Say	
			5 minutes

MORE PRACTICE

Prompt writing.

Why do you think planning and building the Big Dig took several years? Why were so many people involved? Use specific details from the selection to support your ideas.

Homework

Practice Book, p. 35, Sequence

ACTIVITY **1** Word Work

Amazing Words Vocabulary

To Do	To Say	*5–10 minutes*

Extend word knowledge.

Develop word meaning.

Scaffold instruction.

Write *energy* on the board or a transparency.

Use the word *energy* to extend word knowledge. **Remember we read this word earlier this week and learned its meaning. How do you feel when you are full of *energy*? What can make you feel that way?** Invite diverse responses. **There are many other words related to the word *energy*. Let's look at and think about some of them.**

Write *energies, energetic, energize.*

Help students read each word. Say: **How is the plural form of *energy* formed?** (change *y* to *i*, add *-es*) **What cute things might an *energetic* kitten do? What annoying or disruptive things might an *energetic* puppy do? What fun ideas could you think of to *energize* a dull party?**

MORE PRACTICE

Deepen understanding of *energy*.

Have students think of as many sources as they can of *energy* in use today, such as gas, oil, coal, sun, wind, water, and electricity. **What provides the *energy* for a car? a toy? a lamp? a skateboard? How does a person act or feel who is low on *energy*? Why might a person feel that way? What can the person do to reverse that feeling?**

ACTIVITY **2** Comprehension

Skill and Strategy Practice

To Do	To Say	*5 minutes*

Scaffold instruction.

Review sequence (homework).

Ask volunteers to read the passage and share answers from Practice Book p. 35. Reiterate the value of finding sequence. **When you read, think about sequence to help you remember events or how things work. Follow a sequence of events or steps to help you complete something accurately, or to explain how things work. Look for key words, dates, times, or other clues. Imagine chunks of time, such as *before, during,* and *after.***

Practice strategic prereading.

See Routine Card 2.

Discuss Genre Read the title and the first paragraph on p. 98 in the Student Reader. Model determining genre.

Think aloud.

This sounds like fiction because it starts off by introducing a character and setting the scene. The illustrations show skateboards, so I think this story might have something to do with skateboarding. I bet the kids will have a problem to solve or a goal to reach.

Review story structure.

Ask Questions **What questions do you ask yourself to help you understand a fictional story?** (What is the problem or goal? How is the problem solved or the goal reached?) **As you read this story, ask these questions and look for the answers.**

ACTIVITY 3 Read a Passage

Read for Comprehension "All the Right Moves," pp. 98–105

10–15 minutes

	To Do	To Say
Scaffold instruction.	Monitor student engagement.	**Read** Have students read pp. 98–105 on their own and then discuss. For students who need more help, stop at the end of each page to discuss. After reading, ask questions.
	See Routine Card 3.	**Who are the main characters?** (twins Rob and Rosie) **How might you describe them?** (active, energetic, enthusiastic)
		What goal do Rob and Rosie have? (to get their dad to build them a skateboard ramp)
		Why does Dad hesitate? (Rob and Rosie don't do their chores.)
		What plan do the twins develop? (They borrow drawings for how to build a ramp; they agree to do their chores as their part of the project.)
		What does the title mean? (Rob and Rosie make the right moves by completing their chores, and this encourages Dad to build the ramp.)
	Model using context for word meaning.	Read aloud the paragraph with *contribution* on p. 103. Explain how the paragraph provides clues to the meaning of *contribution*.
Assess comprehension.	Monitor understanding.	**After Reading** Have students discuss the What Do You Think? question. Prompt them to organize their responses in sequence, based on details given in the story. Listen as they talk to assess comprehension.
MORE PRACTICE		**Reread** Have students reread pp. 100–101 and then explain why Mom and Dad feel frustrated about how Rosie and Rob handle their household responsibilities.

Reread for Fluency "All the Right Moves," pp. 102–103

5–10 minutes

	To Do	To Say
CORRECTIVE FEEDBACK	Pair students. Monitor paired reading.	Students read aloud pp. 102–103, switching readers at the end of each paragraph. Have partners reread; now the other partner begins. For optimal fluency, students should reread three or four times. Give feedback, using Routine Card 4. You may want to have students read along with the DVD-ROM.
MORE PRACTICE	**READERS' THEATER**	Work with a group of three students to adapt pp. 102–103 as a radio play. Have students rehearse reading the parts, with one student serving as the narrator, one as Rob, and one as Rosie.

ACTIVITY 4 Write

Response to Literature

5 minutes

	To Do	To Say
Prompt personal narrative.	Review pp. 104–105. Writing elements: organization, focus	**In this passage, Rosie and Rob focus on getting Dad to build a skateboard ramp for them by promising to do their chores and homework. Think about a time when you wanted something. What was it, and how did you work to get it?** (Students should focus on one goal and how they reached it. Transitions should connect ideas.)

ACTIVITY 1 Read a Passage

Read Together *"Why Do We Work?"* pp. 106–107

10 minutes

	To Do	**To Say**
Scaffold instruction.	Review sequence.	Have students preview pp. 106–107. **This article talks about the variety of rewards people can get from a job well done. In this article, think about how the** *contributions* **involved in a job can mean two things: something** *workers* **give and something** *workers* **receive. Also think about the sequence of steps in the advice on how to do a great job.**
	See Routine Card 3.	**Read** Read the article as students follow along. Then read it a second time, having students join in on the text. After reading, ask questions.
		Besides earning money, what other reasons do people have for working? (to increase a skill, to help others, to extend a hobby)
		What three steps does the author suggest you follow to do a good job? (1. Plan ahead; 2. Keep a good attitude; 3. Finish)
Assess comprehension.	Monitor listening comprehension.	**Summarize** Have students review reasons why people work and how to be a successful worker. Discuss how this article fits the unit theme of "Work and Play" as well as the week's theme, "A Job Well Done."

ACTIVITY 2 Build Concepts

Amazing Words Vocabulary

5–10 minutes

	To Do	**To Say**
Review concept and vocabulary.	Display the concept web you began on Day 1.	**This week's question is** *How does working together get the job done?* **How do this week's words relate to the question?** (Have students answer the question, using some of the vocabulary they learned this week.)
		Ask students to add more words to the concept web. Have students explain how each word relates to jobs. Monitor students' understanding of vocabulary as they discuss the web. See Routine Card 5.
MORE PRACTICE	Write *workers* and *gear* on the board.	Have students relate *workers* and *gear.* **Many** *workers* **need special** *gear* **in order to do their jobs safely or effectively. Give some examples that link** *workers* **to their required** *gear.* **What effect might it have on jobs if** *workers* **lost or broke their** *gear?* **How might they make do?**

ACTIVITY 3 Write

Response to Literature "4 You 2 Do," p. 108

| To Do | To Say | 5–10 minutes |

Guide response activities.

To Do
Discuss the directions on p. 108. Tell students to choose one activity to complete. See Routine Card 8.

To Say
Word Play Have students unscramble the words on their own or with a partner. Offer hints (such as the first letter) as needed. It may help students to manipulate letter tiles as an aid to unscrambling the words.

Making Connections Discuss the question in a group. (Answers will vary but might suggest that Rob and Rosie could learn how to make and follow a long-term plan, or learn to manage problems as they arise.)

On Paper Have students brainstorm some answers to the prompt before they write. Have them write on their own. Students can use Practice Book p. 36 to structure their written responses, or you can send the Practice Book page home for them to complete later.

MORE PRACTICE
If you have more time, direct students to complete all the activities.

ACTIVITY 4 Assessment Options

Passage Reading

| To Do | To Say | 10–15 minutes |

Check fluency.

Check comprehension.

To Do
See Routine Card 6.

Take a two-minute timed sample of each student's oral reading.

To Say
While some students are doing Activity 3, determine which students you want to assess this week and choose from these options.

Fluency Have a student read for two minutes from "The Big Dig of Boston." Record the number of correct words read per minute. See p. 184 for monitoring fluency. Be sure each student is assessed at least every other week.

Have students graph their progress on the Fluency Progress Chart, p. 185.

Retelling Have students reread "The Big Dig of Boston" and retell it. Prompt students if necessary. See p. 186 for monitoring retelling.

If you have time, assess every student.

Homework   Practice Book, p. 36, Writing

Unit 2 Week 5 *Our Nation's Capital*

? What happens in our nation's capital?

Objectives *This week students will...*

Vocabulary
- build concepts and vocabulary: *capital, Capitol, dedicated, executive, memorabilia, museum*

Phonics
- read words with the suffixes *-ly, -ful, -ness, -less*
- apply knowledge of word structure to decode multisyllabic words when reading

Text Comprehension
- use main idea to improve comprehension
- write in response to literature
- make connections across text

Fluency
- practice fluency with oral rereading

Word Work *This week's phonics focus is . . .*

Suffixes *-ly, -ful, -ness, -less*

Amazing Words Concept/Amazing Words *Tested Vocabulary*

The week's vocabulary is related to the concept of our nation's capital.
The first appearance of each word in the Student Reader is noted below.

capital	a city where the government of a country or state is located; where laws are made (p. 112)
Capitol	the building in Washington, D.C., in which Congress meets (p. 116)
dedicated	set something apart for a purpose (p. 127)
executive	someone who manages a business or a department of a government (p. 114)
memorabilia	things or events saved for remembering (p. 129)
museum	a building for displaying a collection of objects related to science, ancient life, art, or other subjects (p. 129)

Student Reader Unit 2 *This week students will read the following selections.*

Daily Lesson Plan

	ACTIVITIES	MATERIALS
Day 1	**Build Concepts** Weekly Concept: Our Nation's Capital Vocabulary: *capital, Capitol, dedicated, executive, memorabilia, museum* **Read a Passage** "Birth of the Capital," pp. 112–113 Comprehension: Use Strategies Reread for Fluency **Write** Response to Literature	Student Reader: Unit 2 Routine Cards 2, 4, 5 Tested Vocabulary Cards Student journals Practice Book, p. 37, Vocabulary Student Reader DVD-ROM
Day 2	**Word Work** Phonics: Suffixes *-ly, -ful, -ness, -less* Vocabulary: Deepen word meaning **Comprehension** Main Idea and Supporting Details **Read a Passage** "Working in the White House," pp. 114–117 Reread for Fluency **Write** Response to Literature	Student Reader: Unit 2 Practice Book, p. 37, Vocabulary Graphic Organizer 1 Routine Cards 1, 2, 3, 4, 7 Practice Book, p. 38, Suffixes *-ly, -ful, -ness, -less* Student Reader DVD-ROM
Day 3	**Word Work** Phonics: Suffixes *-ly, -ful, -ness, -less* Vocabulary: Deepen word meaning **Comprehension** Main Idea and Supporting Details **Read a Passage** "Working in the White House," pp. 118–121 Reread for Fluency **Write** Response to Literature	Practice Book, p. 38, Suffixes *-ly, -ful, -ness, -less* Tested Vocabulary Cards Student Reader: Unit 2 Graphic Organizer 1 Routine Cards 1, 2, 3, 4, 7 Practice Book, p. 39, Main Idea and Details Student Reader DVD-ROM
Day 4	**Word Work** Vocabulary: Extend word knowledge **Comprehension** Skill and Strategy Practice **Read a Passage** "White House Pets," pp. 122–129 Reread for Fluency **Write** Response to Literature	Practice Book, p. 39, Main Idea and Details Student Reader: Unit 2 Routine Cards 2, 3, 4 Student Reader DVD-ROM
Day 5	**Read a Passage** "Washington's Wonderful Monuments," pp. 130–133 Comprehension: Main Idea and Supporting Details; Listening **Build Concepts** Vocabulary **Write** Response to Literature: "4 You 2 Do," p. 134 **Assessment Options** Fluency, Comprehension End-of-Unit Test	Student Reader: Unit 2 Routine Cards 3, 5, 8 Practice Book, p. 40, Writing Assessment Book, p. 36

See pp. xvi–xvii for how *My Sidewalks* integrates instructional practices for **ELL.**

ACTIVITY 1 | Build Concepts

Amazing Words **Vocabulary**

| To Do | To Say | *10–15 minutes* |

Develop oral vocabulary.

See Routine Card 6 and p. 207.

Introduce the Concept/Amazing Words with an oral routine prior to displaying them in print. Page 207 in this Teacher's Guide provides specific guidelines for introducing each word.

Develop word meaning.

See Routine Card 5. Discuss pp. 111–113.

Have students read p. 111 and then look at the pictures on pp. 112–113. **What do you notice?** (a map of Washington, D.C., some of the people who were part of the design and building of the capital) **Can you use the word *government* to describe any of these pictures?** (Example: Washington, D.C., is where the *government* is located.)

Scaffold instruction.

Create a concept web.

In the center of a web, write *The Government.* **This week's concept is *our nation's capital,* which is related to *the government.* The *government* is the group of people who manage our country.** Provide examples to demonstrate meaning. **We vote to choose the people who will run our *government.* Our *government* protects our rights and our freedom.**

Add the other vocabulary words.

Concept and Language Goals

Discuss the meaning of each word as it relates to the government, using the glossary as needed. (See p. 110 in this Teacher's Guide for definitions.)

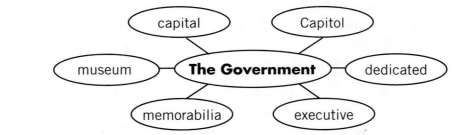

Model the multisyllabic word strategy.

Display each word. Say it as you display it.

Think aloud.

Use the Tested Vocabulary Cards. Follow this routine for each word:

- **Look for Meaningful Parts** Do you recognize any parts of this word? What do these parts mean? Use the parts to read the word.

- **Model** I see most of the word *memory* in *memorabilia.* So *memorabilia* must have something to do with memory. I think *memorabilia* means "things or events worth remembering."

- **Chunk Words with No Recognizable Parts** Model how to chunk the word *museum.* I see a chunk at the beginning of the word: *mu.* I see a part in the middle: *se.* I see a part at the end of the word: *um.* I say each chunk slowly: *mu se um.* I say the chunks fast to make a whole word: *museum.* Is it a real word? Yes, I know the word *museum.*

- Have students practice reading each word.

Read p. 110 with students.

Do you see any of the words we just learned on this page? Together with students, read the sentences on p. 110 describing each selection. Talk about how the concept words might be used in the selections.

MORE PRACTICE

Deepen understanding of *capital.*

Have students demonstrate understanding by answering questions. **Why does a nation need a *capital*? How do you decide where a *capital* should be located, and what it should look like?**

ACTIVITY 2 — Read a Passage

Develop Concepts "Birth of the Capital," pp. 112–113

10–15 minutes

	To Do	To Say
Practice strategic prereading.	See Routine Card 2. Think aloud.	**Discuss Genre** Read the title on p. 112 and have students look at the illustrations on pp. 112–113. Model determining genre. **The illustrations and map are clues that this is nonfiction. They look like pictures of real places, people, and events. I think this article will tell me about the building of the capital.**
Scaffold instruction.	Review text structure.	**Ask Questions** What questions do you ask yourself to help you understand nonfiction? (What did I learn? What is this mainly about?) As you read this article, ask these questions and look for the answers.
Guide comprehension. **Develop language and concepts.**	Read pp. 112–113 aloud.	**Read** Read the article as students follow along. Then read it a second time, having students join in. If necessary, stop at the end of each paragraph to check comprehension. Ask questions to promote discussion and develop the concept. • **What were the first capitals of the United States?** (New York, Philadelphia) • **Why was Washington, D.C., a good location for a new capital?** (It was in the center of the thirteen states and close to both the North and the South.) • **What President helped to plan the capital city?** (George Washington) • **What words on the concept web could help you describe the nation's capital?**
MORE PRACTICE		Have students reread "Birth of the Capital." As they read, tell them to make a list of facts about the new capital to share with family members tonight.

Reread for Fluency "Birth of the Capital," p. 113

5 minutes

	To Do	To Say
CORRECTIVE FEEDBACK	Monitor oral reading.	**Read p. 113 aloud. Reread the page three or four times so your reading gets better each time.** Give feedback on students' oral reading, using the *if . . . then* statements on Routine Card 4. Model fluent reading if necessary. You may want to have students read along with the DVD-ROM.

ACTIVITY 3 — Write

Response to Literature

5 minutes

	To Do	To Say
Prompt journal writing.	Write on the board or a transparency: *What happens in our nation's capital?*	**Take out your journals. This week we are reading about our nation's capital. The question for this week is: *What happens in our nation's capital?* Write an answer to this question based on what you read today.** Have students write about the topic, using what they read and their own experiences.
Homework	Practice Book, p. 37, Vocabulary	

ACTIVITY 1 Word Work

Phonics Suffixes -ly, -ful, -ness, -less

	To Do	To Say	5–10 minutes
Teach the suffixes -ly, -ful, -ness, -less. **Scaffold instruction.**	Write on the board or a transparency: *sadly, powerful, kindness, breathless.*	Remember, when you read a long word, look for meaningful parts. **What parts do you see in this word?** Frame *sad* and *ly*. This word has the suffix *-ly*. A suffix is a word part added to the end of a base word. The suffix *-ly* means "in a way," or how something is done. So *sadly* describes the way in which something is done. Now look at the word *powerful*. **What is the base word?** *(power)* **What is the suffix?** *(-ful)* The suffix *-ful* means "full of." So *powerful* means "full of power." **What parts do you see in** *kindness? (kind ness)* The suffix *-ness* means "quality of." *Kindness* is the quality of being kind. **What parts do you see in** *breathless? (breath less)* The suffix *-less* means "without." **What does** *breathless* **mean?** *(without breath)*	
	Develop word meaning.	Have students think and converse. **What does it feel like to be** *breathless?* **Why do you feel** *breathless* **after you run?**	
CORRECTIVE FEEDBACK	Write each practice word.	Have students practice reading words that end with *-ly, -ful, -ness*, and *-less.* Correct any words students miss and have them reread the list. **joyful laziness timeless neatly slowly bitterness**	
MORE PRACTICE	Write more practice words.	Have students practice reading words that end with *-ly, -ful, -ness, and -less.* **wildly thoughtful heartless frightful sweetness awareness**	

Amazing Words Vocabulary

	To Do	To Say	5 minutes
Review vocabulary.	Review the homework.	Ask students to go over answers and share their writing from Practice Book p. 37. See Routine Card 1 for the multisyllabic word routine.	
	Deepen understanding of *capital* and *Capitol.*	A *capital* is a city where laws are made. The *Capitol* is the building in Washington where Congress meets. **Why is it important for Congress to be located in the** *capital?* **Can any legislature meet at the** *Capitol?*	

ACTIVITY 2 Comprehension

Main Idea and Supporting Details

	To Do	To Say	5 minutes
Scaffold instruction.	Introduce main idea and supporting details.	Today you will read about real people who work in the White House. When you read nonfiction, it's important to find the main idea. The main idea is usually the most important thing the author has to say about the subject.	
	Model the skill.	For example, if I know that the topic of an article is pet care, I need to look for details that help me figure out what the most important idea about pet care is.	
	Distribute Graphic Organizer 1.	As you read "Working in the White House," look for details that help you identify the main idea. Add these details to your graphic organizers. See Routine Card 7.	

ACTIVITY 3 Read a Passage

Read for Comprehension "Working in the White House," pp. 114–117

10–15 minutes

	To Do	**To Say**
Scaffold instruction.	Monitor student engagement. See Routine Cards 2 and 3.	**Read** Have students read pp. 114–117. Stop at the end of each page to ask questions. Students who can read on their own can do so without stopping. After reading, ask questions to promote discussion. **Why is the President called the chief executive?** (He is the highest executive in our nation.) **What makes the job of White House chef so important?** (She is in charge of feeding the first family and many important guests every day.) **What is the job of the Chief Usher?** (to manage a staff of people who make sure the President's family and guests are comfortable) **What do you think the rest of the article will be about?** (Answers will vary. The title suggests it will tell about other jobs at the White House.)
Model summarizing.	Think aloud.	**Summarize** **What were the first four pages mainly about? What did you learn about working in the White House?** Think aloud to model summarizing. **I learned many details about working at the White House, such as that the chef once served 9,500 meals in one month. But the main thing I learned is that it takes many people to manage all of the work at the White House.**
Develop language and concepts.	Ask questions.	• **Why does it take so many people to keep things running smoothly at the White House?** • **What is special about the White House chef who was hired in 2005?**
MORE PRACTICE	Have students reread p. 117.	**Reread** Have students compare the job of the Chief Usher to that of the White House chef.

Reread for Fluency "Working in the White House," pp. 116–117

5 minutes

	To Do	**To Say**
MORE PRACTICE **CORRECTIVE FEEDBACK**	Pair students. Monitor paired reading.	Students read aloud pp. 116–117, switching readers at each new paragraph. Have partners reread; now the other partner begins. For optimal fluency, students should reread three or four times. Give feedback, using the *if . . . then* statements on Routine Card 4. You may want to have students read along with the DVD-ROM.

ACTIVITY 4 Write

Response to Literature

5 minutes

	To Do	**To Say**
Prompt writing.	Writing elements: organization	**How is the White House similar to and different from most ordinary homes? Use details from the article in your response. Use compare and contrast words such as** *both* **and** *unlike* **to show the similarities and differences.**
Homework		Practice Book, p. 38, Suffixes *-ly, -ful, -ness, -less*

ACTIVITY **1** | # Word Work

Phonics Suffixes -ly, -ful, -ness, -less

	To Do	**To Say**	5 minutes
Review suffixes -ly, -ful, -ness, -less. **Scaffold instruction.**	Review the homework. Discuss *countless* on p. 118 in the Student Reader.	Ask students to share answers from Practice Book p. 38. Point out *countless* on p. 118, paragraph 2. **What parts do you see in this word?** *(count less)* **If there are so many of something that you cannot count them, you can use the word *countless*. If you receive *countless* letters, how many letters have you received?** (too many to count) Point to *daily* on p. 118. **What parts do you see in this word?** *(dai ly)* **What is the base word?** *(day)* **If something happens *daily*, how often does it happen?** (each day)	
MORE PRACTICE	Model spelling words with suffixes.	**Spell and Write** Write *smoothly*. **What suffix has been added to *smooth*? Does the spelling of the base word change when the suffix is added?** Continue with *wonderful* and *likeness*. **Do you know other words that have a suffix?** List responses on the board.	

Amazing Words ## Vocabulary

	To Do	**To Say**	5 minutes
Build vocabulary. **Lead cumulative review.**	Deepen understanding of *executive*.	**An *executive* is someone who manages a business or department of government. Say a sentence using *executive*. In what ways is governing a country similar to managing a business? What qualities should an *executive* have? Why?** Use the Tested Vocabulary Cards to review words from previous weeks.	

ACTIVITY **2** | # Comprehension

Main Idea and Supporting Details

	To Do	**To Say**	5–10 minutes
Scaffold instruction.	Review main idea and supporting details.	**The main idea is usually the most important idea about a topic. Supporting details are the pieces of information that help tell you what the main idea is. As you read "Working in the White House," look for the main idea.**	
Guide practice.	Use Graphic Organizer 1.	**Listen as I read p. 119. I want you to notice that the author is describing the job of Secret Service agents.** Read p. 119. Then ask: **What is the topic?** (Secret Service agents) **What is the most important idea about Secret Service agents?** (They protect people and places in Washington.) **What details support the main idea?** (Secret Service agents protect the White House and other buildings in the capital; they guard the President and the first family; they patrol on foot, bikes, motorcycles, and cars.) **Add supporting details to your graphic organizers.** See Routine Card 7.	
MORE PRACTICE	Have students preview pp. 118–121. Think aloud.	**Read the captions and look at the photos on pp. 118–121. What do you think this section will be about?** (more jobs in the White House) **Why do you think so?** Think aloud to model using illustrations and captions to predict. **The captions make me think the article will describe more jobs at the White House, From the photos I think the article will tell more about what it's like to work there.**	

ACTIVITY **3** Read a Passage

Read for Comprehension "Working in the White House," pp. 118–121

10–15 minutes

	To Do	**To Say**
Scaffold instruction.	Monitor student engagement. See Routine Cards 2 and 3.	**Read** Have students read pp. 118–121. Stop at the end of each page to ask questions. Students who can read on their own can do so without stopping. After reading, ask questions to promote discussion. **Why was the Internet Director job created?** (Many people now use e-mail to communicate with the White House.) **Who does the Secret Service protect besides the President?** (the President's family) **Why is it important for the White House to always look its best?** (because many visitors take tours of the White House)
Review the phonics skill.	Point out *wonderful* on p. 121.	Remind students that the suffix *-ful* means "full of." Demonstrate framing the root word *wonder* and the suffix *-ful*. Have students blend the parts to read the word. See Routine Card 1.
Assess comprehension.	Monitor understanding. Summarize.	**After Reading** Have students discuss the What Do You Think? question. Prompt them to identify the main idea of the article as they answer the question. Listen as they talk to assess comprehension. **What is this mainly about? What did you learn?** Work with students to summarize the selection.
MORE PRACTICE	Have students reread p. 119.	**Reread** As they read, tell students to note all of the important jobs that Secret Service agents do. After they read, have them explain why the job of the Secret Service is so important.

Reread for Fluency "Working in the White House," p. 120

5 minutes

	To Do	**To Say**
CORRECTIVE FEEDBACK	Monitor oral reading.	**Read p. 120 aloud. Reread the page three or four times so your reading gets better each time.** Give feedback on students' oral reading, using the *if . . . then* statements on Routine Card 4. Model fluent reading if necessary. You may want to have students read along with the DVD-ROM.

ACTIVITY **4** Write

Response to Literature

5 minutes

	To Do	**To Say**
MORE PRACTICE	Prompt writing.	**Why do you think people who work at the White House usually keep their jobs for such a long time? Provide information that supports your opinion. Use complete sentences to express your thoughts.**

Homework	Practice Book, p. 39, Main Idea and Details

4

Word Work

Amazing Words Vocabulary

	To Do	To Say	5–10 minutes

Extend word knowledge.

Write on the board or a transparency: *We sent all of the Civil War* <u>memorabilia</u> *to the* <u>museum</u>.

Use the word *memorabilia* to extend word knowledge. **Remember we read this word earlier this week. We looked for meaningful parts and we noticed most of the word** *memory*. **Today, I want to talk about other words related to** *memory*.

Explore words related to memory.

A *memory* is a person, thing, or event that you can remember. *Memorabilia* are things or events worth remembering. **Can you think of other words that relate to** *memory?* (memorable, memorial, memorize) Write words as students name them, and add some of your own. Talk about the meanings of the words. **How are all of these word meanings similar?** (Each has something to do with remembering.)

Scaffold instruction.

Develop word meaning.

How does collecting and saving *memorabilia* **help us to preserve our** *memories?* **In what ways are** *memorabilia* **and** *memories* **different?**

MORE PRACTICE

Deepen understanding of *memorabilia* and *dedicated*.

Have individual students or partners use the two words *memorabilia* and *dedicate* in sentences. (For example: My mom has *memorabilia* from our vacation trip, such as postcards. Grandpa *dedicated* a poem he wrote to our family.) Share sentences. Ask: **How is** *dedicating* **an object to the memory of someone or something similar to saving** *memorabilia?*

Comprehension

Skill and Strategy Practice

	To Do	To Say	5 minutes

Scaffold instruction.

Review main idea (homework).

Ask volunteers to read the passage and share answers from Practice Book p. 39. Remind students of the importance of finding the main idea. **When you read nonfiction, finding the main idea can help you to better understand what you read. One way to help identify the main idea is to ask yourself, "Is this the most important idea about the topic?" Remember to look for details that support the main idea.**

Practice strategic prereading.

See Routine Card 2.

Discuss Genre Read the title and the first paragraph on p. 122 in the Student Reader. Model determining genre.

Think aloud.

I first thought this might be nonfiction because of the photographs and illustrations. They look like pictures of real people and animals.

Review text structure.

Ask Questions What questions do you ask yourself to help you understand nonfiction? (What did I learn? What is this mainly about?) **As you read this article, ask these questions and look for the answers.**

ACTIVITY 3 Read a Passage

Read for Comprehension "White House Pets," pp. 122–129

	To Do	To Say	
			10–15 minutes

Scaffold instruction.

To Do: Monitor student engagement.

See Routine Card 3.

To Say: **Read** Have students read pp. 122–129 on their own and then discuss. For students who need more help, stop at the end of each page to discuss. After reading, ask questions.

What are some of the unusual pets that have lived in the White House? (parrots, ponies, elephants, sheep, tigers, goats, alligators, bears, hyena, zebra, hippo, wallaby)

Which President had the greatest number of pets? (Teddy Roosevelt)

What did President Coolidge believe about people who did not have pets? (A person who didn't have pets shouldn't be President.)

Where can you go to learn more about White House pets? (the Presidential Pet Museum)

Assess comprehension.

To Do: Monitor understanding.

To Say: **After Reading** Have students discuss the What Do You Think? question. Prompt them to identify the main idea of the article in their response. Listen as they talk, to assess comprehension.

MORE PRACTICE

To Say: **Reread** Have students reread pp. 126–127 and then describe what happened to Whiskers the goat.

Reread for Fluency "White House Pets," pp. 122–125

	To Do	To Say	
			5–10 minutes

CORRECTIVE FEEDBACK

To Do: Pair students. Monitor paired reading.

To Say: Students read aloud pp. 122–125, switching readers at the end of each paragraph. Have partners reread; now the other partner begins. For optimal fluency, students should reread three or four times. Give feedback, using Routine Card 4. You may want to have students read along with the DVD-ROM.

MORE PRACTICE

To Do: READERS' THEATER

To Say: Work with a group of students to adapt pp. 126–127 as a scene. Have students rehearse reading the parts, with three narrators for the parts about Presidents Coolidge, Harrison, and Harding and three students silently acting out the Presidents' actions.

ACTIVITY 4 Write

Response to Literature

	To Do	To Say	
			5 minutes

Prompt expository writing.

To Do: Review pp. 122–129.

Writing elements: focus, organization

To Say: **What is the main idea of "White House Pets?"** Use details from the article to support your answer. (Students should focus on the article's main idea; all details should support the main idea. Transition words should connect ideas.)

ACTIVITY 1 Read a Passage

Read Together "Washington's Wonderful Monuments," pp. 130–133

10 minutes

	To Do	**To Say**
Scaffold instruction.	Review main idea. See Routine Card 3.	Have students preview pp. 130–133. **This article tells about famous sights in our nation's capital. As you read, look for an important idea about these famous sights, and the details that support it.**
		Read Read the article as students follow along. Then read it a second time, having students join in on the text. After reading, ask questions.
		What can you do at the Capitol? (watch Congress at work)
		Whom does the Washington Monument honor? (It honors our nation's first President, George Washington.)
		What are two famous memorials you can visit while in Washington, D.C.? (Lincoln Memorial and Jefferson Memorial)
Assess comprehension.	Monitor listening comprehension.	**Summarize** Have students describe each of the sights mentioned in the article, including the features that make them unique.

ACTIVITY 2 Build Concepts

Amazing Words Vocabulary

5–10 minutes

	To Do	**To Say**
Review concept and vocabulary.	Display the concept web you began on Day 1.	**This week's question is *What happens in our nation's capital?* How do this week's words relate to the question?** (Have students answer the question, using some of the vocabulary they learned this week.)
		Ask students to add more words to the concept web. Have students explain how each word relates to the government. Monitor students' understanding of vocabulary as they discuss the web. See Routine Card 5.
MORE PRACTICE	Write *museum* and *memorabilia* on the board.	Have students relate *museum* and *memorabilia*. **Give an example of the kind of *memorabilia* you might find in a *museum*. Why is it important to keep some *memorabilia* in *museums*? What can we learn about our country's history from presidential *memorabilia*?**

ACTIVITY 3 Write

Response to Literature "4 You 2 Do," p. 134

To Do | **To Say**

5–10 minutes

Guide response activities.

Discuss the directions on p. 134. Tell students to choose one activity to complete. See Routine Card 8.

Word Play Have students replace the *x*'s with the correct letters on their own and then meet with a partner to compare responses.

Making Connections Discuss the question in a group. (Answers will vary, but students should offer an opinion and explain their reasoning. For example, a student may respond that she would prefer to visit the White House because it would be interesting to see where our Presidents live.)

On Paper Have students brainstorm some answers to the prompt before they write. Have them write on their own. Students can use Practice Book p. 40 to structure their written response, or you can send the Practice Book page home for them to complete later.

MORE PRACTICE

If you have more time, direct students to complete all the activities.

ACTIVITY 4 Assessment Options

End-of-Unit Test

To Do | **To Say**

10–15 minutes

Assess fluency and compre-hension.

Use Assessment Book, p. 36.

Options for end-of-unit assessment are available in the Assessment Book, p. 36.

Homework Practice Book, p. 40, Writing

Unit 3 Week 1 *Nature's Designs*

? What can we learn from patterns in nature?

Objectives *This week students will...*

Vocabulary
- build concepts and vocabulary: *arrangement, available, landscape, patterns, repeats, reveal, snowfall*

Phonics
- read words with vowel combinations: long *a* spelled *ai, ay*
- apply knowledge of word structure to decode multisyllabic words when reading

Text Comprehension
- use sequence to improve comprehension
- write in response to literature
- make connections across text

Fluency
- practice fluency with oral rereading

Word Work *This week's phonics focus is . . .*

Long *a* Spelled *ai, ay*

Amazing Words *Concept/Amazing Words* *Tested Vocabulary*

The week's vocabulary is related to the concept of nature's designs.
The first appearance of each word in the Student Reader is noted below.

arrangement   the order in which things are placed (p. 8)

available   able to be had or gotten (p. 10)

landscape   a view of scenery from one place (p. 11)

patterns   ways in which colors or shapes appear over and over (p. 8)

repeats   does something again (p. 9)

reveal   to make something known; to display or show something (p. 10)

snowfall   snow that has come down and landed in an area (p. 11)

Student Reader Unit 3 *This week students will read the following selections.*

8	**Spectacular Snowflakes**	Expository Nonfiction
12	**Patterns Everywhere**	Expository Nonfiction
20	**The Talking Pot**	Realistic Fiction
28	**Poems**	Poetry
30	**4 You 2 Do**	Activity Page

Daily Lesson Plan

	ACTIVITIES	MATERIALS
Day 1	**Build Concepts** Weekly Concept: Nature's Designs Vocabulary: *arrangement, available, landscape, patterns, repeats, reveal, snowfall* **Read a Passage** "Spectacular Snowflakes," pp. 8–11 Comprehension: Use Strategies Reread for Fluency **Write** Response to Literature	Student Reader: Unit 3 Routine Cards 2, 4, 5 Tested Vocabulary Cards Student journals Practice Book, p. 41, Vocabulary Student Reader DVD-ROM
Day 2	**Word Work** Phonics: Long *a* Spelled *ai, ay* Vocabulary: Deepen word meaning **Comprehension** Sequence **Read a Passage** "Patterns Everywhere," pp. 12–15 Reread for Fluency **Write** Response to Literature	Student Reader: Unit 3 Practice Book, p. 41, Vocabulary Graphic Organizer 6 Routine Cards 1, 2, 3, 4, 7 Practice Book, p. 42, Long *a* Spelled *ai, ay* Student Reader DVD-ROM
Day 3	**Word Work** Phonics: Long *a* Spelled *ai, ay* Vocabulary: Deepen word meaning **Comprehension** Sequence **Read a Passage** "Patterns Everywhere," pp. 16–19 Reread for Fluency **Write** Response to Literature	Practice Book, p. 42, Long *a* Spelled *ai, ay* Tested Vocabulary Cards Student Reader: Unit 3 Graphic Organizer 6 Routine Cards 1, 2, 3, 4, 7 Practice Book, p. 43, Sequence Student Reader DVD-ROM
Day 4	**Word Work** Vocabulary: Extend word knowledge **Comprehension** Skill and Strategy Practice **Read a Passage** "The Talking Pot" pp. 20–27 Reread for Fluency **Write** Response to Literature	Practice Book, p. 43, Sequence Student Reader: Unit 3 Routine Cards 2, 3, 4 Student Reader DVD-ROM
Day 5	**Read a Passage** Poems, pp. 28–29 Comprehension: Sequence; Listening **Build Concepts** Vocabulary **Write** Response to Literature: "4 You 2 Do," p. 30 **Assessment Options** Fluency Comprehension	Student Reader: Unit 3 Routine Cards 3, 5, 6, 8 Fluency Progress Chart, p. 185 Practice Book, p. 44, Writing

See pp. xvi–xvii for how *My Sidewalks* integrates instructional practices for ELL.

ACTIVITY **1** Build Concepts

Amazing Words **Vocabulary**

| To Do | To Say | 10–15 minutes |

Develop oral vocabulary.

See Routine Card 6 and p. 208.

Introduce the Concept/Amazing Words with an oral routine prior to displaying them in print. Page 208 in this Teacher's Guide provides specific guidelines for introducing each word.

Develop word meaning.

See Routine Card 5. Discuss pp. 7–11.

Have students read p. 7 and then look at the pictures on pp. 8–11. **What do the pictures show?** (snow-covered trees, snowflakes, a snowman) **Can you use the words *nature* and *designs* to describe the pictures?** (Example: Sometimes interesting *designs* appear in *nature*.)

Scaffold instruction.

Create a concept web.

In the center of a web, write *Nature's Designs*. **This week's concept is *nature's designs*. *Nature's designs* are patterns that occur in nature.** Provide an example to demonstrate meaning. **Snowflakes are examples of *nature's designs*.**

Add the other vocabulary words.

Discuss the meaning of each word as it relates to nature's designs, using the glossary as needed. (See p. 122 in this Teacher's Guide for definitions.)

Concept and Language Goals

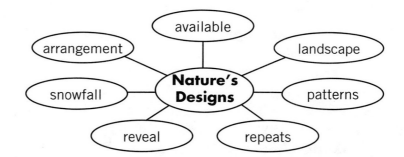

Model the multisyllabic word strategy.

Display each word. Say it as you display it.

Use the Tested Vocabulary Cards. Follow this routine for each multisyllabic word.

- **Look for Meaningful Parts** Do you recognize any parts of this word? What do these parts mean? Use the parts to read the word. Be sure students notice the following: *arrange, land, snow, fall.*

Think aloud.

- **Model** I recognize the word *arrange* at the beginning of *arrangement*. I know *arrange* means "to put things in a certain order." I also see the suffix *-ment* at the end of the word. I know *-ment* can mean "the result of something." So an *arrangement* must be the result of arranging something. Discuss other words with this suffix: *amazement, enjoyment, measurement.*

Point to *available*.

- **Chunk Words with No Recognizable Parts** Model how to chunk the word *available*. I see a chunk at the beginning of the word: *a.* I see another chunk after that: *vail,* I see a chunk after that: *a,* and a part at the end: *ble.* I say each chunk slowly: *a vail a ble.* I say the chunks fast to make a whole word: *available.* Is it a real word? Yes, I know the word *available.*

- Have students practice reading each word.

Preview.

Read p. 6 with students.

Do you see any of the words we just learned on this page? Together with students, read the sentences on p. 6 describing each selection. Talk about how the vocabulary words might be used in the selections.

MORE PRACTICE

Deepen understanding of *nature*.

Have students demonstrate understanding by answering questions. **Which one is an example of something in *nature*, a bird flying or a painting of a bird? What are some examples of things you see in *nature*?**

ACTIVITY 2 Read a Passage

Develop Concepts "Spectacular Snowflakes," pp. 8–11

10–15 minutes

	To Do	**To Say**
Practice strategic prereading.	See Routine Card 2.	**Discuss Genre** Read the title on p. 8 and have students look at the pictures on pp. 8–11. Model determining genre.
	Think aloud.	**The photographs are a clue that this is nonfiction. They look like photos of real places. I think this article will tell me about how snowflakes are made and how they are shaped.**
Scaffold instruction.	Review text structure.	**Ask Questions** **What questions do you ask yourself to help you understand nonfiction?** (What did I learn? What is this mainly about?) **As you read this article, ask these questions and look for the answers.**
Guide comprehension.	Read pp. 8–11 aloud.	**Read** the article as students follow along. Then read it a second time, having students join in. If necessary, stop at the end of each paragraph to check comprehension. Ask questions to promote discussion and develop the concept.
Develop language and concepts.		• **Where does a snowflake begin?**
		• **What kind of pattern does a snowflake form?**
		• **Why is each snowflake different?**
		• **What words on the concept web could help you describe snowflakes?**
MORE PRACTICE		Have students reread "Spectacular Snowflakes." As they read, tell them to write an explanation of how snowflakes are formed to share with family members tonight.

Reread for Fluency "Spectacular Snowflakes," p. 9

5 minutes

	To Do	**To Say**
CORRECTIVE FEEDBACK	Monitor oral reading.	**Read p. 9 aloud. Reread the page three or four times so your reading gets better each time.** Give feedback on students' oral reading, using the *if . . . then* statements on Routine Card 4. Model fluent reading if necessary. You may want to have students read along with the DVD-ROM.

ACTIVITY 3 Write

Response to Literature

5 minutes

	To Do	**To Say**
Prompt journal writing.	Write on the board or a transparency: *What can we learn from patterns in nature?*	**Take out your journals. This week we are reading about nature's designs. Our question for this week is: *What can we learn from patterns in nature?* Write an answer to this question based on what you read today.** Have students write about the topic, using what they read and their own experiences.
Homework		Practice Book, p. 41, Vocabulary

2

Word Work

Phonics Long *a* Spelled *ai, ay*

	To Do	**To Say**	5–10 minutes
Teach words with long *a* spelled *ai, ay*. **Scaffold instruction.**	Write on the board or a transparency: *They decided to* <u>proclaim</u> *him the winner.* Develop word meaning. Write *always*.	Remember, when two vowels appear together in a word or syllable, the first vowel usually stands for its long sound and the second is silent. What parts do you see in *proclaim*? Frame *pro claim*. **What vowel sound do you hear in the second syllable?** (long *a*) Point out to students that the *i* in the vowel combination *ai* is silent. Have students think and converse. **If you *proclaim* something, you declare it publicly. What kinds of things do people *proclaim*? Why?** **Here is another word with two vowels together. What parts do you see in *always*?** *(al ways)* **What vowel sound do you hear in the second syllable?** (long *a*) **The letters *ay* usually stand for the sound long *a*.**	
CORRECTIVE FEEDBACK	Write each practice word.	Have students practice reading these words with long *a* spelled *ai* or *ay*. Correct any words students miss and have them reread the list. **birthday subway replay fainted exclaim raindrop**	
MORE PRACTICE	Write more practice words.	Have students practice reading these words with long *a* spelled *ai* or *ay*. **Saturday maybe crayfish regain contain explain**	

Amazing Words Vocabulary

	To Do	**To Say**	5 minutes
Review vocabulary.	Review the homework. Deepen word understanding of *patterns*.	Ask students to go over answers and share their writing from Practice Book p. 41. See Routine Card 1 for the multisyllabic word routine. **Remember, *patterns* are the ways in which colors or shapes appear over and over again in order. What are some examples of *patterns* you see in your daily life? What are some things you can use to create *patterns*?**	

Comprehension

Sequence

	To Do	**To Say**	5 minutes
Scaffold instruction.	Introduce sequence.	Today you will read about different patterns found in nature, including the pattern you see when a rainbow is formed. When you read about how real things happen, it's important to keep track of the sequence, or order. Keeping track of the sequence may help you to understand what you read. Words like *first, next,* and *finally* can give you clues to the sequence. Sometimes the order of words in a list gives clues.	
	Model the skill.	For example, if I read that the colors of the rainbow are always in the same order, with red appearing first in the list, I know that red is always the first color in the sequence of colors in a rainbow.	
	Distribute Graphic Organizer 6.	As you read "Patterns Everywhere," look for words that help you understand patterns in nature and how they are formed. You can add these details to your graphic organizers. See Routine Card 7.	

ACTIVITY 3 Read a Passage

Read for Comprehension "Patterns Everywhere," pp. 12–15

10–15 minutes

	To Do	To Say
Scaffold instruction.	Monitor student engagement.	**Read** Have students read pp. 12–15. Stop at the end of each page to ask questions. Students who can read on their own can do so without stopping. After reading, ask questions to promote discussion.
	See Routine Cards 2 and 3.	**What three patterns in nature does the article mention?** (patterns of fives, spirals, and color patterns)
		Where can you see patterns of fives? (starfish, flower petals, sand dollars, seeds inside an apple)
		How is the arrangement of seeds inside an apple like the shape of a starfish? (Both have a five-pointed star shape.)
		What do you think the rest of the article will be about? (Answers will vary. The title suggests it will tell more about patterns in nature.)
Model summarizing.	Think aloud.	**Summarize What were the first four pages mainly about? What did you learn about patterns in nature?** Think aloud to model summarizing. **I learned some details about patterns of fives in nature, such as that you can see patterns of fives in starfish, apple seeds, and flower petals. But the main thing I learned was that there are patterns in nature all around us.**
Develop language and concepts.	Ask questions.	• **What kind of pattern do many plants have in common?** • **How is the arrangement of seeds in an okra plant similar to many flower petal arrangements?**
MORE PRACTICE	Have students reread p. 14.	**Reread** Have students describe the pattern similarities between starfish, sand dollars, and apple seeds.

Reread for Fluency "Patterns Everywhere," p. 12–13

5 minutes

	To Do	To Say
MORE PRACTICE **CORRECTIVE FEEDBACK**	Pair students. Monitor paired reading.	Students read aloud pp. 12–13, switching readers at each new paragraph. Have partners reread; now the other partner begins. For optimal fluency, students should reread three or four times. Give feedback, using the *if . . . then* statements on Routine Card 4. You may want to have students read along with the DVD-ROM.

ACTIVITY 4 Write

Response to Literature

5 minutes

	To Do	To Say
Prompt writing.	Writing elements: support	**What are some patterns of fives found in nature that are described in "Patterns Everywhere"? Use details from the article to support your answer.**
Homework		Practice Book, p. 42, Long *a* Spelled *ai, ay*

ACTIVITY 1 — Word Work

Phonics Long *a* Spelled *ai, ay*

	To Do	To Say	5 minutes
Review long *a* spelled *ai, ay*. **Scaffold instruction.**	Review the homework. Discuss *rain* on p. 13 in the Student Reader.	Ask students to share answers from Practice Book p. 42. Point out *rain* on p. 13, paragraph 1. **Remember, when two vowels appear together in a word or syllable, the first usually stands for its long sound and the second is silent. What vowel sound do you hear in the word *rain*?** (long *a*) **Which vowel is silent?** (*i*) Then point to *displays* on p. 13, paragraph 1. **What parts do you see in this word?** (*dis plays*) **What vowel sound do you hear in the second syllable?** (long *a*) **Remember, the letters *ay* usually stand for the sound long *a*.** Ask students to think of other words with the vowel combinations *ai* and *ay*.	
MORE PRACTICE	Model spelling words with the long *a* vowel sound.	**Spell and Write** Write *rain* and *play*. Say *gain*. **What vowel sound do you hear in this word? What letters spell that vowel sound?** Underline *ai*. Continue with *play (ay)*. **What other words do you know that have these vowel patterns?**	

Amazing Words — Vocabulary

	To Do	To Say	5 minutes
Build vocabulary.	Deepen understanding of *landscape*.	Read aloud the first paragraph on p. 13. **The picture gives a clue to the meaning of the word *landscape*. What does the picture show?** (the rainbow stretching over the land) **Say a sentence using *landscape*. Describe the *landscape* outside your window.**	
Lead cumulative review.		Use the Tested Vocabulary Cards to review words from previous weeks.	

ACTIVITY 2 — Comprehension

Sequence

	To Do	To Say	5–10 minutes
Scaffold instruction.	Review sequence.	**An author gives you clues to the sequence. Look for dates, phrases, the order of words in a list, and words such as *first, then, next,* or *finally*. As you read "Patterns Everywhere," try to put the colors of a rainbow in the correct sequence.**	
Guide practice.	Use Graphic Organizer 6.	**Listen as I read p. 18. I want you to notice how the author describes the colors of a rainbow.** Read p. 18. Then ask: **Which of the colors always comes first?** (red) **Which comes next?** (orange) **Which comes last?** (purple) **Add these sequence words to your graphic organizers.** See Routine Card 7.	
MORE PRACTICE	Have students preview pp. 16–19.	**Read the captions and look at the photographs on pp. 16–19. What do you think this section will be about?** (spiral patterns, color patterns) **Why do you think so?** Think aloud to model using captions and pictures to predict.	
	Think aloud.	**The captions and pictures make me think the article will tell about different places in nature where you can find spiral patterns and color patterns.**	

ACTIVITY **3** Read a Passage

Read for Comprehension "Patterns Everywhere," pp. 16–19

10–15 minutes

	To Do	To Say
Scaffold instruction.	Monitor student engagement.	**Read** Have students read pp. 16–19. Stop at the end of each page to ask questions. Students who can read on their own can do so without stopping. After reading, ask questions to promote discussion.
	See Routine Cards 2 and 3.	**Where can you see spiral patterns in nature?** (some seashells, flower seeds, bighorn sheep horns, ferns, hurricanes, galaxies)
		Why do spiral patterns appear so often in nature? (They might take the least amount of energy to grow.)
		When do rainbows form? (when light shines through tiny drops of water)
		Where can you see a color pattern that is like the one in a rainbow? (prism, soap bubbles, looking through a lawn sprinkler on a sunny day)
Review the phonics skill.	Point out *rainbow* on p. 18, paragraph 1.	Remind students that the vowel combination *ai* is pronounced with the sound long *a*. Demonstrate framing the word parts *rain bow*. Have students blend the parts to read the word. See Routine Card 1.
Assess comprehension.	Monitor understanding.	**After Reading** Have students discuss the What Do You Think? question. Prompt them to use sequence words in their responses. Listen as they talk to assess comprehension.
	Summarize.	**What is this mainly about? What did you learn?** Work with students to summarize the selection.
MORE PRACTICE	Have students reread p. 18.	**Reread** As they read, tell students to note the order of the colors in a rainbow. After they read, have them recite the correct order of all the colors, beginning with red.

Reread for Fluency "Patterns Everywhere," p. 16–17

5 minutes

	To Do	To Say
CORRECTIVE FEEDBACK	Monitor oral reading.	**Read pp. 16–17 aloud. Reread the page three or four times so your reading gets better each time.** Give feedback on students' oral reading, using the *if . . . then* statements on Routine Card 4. Model fluent reading if necessary. You may want to have students read along with the DVD-ROM.

ACTIVITY **4** Write

Response to Literature

5 minutes

	To Do	To Say
MORE PRACTICE	Prompt writing.	**Think of another shape pattern or color pattern in nature. Describe the pattern and where it appears. Focus your ideas on your topic.**
Homework		Practice Book, p. 43, Sequence

ACTIVITY 1 | Word Work

Amazing Words **Vocabulary**

| **To Do** | **To Say** | *5–10 minutes* |

Extend word knowledge.

Write on the board or a transparency: *A heavy snowfall can quickly cover the ground.*

Use the word *snowfall* to extend word knowledge. **Remember, we read this word earlier this week.** *Snowfall* **is a compound word made up of the words** *snow* **and** *fall.* **It means "the snow that has fallen on the ground."**

Teach compound words with *snow*.

There are other compound words that also contain the word *snow*. **Can you think of other words beginning with the word** *snow*? *(snowball, snowman, snowflake, snowplow, snowshoe, snowstorm)* Write words as students name them and add some of your own. Talk about the meanings of the words and how they relate to each other.

Scaffold instruction.

Develop word meaning.

What outdoor activities can you do after a heavy *snowfall*? **During what season do most** *snowfalls* **occur?**

MORE PRACTICE

Deepen understanding of *landscape* and *snowfall*.

Have individual students or partners use the two words *landscape* and *snowfall* in a sentence. (For example: A heavy *snowfall* can change the *landscape* into a winter wonderland.) Share sentences. Ask: **Does a rainfall change the** *landscape* **the way that a** *snowfall* **does? Explain.**

ACTIVITY 2 | Comprehension

Skill and Strategy Practice

| **To Do** | **To Say** | *5 minutes* |

Scaffold instruction.

Review sequence (homework).

Ask volunteers to read the passage and share answers from Practice Book p. 43. Remind students of the importance of following the sequence. **When you read a story, the sequence of events is often important. There might be clue words to the order in which things happen. Look for these words. It may also help you to picture in your mind the events as they happen.**

Practice strategic prereading.

See Routine Card 2.

Discuss Genre Read the title and the first two paragraphs on p. 20 in the Student Reader. Model determining genre.

Think aloud.

I first thought this might be fiction because of the illustrations. When I read the first paragraph, I knew it was fiction because of the description of what the character, Justin, sees and thinks.

Review story structure.

Ask Questions What questions do you ask yourself to help you understand a fictional story? (What is the problem or goal? How is the problem solved or the goal reached?) **As you read this story, ask these questions and look for the answers.**

ACTIVITY 3 Read a Passage

Read for Comprehension "The Talking Pot," pp. 20–27

10–15 minutes

	To Do	**To Say**
Scaffold instruction.	Monitor student engagement.	**Read** Have students read pp. 20–27 on their own and then discuss. For students who need more help, stop at the end of each page to discuss. After reading, ask questions.
	See Routine Card 3.	**Who are the main characters in this story?** (Justin and his grandmother) **What is the setting?** (a village in the New Mexico desert)
		What does Justin's grandmother do? (She makes clay pots.) **What are the patterns on the pots based on?** (things in nature, such as clouds, birds, fish, snakes, and waves)
		What problem is Justin faced with? (He has to choose a design for his pot.)
		What design does Justin choose for his pot? (Black Mesa) **Why is this a good choice?** (It shows where he lives; it's a part of nature.)
Assess comprehension.	Monitor understanding.	**After Reading** Have students discuss the What Do You Think? question. Prompt them to use sequence words in their answer. Listen as they talk to assess comprehension.
MORE PRACTICE		**Reread** Have students reread p. 26 and explain why Justin was worried about choosing a design.

Reread for Fluency "The Talking Pot," pp. 24–25

5–10 minutes

	To Do	**To Say**
CORRECTIVE FEEDBACK	Pair students. Monitor paired reading.	Students read aloud pp. 24–25, switching readers at the end of each paragraph. Have partners reread; now the other partner begins. For optimal fluency, students should reread three or four times. Give feedback, using Routine Card 4. You may want to have students read along with the DVD-ROM.
MORE PRACTICE	**READERS' THEATER**	Work with a group of three students to adapt pp. 24–25 as a scene. Have students rehearse reading the parts, with one student as the narrator, one as Justin, and one as Justin's grandmother.

ACTIVITY 4 Write

Response to Literature

5 minutes

	To Do	**To Say**
Prompt expository writing.	Review pp. 23–25. Writing elements: organization, conventions	Describe the sequence of steps that Justin's grandmother takes to make a pot. Begin with rolling out the clay and end with baking the painted pot. Use sequence words in your description. Use correct grammar and spelling to clearly express your ideas.

ACTIVITY 1 Read a Passage

Read Together Poems, pp. 28–29

	To Do	**To Say**	*10 minutes*
Scaffold instruction.	Review sequence.	Have students preview pp. 28–29. **These poems describe snowflakes and "sunflakes," flakes made out of sun. As you read, pay attention to the sequence, or order, in which things happen in each poem. Following the sequence can help you better understand the poems.**	
	See Routine Card 3.	**Read** Read the poems as students follow along. Then read them a second time, having students join in. After reading, ask questions.	
		Who is the narrator speaking to in "I Wish I Knew"? (winter)	
		What does the narrator want to know? (how snowflake designs are made)	
		What is the author of "Sunflakes" describing? (flakes made out of sun)	
		What kinds of things could you do with sunflakes? (build a sunman, have a sunball fight, go sledding in July)	
Assess comprehension.	Monitor listening comprehension.	**Summarize** Have students tell what each poem is about and what images the author uses to create the mood of the poem.	

ACTIVITY 2 Build Concepts

Amazing Words Vocabulary

	To Do	**To Say**	*5–10 minutes*
Review concept and vocabulary.	Display the concept web you began on Day 1.	**This week's question is:** *What can we learn from patterns in nature?* **How do this week's words relate to the question?** (Have students answer the question, using some of the vocabulary they learned this week.)	
		Ask students to add more words to the concept web. Have students explain how each word relates to patterns in nature. Monitor students' understanding of vocabulary as they discuss the web. See Routine Card 5.	
MORE PRACTICE	Write *patterns* and *arrangement* on the board.	Have students relate *patterns* and *arrangement*. **Give an example of an** *arrangement* **of colors or shapes that result in a** *pattern*. **What** *arrangements* **or** *patterns* **have you seen inside or outside a building?**	

ACTIVITY **3** | Write

Response to Literature "4 You 2 Do," p. 30

| | To Do | To Say | *5–10 minutes* |

Guide response activities.

Discuss the directions on p. 30. Tell students to choose one activity to complete. See Routine Card 8.

Word Play Have students write their answers on their own and then meet with a partner to share and compare responses.

Making Connections Discuss the question in a group. (Answers will vary but should mention one of the patterns described in the selections, including snowflakes, spirals, fives, and colors.)

On Paper Have students brainstorm some answers to the prompt before they write. Have them write on their own. Students can use Practice Book, p. 44 to structure their written responses, or you can send the Practice Book page home for them to complete later.

MORE PRACTICE

If you have more time, direct students to complete all of the activities.

ACTIVITY **4** | Assessment Options

Passage Reading

| | To Do | To Say | *10–15 minutes* |

See Routine Card 6.

While some students are doing Activity 3, determine which students you want to assess this week and choose from these options.

Check fluency.

Take a two-minute timed sample of each student's oral reading.

Fluency Have a student read for two minutes from "The Talking Pot!" Record the number of correct words read per minute. See p. 184 for monitoring fluency. Be sure each student is assessed at least every other week.

Have students graph their progress on the Fluency Progress Chart, p. 185.

Check comprehension.

Retelling Have students reread "The Talking Pot!" and retell it. Prompt students if necessary. See p. 186 for monitoring retelling.

If you have time, assess every student.

Homework

Practice Book, p. 44, Writing

Unit 3 Week 2 *Animal Journeys*

Why do animals migrate?

Objectives *This week students will...*

Vocabulary
- build concepts and vocabulary: *migrate, observe, refuges, shelter, zones*

Phonics
- read words that contain syllables with vowel combinations: long *e* spelled *e, ee, ea*
- apply knowledge of word structure to decode multisyllabic words when reading

Text Comprehension
- use main idea to improve comprehension
- write in response to literature
- make connections across text

Fluency
- practice fluency with oral rereading

Word Work *This week's phonics focus is . . .*

Long *e* Spelled *e, ee, ea*

Amazing Words Concept/Amazing Words *Tested Vocabulary*

The week's vocabulary is related to the concept of animal journeys, or migration. The first appearance of each word in the Student Reader is noted below.

migrate	to go from one place to another when the seasons change (p. 34)
observe	to look at something carefully in order to learn about it; study (p. 48)
refuges	shelters or protection from danger or trouble (p. 44)
shelter	something that covers or protects you from weather, danger, or attack (p. 46)
zones	the five great divisions of the earth's surface, bounded by imaginary lines going around the earth parallel to the equator (p. 38)

Student Reader Unit 3 *This week students will read the following selections.*

Daily Lesson Plan

	ACTIVITIES	MATERIALS
Day 1	**Build Concepts** Weekly Concept: Animal Journeys Vocabulary: *migrate, observe, refuges, shelter, zones* **Read a Passage** "Animals on the Move," pp. 34–37 Comprehension: Use Strategies Reread for Fluency **Write** Response to Literature	Student Reader: Unit 3 Routine Cards 2, 4, 5 Tested Vocabulary Cards Student journals Practice Book, p. 45, Vocabulary Student Reader DVD-ROM
Day 2	**Word Work** Phonics: Long *e* Spelled *e, ee, ea* Vocabulary: Deepen word meaning **Comprehension** Main Idea and Supporting Details **Read a Passage** "Flight for Survival," pp. 38–41 Reread for Fluency **Write** Response to Literature	Student Reader: Unit 3 Practice Book, p. 45, Vocabulary Graphic Organizer 1 Routine Cards 1, 2, 3, 4, 7 Practice Book, p. 46, Long *e* Spelled *e,* *ee, ea* Student Reader DVD-ROM
Day 3	**Word Work** Phonics: Long *e* Spelled *e, ee, ea* Vocabulary: Deepen word meaning **Comprehension** Main Idea and Supporting Details **Read a Passage** "Flight for Survival," pp. 42–45 Reread for Fluency **Write** Response to Literature	Practice Book, p. 46, Long *e* Spelled *e,* *ee, ea* Tested Vocabulary Cards Student Reader: Unit 3 Graphic Organizer 1 Routine Cards 1, 2, 3, 4, 7 Practice Book, p. 47, Main Idea and Details Student Reader DVD-ROM
Day 4	**Word Work** Vocabulary: Extend word knowledge **Comprehension** Skill and Strategy Practice **Read a Passage** "Wildlife Welcome!" pp. 46–53 Reread for Fluency **Write** Response to Literature	Practice Book, p. 47, Main Idea and Details Student Reader: Unit 3 Routine Cards 2, 3, 4 Student Reader DVD-ROM
Day 5	**Read a Passage** "Where Birds Vacation," pp. 54–55 Comprehension: Main Idea; Listening **Build Concepts** Vocabulary **Write** Response to Literature: "4 You 2 Do," p. 56 **Assessment Options** Fluency Comprehension	Student Reader: Unit 3 Routine Cards 3, 5, 6, 8 Fluency Progress Chart, p. 185 Practice Book, p. 48, Writing

See pp. xvi–xvii for how *My Sidewalks* integrates instructional practices for ELL.

Amazing Words **Vocabulary**

| | **To Do** | **To Say** | *10–15 minutes* |

Develop oral vocabulary.

See Routine Card 6 and p. 209.

Introduce the Concept/Amazing Words with an oral routine prior to displaying them in print. Page 209 in this Teacher's Guide provides specific guidelines for introducing each word.

Develop word meaning.

See Routine Card 5. Discuss pp. 33–37.

Have students read p. 33 and then look at the pictures on pp. 34–37. **What do you notice?** (different birds, animals, and insects) **Can you use the word** *journeys* **to describe any of these pictures?** (Example: Some animals make *journeys* each year to survive.)

Scaffold instruction.

Create a concept web.

In the center of a web, write *Animal Journeys.* **This week's concept is** *animal journeys.* **A** *journey* **is a trip from one place to another.** Provide an example to demonstrate meaning. **The** *journeys* **of humpback whales happen each winter when the whales swim to warmer waters.**

Add the other vocabulary words.

Discuss the meaning of each word as it relates to animal journeys, using the glossary as needed. (See p. 134 in this Teacher's Guide for definitions.)

Concept and Language Goals

Model the multisyllabic word strategy.

Display each word. Say it as you display it.

Use the Tested Vocabulary Cards. Follow this routine for each word:

- **Look for Meaningful Parts** Remind students to look for meaningful parts. **As you say each word, ask yourself: Do I see any parts I know?**

- **Chunk Words with No Recognizable Parts** Model how to chunk the word *shelter* to read it.

Think aloud.

- **Model** I see a chunk at the beginning of the word: *shel.* I see a part at the end of the word: *ter.* I say each chunk slowly: *shel ter.* I say the chunks fast to make a whole word: *shelter.* Is it a real word? Yes, I know the word *shelter.*

- Have students practice reading each word.

Read p. 32 with students.

Do you see any of the words we just learned on this page? Together with students, read the sentences on p. 32 describing each selection. Talk about how the concept words might be used in the selections.

MORE PRACTICE

Deepen understanding of *migrate.*

Have students demonstrate understanding by answering questions. **Which animal** *migrates,* **a zebra that travels to another region to find water during the dry season, or a horse that travels back to the barn in search of food? Why? What are some of the factors that might cause animal** *migration?*

ACTIVITY 2 Read a Passage

Develop Concepts "Animals on the Move," pp. 34–37

	To Do	To Say	*10–15 minutes*

Practice strategic prereading.

See Routine Card 2.

Think aloud.

Discuss Genre Read the title on p. 34 and have students look at the photographs on pp. 34–37. Model determining genre.

The photographs are a clue that this is nonfiction. They look like photos of real animals and insects. I think this article will tell me why animals migrate.

Scaffold instruction.

Review text structure.

Ask Questions What questions do you ask yourself to help you understand nonfiction? (What did I learn? What is this mainly about?) **As you read this article, ask these questions and look for the answers.**

Guide comprehension.

Read pp. 34–37 aloud.

Read Read the article as students follow along. Then read it a second time, having students join in. If necessary, stop at the end of each paragraph to check comprehension. Ask questions to promote discussion and develop the concept.

Develop language and concepts.

- Why do animals usually migrate from one place to another?
- Which animals migrate in order to start new families?
- What are some of the dangers animals face on their journeys?
- How do animals stay on course during the journey?
- What words on the concept web could help you describe animal journeys?

MORE PRACTICE

Have students reread "Animals on the Move." As they read, tell them to make a list of the reasons why animals migrate to share with family members tonight.

Reread for Fluency "Animals on the Move," p. 37

	To Do	To Say	*5 minutes*

CORRECTIVE FEEDBACK

Monitor oral reading.

Read p. 37 aloud. Reread the page three or four times so your reading gets better each time. Give feedback on students' oral reading, using the *if . . . then* statements on Routine Card 4. Model fluent reading if necessary. You may want to have students read along with the DVD-ROM.

ACTIVITY 3 Write

Response to Literature

	To Do	To Say	*5 minutes*

Prompt journal writing.

Write on the board or a transparency: *Why do animals migrate?*

Take out your journals. This week we are reading about animal journeys. Our question for this week is: *Why do animals migrate?* **Write an answer to this question based on what you read today.** Have students write about the topic, using what they read and their own experiences.

Homework   Practice Book, p. 45, Vocabulary

ACTIVITY **1** # Word Work

Phonics Long e Spelled e, ee, ea

	To Do	**To Say**	

5–10 minutes

Teach long e spelled e, ee, ea.

Write on the board or a transparency: *The animals moved* <u>deeper</u> *into the forest as the* <u>seasons</u> *changed.*

Remember, when you read a long word, look for meaningful parts. What parts do you see in this word? Frame *deep er.*

You know that vowels have long and short sounds. Point to the first syllable in *deeper.* What vowel sound do you hear in the first syllable of this word? (long *e*) Two vowels in a row usually make the long vowel sound of the first letter. When you see the vowels *ee* or *ea* together in a word, they usually make the long *e* sound. What parts do you see in *seasons? (sea sons)* What vowel sound do you hear in the first syllable? (long *e*)

Scaffold instruction.

Develop word meaning.

Have students think and converse. **What signs in nature tell you that the *seasons* are changing? Why do some animals behave differently during different *seasons*?**

Write *ecology.*

What parts do you see in this word? *(e col o gy)* **What vowel sound do you hear in the first syllable?** (long *e*) **The vowel *e* alone can also stand for the long *e* sound.**

CORRECTIVE FEEDBACK

Write each practice word.

Have students practice reading these words with long *e* spelled *e, ee, ea.* Correct any words students miss and have them reread the list.

eastern	ordeal	needed	freedom	maybe	downstream

MORE PRACTICE

Write more practice words.

Have students practice reading these words with long *e* spelled *e, ee, ea.*

southeast	eagerly	between	sleepless	leaving	reason

Amazing Words Vocabulary

	To Do	**To Say**	

5 minutes

Review vocabulary.

Review the homework.

Ask students to go over answers and share their writing from Practice Book p. 45. See Routine Card 1 for the multisyllabic word routine.

Deepen understanding of *observe.*

Remember, *observe* means "to see and note." If a scientist wants to understand an animal's behavior, he might *observe* it in its natural habitat. Why? If you *observe* an egg hatching, do you see it yourself, or do you hear about it from someone else?

ACTIVITY **2** # Comprehension

Main Idea and Supporting Details

	To Do	**To Say**	

5 minutes

Scaffold instruction.

Introduce main idea and supporting details.

Today you will read about birds that migrate. When you read nonfiction, identifying the main idea can help you better understand what you read. To find the main idea, ask yourself: Who or what is this article about? What is the most important idea about the topic? What are some details that support or tell about the most important idea?

Model the skill.

For example, if I know that the topic of an article is migratory birds, then I need to pay attention to figure out what the most important idea about migratory birds is.

Distribute Graphic Organizer 1.

As you read "Flight for Survival," look for the most important or main idea about the topic, as well as details that support the main idea. Add these supporting details to your graphic organizers. See Routine Card 7.

ACTIVITY **3** Read a Passage

Read for Comprehension "Flight for Survival," pp. 38–41

10–15 minutes

	To Do	**To Say**
Scaffold instruction.	Monitor student engagement. See Routine Cards 2 and 3.	**Read** Have students read pp. 38–41. Stop at the end of each page to ask questions. Students who can read on their own can do so without stopping. After reading, ask questions to promote discussion. **Why do birds fly to warmer zones?** (to search for food and warmth) **How do birds prepare for their long flights?** (They eat extra food before leaving.) **What helps birds find their way?** (They use landmarks, and the sun, stars, and winds to guide them.) **What do you think the rest of the article will be about?** (Answers will vary. The title suggests it will tell more about migrating birds.)
Model summarizing.	Think aloud.	**Summarize** What were the first four pages mainly about? What did you learn about flying for survival? Think aloud to model summarizing. **I learned many details about migrating birds, such as their bodies are made for long flights. But the main thing I learned is that birds migrate in order to survive.**
Develop language and concepts.	Ask questions.	• **In what ways are bird's bodies designed for long flights?** • **Why do some birds travel at night?**
MORE PRACTICE	Have students reread p. 40.	**Reread** Tell students to draw a picture of birds flying south over one of the landmarks described.

Reread for Fluency "Flight for Survival," pp. 38–39

5 minutes

	To Do	**To Say**
MORE PRACTICE **CORRECTIVE FEEDBACK**	Pair students. Monitor paired reading.	Students read aloud pp. 38–39, switching readers at each new paragraph. Have partners reread; now the other partner begins. For optimal fluency, students should reread three or four times. Give feedback using the *if . . . then* statements on Routine Card 4. You may want to have students read along with the DVD-ROM.

ACTIVITY **4** Write

Response to Literature

5 minutes

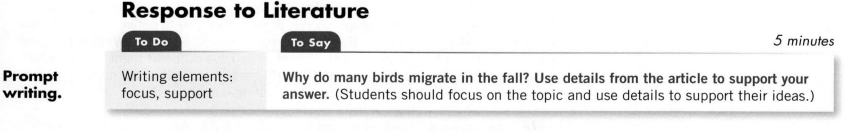

	To Do	**To Say**
Prompt writing.	Writing elements: focus, support	**Why do many birds migrate in the fall? Use details from the article to support your answer.** (Students should focus on the topic and use details to support their ideas.)
Homework		Practice Book, p. 46, Long *e* Spelled *e, ee, ea*

3

Word Work

Phonics Long *e* Spelled *e, ee, ea*

	To Do	To Say	5 minutes
Review long e spelled e, ee, ea. **Scaffold instruction.**	Review the homework. Discuss *seasons* on p. 45, paragraph 2, in the Student Reader.	Ask students to share answers from Practice Book p. 46. Point out *seasons* on p. 45. **Remember, when you see the letters *e*, and *ee* or *ea* together in a word, they usually make the long *e* sound. What parts do you see in this word?** *(sea sons)* **What vowel sound do you hear in the first syllable?** (long *e*) Then point to *needed* on p. 43. **What parts do you see in this word?** *(need ed)* **What vowel sound do you hear in the first syllable?** (long *e*) Ask students to look for other words with vowel combinations *ee* and *ea* that make the long *e* sound.	
MORE PRACTICE	Model spelling words with the long *e* vowel sound.	**Spell and Write** Write *sheep* and *each*. Say *sheep*. **What vowel sound do you hear in this word? What letters spell that vowel sound?** Underline *ee*. Continue with *each* (*ea*). **Look for long *e* words in the selections and tell what letters spell the long *e* sound.**	

Amazing Words Vocabulary

	To Do	To Say	5 minutes
Build vocabulary.	Deepen understanding of *refuges* and *shelter*.	Read aloud p. 44. **The author gives a clue to the meaning of *refuges* by describing how the swans were cared for at the *refuges*. We learned another word this week that is a synonym for *refuge*. Write *refuge* and *shelter*. Say a sentence using *refuge* and *shelter*. Why is it so important for animals to have *shelter* in the winter?**	
Lead cumulative review.		Use the Tested Vocabulary Cards to review words from previous weeks.	

Comprehension

Main Idea and Supporting Details

	To Do	To Say	5–10 minutes
Scaffold instruction.	Review main idea and supporting details.	**To find the main idea, remember to ask yourself what the most important idea about the topic is. Sometimes, you have to figure out the main idea yourself and state it in your own words. Make sure the main idea you have identified makes sense and that it is supported by details in the article.**	
Guide practice.	Use Graphic Organizer 1.	**Listen as I read the last paragraph on this page. I want you to notice that the author is describing the way birds fly.** Read p. 41, paragraph 3. Then ask: **What is the most important idea in this paragraph?** (Different birds have different flight styles.) **What is one detail that supports this idea?** (Canada geese flap their wings nonstop.) **Add this detail to your graphic organizers.** See Routine Card 7.	
MORE PRACTICE	Have students preview pp. 42–45.	**Read the captions and look at the photos on pp. 42–45. What do you think this section will be about?** (different migratory birds and how they fly) **Why do you think so?** Think aloud to model using captions and illustrations to predict.	
	Think aloud.	**The captions make me think the article will describe different ways that birds fly when they migrate. From the pictures I think the article will tell about different types of migratory birds, such as Canada geese.**	

ACTIVITY 3 | Read a Passage

Read for Comprehension "Flight for Survival," pp. 42–45

10–15 minutes

	To Do	To Say
Scaffold instruction.	Monitor student engagement.	**Read** Have students read pp. 42–45. Stop at the end of each page to ask questions. Students who can read on their own can do so without stopping. After reading, ask questions to promote discussion.
	See Routine Cards 2 and 3.	**Why do geese fly in a V shape?** (in order to save energy, and so that they can see and hear each other)
		What caused trumpeter swans to change their migration habits? (They were cared for and fed at wildlife refuges, so they got used to having food available in the winter and changed their migration paths.)
		When do migrating birds fly north again? (when the days get longer)
	Model using context for word meaning.	Read aloud the paragraph with *soaring* on p. 43. Explain how the sentence "They spread out their wings and ride the wind" provides clues to the meaning of *soaring* by describing what *soaring* birds look like.
Assess comprehension.	Monitor understanding.	**After Reading** Have students discuss the What Do You Think? question. Prompt them to identify the main idea as they answer the question. Listen as they talk to assess comprehension.
	Summarize.	**What is this mainly about? What did you learn?** Work with students to summarize the selection.
MORE PRACTICE	Have students reread p. 44.	**Reread** As they read, tell students to describe the causes that led to the trumpeter swans' adaptation to colder weather.

Reread for Fluency "Flight for Survival," p. 45

5 minutes

	To Do	To Say
CORRECTIVE FEEDBACK	Monitor oral reading.	**Read p. 45 aloud. Reread the page three or four times so your reading gets better each time.** Give feedback on students' oral reading, using the *if . . . then* statements on Routine Card 4. Model fluent reading if necessary. You may want to have students read along with the DVD-ROM.

ACTIVITY 4 | Write

Response to Literature

5 minutes

	To Do	To Say
MORE PRACTICE	Prompt writing.	**What challenges do migrating birds face each year on their long journeys south? Use details from the article to support your ideas.**
Homework		Practice Book, p. 47, Main Idea and Details

ACTIVITY 1 Word Work

Amazing Words Vocabulary

	To Do	To Say	
			5–10 minutes

Extend word knowledge.

Teach *observant* and *observatory*.

Scaffold instruction.

Write on the board or a transparency: *We often observe the birds bringing food to their babies.*

Use the word *observe* to extend word knowledge. **Remember, we read this word earlier this week and learned that it means "to look at something carefully in order to learn about it." Today we'll look at other words that are related to *observe*.**

The word *observant* means "quick to notice things." Would *observant* people notice a change in the weather right away, or would they take a while to notice? Why is it important for scientists to be *observant*?

An *observatory* is a building equipped with telescopes and other devices for studying the stars, planets, weather conditions, and so on. Who would use an *observatory*, an astronomer or a veterinarian? Why? Talk about the meanings of the three words, and discuss how they are related. Have students practice pronouncing all the words.

Develop word meaning.

What do we learn when we *observe* animals in their natural habitats?

MORE PRACTICE

Deepen understanding of *observe*.

Have individual students or partners use the word *observe* in a sentence. (For example: You can *observe* birds in their natural environment by setting up a birdfeeder or a birdbath in your yard.) Share sentences. Ask: **When you *observe* an animal's behavior, are you interacting with the animal, or just watching?**

ACTIVITY 2 Comprehension

Skill and Strategy Practice

	To Do	To Say	
			5 minutes

Scaffold instruction.

Review main idea (homework).

Ask volunteers to read the passage and share answers from Practice Book p. 47. Remind students of the importance of identifying the main idea. **Sometimes an author will state the main idea directly. Other times, the author will leave it up to the reader to find the main idea. When you look for the main idea, ask yourself, "What is the most important point the author is trying to make?"**

Practice strategic prereading.

See Routine Card 2.

Discuss Genre Read the title and the first paragraph on p. 46 in the Student Reader. Model determining genre.

Think aloud.

I first thought this might be nonfiction because of the photographs. They look like photos of real animals and insects.

Review text structure.

Ask Questions What questions do you ask yourself to help you understand nonfiction? (What did I learn? What is this mainly about?) **As you read this article, ask these questions and look for the answers.**

ACTIVITY 3 # Read a Passage

Read for Comprehension "Wildlife Welcome!" pp. 46–53

10–15 minutes

	To Do	To Say
Scaffold instruction.	Monitor student engagement.	**Read** Have students read pp. 46–53 on their own and then discuss. For students who need more help, stop at the end of each page to discuss. After reading, ask questions.
	See Routine Card 3.	**What are the three keys to attracting wildlife?** (water, shelter, food) **How do these keys relate to animal migration?** (They are the same basic survival needs that lead some animals to migrate.)
		Why is it difficult for animals to get water in the summer and winter? (Water can freeze in winter or dry up in summer.)
		Why do toads seek shelter in shady places? (to stay cool and damp)
		How do bats help people? (They feed on annoying insects.)
		What is the best food for attracting animals and insects? (plants)
Assess comprehension.	Monitor understanding.	**After Reading** Have students discuss the What Do You Think? question. Prompt them to identify the main idea of the article as they respond. Listen as they talk to assess comprehension.
MORE PRACTICE		**Reread** Have students reread pp. 47–48 and then explain why water is so important to wild animals.

Reread for Fluency "Wildlife Welcome!" pp. 49–51

5–10 minutes

	To Do	To Say
CORRECTIVE FEEDBACK	Pair students. Monitor paired reading.	Students read aloud pp. 49–51, switching readers after each paragraph. Have partners reread; now the other partner begins. For optimal fluency, students should reread three or four times. Give feedback, using Routine Card 4. You may want to have students read along with the DVD-ROM.
MORE PRACTICE	**READERS' THEATER**	Work with students to adapt pp. 47–53 as a public service announcement for broadcast on radio, describing the importance of water, shelter, and food for migrating animals.

ACTIVITY 4 # Write

Response to Literature

5 minutes

	To Do	To Say
Prompt personal narrative.	Review pp. 46–53. Writing elements: focus, support	**How would you attract and protect the animals featured in "Wildlife Welcome!"? Use details from the article to support your answer.** (Students should use details that support their main ideas.)

Read a Passage

Read Together "Where Birds Vacation," pp. 54–55

	To Do	**To Say**	*10 minutes*
Scaffold instruction.	Review main idea.	Have students preview pp. 54–55. **This article tells about birdhouses that come in all different shapes and sizes. Remember, when you read nonfiction, try to find the main or most important idea about the topic. Then look for details that support the main idea.**	
	See Routine Card 3.	**Read** Read the article as students follow along. Then read it a second time, having students join in on the text. After reading, ask questions.	
		How were the birdhouses that the Australian students made different from the houses they made for people? (They were the same, only smaller.)	
		What was the first birdhouse in Doug Harnes's Birdhouse City? (a model of an old hotel)	
		How many birdhouses are there in Birdhouse City? (over 90 birdhouses)	
Assess comprehension.	Monitor listening comprehension.	**Summarize** Have one student describe the similarities and differences between the birdhouses described in the article and regular houses.	

Build Concepts

Amazing Words Vocabulary

	To Do	**To Say**	*5–10 minutes*
Review concept and vocabulary.	Display the concept web you began on Day 1.	**This week's question is *Why do animals migrate?* How do this week's words relate to the question?** (Have students answer the question, using some of the vocabulary they learned this week.)	
		Ask students to add more words to the concept web. Have students explain how each word relates to animal journeys. Monitor students' understanding of vocabulary as they discuss the web. See Routine Card 5.	
MORE PRACTICE	Write *migrate* and *observe* on the board.	Have students relate *migrate* and *observe.* **Give an example of an animal that *migrates.* When scientists *observe migratory* animals, what do they learn about their habits?**	

ACTIVITY 3 | Write

Response to Literature "4 You 2 Do," p. 56

	To Do	**To Say**	*5–10 minutes*

Guide response activities.

Discuss the directions on p. 56. Tell students to choose one activity to complete. See Routine Card 8.

Word Play Have students find words on their own and then meet with a partner to share their responses.

Making Connections Discuss the question in a group. (Possible answers: make suet feeders, install birdbaths, plant flowers, fruit bushes, and install birdhouses or bat houses)

On Paper Have students brainstorm some answers to the prompt before they write. Have them write on their own. Students can use Practice Book p. 48 to structure their written responses, or you can send the Practice Book page home for them to complete later.

MORE PRACTICE

If you have more time, direct students to complete all the activities.

ACTIVITY 4 | Assessment Options

Passage Reading

	To Do	**To Say**	*10–15 minutes*

See Routine Card 6.

While some students are doing Activity 3, determine which students you want to assess this week and choose from these options.

Check fluency.

Take a two-minute timed sample of each student's oral reading.

Fluency Have a student read for two minutes from "Flight for Survival." Record the number of correct words read per minute. See p. 184 for monitoring fluency. Be sure each student is assessed at least every other week.

Have students graph their progress on the Fluency Progress Chart, p. 185.

Check comprehension.

Retelling Have students reread "Flight for Survival" and retell it. Prompt students if necessary. See p. 186 for monitoring retelling.

If you have time, assess every student.

Homework   Practice Book, p. 48, Writing

Unit 3 Week 3 *Our Spinning Planet*

How do day and night affect people and animals?

Objectives *This week students will...*

Vocabulary
- build concepts and vocabulary: *dazed, hemisphere, nocturnal, revolution, rotation, vacation*

Phonics
- read contractions
- apply knowledge of word structure to decode multisyllabic words when reading

Text Comprehension
- draw conclusions to improve comprehension
- write in response to literature
- make connections across text

Fluency
- practice fluency with oral rereading

Word Work *This week's phonics focus is . . .*

Contractions

Amazing Words Concept/Amazing Words *Tested Vocabulary*

The week's vocabulary is related to the concept of our spinning planet, which relates to day and night. The first appearance of each word in the Student Reader is noted below.

dazed	unable to think clearly (p. 70)
hemisphere	one half of the Earth's surface (p. 62)
nocturnal	active in the night (p. 67)
revolution	a movement in a circle or curve around some point (p. 62)
rotation	the act of turning around a center (p. 61)
vacation	a time when you are not at school or at work (p. 70)

Student Reader Unit 3 *This week students will read the following selections.*

60	**Night and Day**	Expository Nonfiction
62	**The Amazing Skies of the North**	Expository Nonfiction
70	**Plane Tired!**	Realistic Fiction
78	**Alaskan Animals**	Photo Essay
82	**4 You 2 Do**	Activity Page

Daily Lesson Plan

	ACTIVITIES	MATERIALS
Day 1	**Build Concepts** Weekly Concept: Our Spinning Planet Vocabulary: *dazed, hemisphere, nocturnal, revolution,* *rotation, vacation* **Read a Passage** "Night and Day," pp. 60–61 Comprehension: Use Strategies Reread for Fluency **Write** Response to Literature	Student Reader: Unit 3 Routine Cards 2, 4, 5 Tested Vocabulary Cards Student journals Practice Book, p. 49, Vocabulary Student Reader DVD-ROM
Day 2	**Word Work** Phonics: Contractions Vocabulary: Deepen word meaning **Comprehension** Draw Conclusions **Read a Passage** "The Amazing Skies of the North," pp. 62–65 Reread for Fluency **Write** Response to Literature	Student Reader: Unit 3 Practice Book, p. 49, Vocabulary Graphic Organizer 2 Routine Cards 1, 2, 3, 4, 7 Practice Book, p. 50, Contractions Student Reader DVD-ROM
Day 3	**Word Work** Phonics: Contractions Vocabulary: Deepen word meaning **Comprehension** Draw Conclusions **Read a Passage** "The Amazing Skies of the North," pp. 66–69 Reread for Fluency **Write** Response to Literature	Practice Book, p. 50, Contractions Tested Vocabulary Cards Student Reader: Unit 3 Graphic Organizer 2 Routine Cards 1, 2, 3, 4, 7 Practice Book, p. 51, Draw Conclusions Student Reader DVD-ROM
Day 4	**Word Work** Vocabulary: Extend word knowledge **Comprehension** Skill and Strategy Practice **Read a Passage** "Plane Tired!" pp. 70–77 Reread for Fluency **Write** Response to Literature	Practice Book, p. 51, Draw Conclusions Student Reader: Unit 3 Routine Cards 2, 3, 4 Student Reader DVD-ROM
Day 5	**Read a Passage** "Alaskan Animals," pp. 78–81 Comprehension: Draw Conclusions; Listening **Build Concepts** Vocabulary **Write** Response to Literature: "4 You 2 Do," p. 82 **Assessment Options** Fluency Comprehension	Student Reader: Unit 3 Routine Cards 3, 5, 6, 8 Fluency Progress Chart, p. 185 Practice Book, p. 52, Writing

See pp. xvi–xvii for how *My Sidewalks* integrates instructional practices for ELL.

ACTIVITY 1 Build Concepts

Amazing Words Vocabulary

To Do	**To Say**	*10–15 minutes*

Develop oral vocabulary.

See Routine Card 6 and p. 210.

Introduce the Concept/Amazing Words with an oral routine prior to displaying them in print. Page 210 in this Teacher's Guide provides specific guidelines for introducing each word.

Develop word meaning.

See Routine Card 5. Discuss pp. 59–61.

Have students read p. 59 and then look at the pictures on pp. 60–61. **What do you notice?** (views of the Earth in different amounts of shadow and light) **Can you use the word *rotation* to describe these pictures?** (Example: Nighttime occurs when the Earth's *rotation* causes part of the Earth to face away from the sun.)

Scaffold instruction.

Create a concept web.

In the center of a web, write *Day and Night.* **This week's concept is *our spinning planet,* which is related to *day and night.*** Provide an example to demonstrate meaning. **The Earth makes one rotation each day. When a part of the Earth faces away from the sun it is night in that part, and when it faces into the sun, it is day.**

Add the other vocabulary words.

Discuss the meaning of each word as it relates to day and night, using the glossary as needed. (See p. 146 in this Teacher's Guide for definitions.)

Concept and Language Goals

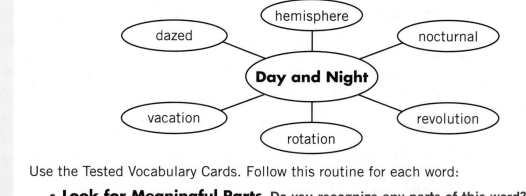

Model the multisyllabic word strategy.

Display each word. Say it as you display it.

Use the Tested Vocabulary Cards. Follow this routine for each word:

- **Look for Meaningful Parts** **Do you recognize any parts of this word? What do these parts mean? Use the parts to read the word.** As you introduce the words, be sure students notice the following: *sphere, re-* ("back" or "again"), and *rotate.*

- **Chunk Words with No Recognizable Parts** Model how to chunk the word *nocturnal* to read it.

Think aloud.

- **Model** **I see a chunk at the beginning of the word: *noc.* I see a part in the middle: *turn.* I see a part at the end of the word: *al.* I say each chunk slowly: *noc turn al.* I say the chunks quickly to make a whole word: *nocturnal.* Is it a real word? Yes, I know the word *nocturnal.***

- Have students practice reading each word.

Read p. 58 with students.

Do you see any of the words we just learned on this page? Together with students, read the sentences on p. 58 describing each selection. Talk about how the concept words might be used in the selections.

MORE PRACTICE

Deepen understanding of *rotation.*

Have students demonstrate understanding by answering questions. **Which is an example of a *rotation,* the hour hand on a clock moving one full time around, or the Earth moving around the sun? Why? Does an object that *rotates* spin in a circle, or move in a straight line?**

ACTIVITY 2 Read a Passage

Develop Concepts "Night and Day," pp. 60–61

10–15 minutes

	To Do	To Say
Practice strategic prereading.	See Routine Card 2. Think aloud.	**Discuss Genre** Read the title on p. 60 and have students look at the pictures on pp. 60–61. Model determining genre. **The photographs are a clue that this is nonfiction. They look like real photos of the Earth. I think this article will tell about what causes night and day on Earth.**
Scaffold instruction.	Review text structure.	**Ask Questions** What questions do you ask yourself to help you understand nonfiction? (What did I learn? What is this mainly about?) **As you read this article, ask these questions and look for the answers.**
Guide comprehension. **Develop language and concepts.**	Read pp. 60–61 aloud.	**Read** Read the article as students follow along. Then read it a second time, having students join in. If necessary, stop at the end of each paragraph to check comprehension. Ask questions to promote discussion and develop the concept. • **What star is nearest to Earth?** (the sun) • **What causes the sun to appear as if it is rising and setting each day?** (The Earth is rotating, or spinning, on its axis.) • **In the course of a day, why are some places in daylight while others are in darkness?** (because the sun doesn't shine on all of the Earth at once) • **What words on the concept web could help you describe night and day?**

MORE PRACTICE Have students reread "Night and Day." As they read, tell them to write descriptions of what causes night and day to share with family members tonight.

Reread for Fluency "Night and Day," p. 61

5 minutes

	To Do	To Say
CORRECTIVE FEEDBACK	Monitor oral reading.	**Read p. 61 aloud. Reread the page three or four times so your reading gets better each time.** Give feedback on students' oral reading, using the *if... then* statements on Routine Card 4. Model fluent reading if necessary. You may want to have students read along with the DVD-ROM.

ACTIVITY 3 Write

Response to Literature

5 minutes

	To Do	To Say
Prompt journal writing.	Write on the board or a transparency: *How do day and night affect people and animals?*	**Take out your journals. This week we are reading about day and night. Our question for this week is:** *How do day and night affect people and animals?* **Write an answer to this question based on what you read today.** Have students write about the topic, using what they read and their own experiences.

Homework Practice Book, p. 49, Vocabulary

ACTIVITY **1** Word Work

Phonics Contractions

	To Do	To Say	5–10 minutes
Teach contractions.	Write on the board or a transparency: *The Earth <u>doesn't</u> feel like it's spinning.*	A contraction is a shortened form of a word or group of words. In a contraction, an apostrophe takes the place of the letters that have been removed. Write *does not* on the board. Cross out the *o* in *not* and replace it with an apostrophe. **What two words is *doesn't* a shortened form of?** *(does not)*	
Scaffold instruction.	Write *let's, we'll,* and *I'm.*	**Here are three more contractions. What words is each a shortened form of?** *(let us, we will,* and *I am)* **Which letters does the apostrophe replace in each word?** (the *u* in *us,* the *w* and the *i* in *will,* and the *a* in *am)* Guide students in reading each contraction.	
CORRECTIVE FEEDBACK	Write each practice word.	Have students practice reading these contractions. Correct any words students miss and have them reread the list.	

you'll   won't   wouldn't   couldn't   aren't   could've

MORE PRACTICE	Write more practice words.	Have students practice reading these contractions, and say the original words that were contracted.

that's   shouldn't   didn't   it's   would've   mustn't

Amazing Words Vocabulary

	To Do	To Say	5 minutes
Review vocabulary.	Review the homework.	Ask students to go over answers and share their writing from Practice Book p. 49. See Routine Card 1 for the multisyllabic word routine.	
	Deepen understanding of *revolution.*	Remember, a *revolution* is a movement in a circle or curve around some point. As the Earth rotates, it also travels in a circle around the sun. **Why is this a *revolution?* What else is an example of a *revolution?* Why?**	

ACTIVITY **2** Comprehension

Draw Conclusions

	To Do	To Say	5 minutes
Scaffold instruction.	Introduce drawing conclusions.	Today you will read an article about day and night in the North. Drawing conclusions can help you to better understand what you read. A conclusion is a decision you make about the information in an article, based upon what you read and your own experience.	
	Model the skill.	For example, if I read that the sun doesn't set during the summer in the far Northern Hemisphere, because of the Earth's rotation, I might draw the conclusion that during the winter, the sun also never rises.	
	Distribute Graphic Organizer 2.	As you read "The Amazing Skies of the North," look for details that help you to draw conclusions. Add these details to your graphic organizer. See Routine Card 7.	

ACTIVITY 3 Read a Passage

Read for Comprehension "The Amazing Skies of the North," pp. 62–65

10–15 minutes

	To Do	To Say
Scaffold instruction.	Monitor student engagement. See Routine Cards 2 and 3.	**Read** Have students read pp. 62–65. Stop at the end of each page to ask questions. Students who can read on their own may do so without stopping. After reading, ask questions to promote discussion. **What are the two ways the Earth moves?** (It rotates on its axis, and it revolves around the sun.) **What causes summer?** (the tilt of the Northern Hemisphere of the Earth toward the sun) **What is the Midnight Sun?** (when the summer sun doesn't set in the far Northern Hemisphere) **What do you think the rest of the article will be about?** (Answers will vary. The title suggests it will tell more about seasons in the North.)
Model summarizing.	Think aloud.	**Summarize** What were the first four pages mainly about? What did you learn about the seasons in the Northern Hemisphere? Think aloud to model summarizing. **I learned many details about winter and summer in the Northern Hemisphere, including that the sun doesn't set in the summer at the North Pole. The main thing I learned is that the North is a land of amazing weather.**
Develop language and concepts.	Ask questions.	• **Why do you think the people who live in the North have summer celebrations?** • **Why doesn't the sun ever set at the North Pole during summer?**
MORE PRACTICE	Have students reread p. 65.	**Reread** Tell students to draw a picture that shows what the Midnight Sun Game in Fairbanks might look like.

Reread for Fluency "The Amazing Skies of the North," pp. 62–63

5 minutes

	To Do	To Say
MORE PRACTICE **CORRECTIVE FEEDBACK**	Pair students. Monitor paired reading.	Students read aloud pp. 62–63, switching readers at each new paragraph. Have partners reread; now the other partner begins. For optimal fluency, students should reread three or four times. Give feedback, using the *if... then* statements on Routine Card 4. You may want to have students read along with the DVD-ROM.

ACTIVITY 4 Write

Response to Literature

5 minutes

	To Do	To Say
Prompt writing.	Writing elements: support	**If the sun doesn't set at the North Pole during the summer months, what conclusion can you draw about the sun at the South Pole? Use details to support your conclusion.**
Homework		Practice Book, p. 50, Contractions

Word Work

Phonics Contractions

	To Do	To Say	5 minutes

Review contractions.

Scaffold instruction.

Review the homework. Discuss *doesn't* on p. 64, paragraph 3, in the student Reader.

Ask students to share answers from Practice Book p. 50.

Point out *doesn't* on p. 64. **Remember, a contraction is a shortened form of a word or group of words. In a contraction, an apostrophe takes the place of letters that have been removed. What two words is *doesn't* a shortened form of?** *(does not)* **What letters does the apostrophe replace?** (the *o* in *not*)

Point to *wouldn't* on p. 65. **What two words is *wouldn't* a shortened form of?** *(would not)* **What letter does the apostrophe replace?** (the *o* in *not*) Ask students to look for other contractions, or to form contractions.

MORE PRACTICE

Model spelling contractions.

Spell and Write Write *does* and *not*. **How do we combine these words to make *doesn't*?** Have a volunteer write the contraction. Remind students that the apostrophe takes the place of missing letters. Continue with *would not, is not, and it is.*

Amazing Words Vocabulary

	To Do	To Say	5 minutes

Build vocabulary.

Deepen understanding of *nocturnal*.

Read aloud the last paragraph on p. 67. **The author gives a clue to the meaning of *nocturnal* when she says that "they are like animals that are only active at night."** Write *nocturnal*. **What are some examples of animals that are *nocturnal?*** (bats, owls) **Why do the people who live in Fairbanks during the winter feel like *nocturnal* animals? What skills or attributes do *nocturnal* animals need to have? Why?**

Lead cumulative review.

Use the Tested Vocabulary Cards to review words from previous weeks.

Comprehension

Draw Conclusions

	To Do	To Say	5–10 minutes

Scaffold instruction.

Review drawing conclusions.

Remember to use details from a story or article, as well as your own experience, to draw conclusions as you read. After you draw a conclusion, ask yourself whether it makes sense and whether it can be supported with evidence from the selection.

Guide practice.

Use Graphic Organizer 2.

Listen as I read p. 66. I want you to notice that the author describes some of the activities that take place during the week of the solstice. Read p. 66. Then ask: What conclusions can you draw about how the people of Fairbanks feel about the summer solstice? (They enjoy it.) **How do you know?** (The article says that they have all kinds of games and activities, stores are open all night, and there's even a race.) **Add these details to your graphic organizer. See Routine Card 7.**

MORE PRACTICE

Have students preview pp. 66–69.

Read the captions and look at the photographs on pp. 66–69. What do you think this section will be about? (the seasons and weather in the North) **Why do you think so?** Think aloud to model using captions and illustrations to predict.

Think aloud.

The captions make me think the article will tell more about day and night in the North, and how people cope with or celebrate the amazing darkness and light. The pictures make me think the article will describe some of the celebrations that people in the North have during the winter and summer.

ACTIVITY 3   Read a Passage

Read for Comprehension "The Amazing Skies of the North," pp. 66–69

10–15 minutes

	To Do	To Say
Scaffold instruction.	Monitor student engagement.	**Read** Have students read pp. 66–69. Stop at the end of each page to ask questions. Students who can read on their own may do so without stopping. After reading, ask questions to promote discussion.
	See Routine Cards 2 and 3.	**In what ways is the Midnight Sun Fun Run different from other races?** (It's held late at night; people wear wild costumes.)
		When does the winter solstice occur? (around December 21) **What happens at the North Pole during the winter solstice?** (The sun never rises.)
		How do people celebrate the winter solstice? (with plays, sleigh rides, dog mushing races, and other fun activities)
		What are the Northern Lights? (streams of light that pour across the night sky in winter in the North)
	Model using context for word meaning.	Read aloud the paragraph with *mushing* on p. 68. Explain how the sentence that follows provides a clue to the meaning of *mushing* by describing how the dogs pull sleds across the ice.
Assess comprehension.	Monitor understanding.	**After Reading** Have students discuss the What Do You Think? question. Prompt them to draw conclusions about the Northern Lights as they answer the question. Listen as they talk to assess comprehension.
	Summarize.	**What is this mainly about? What did you learn?** Work with students to summarize the selection.
MORE PRACTICE	Have students reread pp. 67–68.	**Reread** As they read, tell students to note details about the winter solstice celebrations. Have them add these details to their graphic organizers. After they read, have them draw conclusions about how the people of Fairbanks feel about the extreme darkness of winter.

Reread for Fluency "The Amazing Skies of the North," p. 69

5 minutes

	To Do	To Say
CORRECTIVE FEEDBACK	Monitor oral reading.	**Read p. 69 aloud. Reread the page three or four times so your reading gets better each time.** Give feedback on students' oral reading, using the *if . . . then* statements on Routine Card 4. Model fluent reading if necessary. You may want to have students read along with the DVD-ROM.

ACTIVITY 4   Write

Response to Literature

5 minutes

	To Do	To Say
MORE PRACTICE	Prompt writing.	**How are the celebrations of the summer and winter solstices similar? Use exact words and complete sentences to express your ideas.**
Homework		Practice Book, p. 51, Draw Conclusions

ACTIVITY 1 · Word Work

Amazing Words **Vocabulary**

	To Do	To Say	5–10 minutes
Extend word knowledge. **Teach prefix re-.**	Write on the board or a transparency: *The wheel made one <u>revolution</u> before coming to a stop.*	Use the word *revolution* to extend word knowledge. **Remember, we read this word earlier this week. We looked for meaningful parts and we noticed the prefix *re-*. We can use this prefix to read other words.** **The prefix *re-* can mean "back." A *revolution* is a movement in a circle or curve that comes back to the starting point. Can you think of other words beginning with *re-*?** *(react, rewind, rebound, retrace, replace, refund)* Write words as students name them and add some of your own. Talk about the meanings of the words. Have students practice pronouncing all of the words.	
Scaffold instruction.	Develop word meaning.	**How long does one *revolution* of the Earth around the sun take? Does the Earth's *revolution* around the sun ever stop?**	
MORE PRACTICE	Deepen understanding of *revolution* and *rotation*.	Have individual students or partners use the two words *revolution* and *rotation* in a sentence. (For example: The *rotation* of the Earth occurs as the Earth moves in a *revolution* around the sun.) Share sentences. Ask: **How is the *rotation* of the Earth different from the *revolution* of the Earth?**	

ACTIVITY 2 · Comprehension

Skill and Strategy Practice

	To Do	To Say	5 minutes
Scaffold instruction.	Review drawing conclusions (homework).	Ask volunteers to read the passage and share answers from Practice Book p. 51. Remind students of the importance of drawing conclusions. **When you read a story, you can draw conclusions about characters and events. As you read, ask yourself why events happen and why characters behave the way they do. Use the information in the story and what you already know to draw conclusions. Be sure to ask yourself, "Do my conclusions make sense? Can I support them with details from the story?"**	
Practice strategic prereading.	See Routine Card 2.	**Discuss Genre** Read the title and the first paragraph on p. 70 in the Student Reader. Model determining genre.	
	Think aloud.	**I first thought this might be fiction because of the illustrations. When I read the first paragraph, I knew it was fiction because of the way the narrator speaks.**	
	Review story structure.	**Ask Questions** **What questions do you ask yourself to help you understand a fictional story?** (What is the problem or goal? How is the problem solved or the goal reached?) **As you read this story, ask these questions and look for the answers.**	

ACTIVITY 3 Read a Passage

Read for Comprehension "Plane Tired!" pp. 70–77

	To Do	To Say
		10–15 minutes
Scaffold instruction.	Monitor student engagement.	**Read** Have students read pp. 70–77 on their own and then discuss. For students who need more help, stop at the end of each page to discuss. After reading, ask questions.
	See Routine Card 3.	**Who tells the story?** (Mark) **Who are the main characters?** (Mark, his parents, his sister Rebecca, and her roommate Marie)
		What is the setting? (Paris, France)
		What problem does Mark face? (His jet lag is making him dazed and sleepy.)
		What famous place do Mark and his family visit? (the Louvre)
		Why do Mark and his parents return to their hotel? (Mark falls asleep at the museum.)
Assess comprehension.	Monitor understanding.	**After Reading** Have students discuss the What Do You Think? question. Prompt them to draw conclusions based on details in the story. Listen as they talk to assess comprehension.
MORE PRACTICE		**Reread** Have students reread pp. 74–75 and then describe the things that Mark saw at the museum.

Reread for Fluency "Plane Tired!" pp. 74–77

	To Do	To Say
		5–10 minutes
CORRECTIVE FEEDBACK	Pair students. Monitor paired reading.	Students read aloud pp. 74–77, switching readers at the end of each paragraph. Have partners reread; now the other partner begins. For optimal fluency, students should reread three or four times. Give feedback, using Routine Card 4. You may want to have students read along with the DVD-ROM.
MORE PRACTICE	**READERS' THEATER**	Work with a group of three students to adapt pp. 73–74 as a radio play. Have students rehearse reading the parts: narrator, Mark, and Rebecca. Then have them perform for the class.

ACTIVITY 4 Write

Response to Literature

	To Do	To Say
		5 minutes
Prompt descriptive writing.	Review pp. 76–77. Writing elements: focus, support	**Describe how Mark's experience in Paris might have been different if he didn't have jet lag. Use details from the story to support your answer.** (Students should focus on their topic and use descriptive details to support their ideas.)

ACTIVITY 1 Read a Passage

Read Together "Alaskan Animals," pp. 78–81

10 minutes

	To Do	**To Say**
Scaffold instruction.	Review drawing conclusions.	Have students preview pp. 78–81. **This article tells about animals that are active during the day, and animals that are active during the night. As you read, use the information in the selection, as well as what you know, to draw conclusions about nocturnal and diurnal animals.**
	See Routine Card 3.	**Read** Read the photo essay as students follow along. Then read it a second time, having students join in on the text. After reading, ask questions.
		What are diurnal animals? (animals that are active during the day)
		Why do eagles hunt during the day? (They can use their sharp eyesight to spot fish.)
		What do many nocturnal animals do during the day? (They sleep in burrows or dens.)
		What animals prey on moose? (bears and wolves)
Assess comprehension.	Monitor listening comprehension.	**Summarize** Have one student describe the traits that the nocturnal animals share, and one student describe the traits that the diurnal animals share.

ACTIVITY 2 Build Concepts

Amazing Words Vocabulary

5–10 minutes

	To Do	**To Say**
Review concept and vocabulary.	Display the concept web you began on Day 1.	**This week's question is** *How do day and night affect people and animals?* **How do this week's words relate to the question?** (Have students answer the question, using some of the vocabulary they learned this week.)
		Ask students to add more words to the concept web. Have students explain how each word relates to day and night. Monitor students' understanding of vocabulary as they discuss the web. See Routine Card 5.
MORE PRACTICE	Write *dazed* and *vacation* on the board.	Have students relate *dazed* and *vacation.* **How can traveling make you** *dazed?* **Do you get** *dazed* **from jet lag every time you take a** *vacation?* **Explain. How can being** *dazed* **from jet lag affect your** *vacation?*

ACTIVITY 3 | Write

Response to Literature "4 You 2 Do," p. 82

To Do | **To Say** | *5–10 minutes*

Guide response activities.

Discuss the directions on p. 82. Tell students to choose one activity to complete. See Routine Card 8.

Word Play Have students work with partners to find the rhyming answers.

Making Connections Discuss the question in a group. (Possible answer: People in Alaska and travelers have to adjust to having sunlight at times of the day when they are used to having darkness.)

On Paper Have students brainstorm some answers to the prompt before they write. Have them write on their own. Students can use Practice Book p. 52 to structure their written responses, or you can send the Practice Book page home for them to complete later.

MORE PRACTICE

If you have more time, direct students to complete all the activities.

ACTIVITY 4 | Assessment Options

Passage Reading

To Do | **To Say** | *10–15 minutes*

See Routine Card 6.

While some students are doing Activity 3, determine which students you want to assess this week and choose from these options.

Check fluency.

Take a two-minute timed sample of each student's oral reading.

Fluency Have a student read for two minutes from "Plane Tired!" Record the number of correct words read per minute. See p. 184 for monitoring fluency. Be sure each student is assessed at least every other week.

Have students graph their progress on the Fluency Progress Chart, p. 185.

Check comprehension.

Retelling Have students reread "Plane Tired!" and retell it. Prompt students if necessary. See p. 186 for monitoring retelling.

If you have time, assess every student.

Homework

Practice Book, p. 52, Writing

Unit 3 Week 4 *Storms*

What can you learn about weather?

Objectives *This week students will...*

Vocabulary
- build concepts and vocabulary: *behavior, coast, inland, phenomenon, tsunami, unpredictable*

Phonics
- read words long *o* spelled *oa, ow*
- apply knowledge of word structure to decode multisyllabic words when reading

Text Comprehension
- compare and contrast to improve comprehension
- write in response to literature
- make connections across text

Fluency
- practice fluency with oral rereading

Word Work *This week's phonics focus is . . .*

Long *o* Spelled *oa, ow*

Amazing Words Concept/Amazing Words *Tested Vocabulary*

The week's vocabulary is related to the concept of storms.
The first appearance of each word in the Student Reader is noted below.

behavior   way of acting (p. 89)

coast   land along the sea (p. 88)

inland   away from the coast or the border (p. 101)

phenomenon   someone or something that is extraordinary or remarkable (p. 86)

tsunami   a long, high ocean wave caused by an underwater earthquake, or submarine landslide, or other disturbance (p. 88)

unpredictable   not able to be described or depended on; uncertain (p. 96)

Student Reader Unit 3 *This week students will read the following selections.*

86	**Weird Weather**	Expository Nonfiction
88	**How Did the Animals Know?**	Expository Nonfiction
96	**Taito and the Gulls**	Realistic Fiction
104	**Is It Going to Rain?**	How-to Article
108	**4 You 2 Do**	Activity Page

Daily Lesson Plan

	ACTIVITIES	MATERIALS
Day 1	**Build Concepts** Weekly Concept: Storms Vocabulary: *behavior, coast, inland, phenomenon, tsunami, unpredictable* **Read a Passage** "Weird Weather," pp. 86–87 Comprehension: Use Strategies Reread for Fluency **Write** Response to Literature	Student Reader: Unit 3 Routine Cards 2, 4, 5 Tested Vocabulary Cards Student journals Practice Book, p. 53, Vocabulary Student Reader DVD-ROM
Day 2	**Word Work** Phonics: Long *o* Spelled *oa, ow* Vocabulary: Deepen word meaning **Comprehension** Compare and Contrast **Read a Passage** "How Did the Animals Know?" pp. 88–91 Reread for Fluency **Write** Response to Literature	Student Reader: Unit 3 Practice Book, p. 53, Vocabulary Graphic Organizer 4 Routine Cards 1, 2, 3, 4, 7 Practice Book, p. 54, Long *o* Spelled *oa, ow* Student Reader DVD-ROM
Day 3	**Word Work** Phonics: Long *o* Spelled *oa, ow* Vocabulary: Deepen word meaning **Comprehension** Compare and Contrast **Read a Passage** "How Did the Animals Know?" pp. 92–95 Reread for Fluency **Write** Response to Literature	Practice Book, p. 54, Long *o* Spelled *oa, ow* Tested Vocabulary Cards Student Reader: Unit 3 Graphic Organizer 4 Routine Cards 2, 3, 4, 7 Practice Book, p. 55, Compare and Contrast Student Reader DVD-ROM
Day 4	**Word Work** Vocabulary: Extend word knowledge **Comprehension** Skill and Strategy Practice **Read a Passage** "Taito and the Gulls," pp. 96–103 Reread for Fluency **Write** Response to Literature	Practice Book, p. 55, Compare and Contrast Student Reader: Unit 3 Routine Cards 2, 3, 4 Student Reader DVD-ROM
Day 5	**Read a Passage** "Is It Going to Rain?" pp. 104–107 Comprehension: Compare and Contrast; Listening **Build Concepts** Vocabulary **Write** Response to Literature: "4 You 2 Do," p. 108 **Assessment Options** Fluency Comprehension	Student Reader: Unit 3 Routine Cards 3, 5, 6, 8 Fluency Progress Chart, p. 185 Practice Book, p. 56, Writing

See pp. xvi–xvii for how *My Sidewalks* integrates instructional practices for ELL.

Build Concepts

Amazing Words **Vocabulary**

	To Do	**To Say**	*10–15 minutes*

Develop oral vocabulary.	See Routine Card 6 and p. 211.	Introduce the Concept/Amazing Words with an oral routine prior to displaying them in print. Page 211 in this Teacher's Guide provides specific guidelines for introducing each word.
Develop word meaning.	See Routine Card 5. Discuss pp. 85–87.	Have students read p. 85 and then look at the pictures on pp. 86–87. **What do you notice?** (cats, dogs, frogs, a sun) **Can you use the word** *phenomenon* **to describe any of these pictures?** (Example: Frogs falling from the sky is a weather *phenomenon.*)
Scaffold instruction.	Create a concept web.	In the center of a web, write *Storms.* **This week's concept is** *storms.* **Some storms can produce a weather** *phenomenon.* Provide an example to demonstrate meaning. **A tsunami wave is a** *phenomenon* **because it is such an unusual occurrence.**
	Add the other vocabulary words.	Discuss the meaning of each word as it relates to storms, using the glossary as needed. (See p. 158 in this Teacher's Guide for definitions.)
	Concept and Language Goals	

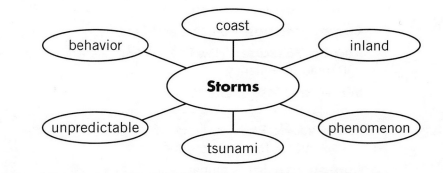

Model the multisyllabic word strategy.	Display each word. Say it as you display it.	Use the Tested Vocabulary Cards. Follow this routine for each word:
		• **Look for Meaningful Parts** Do you recognize any parts of this word? What do these parts mean? Use the parts to read the word. As you introduce the words, be sure students notice the following: *in, land, un-* ("not"), *predictable.*
	Think aloud.	• **Model** I see *in* and *land* in the word *inland.* I know this is a compound word. I think this word means "away from the coast or the border."
	Point to *behavior.*	• **Chunk Words with No Recognizable Parts** Model how to chunk the word *behavior:* I see a chunk at the beginning of the word: *be.* I see a part in the middle: *hav.* I see a part at the end of the word: *ior.* I say each chunk slowly: *be hav ior.* I say the chunks quickly to make a whole word: *behavior.* Is it a real word? Yes, I know the word *behavior.*
		• Have students practice reading each word.
Preview.	Read p. 84 with students.	**Do you see any of the words we just learned on this page?** Together with students, read the sentences on p. 84 describing each selection. Talk about how the concept words might be used in the selections.
MORE PRACTICE	Deepen understanding of *phenomenon.*	Have students demonstrate understanding by answering questions. **Which one is a** *phenomenon,* **a rain shower while the sun is shining, or a snowstorm in winter? Why? If something is a** *phenomenon,* **is it ordinary or is it unusual? What makes something a** *phenomenon?*

ACTIVITY **2** Read a Passage

Develop Concepts "Weird Weather," pp. 86–87

10–15 minutes

	To Do	**To Say**
Practice strategic prereading.	See Routine Card 2. Think aloud.	**Discuss Genre** Read the title on p. 86 and have students look at the photographs on pp. 86–87. Model determining genre. The title and photographs are a clue that this is nonfiction. The photos look like strange weather conditions. I think this article will tell me about strange weather and what causes it.
Scaffold instruction.	Review text structure.	**Ask Questions** What questions do you ask yourself to help you understand nonfiction? (What did I learn? What is this mainly about?) As you read this article, ask these questions and look for the answers.
Guide comprehension. **Develop language and concepts.**	Read pp. 86–87 aloud.	**Read** Read the article as students follow along. Then read it a second time, having students join in. If necessary, stop at the end of each paragraph to check comprehension. Ask questions to promote discussion and develop the concept. • **What makes something a phenomenon?** (It can be explained, but it is strange.) • **What causes a shower of frogs?** (Strong winds pick up frogs from a pond and when the wind dies down, the frogs fall back to Earth.) • **What causes a sun halo?** (Sunlight reflects off of ice crystals in a cloud.) • **What words on the concept web could help you describe weird weather?**

MORE PRACTICE	Have students reread "Weird Weather." As they read, tell them to make lists of the different weather phenomena described in the article to share with family members tonight.

Reread for Fluency "Weird Weather," p. 87

5 minutes

	To Do	**To Say**
CORRECTIVE FEEDBACK	Monitor oral reading.	Read p. 87 aloud. Reread the page three or four times so your reading gets better each time. Give feedback on students' oral reading, using the *if... then* statements on Routine Card 4. Model fluent reading if necessary. You may want to have students read along with the DVD-ROM.

ACTIVITY **3** Write

Response to Literature

5 minutes

	To Do	**To Say**
Prompt journal writing.	Write on the board or a transparency: *What can you learn about weather?*	Take out your journals. This week we are reading about storms. Our question for this week is: *What can you learn about weather?* Write an answer to this question based on what you read today. Have students write about the topic, using what they read and their own experiences.
Homework		Practice Book, p. 53, Vocabulary

2

Word Work

Phonics Long *o* Spelled *oa, ow*

	To Do	**To Say**	*5–10 minutes*
Teach long *o* spelled *oa*, *ow*.	Write on the board or on a transparency: *We drove along the coastal highway.*	When two vowels appear together in a word or syllable, the first usually stands for its long sound and the second is silent. What parts do you see in this word? *(coast al)* What vowels appear together in the first syllable? *(o and a)* What vowel sound do you hear in the first syllable? (long *o*)	
Scaffold instruction.	Write *rainbow*.	The letters *ow* can also stand for the sound long *o* or the diphthong /ou/, where each letter contributes to the sound heard. What parts do you see in this word? *(rain bow)* What vowel sound do you hear in the second syllable? (long *o*) Guide students in blending the word parts into the whole word.	
	Develop word meaning.	Have students think and converse. **During a storm, *coastal* areas are often the most affected. Why? What kinds of storms happen most frequently in *coastal* areas?**	
CORRECTIVE FEEDBACK	Write each practice word.	Have students practice reading these words with long *o* spelled *oa, ow*. Correct any words students miss and have them reread the list.	
		floating foamy loaded bowling follow	
MORE PRACTICE	Write more practice words.	Have students practice reading these words with long *o* spelled *oa, ow*.	
		charcoal tugboat bloated outgrow swallow slowly	

Amazing Words **Vocabulary**

	To Do	**To Say**	*5 minutes*
Review vocabulary.	Review the homework.	Ask students to go over answers and share their writing from Practice Book p. 53. See Routine Card 1 for the multisyllabic word routine.	
	Deepen understanding of *coast*.	**Remember, the *coast* is the land along the sea. When a hurricane hits, many towns along the *coast* are badly damaged. Why do people still live on the *coast?***	

Comprehension

Compare and Contrast

	To Do	**To Say**	*5 minutes*
Scaffold instruction.	Introduce compare and contrast.	**Today you will read about how animals' instincts can help save their lives. When you read, it's important to compare and contrast in order to better understand what you're reading. Compare and contrast by finding ways in which two or more things are alike and different.**	
	Model the skill.	**For example, if I am comparing and contrasting humans and animals, and I read that humans can't smell the chemical changes in the air before a storm, but dogs can, I know that this is one way that humans and animals are different.**	
	Distribute Graphic Organizer 4.	**As you read "How Did the Animals Know?" look for information that helps you compare and contrast how different animals respond to danger. Add this information to your graphic organizer.** See Routine Card 7.	

ACTIVITY 3 Read a Passage

Read for Comprehension "How Did the Animals Know?" pp. 88–91

10–15 minutes

	To Do	To Say
Scaffold instruction.	Monitor student engagement. See Routine Cards 2 and 3.	**Read** Have students read pp. 88–91. Stop at the end of each page to ask questions. Students who can read on their own can do so without stopping. After reading, ask questions to promote discussion. **Why was the tsunami so devastating?** (People didn't know it was coming because they didn't have a warning system.) **On p. 89, what is one of nature's warning systems?** (the behavior of animals before a storm) **Why do dogs act strangely before a storm?** (Their sense of smell is so strong; they can smell changes in the air before a storm.) **What do you think the rest of the article will be about?** (Answers will vary. The title suggests that it will tell more about how animals sense danger.)
Model summarizing.	Think aloud.	**Summarize** **What were the first four pages mainly about? What did you learn about animals' ability to sense danger?** Think aloud to model summarizing. **I learned many details about how animals sense danger, such as the way dogs can smell changes in the air before a storm. The main thing I learned is that people should pay attention to animal behavior in order to protect themselves from dangerous weather.**
Develop language and concepts.	Ask questions.	• **How do dogs behave before a storm?** • **How would an early warning system have helped people affected by the tsunami?**
MORE PRACTICE	Have students reread p. 91.	**Reread** Tell students to draw a picture of the dog warning the girl about the tsunami danger.

Reread for Fluency "How Did the Animals Know?" pp. 89–90

5 minutes

	To Do	To Say
MORE PRACTICE **CORRECTIVE FEEDBACK**	Pair students. Monitor paired reading.	Students read aloud pp. 89–90, switching readers at each new paragraph. Have partners reread; now the other partner begins. For optimal fluency, students should reread three or four times. Give feedback, using the *if... then* satements on Routine Card 4. You may want to have students read along with the DVD-ROM.

ACTIVITY 4 Write

Response to Literature

5 minutes

	To Do	To Say
Prompt writing.	Writing elements: support, organization	**Compare and contrast the behavior of the humans before the tsunami hit with the behavior of the animals. Use details from the article to support your ideas. Include words that compare and contrast, such as *both* and *unlike*.**
Homework		Practice Book, p. 54, Long *o* Spelled *oa, ow*

ACTIVITY 1 ## Word Work

Phonics Long *o* Spelled *oa, ow*

To Do	To Say	5 minutes

Review long *o* spelled *oa, ow*.

Scaffold instruction.

Review the homework. Discuss *swallowed* on p. 89 in the student Reader.

Ask students to share answers from Practice Book p. 54.

Point out *swallowed* on p. 89, paragraph 1. **Remember, *oa* and *ow* can stand for the sound long *o* in a word or syllable. What parts do you see in this word?** (swal lowed) **What vowel sound do you hear in the second syllable?** (long *o*)

Then point to *approaching* on p. 95, paragraph 2. **What parts do you see in this word?** (ap proach ing) **What vowel sound do you hear in the second syllable?** (long *o*) Ask students to identify other words with the vowel combinations *oa* and *ow*.

MORE PRACTICE

Model spelling words with the long *o* vowel sound.

Spell and Write Write *snow* and *coasts*. Say *snow*. **What vowel sound do you hear in this word? What letters spell that vowel sound?** Underline *ow*. Continue with *coasts* (*oa*). **Look for long *o* words and tell what letters spell this sound.**

Amazing Words ### Vocabulary

To Do	To Say	5 minutes

Build vocabulary.

Lead cumulative review.

Deepen understanding of *tsunami* and *behavior*.

Read aloud p. 91. **How did sensing the danger of the *tsunami* help the family dog and the young girl to survive? What *behavior* did the girl pick up on?** Write *tsunami* and *behavior*. **Say a sentence using *tsunami* and *behavior*. How can an early warning help people to survive a *tsunami*?**

Use the Tested Vocabulary Cards to review words from previous weeks.

ACTIVITY 2 ## Comprehension

Compare and Contrast

To Do	To Say	5–10 minutes

Scaffold instruction.

Review compare and contrast.

When you compare and contrast you look for ways that things are similar and different. Organizing information this way can help you to better understand what you read. As you read "How Did the Animals Know?" look for similarities and differences in the ways that the animals sense and respond to danger.

Guide practice.

Use Graphic Organizer 4.

Listen as I read p. 92. I want you to notice how the author describes the ways that birds and fish acted when they sensed danger. Read p. 92. Then ask: **How was the behavior of the flamingos and the animals on land similar?** (Both left the coast.) **How was the response of the flamingos and the response of the birds in the air different?** (The flamingos flew to higher elevations, while the birds flew in a different direction.) **Add these details to your graphic organizers.** See Routine Card 7.

MORE PRACTICE

Have students preview pp. 92–95.

Read the captions and look at the photos on pp. 92–95. What do you think this section will be about? (more about the ways that animals sense danger) **Why do you think so?** Think aloud to model using captions and illustrations to predict.

Think aloud.

The captions make me think the article is about how animals behave when they sense danger, and the ways humans might interpret this behavior. From the pictures, I think this section will tell about the ways wildlife reacts to danger.

ACTIVITY **3** Read a Passage

Read for Comprehension "How Did the Animals Know?" pp. 92–95

10–15 minutes

	To Do	To Say
Scaffold instruction.	Monitor student engagement.	**Read** Have students read pp. 92–95. Stop at the end of each page to ask questions. Students who can read on their own can do so without stopping. After reading, ask questions to promote discussion.
	See Routine Cards 2 and 3.	**On p. 92, how did the birds in the air know to fly in a different direction?** (They saw how the schools of fish in the water were swimming.) **Why did animals on land leave areas along the coast?** (They saw the birds flying in a different direction.)
		How did the zoo animals behave before the tsunami? (They tried to break free; they backed into the corners of their cages; they refused to eat.)
		What warning signal did the tourists in Thailand get? (the strange behavior of the elephants)
		What two warning systems do we have in the United States? (weather reports; signals from nature and animals)
Assess comprehension.	Monitor understanding.	**After Reading** Have students discuss the What Do You Think? question. Prompt them to find details in the article to support their responses. Listen as they talk to assess comprehension.
	Summarize.	**What is this mainly about? What did you learn?** Work with students to summarize the selection.
MORE PRACTICE	Have students reread p. 94.	**Reread** As they read, tell students to note the similarities and differences between the ways that animals and humans sense and prepare for danger. Have students add these details to their graphic organizers. After they read, have them tell why animals are better prepared for danger than humans.

Reread for Fluency "How Did the Animals Know?" p. 95

5 minutes

	To Do	To Say
CORRECTIVE FEEDBACK	Monitor oral reading.	**Read p. 95 aloud. Reread the page three or four times so your reading gets better each time.** Give feedback on students' oral reading, using the *if... then* statements on Routine Card 4. Model fluent reading if necessary. You may want to have students read along with the DVD-ROM.

ACTIVITY **4** Write

Response to Literature

5 minutes

	To Do	To Say
MORE PRACTICE	Prompt writing.	**If a storm was approaching, what kind of behavior might you see in dogs, birds, and other animals? Use details from the article to support your answer.** (Students should cite examples from the article that support their ideas.)
Homework		Practice Book, p. 55, Compare and Contrast

ACTIVITY 1 Word Work

Amazing Words Vocabulary

	To Do	**To Say**	*5–10 minutes*

Extend word knowledge.

Write on the board or a transparency: *The weather in winter is often* <u>unpredictable</u>.

Use the word *unpredictable* to extend word knowledge. **Remember we read this word earlier this week. We looked for meaningful parts, and we noticed the word** *predictable*. **Today I want you to notice the prefix** *un-*. **We can use this prefix to read other words.**

Teach prefix *un-*.

Scaffold instruction.

The prefix *un-* means "not." So *unpredictable* means "not predictable," or "not certain." Can you think of other words beginning with *un-*? (*unfair, unkind, unselfish, unsteady, untangle, untruthful*) Write words as students name them and add some of your own. Talk about the meanings of the words, then practice pronouncing all of the words.

Is the weather always *unpredictable?* Why? What other things are always *unpredictable*?

MORE PRACTICE

Deepen understanding of *unpredictable*.

Have individual students or partners use *unpredictable* in a sentence. (For example: The hurricane's path was *unpredictable* and caused a disaster in many coastal areas.) Share sentences. Ask: **Why is *unpredictable* weather more likely to cause a disaster?**

ACTIVITY 2 Comprehension

Skill and Strategy Practice

	To Do	**To Say**	*5 minutes*

Scaffold instruction.

Review compare and contrast (homework).

Ask volunteers to read the passage and share answers from Practice Book p. 55. Remind students of the importance of comparing and contrasting. **When you read a story, comparing and contrasting the events, characters, and settings can help you better understand what you read. You can also compare and contrast what happens in a story to something that has happened in another story or in your own life.**

Practice strategic prereading.

See Routine Card 2.

Discuss Genre Read the title and the first paragraph on p. 96 in the Student Reader. Model determining genre.

Think aloud.

I first thought this might be fiction because of the illustrations. When I read the first paragraph, I knew it was fiction because of the description of the narrator running along the beach.

Review story structure.

Ask Questions What questions do you ask yourself to help you understand a fictional story? (What is the problem or goal? How is the problem solved or the goal reached?) **As you read this story, ask these questions and look for the answers.**

ACTIVITY **3** Read a Passage

Read for Comprehension "Taito and the Gulls," pp. 96–103

10–15 minutes

	To Do	To Say
Scaffold instruction.	Monitor student engagement.	**Read** Have students read pp. 96–103 on their own and then discuss. For students who need more help, stop at the end of each page to discuss. After reading, ask questions.
	See Routine Card 3.	**Who is telling this story?** (Taito, an Arawak boy) **Who are the main characters?** (Taito, his mother, father, and great-grandfather)
		Where does the story take place? (on an island)
		Why can't Taito attend the feast? (He wasted his time watching the gulls when he was supposed to be catching fish.)
		What advice does Taito's great-grandfather give him? (Observe and learn from the animals.)
		What does Taito observe the gulls doing? (He sees them suddenly fly inland.) **What does the gulls' behavior mean?** (It is a sign that bad weather is coming.)
		What comparison does Taito make between the gulls and his people at the end of the story? (The gulls, like his people, are safe and have returned home.)
Assess comprehension.	Monitor understanding.	**After Reading** Have students discuss the What Do You Think? question. Prompt them to find as many similarities and differences as they can. Listen as they talk to assess comprehension.
MORE PRACTICE		**Reread** Have students reread pp. 99–100 and then explain why Taito feels bad to have disappointed his great-grandfather.

Reread for Fluency "Taito and the Gulls," pp. 101–102

5–10 minutes

	To Do	To Say
CORRECTIVE FEEDBACK	Pair students. Monitor paired reading.	Students read aloud pp. 101–102, switching readers at the end of each paragraph. Have partners reread; now the other partner begins. For optimal fluency, students should reread three or four times. Give feedback, using Routine Card 4. You may want to have students read along with the DVD-ROM.
MORE PRACTICE	**READERS' THEATER**	Work with a group of students to adapt pp. 97–98 as a scene. Have students rehearse reading the parts, with one student as the narrator, another as Taito, and the others as Taito's mother and father.

ACTIVITY **4** Write

Response to Literature

5 minutes

	To Do	To Say
Prompt expository writing.	Review pp. 96–103. Writing elements: focus, support	**What does Taito learn about the weather from his great-grandfather?** Use details from the story to support your main ideas.

ACTIVITY 1 — Read a Passage

Read Together "Is It Going to Rain?" pp. 104–107

	To Do	**To Say**	
Scaffold instruction.	Review compare and contrast.	Have students preview pp. 104–107. **This article tells how to make and use a barometer. Comparing and contrasting information from an article with what you already know can help you to better understand what you read. As you read about how to use the barometer, compare and contrast it to other methods for predicting the weather.**	*10 minutes*
	See Routine Card 3.	**Read** Read the article as students follow along. Then read it a second time, having students join in on the text. After reading, ask questions.	
		What is a barometer used for? (It measures air pressure and can help you to tell whether or not it's going to rain.)	
		What does it mean when the water level in your barometer drops? (The air pressure has decreased and rain is likely.)	
		Why should you add food coloring to the water in your barometer? (to help you see the water level)	
Assess comprehension.	Monitor listening comprehension.	**Summarize** Have one student explain how to make a barometer while others add any missing details.	

ACTIVITY 2 — Build Concepts

 **Vocabulary**

	To Do	**To Say**	
Review concept and vocabulary.	Display the concept web you began on Day 1.	**This week's question is *What can you learn about weather?* How do this week's words relate to the question?** (Have students answer the question, using some of the vocabulary they learned this week.)	*5–10 minutes*
		Ask students to add more words to the concept web. Have students explain how each word relates to storms. Monitor students' understanding of vocabulary as they discuss the web. See Routine Card 5.	
MORE PRACTICE	Write *inland* and *coast* on the board.	Have students relate *inland* and *coast.* **Give an example of a type of storm or weather that animals and humans on the *coast* would need to go *inland* in order to survive. Why is it often safer to be *inland* during a storm?**	

ACTIVITY 3 | Write

Response to Literature "4 You 2 Do," p. 108

5–10 minutes

	To Do	**To Say**
Guide response activities.	Discuss the directions on p. 108. Tell students to choose one activity to complete. See Routine Card 8.	**Word Play** Have students find the answers on their own. Then have them work with a partner to try to spell *phenomenon* using the clues they found. **Making Connections** Discuss the question in a group. (Possible answer: Birds flew from their usual spots to higher or safer ground.) **On Paper** Brainstorm some possible animals to use with the group before students draw. Have them write their comic strips on their own. Students can use Practice Book p. 56 to structure their written responses, or you can send the Practice Book page home for them to complete later.
MORE PRACTICE		If you have more time, direct students to complete all the activities.

ACTIVITY 4 | Assessment Options

Passage Reading

10–15 minutes

	To Do	**To Say**
	See Routine Card 6.	While some students are doing Activity 3, determine which students you want to assess this week and choose from these options.
Check fluency.	Take a two-minute timed sample of each student's oral reading.	**Fluency** Have a student read for two minutes from "Taito and the Gulls." Record the number of correct words read per minute. See p. 184 for monitoring fluency. Be sure each student is assessed at least every other week. Have students graph their progress on the Fluency Progress Chart, p. 185.
Check comprehension.		**Retelling** Have students reread "Taito and the Gulls" and retell it. Prompt students if necessary. See p. 186 for monitoring retelling.
		If you have time, assess every student.
Homework		Practice Book, p. 56, Writing

Unit 3 Week 5 *Going Green*

How can we protect nature?

Objectives *This week students will...*

Vocabulary
- build concepts and vocabulary: *benefits, cells, electricity, hydrogen, resources, solar*

Phonics
- prefixes *mis-, non-, over-, pre-, mid-*
- apply knowledge of word structure to decode multisyllabic words when reading

Text Comprehension
- use main idea to improve comprehension
- write in response to literature
- make connections across text

Fluency
- practice fluency with oral rereading

Word Work *This week's phonics focus is . . .*

Prefixes *mis-, non-, over-, pre-, mid-*

Amazing Words Concept/Amazing Words *Tested Vocabulary*

The week's vocabulary is related to the concept of going green, which is related to the environment. The first appearance of each word in the Student Reader is noted below.

benefits	things that help someone or something (p. 124)
cells	units in devices for converting chemical or solar energy into electricity (p. 119)
electricity	energy that can produce light, heat, or motion (p. 118)
hydrogen	a colorless gas that burns easily (p. 118)
resources	things that will meet needs (p. 116)
solar	of or from the sun (p. 119)

Student Reader Unit 3 *This week students will read the following selections.*

112	**Recycling**	Expository Nonfiction
116	**Safer Energy**	Expository Nonfiction
124	**Racing with the Sun**	Expository Nonfiction
132	**Let's Save the Planet!**	Expository Nonfiction
134	**4 You 2 Do**	Activity Page

Daily Lesson Plan

	ACTIVITIES	MATERIALS

Day 1	**Build Concepts** Weekly Concept: Going Green
	    Vocabulary: *benefits, cells, electricity, hydrogen, resources, solar*
	Read a Passage "Recycling," pp. 112–115
	    Comprehension: Use Strategies
	    Reread for Fluency
	Write Response to Literature
		Student Reader: Unit 3
		Routine Cards 2, 4, 5
		Tested Vocabulary Cards
		Student journals
		Practice Book, p. 57, Vocabulary
		Student Reader DVD-ROM

Day 2	**Word Work** Phonics: Prefixes *mis-, non-, over-, pre-, mid-*
	    Vocabulary: Deepen word meaning
	Comprehension Main Idea
	Read a Passage "Safer Energy," pp. 116–120
	    Reread for Fluency
	Write Response to Literature
		Student Reader: Unit 3
		Practice Book, p. 57, Vocabulary
		Graphic Organizer 1
		Routine Cards 1, 2, 3, 4, 7
		Practice Book, p. 58,
		    Prefixes *mis-, non-, over-, pre-, mid-*
		Student Reader DVD-ROM

Day 3	**Word Work** Phonics: Prefixes *mis-, non-, over-, pre-, mid-*
	    Vocabulary: Deepen word meaning
	Comprehension Main Idea
	Read a Passage "Safer Energy," pp. 121–123
	    Reread for Fluency
	Write Response to Literature
		Practice Book, p. 58,
		    Prefixes *mis-, non-, over-, pre-, mid-*
		Tested Vocabulary Cards
		Student Reader: Unit 3
		Graphic Organizer 1
		Routine Cards 1, 2, 3, 4, 7
		Practice Book, p. 59, Main Idea and Details
		Student Reader DVD-ROM

Day 4	**Word Work** Vocabulary: Extend word knowledge **Comprehension** Skill and Strategy Practice **Read a Passage** "Racing with the Sun," pp. 124–131 Reread for Fluency **Write** Response to Literature	Practice Book, p. 59, Main Idea and Details Student Reader: Unit 3 Routine Cards 2, 3, 4 Student Reader DVD-ROM

Day 5	**Read a Passage** "Let's Save the Planet!" pp. 132–133
	    Comprehension: Main Idea; Listening
	Build Concepts Vocabulary
	Write Response to Literature: "4 You 2 Do," p. 134
	Assessment Options Fluency, Comprehension
	    End-of-Unit Test
		Student Reader: Unit 3
		Routine Cards 3, 5, 8
		Practice Book, p. 60, Writing
		Assessment Book, p. 42

See pp. xvi–xvii for how *My Sidewalks* integrates instructional practices for ELL.

ACTIVITY 1 Build Concepts

Amazing Words Vocabulary

| | **To Do** | **To Say** | *10–15 minutes* |

Develop oral vocabulary.
See Routine Card 6 and p. 212.

Introduce the Concept/Amazing Words with an oral routine prior to displaying them in print. Page 212 in this Teacher's Guide provides specific guidelines for introducing each word.

Develop word meaning.
See Routine Card 5. Discuss pp. 111–115.

Have students read p. 111 and then look at the pictures on pp. 112–115. **What do you notice?** (aluminum cans, old newspapers, a cell phone, balloons) **Can you use the word *environment* to describe any of these pictures?** (Example: We can help protect the *environment* by recycling old cans and newspapers.)

Scaffold instruction.
Create a concept web.

In the center of a web, write *The Environment.* **This week's concept is *going green*, which is related to the *environment*. The *environment* is all of the surrounding influences, such as air, water, and soil, that affect the growth of living things.** Provide an example to demonstrate meaning. **It's important not to pollute our rivers and streams, because they are part of our *environment*.**

Add the other vocabulary words.

Concept and Language Goals

Discuss the meaning of each word as it relates to the environment, using the glossary as needed. (See p. 170 in this Teacher's Guide for definitions.)

Model the multisyllabic word strategy.
Display each word. Say it as you display it.

Use the Tested Vocabulary Cards. Follow this routine for each word:

- **Look for Meaningful Parts** Remind students to look for meaningful parts. **As you say each word, ask yourself: Do I see any parts I know?**

- **Chunk Words with No Recognizable Parts** Model how to chunk the word *hydrogen* to read it.

Think aloud.

- **Model** I see a chunk at the beginning of the word: *hy.* I see a part in the middle: *dro.* I see a part at the end of the word: *gen.* I say each chunk slowly: *hy dro gen.* I say the chunks fast to make a whole word: *hydrogen.* Is it a real word? Yes, I know the word *hydrogen.*

- Have students practice reading each word.

Preview.
Read p. 110 with students.

Do you see any of the words we just learned on this page? Together with students, read the sentences on p. 110 describing each selection. Talk about how the vocabulary words might be used in the selections.

MORE PRACTICE
Deepen understanding of *environment.*

Have students demonstrate understanding by answering questions. **Which one is part of our *environment*, the air we breathe, or the cars that we drive? Why? If something is part of the *environment*, is it a living thing or is it man-made? How can we protect our *environment*?**

ACTIVITY **2**   Read a Passage

Develop Concepts "Recycling," pp. 112–115

10–15 minutes

	To Do	To Say
Practice strategic prereading.	See Routine Card 2. Think aloud.	**Discuss Genre** Read the title on p. 112 and have students look at the illustrations on pp. 112–115. Model determining genre. **The photographs are a clue that this is nonfiction. They look like photos of real objects. I think this article will tell about how to recycle objects like these and why recycling is important.**
Scaffold instruction.	Review text structure.	**Ask Questions** **What questions do you ask yourself to help you understand nonfiction?** (What did I learn? What is this mainly about?) **As you read this article, ask these questions and look for the answers.**
Guide comprehension. **Develop language and concepts.**	Read pp. 112–115 aloud.	**Read** Read the article as students follow along. Then read it a second time, having students join in. If necessary, stop at the end of each paragraph to check comprehension. Ask questions to promote discussion and develop the concept. • **Why is it important to recycle soda cans?** (They can be melted down and made into something else instead of just becoming trash.) • **Where does trash end up?** (underground, in the ocean) • **Why are plastic bags and balloons harmful?** (When they're dumped in the ocean, they can choke and kill sea turtles, fish, and seals.) • **What words on the concept web could help you describe recycling?**
MORE PRACTICE		Have students reread "Recycling." As they read, tell them to make a list of the reasons why recycling is so important. Have them share their lists with family members tonight.

Reread for Fluency "Recycling," p. 114

5 minutes

	To Do	To Say
CORRECTIVE FEEDBACK	Monitor oral reading.	**Read p. 114 aloud. Reread the page three or four times so your reading gets better each time.** Give feedback on students' oral reading, using the *if . . . then* statements on Routine Card 4. Model fluent reading if necessary. You may want to have students read along with the DVD-ROM.

ACTIVITY **3**   Write

Response to Literature

5 minutes

	To Do	To Say
Prompt journal writing.	Write on the board or a transparency: *How can we protect nature?*	**Take out your journals. This week we are reading about the environment. Our question for this week is:** *How can we protect nature?* **Write an answer to this question based on what you read today.** Have students write about the topic, using what they read and their own experiences.
Homework		Practice Book, p. 57, Vocabulary

ACTIVITY 1 | Word Work

Phonics Prefixes *mis-, non-, over-, pre-, mid-*

5–10 minutes

	To Do	**To Say**
Teach the prefixes *mis-, non-, over-, pre-, mid-*.	Write on the board or a transparency: *It was our <u>misfortune</u> to run into bad weather on our hike.*	Remember, when you read a long word, look for meaningful parts. Do you see any familiar parts in this word? Frame *fortune.* The word *fortune* means "luck." Today I want you to notice the prefix, *mis-.* The prefix *mis-* means "bad," "badly," or "wrongly." So *misfortune* means bad fortune or bad luck. Knowing the meanings of prefixes can help you read and understand other words.
Scaffold instruction.	Write *nonliving, oversized, prepaid,* and *midweek.*	Read these words aloud. What prefixes do you see? *(non-, over-, pre-, and mid-)* Discuss the meanings of the prefixes and the words. **The prefix *non-* means "not." The prefix *over-* means "over" or "too much." The prefix *pre-* means "before," and *mid-* means "middle." If a piece of rock is *nonliving*, what does that mean?** (It has no life at all.) **What does an *oversized* book look like?** (very large) **If your vacation is *prepaid*, do you have to pay when it is done?** (no) **What day of the week falls *midweek*?** (Wednesday)
CORRECTIVE FEEDBACK	Write each practice word.	Have students practice reading words with prefixes: *mis-, non-, over-, pre-,* and *mid-.* Correct any words students miss and have them reread the list. **nonfiction** **overpriced** **premature** **midseason**
MORE PRACTICE	Write more practice words.	Have students practice reading words that start with prefixes. **misunderstand** **overactive** **precaution** **midstream**

Amazing Words Vocabulary

5 minutes

	To Do	**To Say**
Review vocabulary.	Review the homework.	Ask students to go over answers and share their writing from Practice Book p. 57. See Routine Card 1 for the multisyllabic word routine.
	Deepen understanding of *electricity.*	Remember, *electricity* is a form of energy. Many people heat their homes with *electricity.* What is another example of something that you use *electricity* for? Would our lives be different without *electricity?* Why?

ACTIVITY 2 | Comprehension

Main Idea

5 minutes

	To Do	**To Say**
Scaffold instruction.	Introduce main idea.	Today you will read about new energy sources. When you read nonfiction, identifying the main idea can help you better understand the information that you read. To find the main idea, ask yourself: Who or what is this article about? What is the most important idea about the topic? What are some details that support or tell about the main idea?
	Model the skill.	For example, if I know that the topic of an article is energy sources, then I need to pay attention to try to find the most important idea about energy sources. As I read, I can look for details that support or tell more about the main idea.
	Distribute Graphic Organizer 1.	As you read "Safer Energy," look for the main idea and supporting details. Add these details to your graphic organizer. See Routine Card 7.

ACTIVITY 3 Read a Passage

Read for Comprehension "Safer Energy," pp. 116–120

10–15 minutes

	To Do	**To Say**
Scaffold instruction.	Monitor student engagement.	**Read** Have students read pp. 116–120. Stop at the end of each page to ask questions. Students who can read on their own can do so without stopping. After reading, ask questions to promote discussion.
	See Routine Cards 2 and 3.	**What does it mean if a resource is nonrenewable?** (Once it is gone, it cannot be replaced.)
		Why isn't gasoline a good fuel source? (It causes air pollution.)
		What are two alternative fuel sources that scientists are hopeful about? (hydrogen and solar power) **Why?** (Hydrogen is easy to make and use, and it's cleaner than gasoline or electricity. Solar energy can be stored, and it's free.)
		What do you think the rest of the article will be about? (Answers will vary. The title suggests that it will tell more about cleaner and safer energy alternatives.)
Model summarizing.	Think aloud.	**Summarize What were the first five pages mainly about? What did you learn about the search for safer energy sources?** Think aloud to model summarizing. **I learned a lot of details about energy sources, like the fact that solar energy can be stored in batteries. But the main thing I learned is that it's important for us to find new, cleaner sources of energy to replace nonrenewable energy resources.**
Develop language and concepts.	Ask questions.	• **How might cars contribute to global warming?**
		• **Why is hydrogen a good source of energy?**
MORE PRACTICE	Have students reread p. 120.	**Reread** Tell students to draw a picture of a building that uses solar power as an energy source.

Reread for Fluency "Safer Energy," pp. 118–119

5 minutes

	To Do	**To Say**
MORE PRACTICE **CORRECTIVE FEEDBACK**	Pair students. Monitor paired reading.	Students read aloud pp. 118–119, switching readers at each new paragraph. Have partners reread; now the other partner begins. For optimal fluency, students should reread three or four times. Give feedback, using the *if . . . then* statements on Routine Card 4. You may want to have students read along with the DVD-ROM.

ACTIVITY 4 Write

Response to Literature

5 minutes

	To Do	**To Say**
Prompt writing.	Writing elements: Support, conventions	**What energy sources does the natural environment provide us with? Include details from the article in your answer. Use correct spelling and punctuation to express your ideas.**
Homework		Practice Book, p. 58, Prefixes *mis-, non-, over-, pre-, mid-*

ACTIVITY **1** # Word Work

Phonics Prefixes *mis-, non-, over-, pre-, mid-*

		5 minutes
	To Do	**To Say**
Review prefixes *mis-, non-, over-, pre-, mid-*.	Review the homework. Discuss *nonrenewable* on p. 116 in the Student Reader.	Ask students to share answers from Practice Book p. 58.
Scaffold instruction.		Point out *nonrenewable* on p. 116, paragraph 2. **Remember, we can use prefixes to read unfamiliar words. What prefix do you see in this word?** *(non-)* **What does *non-* mean?** ("not") **There's another prefix here, *re-*, which means "again." Something *renewable* can be made new again. How about if it is *nonrenewable*?** (It cannot.)
		Remind students that before they read each selection they preview it. Write *preview* on the board. **What prefix do you see?** *(pre-)* **What does *pre-* mean?** ("before") **What do you do when you preview something?** ("look at it before") Ask students to think of other words with prefixes *mis-, non-, over-, pre-,* and *mid-.* Discuss their meanings.
MORE PRACTICE	Model spelling words with prefixes.	**Spell and Write** Write *nonstop.* **What prefix has been added to *stop?* Does the spelling of the base word change when the prefix is added?**

Amazing Words Vocabulary

		5 minutes
	To Do	**To Say**
Build vocabulary.	Deepen understanding of *resource* and *hydrogen.*	Read aloud the second paragraph on p. 116. **The author gives a clue to the meaning of *resource.* What examples of *resources* does the author give?** (coal, oil, and natural gas) **We learned another word this week that describes an energy *resource.*** Write *resource* and *hydrogen.* **Say a sentence using *resource* and *hydrogen.* Why might *hydrogen* be a better energy *resource* than coal, oil, or natural gas?**
Lead cumulative review.		Use the Tested Vocabulary Cards to review words from previous weeks.

ACTIVITY **2** # Comprehension

Main Idea

		5–10 minutes
	To Do	**To Say**
Scaffold instruction.	Review main idea.	**To find the main idea, remember to ask yourself what the author's most important idea about the topic is. Sometimes, you have to figure out the main idea yourself and state it in your own words. Make sure the main idea you have identified makes sense and that it is supported by details in the article.**
Guide practice.	Use Graphic Organizer 1.	**Listen as I read p. 123. I want you to notice the author is writing about using wind, sun, and water as energy sources. What is the most important idea about wind, sun, and water on this page?** (Wind, sun, and water are good sources of energy.) **What details support this idea?** (They are all renewable, they are easily collected, and they are clean.) **Add these details to your graphic organizer.** See Routine Card 7.
MORE PRACTICE	Have students preview pp. 121–123.	**Read the captions and look at the photos on pp. 121–123. What do you think this section will be about?** (more about the search for clean and renewable energy) **Why do you think so?** Think aloud to model using captions and illustrations to predict.
	Think aloud.	**The captions and pictures make me think the article will describe how we can use wind farms, dams, and ocean waves as possible energy sources.**

ACTIVITY 3 Read a Passage

Read for Comprehension "Safer Energy," pp. 121–123

10–15 minutes

	To Do	**To Say**
Scaffold instruction.	Monitor student engagement.	**Read** Have students read pp. 121–123. Stop at the end of each page to ask questions. Students who can read on their own can do so without stopping. After reading, ask questions to promote discussion.
	See Routine Cards 2 and 3.	**How does wind produce energy?** (The wind spins the blades on a giant tower, and the spinning blades produce electricity.)
		What was hydropower used for years ago? (grinding grain and watering crops)
		Why is water such a good resource? (It is renewable.)
	Model using context for word meaning.	Read aloud the paragraph with *turbine* on p. 122. Explain how the final sentence on the page and the words *barrel* and *wheel* provide clues to the meaning of *turbine* by describing how it works and what it looks like.
Assess comprehension.	Monitor understanding.	**After Reading** Have students discuss the What Do You Think? question. Prompt them to identify the main idea as they answer the question. Listen as they talk to assess comprehension.
	Summarize.	**What is this mainly about? What did you learn?** Work with students to summarize the selection.
MORE PRACTICE	Have students reread p. 122.	**Reread** As they read, tell students to describe how dams use water to produce electricity. After they read, have them tell why water is a good energy source.

Reread for Fluency "Safer Energy," p. 121

5 minutes

	To Do	**To Say**
CORRECTIVE FEEDBACK	Monitor oral reading.	**Read p. 121 aloud. Reread the page three or four times so your reading gets better each time.** Give feedback on students' oral reading, using the *if . . . then* statements on Routine Card 4. Model fluent reading if necessary. You may want to have students read along with the DVD-ROM.

ACTIVITY 4 Write

Response to Literature

5 minutes

	To Do	**To Say**
MORE PRACTICE	Prompt writing.	**Why are wind, water, and sun such good sources of energy? Use details from the article to support your answer.**
	Homework	Practice Book, p. 59, Main Idea and Details

ACTIVITY 1 Word Work

Amazing Words ## Vocabulary

	To Do	**To Say**	*5–10 minutes*

Extend word knowledge.

Teach root word *hydr*.

Scaffold instruction.

Write on the board or a transparency:
<u>Hydrogen</u> can be used as fuel for cars.

Use the word *hydrogen* to extend word knowledge. **Remember, we read this word earlier this week. We chunked it to pronounce it, but we might also have noticed the Greek root word *hydr*. We can use this root to read other words.**

The root word *hydr* means "water." *Hydrogen* **is a colorless gas that can combined with oxygen to form water.** (H_2O) **Can you think of other words that contain the root word *hydr*?** (*hydrant, hydroelectric, hydrate, hydraulic, hydrofoil, hydrophobia, dehydrated*) Write words as students name them and add some of your own. Talk about the meanings of the words and how they relate to water. Point out that the *y* in *hydr* is pronounced with the sound long *i*.

Develop word meaning.

Is *hydrogen* a renewable energy source? Why?

MORE PRACTICE

Deepen understanding of *hydrogen* and *solar*.

Have individual students or partners use the two words *hydrogen* and *solar* together in sentences. (For example: Both *hydrogen* and *solar* energy can be used to generate electricity.) Share sentences. Ask: **Why are *hydrogen* and *solar* energy such good alternative energy resources?**

ACTIVITY 2 Comprehension

Skill and Strategy Practice

	To Do	**To Say**	*5 minutes*

Scaffold instruction.

Review main idea (homework).

Ask volunteers to read the passage and share answers from Practice Book p. 59. Remind students of the importance of finding the main idea. **Sometimes an author will state the main idea directly. Other times, the author will leave it up to the reader to find the main idea. When you look for the main idea, ask yourself, "What is the most important point the author is trying to make?"**

Practice strategic prereading.

See Routine Card 2. Think aloud.

Discuss Genre Read the title and p. 124 in the Student Reader. Model determining genre.

I first thought this might be nonfiction because of the photographs. They look like pictures of real cars. When I read the first page, I knew it was nonfiction because of the description of solar cars.

Review text structure.

Ask Questions What questions do you ask yourself to help you understand nonfiction? (What did I learn? What is this mainly about?) **As you read this article, ask these questions and look for the answers.**

ACTIVITY 3 Read a Passage

Read for Comprehension "Racing with the Sun," pp. 124–131

10–15 minutes

	To Do	**To Say**
Scaffold instruction.	Monitor student engagement. See Routine Card 3.	**Read** Have students read pp. 124–131 on their own and then discuss. For students who need more help, stop at the end of each page to discuss. After reading, ask questions. **How do solar cells work?** (They collect and change sunlight into energy cars can use.) **What are the benefits of solar energy?** (It doesn't pollute the environment, and it is renewable.) **What are the drawbacks of solar cells?** (They don't store enough power for everyday use, and they can only run during the day.) **Where did the 2005 North American Solar Challenge race begin and end?** (It began in Austin, Texas, and ended in Canada.) **On what kind of days do solar cars go faster and farther?** (bright, sunny days) **Why?** (They depend on sunlight for energy.)
Review the phonics skill.	Point out *midway* on p. 129, paragraph 1.	Remind students that they learned the prefix *mid-*, which means "middle." Demonstrate framing the word parts *mid* and *way*. Have students blend the parts to read the word. Use the prefix *mid-* to figure out the meaning of the word.
Assess comprehension.	Monitor understanding.	**After Reading** Have students discuss the What Do You Think? question. Prompt them to identify the main idea of the article. Listen to assess comprehension.
MORE PRACTICE		**Reread** Have students reread pp. 129–131 and describe the last half of the race.

Reread for Fluency "Racing with the Sun," pp. 124–127

5–10 minutes

	To Do	**To Say**
CORRECTIVE FEEDBACK	Pair students. Monitor paired reading.	Students read aloud pp. 124–127, switching readers at the end of each paragraph. Have partners reread; now the other partner begins. For optimal fluency, students should reread three or four times. Give feedback, using Routine Card 4. You may want to have students read along with the DVD-ROM.
MORE PRACTICE	**READERS' THEATER**	Work with groups to adapt pp. 129–131 as a radio broadcast. Have students divide the lines and then rehearse reading as sports announcers for the race.

ACTIVITY 4 Write

Response to Literature

5 minutes

	To Do	**To Say**
Prompt expository writing.	Review pp. 124–131. Writing elements: focus, support, conventions	**What is the main idea of "Racing with the Sun"? Include details from the article to support your answer. Use complete sentences to express your ideas.** (Students should establish a main idea and provide details that support it.)

ACTIVITY 1   Read a Passage

Read Together "Let's Save the Planet!" pp. 132–133

10 minutes

	To Do	**To Say**
Scaffold instruction.	Review main idea.	Have students preview pp. 132–133. **This article tells about different children who have helped protect the environment. When you read nonfiction, identifying the main idea can help you better understand what you read. Look for supporting details to help you determine the main idea.**
	See Routine Card 3.	**Read** Read the article as students follow along. Then read it a second time, having students join in on the text. After reading, ask questions.
		What are the President's Environmental Youth Awards? (awards given each year to kids who do projects that help protect the environment)
		What are some examples of projects that kids have won PEYA awards for? (recycling, creating bike trails, putting up nest boxes for rare birds)
Assess comprehension.	Monitor listening comprehension.	**Summarize** Have one student describe the different kinds of environmental projects that kids might do to show their commitment to protecting the Earth and its resources.

ACTIVITY 2   Build Concepts

Amazing Words Vocabulary

5–10 minutes

	To Do	**To Say**
Review concept and vocabulary.	Display the concept web you began on Day 1.	**This week's question is *How can we protect nature?* How do this week's words relate to the question?** (Have students answer the question, using some of the vocabulary they learned this week.)
		Ask students to add more words to the concept web. Have students explain how each word relates to the environment. Monitor students' understanding of vocabulary as they discuss the web. See Routine Card 5.
MORE PRACTICE	Write *resources* and *benefits* on the board.	Have students relate *resources* and *benefits*. **Give an example of a nonrenewable energy *resource*. Now give an example of a renewable energy *resource*. What are the environmental *benefits* of using renewable energy *resources*? How do we *benefit* from finding alternative energy *resources*?**

ACTIVITY 3 Write

Response to Literature "4 You 2 Do," p. 134

5–10 minutes

Guide response activities.

To Do

Discuss the directions on p. 134.
Tell students to choose one activity to complete. See Routine Card 8.

To Say

Word Play Have students work individually or in pairs to write their advertisements and then meet as a class to share them.

Making Connections Discuss the question in a group. (Answers should include hydrogen, solar power, wind, or other renewable resources that students read about, as well as the advantages of using them.)

On Paper Have students brainstorm some answers to the prompt before they write. Have them write on their own. Students can use Practice Book p. 60 to structure their written responses, or you can send the Practice Book page home for them to complete later.

MORE PRACTICE

If you have more time, direct students to complete all the activities.

ACTIVITY 4 Assessment Options

End-of-Unit Test

10–15 minutes

Assess fluency and comprehension.

To Do

Use Assessment Book, p. 48.

To Say

Options for end-of-unit assessment are available in the Assessment Book, p. 48.

Homework Practice Book, p. 60, Writing

Resources

Contents

Monitoring Fluency

Ongoing assessment of student reading fluency is one of the most valuable measures we have of students' reading skills. One of the most effective ways to assess fluency is taking timed samples of students' oral reading and measuring the number of words correct per minute (WCPM).

Fluency Goals

Level D End-of-Year Goal = 110–130 WCPM

Target Goals by Unit:

Unit 1 60 to 80 WCPM

Unit 2 70 to 90 WCPM

Unit 3 80 to 100 WCPM

Unit 4 90 to 110 WCPM

Unit 5 100 to 120 WCPM

Unit 6 110 to 130 WCPM

How to Measure Words Correct Per Minute—WCPM

Timed Reading of the Text

Make a copy of the text for yourself and have one for the student. Tell the student: **As you read this aloud, I want you to do your best reading. Read as quickly as you can without making mistakes. That doesn't mean it's a race. Just do your best reading. When I say *begin,* start reading.**

As the student reads, follow along in your copy. Mark words that are read incorrectly. Definitions and examples of these reading errors are given on p. 192.

Incorrect	Correct
• omissions	• self-corrections within 3 seconds
• substitutions	• repeated words
• mispronunciations	
• insertions	

After One Minute

At the end of one minute, draw a line after the last word that was read. Have the student finish reading but don't count any words beyond one minute. Arrive at the words correct per minute—WCPM—by counting the total number of words that the student read correctly in one minute.

Fluency Progress Chart

Copy the chart on the next page. Use it to record each student's progress across the year. Assist students in recording their scores on the chart and setting goals for the future.

Interpreting Results

Fluency goals are estimates, and students will vary considerably in their progress based on many factors. Also, student progress will depend greatly on where they start with respect to WCPM. Level D End-of-Year goals are the same as for students without reading difficulties at the end of Grade 4.

Fluency Progress Chart, Level D

Student's Name _____

140																														
135																														
130																														
125																														
120																														
115																														
110																														
105																														
100																														
95																														
90																														
85																														
80																														
75																														
70																														
65																														
60																														
55																														
50																														
45																														
	1	2	3*	4	5*	1	2	3*	4	5*	1	2	3*	4	5*	1	2	3*	4	5*	1	2	3*	4	5*	1	2	3*	4	5*
	Unit 1					Unit 2					Unit 3					Unit 4					Unit 5					Unit 6				

* = Fluency Assessment Using Unfamiliar Text

Monitoring Retelling

Retelling is a way to monitor and assess comprehension. Through retelling, students show whether they understand story grammar and can follow sequence, grasp main ideas, and draw conclusions about what they read. Help students learn how to retell by giving them many opportunities to retell stories and nonfiction selections. Scaffold their retellings by prompting them to tell more.

How to Do a Retelling

Have the student read quietly. If the student has difficulty with the passage, you may read it aloud.

Tell the student: **Read the story quietly to yourself. When you finish reading, I will ask you to tell me about what you read.**

When the student has finished, or when you have finished reading aloud, ask:

- (For fiction) **What happened in the story?**
- (For nonfiction) **What was the selection mostly about?**

Prompts for Retelling

If a retelling is incomplete, use prompts to encourage the student to tell more.

Narrative Prompts

- **Who is in the story?**
- **Where and when does the story take place?**
- **What is the problem or goal?**
- **How is the problem solved or the goal reached?**

Expository Prompts

- **What did you learn about _____?**
- **What are the most important ideas?**

Looking Back

Encourage students to look back in the text to find answers or to confirm their answers.

- **Let's check the book to make sure.**
- **Show me where the book tells you that.**
- **Where can we look in the book to find the answer?**

See Assessment Book, pp. 10–13, for scoring rubrics for retelling. Use the rubrics to help students move toward a fluent retelling.

Using End-of-Unit Assessment Results

To make instructional decisions at the end of each unit, consider scores for

- Unit Test
- Benchmark Reader reading

Record Scores

Several forms are provided for recording students' progress across the year.

- Record Sheet for Unit Tests: Record scores for each Unit Test. See the Assessment Book, p. 16.
- Fluency Progress Chart: Record each student's WCPM across the year. See p. 185.
- Retelling Charts: Record the student's retelling scores for each unit. See the Assessment Book, pp. 12–14.

Questions to Consider

- Has the student's performance met expectations for daily lessons?
- What can the student read alone? What can the student read with supervision?
- Is the student progressing toward grade-level goals?

Evaluate Student Progress

To move into the next unit of *My Sidewalks*, the student should

- score 80% or better on the Unit Test
- be able to read and retell the end-of-unit Benchmark Reader accurately
- be capable of working in the Level D group based on teacher judgment

If . . . the student's scores indicate a specific weakness in one area of literacy, such as fluency or comprehension,

then . . . focus the student's instruction and practice on that area.

If . . . the student has not met the fluency benchmarks for the unit,

then . . . consider that the benchmark WCPM at the high end of the range are more typical of on-level students, and students in intensive intervention may be progressing well even if they are not meeting fluency benchmarks.

The student may be more appropriately placed in *My Sidewalks*, Level C if the student

- scores 60% or lower on Unit Tests
- is struggling to keep up with the Level D group
- is unable to decode the simplest word types

Exiting MY SiDEWALKS

In Level D of *My Sidewalks,* there are two opportunities for students to exit the program—at midyear and at the end of the year. Many factors govern decisions concerning instruction for individual students. Understandably, guidelines in your school or district regarding adequate yearly progress, in addition to processes such as Individualized Education Plans, will influence each student's placement in or exit from any intervention program.

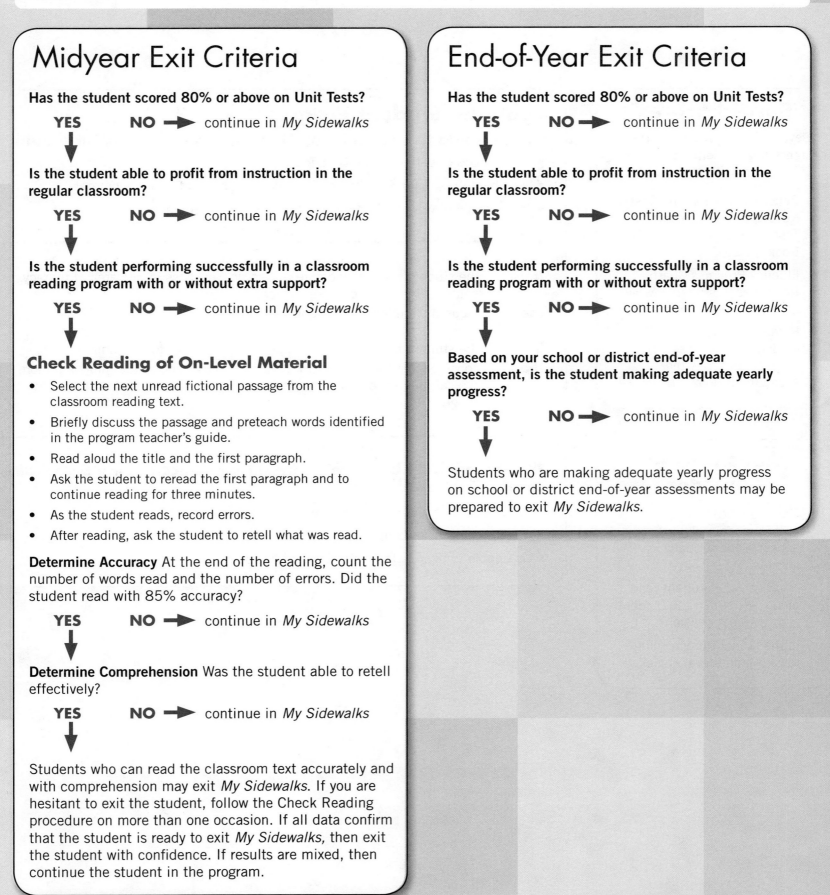

Midyear Exit Criteria

Has the student scored 80% or above on Unit Tests?

YES   **NO** ➡ continue in *My Sidewalks*

Is the student able to profit from instruction in the regular classroom?

YES   **NO** ➡ continue in *My Sidewalks*

Is the student performing successfully in a classroom reading program with or without extra support?

YES   **NO** ➡ continue in *My Sidewalks*

Check Reading of On-Level Material

- Select the next unread fictional passage from the classroom reading text.
- Briefly discuss the passage and preteach words identified in the program teacher's guide.
- Read aloud the title and the first paragraph.
- Ask the student to reread the first paragraph and to continue reading for three minutes.
- As the student reads, record errors.
- After reading, ask the student to retell what was read.

Determine Accuracy At the end of the reading, count the number of words read and the number of errors. Did the student read with 85% accuracy?

YES   **NO** ➡ continue in *My Sidewalks*

Determine Comprehension Was the student able to retell effectively?

YES   **NO** ➡ continue in *My Sidewalks*

Students who can read the classroom text accurately and with comprehension may exit *My Sidewalks.* If you are hesitant to exit the student, follow the Check Reading procedure on more than one occasion. If all data confirm that the student is ready to exit *My Sidewalks,* then exit the student with confidence. If results are mixed, then continue the student in the program.

End-of-Year Exit Criteria

Has the student scored 80% or above on Unit Tests?

YES   **NO** ➡ continue in *My Sidewalks*

Is the student able to profit from instruction in the regular classroom?

YES   **NO** ➡ continue in *My Sidewalks*

Is the student performing successfully in a classroom reading program with or without extra support?

YES   **NO** ➡ continue in *My Sidewalks*

Based on your school or district end-of-year assessment, is the student making adequate yearly progress?

YES   **NO** ➡ continue in *My Sidewalks*

Students who are making adequate yearly progress on school or district end-of-year assessments may be prepared to exit *My Sidewalks.*

Matching Students to Text

Providing students with reading materials they can and want to read is an important step toward developing fluent readers. A fluency test allows you to determine each student's instructional and independent reading level. Information on how to administer a fluency test is provided on pp. 191–192.

Instructional Reading Level

Only approximately 1 in 10 words will be difficult when reading a selection from the Student Reader for students in the *My Sidewalks* intervention program. Students reading at their instructional level need teacher support and benefit from guided instruction.

Independent Reading Level

Students should read regularly in independent-level texts in which no more than approximately 1 in 20 words is difficult for the reader. Other factors that make a book easy to read include the student's interest in the topic, the amount of text on a page, how well illustrations support meaning, and the complexity and familiarity of the concepts.

Guide students in learning how to self-select books at their independent reading level. As you talk about a book with students, discuss the challenging concepts in it, list new words students find in sampling the book, and ask students about their familiarity with the topic. A blackline master to help students evaluate books for independent reading is provided on p. 190.

Self-Selected/Independent Reading

While oral reading allows you to assess students' reading level and fluency, independent reading is of crucial importance to students' futures as readers and learners. Students need to develop their ability to read independently for increasing amounts of time.

- Specify the amount of time you wish students to read independently each week. During the year, gradually increase the amount of time devoted to independent reading.

- Encourage students to read to a partner or a family member.

- Help students track the amount of time they read independently and the number of pages they read in a given amount of time. Tracking will help motivate them to gradually increase their duration and speed. A blackline master for tracking independent reading is provided on p. 190. Check it on a regular basis to monitor progress.

Choosing a Book for Independent Reading

When choosing a book, story, or article for independent reading, consider these questions:

_____ 1.   Do I know something about this topic?

_____ 2.   Am I interested in this topic?

_____ 3.   Do I like reading this kind of book (fiction, fantasy, biography, or whatever)?

_____ 4.   Have I read other things by this author? Do I like this author?

If you say "yes" to at least one of the questions above, continue:

_____ 5.   In reading the first page, was only about 1 of every 20 words hard?

If you say "yes," continue:

_____ 6.   Does the number of words on a page look about right to me?

If you say "yes," the book or article is probably at the right level for you.

Silent Reading

Record the date, the title of the book or article you read, the amount of time you spent reading, and the number of pages you read during that time.

Date	Title	Minutes	Pages

Matching Students to Text

Taking a Fluency Test

A fluency test is an assessment of a student's oral reading accuracy and oral reading fluency. Reading accuracy is based on the number of words read correctly. Reading fluency is based on the reading rate (the number of words correct per minute) and the degree to which a student reads with a "natural flow."

How to Measure Reading Accuracy

1. Choose a text of about 100 to 140 words that is unfamiliar to the student.

2. Make a copy of the text for yourself. Make a copy for the student or have the student read aloud from a book.

3. Give the student the text and have the student read aloud. (You may wish to record the student's reading for later evaluation.)

4. On your copy of the text, mark any miscues or errors the student makes while reading. See the fluency test sample on p. 192, which shows how to identify and mark miscues.

5. Count the total number of words in the text and the total number of errors made by the student. Note: If a student makes the same error more than once, such as mispronouncing the same word multiple times, count it as one error. Self-corrections do not count as actual errors. Use the following formula to calculate the percentage score, or accuracy rate:

$$\frac{\text{Total Number of Words} - \text{Total Number of Errors}}{\text{Total Number of Words}} \times 100 = \text{percentage score}$$

Interpreting the Results

- A student who reads 95–100% of the words correctly is reading at an independent level and may need more challenging text.

- A student who reads 90–94% of the words correctly is reading at an instructional level and will likely benefit from guided instruction.

- A student who reads 89% or fewer of the words correctly is reading at a frustrational level and may benefit most from targeted instruction with lower-level texts and further intervention.

How to Measure Reading Rate (WCPM)

1. Follow Steps 1–3 above.

2. Note the exact times when the student begins and finishes reading.

3. Use the following formula to calculate the number of words correct per minute (WCPM):

$$\frac{\text{Total Number of Words Read Correctly}}{\text{Total Number of Seconds}} \times 60 = \text{words correct per minute}$$

Interpreting the Results

An appropriate reading rate for an on-level fourth-grader is 120–130 WCPM.

Matching Students to Text

Fluency Test Sample

Fluency Test Sample

Ms. Abbot ^H read the list of student pairs. She said, "The last student pair is Miguel and Emi." Miguel groaned aloud.

"What is she going to teach me?" he asked loudly. "She doesn't even speak English!"

Ms. Abbot stared hard at Miguel.

"Miguel, I think this project has a lot ^for me^ to teach you," she said.

My family just moved here from Japan three weeks ago. I am shy about (sc) talking to the other students. I have not made any friends.

At this school, students come from all different backgrounds /bands/. I wanted to meet them. But I didn't feel comfortable speaking English. I learned some English in Japan. But, ~~there~~ three are still so many words I don't know. My mother says I am just homesick.

—from *Paper Birds and Plantains*
My Sidewalks Student Reader, Level D

Miscues

Hesitation
The student hesitates over a word, and the teacher provides the word. Wait several seconds before telling the student what the word is.

Insertion
The student inserts words or parts of words that are not in the text.

Self-Correction
The student reads a word incorrectly but then corrects the error. Do not count self-corrections as actual errors. However, noting self-corrections will help you identify words the student finds difficult.

Mispronunciation/Misreading
The student pronounces or reads a word incorrectly.

Omission
The student omits words or word parts.

Substitution
The student substitutes words or parts of words for the words in the text.

Fluency Test Results ▶

Total Number of Words: **124**

Number of Errors: **5**

Reading Time: **61 seconds**

Reading Accuracy ▶

$$\frac{124 - 5}{124} = \frac{119}{124} = .959 = 96\%$$

Accuracy Percentage Score: **96%**

Reading Rate—WCPM

$$\frac{119}{61} \times 60 = 117.04 = 117 \text{ words}$$
correct per minute

Reading Rate: **117 WCPM**

Scope and Sequence

Concepts of Print and Print Awareness	Level A	Level B	Level C	Level D	Level E
Develop awareness that print represents spoken language and conveys and preserves meaning	•				
Identify parts of a book and their functions (front cover, title, page numbers)	•				
Understand the concept of letter and word (including constancy of words and word boundaries)	•				
Track print (front to back of book, top to bottom of page, left to right on line, sweep back left for next line)	•				
Match spoken to printed words	•				
Know capital and lowercase letter names and match them	•				
Write capital and lowercase letters	•				

Phonemic Awareness	Level A	Level B	Level C	Level D	Level E
Identify sounds that are the same or different	•				
Identify and isolate initial, final, and medial sounds	•				
Blend sounds orally	•	•			
Segment a word into sounds	•	•			
Add or delete phonemes	•	•			

Phonics	Level A	Level B	Level C	Level D	Level E
Understand and apply the *alphabetic principle* that spoken words are composed of sounds that are represented by letters	•				
Know letter-sound relationships	•	•	•		
Blend sounds of letters to decode					
Consonants	•	•			
Consonant blends	•	•	•		

Consonant digraphs	●	●	●		
Vowels					
Short	●	●	●	●	●
Long	●	●	●	●	●
R-controlled	●	●	●	●	●
Digraphs	●	●	●	●	●
Diphthongs		●	●	●	●
Other vowel patterns	●	●	●	●	●
Phonograms/word families	●	●	●		
Decode words with common word parts					
Base words and inflected endings	●	●	●	●	●
Contractions	●	●	●	●	●
Possessives	●	●			
Compounds	●	●	●	●	●
Suffixes and prefixes		●	●	●	●
Blend syllables to decode words					
VC/CV	●	●	●	●	●
Consonant + *le*	●	●	●	●	●
VC/V and V/CV	●	●	●	●	●
VCCCV			●	●	●
V/V			●	●	●

Spelling	Level A	Level B	Level C	Level D	Level E
Use sound-letter knowledge to spell	●	●	●	●	●
Use knowledge of word structure to spell	●	●	●	●	●
Blend multisyllabic words	●	●	●	●	●

Reading Fluency	Level A	Level B	Level C	Level D	Level E
Read aloud fluently with accuracy, comprehension, and appropriate pace/rate	●	●	●	●	●
Practice fluency in a variety of ways, including choral reading, partner/paired reading, repeated oral reading, tape-assisted reading, and Readers' Theater	●	●	●	●	●
Work toward appropriate fluency goals	40–60 WCPM	70–90 WCPM	100–120 WCPM	110–130 WCPM	120–140 WCPM

Vocabulary (Oral and Written)	Level A	Level B	Level C	Level D	Level E
Recognize regular and irregular high-frequency words automatically	●	●			
Recognize and understand lesson vocabulary	●	●	●	●	●
Develop vocabulary through direct instruction, concrete experiences, reading, and listening to text read aloud	●	●	●	●	●
Use concept vocabulary	●	●	●	●	●
Use speaking vocabulary	●	●			
Use knowledge of word structure to figure out word meaning		●	●	●	●
Use context clues					
to confirm word identification	●	●	●		
to determine word meaning of multiple-meaning words, homonyms, homographs			●	●	●
to determine word meaning of unfamiliar words			●	●	●
Understand synonyms and antonyms			●	●	●

Text Comprehension	Level A	Level B	Level C	Level D	Level E
Comprehension Strategies					
Preview the text	●	●	●	●	●
Set and monitor purpose for reading	●	●	●	●	●
Activate and use prior knowledge	●	●	●	●	●
Make predictions	●	●	●	●	●
Ask and answer questions	●	●	●	●	●
Look back in text for answers			●	●	●
Recognize story structure: characters, plot, setting	●	●	●	●	●
Summarize text by retelling stories or identifying main ideas	●	●	●	●	●
Use graphic and semantic organizers			●	●	●
Comprehension Skills					
Compare and contrast	●	●	●	●	●
Draw conclusions		●	●	●	●
Main idea and supporting details	●	●	●	●	●
Sequence of events	●	●	●	●	●
Write in response to text	●	●	●	●	●

Oral Vocabulary Routine

Let's Learn Amazing Words

Use this Oral Vocabulary Routine along with the definitions, examples, letter-sounds, and word parts provided on the following pages to introduce each Amazing Word.

ABOUT ORAL VOCABULARY A student's oral vocabulary development is a predictor of future reading success. Oral vocabulary development boosts students' comprehension as they become fluent readers. Oral vocabulary is informally assessed.

Routine

(1) Introduce the Word Relate the word to the selection in which it appears. Supply a student-friendly definition. Have students say the word. Example:
- **In the story, the puzzle is a *challenge*. A *challenge* is a hard task or a test of someone's abilities. You can also *challenge* someone by inviting or daring him or her to do something, such as take part in a competition. Say the word *challenge* with me, *challenge*.**

(2) Demonstrate Provide familiar examples to demonstrate meaning. When possible, use gestures to help convey meaning. Examples:
- **Running in the 5K race was a *challenge*. It was a *challenge* to write a two-page report. Our school will *challenge* another school to a basketball game.**

(3) Apply Have students demonstrate understanding with a simple activity. Example:
- **Tell me something that is a *challenge* for you. How else might one school *challenge* another?**

(4) Display the Word/Letter-Sounds Write the word on a card and display it on a classroom Amazing Words board. Have students identify some familiar letter-sounds or word parts. Example:
- **This word is *challenge*. Run your hand under the two word parts *chal-lenge* as you read the word.**

(5) Use the Word Ask students to use the word in a sentence. Model a sentence if students need help. Example:
- **Eating with chopsticks is a *challenge* for me.**

Oral Vocabulary Unit 1 Week 1

Let's Learn Amazing Words

Routine *Oral Vocabulary*

backgrounds

❶ *Backgrounds* are past experiences, knowledge, and training.

❷ **EXAMPLES** Most doctors have *backgrounds* in science. People who come from the same place may have similar *backgrounds*.

❸ **APPLY TO THE INSTRUCTION** Have students name a job and tell about the *background* a person probably needs to do it. Have students use *background* in their answer.

❹ **WORD PARTS** Students can identify the two smaller words *back* and *ground* and the plural *-s* ending.

culture

❶ Your *culture* is your way of life, including your foods, language, and celebrations.

❷ **EXAMPLES** Celebrating the harvest each fall is part of many *cultures*. In the Japanese *culture*, many people speak both Japanese and English.

❸ **APPLY TO THE INSTRUCTION** Have children list favorite traditions that are part of their *culture*.

❹ **WORD PARTS** Students can identify the closed syllable *cul-*.

ethnic

❶ People in the same *ethnic* group share the same race, nationality, and culture.

❷ **EXAMPLES** There are many different *ethnic* groups in the United States. Fajitas are an example of an *ethnic* food.

❸ **APPLY TO THE INSTRUCTION** Point out that many communities have *ethnic* street fairs or festivals. Have students give examples of what they might experience at an *ethnic* fair.

❹ **SOUND-SPELLINGS** Students can identify the initial sound-spelling /e/*e*. Students can decode *ethnic*.

homesick

❶ To be *homesick* means to be very sad because you are far from home.

❷ **EXAMPLE** At first, the children felt *homesick*, but after a few days they began to enjoy their vacation.

❸ **APPLY TO THE INSTRUCTION** Have students list words that describe what being *homesick* feels like.

❹ **WORD PARTS** Students can identify the two smaller words *home* and *sick* in the compound word.

translated

❶ When something is *translated*, it is changed from one language into another.

❷ **EXAMPLES** The teacher *translated* the book from Spanish into English. When we traveled to France, a guide *translated* our questions from English into French.

❸ **APPLY TO THE INSTRUCTION** Have students imagine they are traveling in another country. Have them identify things they might need to have *translated*.

❹ **WORD PARTS** Run your hand under the three word parts *trans-la-ted* as students read each part and then read the whole word.

understanding

❶ If you have an *understanding* of something, you know something about it.

❷ **EXAMPLE** After I read the directions, I had a clear *understanding* of how to build the model.

❸ **APPLY TO THE INSTRUCTION** Have students name one word that means the opposite of *understanding* and another word that means about the same as *understanding*.

❹ **WORD PARTS** Run your hand under the four word parts *un-der-stand-ing* as students read each part and then read the whole word.

Oral Vocabulary Unit 1 Week 2

Let's Learn Amazing Words

Definitions, examples, applications, and **sound-spellings** to use with the Oral Vocabulary Routine each week.

Routine *Oral Vocabulary*

area

❶ An *area* is an open space. An *area* is also a place.

❷ **EXAMPLES** They built the baseball field in the *area* next to the school. The *area* where the raccoons live has many trees.

❸ **APPLY TO THE INSTRUCTION** Have students describe the *area* where your school is located.

❹ **WORD PARTS** Run your hand under the three word parts *ar-e-a* as students read each part and then read the whole word.

---

confused

❶ If you are *confused*, you are mixed up or not sure about something.

❷ **EXAMPLE** The hiker was *confused* about which way to go, so he got lost.

❸ **APPLY TO THE INSTRUCTION** Have students tell about a time when they were *confused*.

❹ **WORD PARTS** Students can identify the base word *confuse* and the ending *-ed*.

device

❶ A *device* is something invented for a particular use.

❷ **EXAMPLE** Headphones are a *device* used for talking on the phone hands free.

❸ **APPLY TO THE INSTRUCTION** Have students list examples of *devices* people use to make doing things easier.

❹ **SOUND-SPELLINGS** Identify the sound-spelling /d/d.

---

perspective

❶ A *perspective* is a view of something from a distance.

❷ **EXAMPLE** We had a good *perspective* of the town below from on top of the mountain.

❸ **APPLY TO THE INSTRUCTION** Have students imagine they are first on the rooftop of your school and then in a helicopter flying over your school. Have them compare their *perspectives*.

❹ **WORD PARTS** Run your hand under the three word parts *per-spec-tive* as students read each part and then read the whole word.

pioneers

❶ *Pioneers* are people who do something first, preparing the way for other people.

❷ **EXAMPLES** Long ago, *pioneers* settled in places that became towns. The first woman pilot was a *pioneer;* she led the way for other women.

❸ **APPLY TO THE INSTRUCTION** Have students describe challenges a *pioneer* might face.

❹ **WORD PARTS** Run your hand under the three word parts *pi-o-neers* as students read each part and then read the whole word.

---

territory

❶ *Territory* is a set area. It is also one of the parts of a country.

❷ **EXAMPLES** The farmer's *territory* was marked by a fence. Much of the *territory* in Arizona is desert.

❸ **APPLY TO THE INSTRUCTION** Have students describe a *territory* they have seen or read about.

❹ **WORD PARTS** Run your hand under the four word parts *ter-ri-to-ry* as students read each part and then read the whole word.

voyage

❶ A *voyage* is a journey or trip by water or through air or space.

❷ **EXAMPLE** The *voyage* across the ocean took several days.

❸ **APPLY TO THE INSTRUCTION** Point out that a *voyage* is usually a long trip. Have students give examples of places they might want to take a *voyage* to.

❹ **SOUND-SPELLINGS** Identify the sound-spelling /v/v.

Oral Vocabulary Unit 1 Week 3

Let's Learn Amazing Words

Definitions, examples, applications, and **sound-spellings** to use with the Oral Vocabulary Routine each week.

Routine *Oral Vocabulary*

itineraries

❶ *Itineraries* are travel plans.

❷ **EXAMPLES** Our *itinerary* said we would be traveling to three different cities in one week. We looked at our *itinerary* to see what time we would arrive.

❸ **APPLY TO THE INSTRUCTION** Have students describe some things you might find on an *itinerary*.

❹ **WORD PARTS** Run your hand under the five word parts *i-tin-e-rar-ies* as students read each part and then read the whole word.

journey

❶ If you are on a *journey*, you are on a long trip.

❷ **EXAMPLES** The *journey* began in New York and ended in Florida. When it got cold, the birds *journeyed* south.

❸ **APPLY TO THE INSTRUCTION** Have students tell about a *journey* they have taken or would like to take.

❹ **SOUND-SPELLINGS** Identify the sound-spelling /j/*j*.

miles

❶ A *mile* is a unit for measuring distance.

❷ **EXAMPLE** Her house is one *mile* from the school.

❸ **APPLY TO THE INSTRUCTION** Ask: Which of the following can be measured in *miles*: the distance you walk cross the street, the distance between two towns, the distance you walk in an hour.

❹ **SOUND-SPELLINGS** Identify the sound-spelling /m/*m*. Students can decode *miles*.

mode

❶ A *mode* is a method, or the way something is done.

❷ **EXAMPLE** Walking is a slower *mode* of travel than driving.

❸ **APPLY TO THE INSTRUCTION** Ask students what *mode* of travel they prefer and why.

❹ **SOUND-SPELLINGS** Identify the sound-spelling /m/*m*. Students can decode *mode*.

route

❶ A *route* is a way you choose to get somewhere.

❷ **EXAMPLES** We took the quickest *route* to the party because we were late. The *route* through the city is slower but there is more to look at along the way.

❸ **APPLY TO THE INSTRUCTION** Have students describe the *route* they take from home to school.

❹ **SOUND-SPELLINGS** Identify the sound-spelling /r/*r*.

transportation

❶ *Transportation* is a way to move people or things.

❷ **EXAMPLE** The students depended on the bus for *transportation* to school.

❸ **APPLY TO THE INSTRUCTION** Have students say which of the following can be used for *transportation*: cars, desks, plates, bikes, horses, fences, trains.

❹ **WORD PARTS** Run your hand under the four word parts *trans-por-ta-tion* as students read each part and then read the whole word.

views

❶ A *view* is what you can see from a certain place.

❷ **EXAMPLES** We could see *views* of the ocean and the town from the top of the mountain. The *view* on the boat ride was poor because of the fog.

❸ **APPLY TO THE INSTRUCTION** Have students describe memorable *views* they have seen.

❹ **SOUND-SPELLINGS** Identify the sound-spelling /v/*v*.

Let's Learn Amazing Words

Definitions, examples, applications, and **sound-spellings** to use with the Oral Vocabulary Routine each week.

Routine *Oral Vocabulary*

arid

1 If a place is *arid*, it is very dry.

2 **EXAMPLES** The desert is *arid* because it gets very little rainfall. The *arid* hills looked brown and dry.

3 **APPLY TO THE INSTRUCTION** Have students name one word that means the opposite of *arid* and another word that means about the same as *arid*.

4 **WORD PARTS** Run your hand under the two word parts *ar-id* as students read each part and then read the whole word.

canyon

1 A *canyon* is a narrow valley with high, steep sides.

2 **EXAMPLE** The hike to the stream at the bottom of the *canyon* was dangerous.

3 **APPLY TO THE INSTRUCTION** Have students draw a picture of a *canyon* and describe what it looks like.

4 **WORD PARTS** Students can identify the syllable *can-*.

carved

1 Something that is *carved* has been cut.

2 **EXAMPLES** The artist *carved* a face out of stone. My grandfather *carved* the turkey at dinner.

3 **APPLY TO THE INSTRUCTION** Have students give examples of places or things that look like they have been *carved* by nature.

4 **WORD PARTS** Students can identify the base word *carve* and the ending *-ed*.

cliffs

1 A *cliff* is a steep, rocky slope.

2 **EXAMPLE** The *cliffs* surrounding the village were difficult to climb.

3 **APPLY TO THE INSTRUCTION** Have students pantomime climbing a *cliff*.

4 **SOUND-SPELLINGS** Students can identify the sound-spelling /kl/*cl*.

frontier

1 The *frontier* is the place where the wilderness begins.

2 **EXAMPLE** The explorers were not sure what they would find as they headed into the *frontier*.

3 **APPLY TO THE INSTRUCTION** Ask: Would you rather live in a city or on a *frontier*? Why?

4 **WORD PARTS** Run your hand under the two word parts *fron-tier* as students read each part and then read the whole word.

guide

1 A guide is someone or something that shows the way.

2 **EXAMPLES** The museum *guide* led the school group to the dinosaur exhibit. We followed the *guide* as we hiked to the canyon.

3 **APPLY TO THE INSTRUCTION** Ask: Do you like to explore places with or without a *guide*? Why?

4 **SOUND-SPELLINGS** Students can identify the sound-spelling /g/*g*.

hiking

1 If you are *hiking*, you are taking a long walk.

2 **EXAMPLE** As part of their training, the park rangers went *hiking* every day.

3 **APPLY TO THE INSTRUCTION** Have students list some things they might take along on a *hiking* trip.

4 **WORD PARTS** Students can identify the base word *hike* and the ending *-ing*.

Oral Vocabulary Unit 1 Week 5

Let's Learn Amazing Words

Routine *Oral Vocabulary*

astonishing

❶ If something is *astonishing*, it's amazing or surprising.

❷ **EXAMPLES** The large number of people at the concert was *astonishing*. The cheetah moved with *astonishing* speed.

❸ **APPLY TO THE INSTRUCTION** Ask: What have you seen or read about that is *astonishing*?

❹ **WORD PARTS** Run your hand under the four word parts in *as-ton-ish-ing* as students read each part and then read the whole word.

eruptions

❶ An *eruption* is the bursting out of lava, water, or steam from something.

❷ **EXAMPLES** The volcano's *eruptions* shook the ground. Smoke from the *eruptions* filled the sky.

❸ **APPLY TO THE INSTRUCTION** Have students tell which of these words might be used to describe an *eruption*: rumble, calm, hiss, bubble, burst, silence.

❹ **WORD PARTS** Run your hand under the three word parts *e-rup-tions* as students read each part and then read the whole word.

formed

❶ When something is *formed*, it has taken shape.

❷ **EXAMPLES** Dark clouds are *formed* before a rainstorm. The students *formed* a straight line at the door.

❸ **APPLY TO THE INSTRUCTION** Have students tell what is *formed* when water freezes.

❹ **WORD PARTS** Students can identify the base word *form* and the ending *-ed*.

gigantic

❶ Something that is *gigantic* is very large or powerful.

❷ **EXAMPLES** The *gigantic* rock blocked the entrance to the cave. A *gigantic* wave knocked the surfer off her board.

❸ **APPLY TO THE INSTRUCTION** Have students name a word that means the opposite of *gigantic* and a word that means about the same as *gigantic*.

❹ **WORD PARTS** Run your hand under the three word parts *gi-gan-tic* as students read each part and then read the whole word.

naturally

❶ If something is made *naturally*, it is not made by humans.

❷ **EXAMPLES** The trees in the forest grow *naturally*. Some medicines are grown *naturally*, while others are made by scientists.

❸ **APPLY TO THE INSTRUCTION** Have students give examples of things that are *naturally* made, and examples of things made by humans.

❹ **WORD PARTS** Run your hand under the four word parts *nat-ur-al-ly* as students read each part and then read the whole word.

unbelievable

❶ If you think something is *unbelievable*, you think it is not true.

❷ **EXAMPLE** The band thought that their taking first place at the contest was *unbelievable*.

❸ **APPLY TO THE INSTRUCTION** Have students tell about something they've heard or seen that they thought was *unbelievable*. Have them tell why.

❹ **WORD PARTS** Run your hand under the five word parts *un-be-liev-a-ble* as students read each part and then read the whole word.

Oral Vocabulary Unit 2 Week 1

Let's Learn Amazing Words

Routine *Oral Vocabulary*

awareness

1 If you have an *awareness* of something, you know something about it.

2 **EXAMPLE** They had an *awareness* of the other team's strengths because they had seen them play before.

3 **APPLY TO THE INSTRUCTION** Ask: Why is it important to have an *awareness* of what's going on around you when you ride a bicycle?

4 **WORD PARTS** Run your hand under the three word parts *a-ware-ness* as students read each part and then read the whole word.

comprehend

1 To *comprehend* something is to understand it.

2 **EXAMPLE** The audience could not *comprehend* how the magician made the rabbit disappear.

3 **APPLY TO THE INSTRUCTION** Have students tell which of these is something a person can *comprehend*: fruits, directions, rules, colors, word meaning.

4 **WORD PARTS** Run your hand under the three word parts *com-pre-hend* as students read each part and then read the whole word.

exhibit

1 An *exhibit* is a display.

2 **EXAMPLE** We liked the museum's dinosaur *exhibit* better than the rock *exhibit*.

3 **APPLY TO THE INSTRUCTION** Have students describe a favorite *exhibit* they have seen and tell what they liked about it.

4 **WORD PARTS** Run your hand under the three word parts *ex-hib-it* as students read each part and then read the whole word.

experience

1 An *experience* is an event that you see, do, or live through.

2 **EXAMPLES** Our first *experience* riding horses was when we visited a ranch. He gained *experience* working with children by baby-sitting his little brother.

3 **APPLY TO THE INSTRUCTION** Have students describe a happy *experience* and a scary *experience*.

4 **WORD PARTS** Run your hand under the four word parts *ex-per-i-ence* as students read each part and then read the whole word.

horizons

1 *Horizons* are the ranges of your thinking or interests.

2 **EXAMPLE** She hoped traveling to a foreign country would expand her *horizons*.

3 **APPLY TO THE INSTRUCTION** Tell students that some people pursue interests, such as art classes, to expand their *horizons*. Have students tell about something they'd like to do to expand their *horizons*. Have them use the word *horizons* when they tell about it.

4 **WORD PARTS** Run your hand under the three word parts *ho-ri-zons* as students read each part and then read the whole word.

interactive

1 Something that is *interactive* lets you use more than one sense to learn about it.

2 **EXAMPLE** The children liked the *interactive* music exhibit best because the tune changed every time they pushed the buttons.

3 **APPLY TO THE INSTRUCTION** Have students identify different characteristics of *interactive* exhibits and compare them to non-*interactive* exhibits.

4 **WORD PARTS** Run your hand under the four word parts *in-ter-ac-tive* as students read each part and then read the whole word.

Oral Vocabulary Unit 2 Week 2

Let's Learn Amazing Words

Routine *Oral Vocabulary*

accomplished

❶ If you *accomplished* something, you completed it.

❷ **EXAMPLES** The birds *accomplished* the job of building a nest. After working hard all afternoon, we *accomplished* our goal of cleaning up the park.

❸ **APPLY TO THE INSTRUCTION** Have students describe a task or project they have *accomplished*, and how it made them feel.

❹ **WORD PARTS** Run your hand under the three word parts *ac-com-plished* as students read each part and then read the whole word.

collaboration

❶ A *collaboration* is working together to get something done.

❷ **EXAMPLE** The *collaboration* of musicians and dancers made the show run smoothly.

❸ **APPLY TO THE INSTRUCTION** Have students name a job that would be made easier or better by *collaboration*.

❹ **WORD PARTS** Run your hand under the five word parts *col-lab-o-ra-tion* as students read each part and then read the whole word.

cooperate

❶ People who *cooperate* work together.

❷ **EXAMPLE** We decided to *cooperate* on the project rather than work on our own.

❸ **APPLY TO THE INSTRUCTION** Have students name a word that means the opposite of *cooperate* and a word that means about the same as *cooperate*.

❹ **WORD PARTS** Run your hand under the four word parts *co-op-e-rate* as students read each part and then read the whole word.

members

❶ If you are a *member*, you are a part of a group.

❷ **EXAMPLES** The *members* of the drama club meet after school once a week. All the students in our class are *members* of the class.

❸ **APPLY TO THE INSTRUCTION** Have students identify people, animals, and things that are *members* of a specific group.

❹ **SOUND-SPELLINGS** Identify the sound-spelling /m/*m*. Students can decode *members*.

orchestra

❶ An *orchestra* is a group of musicians who play strings, brass, woodwinds, and percussion instruments.

❷ **EXAMPLES** The orchestra played beautiful music. The violin player was part of the *orchestra*.

❸ **APPLY TO THE INSTRUCTION** Have students list instruments that are played in an *orchestra*.

❹ **WORD PARTS** Run your hand under the three word parts *or-ches-tra* as students read each part and then read the whole word.

teamwork

❶ *Teamwork* is people working together to get something done.

❷ **EXAMPLE** Thanks to *teamwork*, the class collected hundreds of bottles and cans for recycling.

❸ **APPLY TO THE INSTRUCTION** Have students describe a time they relied on *teamwork* to make a job go more quickly or easily.

❹ **WORD PARTS** Run your hand under the two word parts *team-work* as students read each part and then read the whole word.

Oral Vocabulary Unit 2 Week 3

Let's Learn *Amazing Words*

Routine *Oral Vocabulary*

extraordinary

1 When something is *extraordinary*, it is very unusual or special.

2 **EXAMPLE** The storm was terrible, but the rainbow that followed was *extraordinary*.

3 **APPLY TO THE INSTRUCTION** Have students name a word that means the opposite of *extraordinary* and a word that means about the same as *extraordinary*.

4 **WORD PARTS** Run your hand under the five word parts *ex-traor-di-nar-y* as students read each part and then read the whole word.

fantastic

1 Things that are *fantastic* cause wonder or surprise.

2 **EXAMPLES** The fireworks were *fantastic*. The view of the sunset from the beach was *fantastic*.

3 **APPLY TO THE INSTRUCTION** Have students tell about something they think is *fantastic*, and why.

4 **WORD PARTS** Students can identify the syllable *fan-*.

inspiration

1 If something is an *inspiration*, it has a strong effect on what you feel or do.

2 **EXAMPLES** The artist got her *inspiration* from nature. Our *inspiration* for the song we wrote came from bird songs.

3 **APPLY TO THE INSTRUCTION** Have students choose something from nature to use as an *inspiration* for an art project.

4 **WORD PARTS** Run your hand under the four word parts *in-spi-ra-tion* as students read each part and then read the whole word.

sculptures

1 A *sculpture* is a piece of art made from stone, wood, clay, or other material.

2 **EXAMPLES** The stone *sculptures* in the garden looked like real people. The artist used clay to make *sculptures* of animals.

3 **APPLY TO THE INSTRUCTION** Have students sketch a plan for a *sculpture* and describe what materials they would use to make it.

4 **WORD PARTS** Run your hand under the two word parts *sculp-ture* as students read each part and then read the whole word.

skillful

1 A *skillful* person has ability, knowledge, or experience.

2 **EXAMPLE** We could tell the carpenter was *skillful* because the house he built was both sturdy and beautiful.

3 **APPLY TO THE INSTRUCTION** Ask students to describe the similarities and differences between being *skillful* and being talented. Ask which they would rather be and why.

4 **SOUND-SPELLINGS** Students can identify the sound-spelling /sk/*sk*.

Oral Vocabulary Unit 2 Week 4

Let's Learn Amazing Words

Routine *Oral Vocabulary*

career

1 A *career* is a job or profession.

2 **EXAMPLE** My cousin's *career* as a veterinarian is perfect for her because she loves animals.

3 **APPLY TO THE INSTRUCTION** Have students identify the words that name *careers* as you say them: teacher, sister, firefighter, friend, artist, boy, coach.

4 **SOUND-SPELLINGS** Students can identify the sound-spelling /k/*c*.

contribution

1 When you make a *contribution*, you give money, help, or advice.

2 **EXAMPLES** The class made a twenty-dollar *contribution* to help save the rainforest. Her *contribution* to the bake sale was a dozen cookies.

3 **APPLY TO THE INSTRUCTION** Have students discuss *contributions* that people make that are not monetary.

4 **WORD PARTS** Run your hand under the four word parts *con-tri-bu-tion* as students read each part and then read the whole word.

energy

1 *Energy* is the power to work, move, and play.

2 **EXAMPLES** He had so much *energy* he raked all the leaves by himself. Electricity is a source of *energy* that we use.

3 **APPLY TO THE INSTRUCTION** Have students pantomime things you can do when you have *energy*, and how you look when you have no *energy*.

4 **WORD PARTS** Run your hand under the three word parts *en-er-gy* as students read each part and then read the whole word.

gear

1 *Gear* is the equipment needed for an activity.

2 **EXAMPLES** They packed a tent and other *gear* they would need for the camping trip. We had all of our soccer *gear*, including cleats and shin guards.

3 **APPLY TO THE INSTRUCTION** Have students identify *gear* they might need for one of the following: a hike, a trip to the beach, a baseball game, a picnic, a walk in the rain.

4 **SOUND-SPELLINGS** Students can identify the sound-spelling /g/*g*.

option

1 An *option* is a choice.

2 **EXAMPLE** When it began raining, one *option* was to head back to the car, while the other *option* was to keep hiking.

3 **APPLY TO THE INSTRUCTION** Describe a situation, such as losing your lunch money, and have students give *options* of what can be done in that situation.

4 **WORD PARTS** Run your hand under the two word parts *op-tion* as students read each part and then read the whole word.

workers

1 *Workers* are people who do a job.

2 **EXAMPLES** The *workers* finished painting the house on time. The owner praised the *workers* for their skill and hard work.

3 **APPLY TO THE INSTRUCTION** Have students identify some jobs that *workers* in their community do.

4 **WORD PARTS** Run your hand under the two word parts *work-ers* as students read each part and then read the whole word.

Oral Vocabulary Unit 2 Week 5

Let's Learn Amazing Words

Routine *Oral Vocabulary*

capital

1 The *capital* of a state or country is the city where the government is located and where the laws are made.

2 EXAMPLE The *capital* of Wisconsin is Madison.

3 APPLY TO THE INSTRUCTION Have students look at a map and identify the *capital* of your state and neighboring states.

4 WORD PARTS Students can identify the syllable *cap-*.

Capitol

1 The *Capitol* is the building in Washington, D.C., in which Congress meets.

2 EXAMPLE On our tour of Washington, D.C., we visited the *Capitol* and the White House.

3 APPLY TO THE INSTRUCTION Show pictures of the *Capitol*. Have students tell what they notice about the building.

4 WORD PARTS Students can identify the syllable *cap-*.

dedicated

1 If something is *dedicated*, it has been set apart for a purpose.

2 EXAMPLE The author *dedicated* the book to her daughter.

3 APPLY TO THE INSTRUCTION Have students pretend they are authors and tell why they *dedicated* "their book" to someone they know.

4 WORD PARTS Run your hand under the four word parts *ded-i-cat-ed* as students read each part and then read the whole word.

executive

1 An *executive* is someone who runs a business or a department of a government.

2 EXAMPLE Her mother ran the company; she was the top *executive*.

3 APPLY TO THE INSTRUCTION Ask students to name something they think a good *executive* might do. Have them use *executive* in their answer.

4 WORD PARTS Run your hand under the four word parts *ex-ec-u-tive* as students read each part and then read the whole word.

memorabilia

1 *Memorabilia* are things or events saved for remembering.

2 EXAMPLES My brother collects *memorabilia* from baseball games, such as ticket stubs and programs. All of our family's *memorabilia* is stored in the attic.

3 APPLY TO THE INSTRUCTION Ask students what kind of *memorabilia* they collect or would like to collect and why.

4 WORD PARTS Run your hand under the six word parts *mem-or-a-bil-i-a* as students read each part and then read the whole word.

museum

1 A *museum* is a building that displays a collection of objects related to science, ancient life, art, or other subjects.

2 EXAMPLE They visited the science *museum* in order to learn more about electricity.

3 APPLY TO THE INSTRUCTION Have students identify different characteristics of a science *museum* and an art *museum*.

4 WORD PARTS Run your hand under the three word parts *mu-se-um* as students read each part and then read the whole word.

Oral Vocabulary Unit 3 Week 1

Let's Learn Amazing Words

Definitions, examples, applications, and **sound-spellings** to use with the Oral Vocabulary Routine each week.

Routine *Oral Vocabulary*

arrangement

❶ An *arrangement* is the way or order in which things are arranged or set up.

❷ **EXAMPLE** You can use *arrangements* of triangles to make diamonds and squares.

❸ **APPLY TO THE INSTRUCTION** Have volunteers arrange several classroom objects and then describe their *arrangement*.

❹ **WORD PARTS** Run your hand under the three word parts *ar-range-ment* as students say each part and then read the whole word.

---

available

❶ If something is *available*, you can get it or use it.

❷ **EXAMPLE** She was not *available* to baby-sit on Saturday.

❸ **APPLY TO THE INSTRUCTION** Have students say *available* for each thing they can use in your classroom: computer, map, skateboard, markers, blender, rulers.

❹ **WORD PARTS** Run your hand under the four word parts *a-vail-a-ble* as students read each part and then read the whole word.

landscape

❶ A *landscape* is a view of scenery from one place.

❷ **EXAMPLES** The explorers stood on a hill and studied the *landscape*. In summer, the *landscape* outside our door is rolling and green.

❸ **APPLY TO THE INSTRUCTION** Have students describe the *landscape* outside your school.

❹ **WORD PARTS** Students can identify the syllable *land-*.

---

patterns

❶ *Patterns* are the ways in which colors or shapes appear over and over again in order.

❷ **EXAMPLES** The quilt had a *pattern* of red and blue squares. There were interesting *patterns* on the tiles of the kitchen floor.

❸ **APPLY TO THE INSTRUCTION** Have students create *patterns* of shapes or colors and then describe their *patterns*.

❹ **WORD PARTS** Students can identify the syllable *pat-*.

repeats

❶ If you *repeat* something, you do it or make it again.

❷ **EXAMPLE** He *repeats* the dance steps over and over until he knows them by heart.

❸ **APPLY TO THE INSTRUCTION** Have students play a game of telephone. Challenge them to *repeat* exactly what they hear.

❹ **WORD PARTS** Run your hand under the two word parts *re-peats* as students read each part and then read the whole word.

---

reveal

❶ To *reveal* something is to make it known.

❷ **EXAMPLE** The audience asked the performer to *reveal* the secret to the trick.

❸ **APPLY TO THE INSTRUCTION** Have students name a word that means the opposite of *reveal* and a word that means about the same as *reveal*.

❹ **WORD PARTS** Run your hand under the two word parts *re-veal* as students read each part and then read the whole word.

snowfall

❶ *Snowfall* is snow that has fallen in an area.

❷ **EXAMPLES** The *snowfall* was heavy and wet. The *snowfall* covered the trees and houses.

❸ **APPLY TO THE INSTRUCTION** Have students describe what the landscape might look like after a heavy *snowfall*.

❹ **WORD PARTS** Run your hand under the two word parts *snow-fall* as students read each part and then read the whole word.

Oral Vocabulary Unit 3 Week 2

Let's Learn Amazing Words

Routine *Oral Vocabulary*

migrate

1. To *migrate* means to go from one place to another when the seasons change.
2. **EXAMPLES** Many birds *migrate* south each winter. Some animals travel great distances when they *migrate*.
3. **APPLY TO THE INSTRUCTION** Ask: If you were a bird, where would you *migrate* to? Why?
4. **SOUND-SPELLINGS** Identify the sound-spelling /mī/*mi*. Students can decode *migrate*.

observe

1. If you *observe* something, you look at it carefully in order to learn about it.
2. **EXAMPLES** Scientists *observe* people to learn how they behave. We went to the zoo to *observe* the animals.
3. **APPLY TO THE INSTRUCTION** Have students look out your classroom window and tell what they *observe*.
4. **WORD PARTS** Run your hand under the two word parts *ob-serve* as students read each part and then read the whole word.

refuges

1. *Refuges* are shelters that offer protection from danger or trouble.
2. **EXAMPLES** Many people used the school building as a *refuge* from the storm. People in wildlife *refuges* help care for certain animals.
3. **APPLY TO THE INSTRUCTION** Ask students to say a sentence using *refuges*.
4. **WORD PARTS** Run your hand under the three word parts *ref-u-ges* as students read each part and then read the whole word.

shelter

1. A *shelter* is something that covers or protects you from the weather or danger.
2. **EXAMPLES** We ran into the house for *shelter* from the sudden storm. An umbrella provides *shelter* from the rain.
3. **APPLY TO THE INSTRUCTION** Have students list things that can provide *shelter* from the sun.
4. **SOUND-SPELLINGS** Identify the sound-spelling /sh/*sh*. Students can decode *shelter*.

zones

1. A *zone* is any area thought of as different from other areas. A *zone* can also be any of the five great divisions of the Earth's surface.
2. **EXAMPLE** Each of the five *zones* on Earth has a different climate.
3. **APPLY TO THE INSTRUCTION** Have students give examples of different *zones* they are familiar with, such as a quiet zone or a no-food zone.
4. **SOUND-SPELLINGS** Identify the sound-spelling /z/*z*. Students can decode *zones*.

Oral Vocabulary Unit 3 Week 3

Let's Learn Amazing Words

Definitions, examples, applications, and **sound-spellings** to use with the Oral Vocabulary Routine each week.

Routine *Oral Vocabulary*

dazed

❶ If you are *dazed*, you are unable to think clearly.

❷ **EXAMPLES** He was *dazed* after he fell from his bike. Some people feel *dazed* after a long train ride.

❸ **APPLY TO THE INSTRUCTION** Have students name a word that means almost the same as *dazed*.

❹ **WORD PARTS** Students can identify the base word *daze* and the ending *-ed*.

hemisphere

❶ A *hemisphere* is one half of Earth's surface.

❷ **EXAMPLE** The United States is located in the Northern *hemisphere* and the Western *hemisphere*.

❸ **APPLY TO THE INSTRUCTION** Have students look at a globe or atlas. Have them make up sentences using the word *hemisphere* that describe where different countries are located.

❹ **WORD PARTS** Run your hand under the three word parts *hem-i-sphere* as students read each part and then read the whole word.

nocturnal

❶ If something is *nocturnal*, it is active during the night.

❷ **EXAMPLE** *Nocturnal* animals, such as owls, sleep during the day and hunt at night.

❸ **APPLY TO THE INSTRUCTION** Have students discuss whether they would prefer to be *nocturnal*, or active during the day, and why.

❹ **WORD PARTS** Run your hand under the three word parts *noc-tur-nal* as students read each part and then read the whole word.

revolution

❶ A *revolution* is a movement in a circle or curve around some point.

❷ **EXAMPLES** After one *revolution*, the ferris wheel stopped and the passengers got off. It takes a year for Earth to complete a *revolution* around the sun.

❸ **APPLY TO THE INSTRUCTION** Have students demonstrate how one object completes a *revolution* around another object.

❹ **WORD PARTS** Run your hand under the four word parts *rev-o-lu-tion* as students read each part and then read the whole word.

rotation

❶ A *rotation* is the act of turning around a center.

❷ **EXAMPLE** Earth is constantly turning; this *rotation* causes day and night.

❸ **APPLY TO THE INSTRUCTION** Have students demonstrate the movement of an object that is in *rotation*.

❹ **WORD PARTS** Run your hand under the three word parts *ro-ta-tion* as students read each part and then read the whole word.

vacation

❶ If you are on *vacation*, you are resting or taking a break from work, school, or other duties.

❷ **EXAMPLES** The entire school was closed for summer *vacation*. The family went to the country for a *vacation*.

❸ **APPLY TO THE INSTRUCTION** Have students tell which activity someone is more likely to do on a *vacation* and why: swim at the beach or write a report.

❹ **WORD PARTS** Run your hand under the three word parts *va-ca-tion* as students read each part and then read the whole word.

Oral Vocabulary Unit 3 Week 4

Let's Learn **Amazing Words**

Definitions, examples, applications, and **sound-spellings** to use with the Oral Vocabulary Routine each week.

Routine *Oral Vocabulary*

behavior

1 Your *behavior* is the way that you act.

2 **EXAMPLES** The clown's *behavior* was very silly. The dog's *behavior* during the storm showed that he was frightened.

3 **APPLY TO THE INSTRUCTION** Have students demonstrate different kinds of *behavior*.

4 **WORD PARTS** Run your hand under the three word parts *be-hav-ior* as students read each part and then read the whole word.

coast

1 The *coast* is the land along the sea.

2 **EXAMPLES** We could see ships anchored in the water just off the *coast*. The captain's house was located on the *coast* so he'd be near the ocean.

3 **APPLY TO THE INSTRUCTION** Have students describe sights and sounds you might see along a *coast*.

4 **SOUND-SPELLINGS** Identify the sound-spelling /k/*c*. Students can decode *coast*.

inland

1 If something is *inland*, it is away from the coast or the border.

2 **EXAMPLES** The people traveled *inland* in order to escape the storm along the coast. The state capital was located *inland*, far from the sea.

3 **APPLY TO THE INSTRUCTION** Ask students to tell if they would prefer to live *inland* or along a coast and give reasons for their answer.

4 **WORD PARTS** Run your hand under the two word parts *in-land* as students read each part and then read the whole word.

phenomenon

1 A *phenomenon* is someone or something that is extraordinary or remarkable.

2 **EXAMPLES** Everyone thought the winner of the race was a *phenomenon* because she was so young. The meteorite shower was a *phenomenon*.

3 **APPLY TO THE INSTRUCTION** Ask: Is something that is a *phenomenon* likely to happen every day or rarely? Explain.

4 **WORD PARTS** Run your hand under the four word parts *phe-nom-e-non* as students read each part and then read the whole word.

tsunami

1 A *tsunami* is a long, high sea wave caused by an underwater earthquake or other disturbance.

2 **EXAMPLES** The *tsunami* destroyed the seaside town. Everyone moved away from the coast when they heard the *tsunami* was coming.

3 **APPLY TO THE INSTRUCTION** Have students use adjectives to tell what they think a *tsunami* would look and sound like.

4 **WORD PARTS** Run your hand under the three word parts *tsu-na-mi* as students read each part and then read the whole word.

unpredictable

1 If something is *unpredictable*, it is uncertain.

2 **EXAMPLES** The weather in spring can be *unpredictable*. The cat's moods were *unpredictable*.

3 **APPLY TO THE INSTRUCTION** Have students give an example of something that is *unpredictable*.

4 **WORD PARTS** Run your hand under the five word parts *un-pre-dict-a-ble* as students read each part and then read the whole word.

Oral Vocabulary Unit 3 Week 5

Let's Learn Amazing Words

Definitions, examples, applications, and **sound-spellings** to use with the Oral Vocabulary Routine each week.

Routine *Oral Vocabulary*

benefits

❶ *Benefits* are things that help someone or something.

❷ **EXAMPLES** One of the *benefits* of exercise is good health. One of the *benefits* of living in a small town is that you can walk everywhere.

❸ **APPLY TO THE INSTRUCTION** Ask: What are the *benefits* of going to school? Use *benefits* in your answer.

❹ **WORD PARTS** Run your hand under the three word parts *ben-e-fits* as students read each part and then read the whole word.

---

cells

❶ *Cells* are units in devices that change chemical or solar energy into electricity.

❷ **EXAMPLE** The electricity in the house came from solar *cells*.

❸ **APPLY TO THE INSTRUCTION** Ask students to name things that solar *cells* might be used for.

❹ **SOUND-SPELLINGS** Identify the sound-spelling /s/*c*. Students can decode *cells*.

electricity

❶ *Electricity* is energy that can produce light, heat, or motion.

❷ **EXAMPLES** Without *electricity*, our school would have no heat or light. During the storm, we had no *electricity*, so we had to use flashlights to see.

❸ **APPLY TO THE INSTRUCTION** Have students list all of the things they depend on *electricity* for. Discuss what life would be like without *electricity*.

❹ **WORD PARTS** Run your hand under the five word parts *e-lec-tric-i-ty* as students read each part and then read the whole word.

---

hydrogen

❶ *Hydrogen* is a colorless gas that burns easily.

❷ **EXAMPLES** *Hydrogen* combines with oxygen to form water. *Hydrogen* weighs less than any other substance.

❸ **APPLY TO THE INSTRUCTION** Tell students that *hydrogen* is a chemical. Ask them to give examples of other chemicals.

❹ **WORD PARTS** Run your hand under the three word parts *hy-dro-gen* as students read each part and then read the whole word.

---

resources

❶ *Resources* are things that meet needs.

❷ **EXAMPLES** The state's *resources* included a large lake and acres of forest. Scientists are trying to find ways to use the sun and wind as *resources* for energy.

❸ **APPLY TO THE INSTRUCTION** Have students list some of their state or community *resources*.

❹ **WORD PARTS** Run your hand under the three word parts *re-sour-ces* as students read each part and then read the whole word.

solar

❶ Things that are *solar* are of or from the sun.

❷ **EXAMPLES** The house had *solar* panels built into the roof. The school uses *solar* energy to provide electricity.

❸ **APPLY TO THE INSTRUCTION** Have students tell why a car that uses *solar* energy can only run during the day.

❹ **WORD PARTS** Students can identify the syllables *so-* and *-lar*. Students can decode *solar*.

Word List

Unit 1 Week 1 Diversity

Closed Syllables with Short Vowels

absent	different	husbands	practice	
admit	dinner	impress	project	
bonnet	dollar	invent	puppet	
bottle	dragons	lesson	ribbon	
button	eggplant	listen	shepherds	
children	followed	messages	velvet	
cinnamon	fossil	mumbled	understanding	
connect	gallons	mustard	weddings	
cultural	hollow	pancakes	witness	
customs	hundred	plantains		
differ	hundreds	plaster		

Concept Vocabulary

backgrounds
culture
ethnic
homesick
translated
understanding

Unit 1 Week 2 Exploration

Closed Syllables with Long Vowels

admire	confused	intone	tadpole
arrived	device	invite	trombone
arrives	escape	mistake	
compete	escaped	mistakes	
compute	explore	outrage	
concede	inhale	reptile	
confine	inside	subscribe	

Concept Vocabulary

area
confused
device
perspective
pioneers
territory
voyage

Unit 1 Week 3 Travel America

Plurals and Inflected Endings -s, -es, -ies

ants	hundreds	promises	views
attractions	landmarks	raises	volunteers
blisters	lanes	roads	walkers
bridges	looks	routes	walks
cars	lots	shoes	walls
changes	marshmallows	sights	weighs
coaches	miles	sounds	workers
congratulations	Millers	stations	
cousins	millions	stops	crosses
days	months	survivors	crutches
desserts	needs	televisions	
destinations	organizes	things	cities
dollars	parts	tons	companies
ears	passengers	tourists	families
flights	patients	towers	flurries
forms	pictures	towns	itineraries
friends	places	travelers	memories
groups	planes	travels	movies
headphones	pledges	treatments	stories
highways	postcards	valleys	worries
hours	pours	vehicles	

Concept Vocabulary

itineraries
journey
miles
mode
route
transportation
views

Unit 1 Word List

Unit 1 Week 4 The Southwest

Verb Endings

added	lived	tired	filming	
asked	looked	turned	frightening	
attached	loved	used	hiking	
attracted	needed	visited	hoping	
blamed	opened	waited	looking	
called	painted	walked	parking	
carved	passed	wanted	racing	
changed	picked	watched	rising	
chatted	pinned	whispered	running	
created	pointed	wondered	shopping	
destroyed	pounded	worked	sitting	
died	pulled		sleeping	
filmed	reached	baking	slipping	
followed	remembered	biting	standing	
grabbed	roamed	climbing	stunning	
granted	searched	driving	swimming	
herded	sobbed	enjoying	thrilling	
hired	spotted	facing		
improved	starred	falling		
learned	striped	fighting		

Concept Vocabulary

arid
canyon
carved
cliffs
frontier
guide
hiking

Unit 1 Week 5 The West

Prefixes *un-, re-, in-, dis-*

unbelievable	unspoiled	reappear	disagree
unbroken	unspoken	redirect	disapprove
uncertain	unusual	reread	disconnect
unclear	unwelcoming	rerecord	dishonest
		indefinite	
		indirect	
		injustice	
		insincere	

Concept Vocabulary

astonishing
eruptions
formed
gigantic
naturally
unbelievable

Unit 2 Word List

Unit 2 Week 1 New Ideas

Syllables with *r*-Controlled *ar, or, ore*

are	jar	fortune	portrait
artists	large	horizons	sport
bombard	largest	important	tornado
carpet	radar	inform	
carton	solar	information	explore
cartoons	stars	meteorologist	ignore
darling	tarnish	morning	more
darted		north	restore
garlic	for	or	wore
harbor	forgery	order	
hard	forget	performance	
	forgot	popcorn	

Concept Vocabulary

awareness
comprehend
exhibit
experience
horizons
interactive

Unit 2 Week 2 Working Together

Syllables with *r*-Controlled *er, ir, ur*

another	larger	printer	thirty
better	later	quarterback	virtue
certain	members	remember	
certainly	never	reporter	curtain
deliver	newspaper	scenery	future
determined	other	servant	nursery
disaster	others	soccer	pursue
father	percussion	teacher	treasure
gathering	perfect	together	turkey
grandmother	perfume		turn
her	person	circle	turning
interested	players	circus	turtle
ladder	posters	thirteen	

Concept Vocabulary

accomplished
collaboration
cooperate
members
orchestra
teamwork

Unit 2 Week 3 Team Effort

Comparative Endings *-er, -est*

angrier	louder	fastest	safest
bluer	stronger	funniest	scariest
crazier	sturdier	greatest	silliest
earlier	wider	hardest	simplest
fancier		highest	sturdiest
harder	craziest	largest	surest
higher	earliest	lightest	widest
longer	fanciest	longest	

Concept Vocabulary

extraordinary
fantastic
inspiration
sculptures
skillful

Unit 2 Word List

Unit 2 Week 4 A Job Well Done

Open (V/CV) and Closed (VC/V) Syllables

amazed	locate	animals	living
apart	making	body	model
before	music	closet	money
began	nature	columns	planet
camel	never	drawings	positive
famous	notice	elevated	project
female	paper	experienced	promise
fever	papers	family	second
finally	pilot	finish	study
humor	Rosie	finished	
Jamie	safer	glamorous	
legal	solution	knowing	
lemon	super	linen	

Concept Vocabulary

career
contribution
energy
gear
option
workers

Unit 2 Week 5 Our Nation's Capital

Suffixes -ly, -ful, -ness, -less

daily	frightful	awareness	breathless
neatly	joyful	bitterness	countless
sadly	powerful	kindness	heartless
slowly	thoughtful	laziness	timeless
smoothly	wonderful	sweetness	
surprisingly			
wildly			

Concept Vocabulary

capital
Capitol
dedicated
executive
memorabilia
museum

Unit 3 Word List

Long a Spelled ai, ay

available	painted	always	Saturday
claim	plain	birthday	say
contain	proclaim	clay	subway
exclaim	rain	crayfish	today
explain	rainbow	days	way
explained	raindrop	may	
fainted	rained	maybe	
gain	regain	layered	
paint	wait	replay	

Concept Vocabulary

arrangement
available
landscape
patterns
repeats
reveal
snowfall

Long e Spelled e, ee, ea

be	feet	three	heaters
because	free	tree	leading
before	freezer	trees	leaves
ecology	freedom		leaving
equator	freezing	clean	ordeal
even	geese	downstream	reach
maybe	keep	each	read
remember	need	eagerly	reason
	needed	easier	seasons
between	see	easily	southeast
deep	seeds	eastern	streams
deeper	seen	eat	
feed	sheep	heat	
feeders	sleepless	heater	

Concept Vocabulary

migrate
observe
refuges
shelter
zones

Contractions

it's	we'll	couldn't	won't
let's	I'll	didn't	wouldn't
that's	you'll	doesn't	
		mustn't	could've
I'm	aren't	shouldn't	would've
	can't		

Concept Vocabulary

dazed
hemisphere
nocturnal
revolution
rotation
vacation

Unit 3 Word List

Unit 3 Week 4 Storms

Long o Spelled oa, ow

				Concept Vocabulary
approaching	floating	bowling	snow	behavior
bloated	foamy	follow	swallow	coast
charcoal	loaded	outgrow	swallowed	inland
coast	tugboat	rainbow		phenomenon
coastal		slowly		tsunami
				unpredictable

Unit 3 Week 5 Going Green

Prefixes mis-, non-, over-, pre-, mid-

				Concept Vocabulary
misfortune	overactive	precaution	midseason	benefits
misunderstand	overpriced	premature	midstream	cells
	oversized	prepaid	midway	electricity
nonfiction		preview	midweek	hydrogen
nonrenewable				resources
nonstop				solar

Unit 4 Word List

Unit 4 Week 1 Perception

Compound Words

anything	gentleman	sometimes	watercolor
cannot	handcuffed	stovetop	waterfall
Englishman	handcuffs	tabletop	workman
fireman	handmade	underground	
Frenchman	something	underwater	

Concept Vocabulary

illusion
invisible
magician
mysterious
perception
vanish

Unit 4 Week 2 Wild Things

Long *i* Spelled *igh, ie*, Final *y*

brightest	cries	deny	python
fighting	fireflies	dragonfly	satisfy
frightened	lie	dry	shy
higher	replied	fly	shyness
might	terrified	fry	skylight
nighttime		hydrant	try
sighing	cry	July	why
	crying	lullaby	

Concept Vocabulary

communication
instinct
protect
relationships
response
sense
young

Unit 4 Week 3 Secret Codes

Consonant + *le*

able	cycle	purple	stable
angle	doubles	puzzle	stifle
babble	example	rifle	stumble
Bittle	gentle	ripple	tumble
bubble	giggle	scrambles	twinkle
bugle	little	shuffle	uncle
cable	middle	simple	unscramble
crackle	noble	single	visible
cradle	possible	sniffle	

Concept Vocabulary

conceals
creative
exchange
interprets
transmit
visible

Unit 4 **Word List**

Unit 4 Week 4 **Communication**

Diphthongs *ou, ow /ou/*

				Concept Vocabulary
around	surround	clowns	powerful	combine
couches	thousand	coward	touchdown	conversation
countless	touchdown	download	towel	dialect
foundation	without	downstairs	township	phrase
grounded		downtown		region
hourly	allowance	flowering		shouts
shout	breakdown	frowning		symbols

Unit 4 Week 5 **Finding Clues**

Suffixes *-er, -or, -ish, -ous*

				Concept Vocabulary
biker	collector	childish	curious	convince
builder	director	foolish	dangerous	curious
diver	editor	impish	joyous	diver
explorer	inventor	Scottish	monstrous	evidence
officer	investigator	selfish	mysterious	explorer
reporter	senator	sheepish	nervous	investigate
			venomous	scrutiny

Unit 5 Word List

Unit 5 Week 1 Emergencies

Diphthongs *oi, oy*

avoid	pointing	annoying	enjoying
broiler	poisonous	boy	oysters
coins	recoil	boyish	royal
moisture	sirloin	destroyed	royalty
noisiest	viewpoint	disloyal	toys
point	voice	employer	

Concept Vocabulary

dangerous
destroyed
exciting
hazards
hero
profession

Unit 5 Week 2 Past Times

Common Syllables *-ion, -tion, -sion, -ture*

champion	civilizations	traditions	architecture
companion	Constitution	vacation	creature
region	generations		future
religion	irrigation	admission	lecture
	location	division	mature
attractions	pollution	fusion	picture
celebration	station	permission	pictures
civilization	tradition		

Concept Vocabulary

ancient
civilization
society
statue
theater
traditions

Unit 5 Week 3 Adventures and Heroes

Syllables with Vowel Combinations *oo, ew, ue*

bamboo	spoon	knew	blueberry
boots	too	news	clueless
food	toolbox	outgrew	clues
foolish	toolboxes	renew	continued
groom	troop	view	glue
moon		withdrew	true
rooftop	cashew		untrue
scoop	dew	avenue	
soon	few	blue	

Concept Vocabulary

adventure
expeditions
forecasts
unfamiliar
wilderness

Unit 5 Word List

Unit 5 Week 4 Extreme Homes

Vowel Sound in *ball*: *a, al, au, aw, augh, ough*

water	hallway	assault	awful
waterproof	install	Australia	hawkish
	smallest	Australian	jawbone
all	stalking	Australians	outlaw
also	tall	caution	straw
boardwalk	walking	faulty	
called	walls	hauled	daughter
fallen		laundry	coughing
		pauper	

Concept Vocabulary

adapted
architecture
burrow
extreme
homesteaders
prairie

Unit 5 Week 5 The Moon

Suffixes *-hood, -ment, -y, -en*

adulthood	embarrassment	lucky	earthen
brotherhood	enjoyment	messy	golden
childhood	improvement	salty	wooden
		shadowy	
amazement	cloudy		
contentment	dirty	ashen	

Concept Vocabulary

astronaut
astronomers
craters
mission
myths
satellite

Unit 6 Word List

Unit 6 Week 1 Opportunity Knocks

Syllables with Short e Spelled ea

breakfast	headline	ready	unhealthy
breath	heaven	spread	wealth
feather	heavier	steady	weather
gingerbread	instead	sweating	
head	read	threatening	

Concept Vocabulary
circumstances
conviction
devised
model
procrastinates
suggested

Unit 6 Week 2 Challenges

Syllables with Vowels oo in foot, u in put

barefoot	crooked	underfoot	pushed
book	driftwood	unhook	put
boyhood	football		putting
cookbook	goodness	input	
cookie	outlook	output	

Concept Vocabulary
achieved
furious
hurdles
perseverance
personality
timid

Unit 6 Week 3 American Journeys

Syllables with Long i: -ind, -ild, Long o: -ost, -old

find	rewind	almost	behold
findings		ghostly	cold
grinder	childhood	hostess	household
kind	mildly	most	resold
kindness	wildlife	outpost	
remind		utmost	

Concept Vocabulary
appreciate
awkward
barrier
immigration
international
occupations

Unit 6 **Word List**

Unit 6 Week 4 Grand Gestures

Syllables V/V

created	idea	piano	rodeo
diary	Indiana	poetry	ruined
diet	iodine	quiet	science
doing	librarian	radio	sundial
experience	meteor	react	triumph
flying	museum	real	video
fuel	nutrient	realize	violets

Concept Vocabulary

apply
determined
distinguishes
efficient
headway
progress

Unit 6 Week 5 Space

Related Words

astronomer	imaginary	scenery	telegraph
astronomy	imagination	scenes	telepathy
discover	imagine	scenic	telephone
discovered	real	science	telescope
discovery	realistic	science fiction	television
future	relate	scientific	universal
futuristic	relationship	scientist	universe
imagery	relative	telecommute	university
images	scenario	telegram	

Concept Vocabulary

complex
futuristic
galaxy
scientific
telescope
universe

Student's Name _____ Date _____

Level D *My Sidewalks*

Observation Checklist

Use this checklist to record your observations of students' reading skills and behaviors.

	Always (Proficient)	Sometimes (Developing)	Rarely (Novice)
Applies knowledge of letter-sounds to decode words			
Uses word structure and syllabication to decode longer words			
Reads at an appropriate reading rate			
Reads with appropriate intonation and stress			
Uses concept vocabulary in discussion			
Previews and uses prior knowledge to understand text			
Asks questions while reading			
Recognizes main ideas			
Recognizes sequence			
Makes comparisons and contrasts			
Draws conclusions to understand text			
Understands story structure (character, setting, plot)			
Summarizes plot or main ideas accurately			
Responds thoughtfully to the text			

General Comments

Word Parts

Students need to become familiar with meaningful parts of words so they can recognize them instantly as they read. This will improve both their reading fluency and the size of their vocabulary. Teach the meaning and pronunciation of these common word parts whenever students encounter them in words they are reading.

Common Prefixes	Meaning	Examples
bi-	two	bicycle
bio-	life	biology
dis-	not; opposite	disagree, disarm, disobey, disrespect
geo-	earth	geology
in-, im-, il-, ir-	not	injustice, insane, impolite, impossible, illegal, illiterate, irregular, irresponsible
micro-	small	microscope
mid-	during; middle	midnight, midsummer, midyear
mis-	bad; not; wrongly	misbehave, misfire, misspell, misunderstand
mono-	one	monologue, monorail
non-	not	nonfiction, nonstop, nonviolent
out-	surpassing	outbid, outdo, outlive
over-	over; too much	overdo, overlook, overpriced
photo-	light	photocopy, photosynthesis
post-	after	postwar
pre-	before	preview
re-	again	redo, retell, return, rewrite
tele-	far; distant	telescope, telephone, telegraph, television
tri-	three	triplets
un-	not	undo, unkind, uncut, unhappy, unsafe, unlucky
under-	below; less than	underpriced, underground, undercover

Common Suffixes	Meaning	Examples
-er, -or	doer; one who	teacher, painter, writer, actor, sailor, visitor, inventor
-ful	full of	careful, hopeful, helpful, wonderful
-hood	state or quality of	childhood, falsehood, adulthood
-ish	relating to	foolish, childish, selfish
-ism, -ist	belief in; one who believes in; one who is	communism, capitalism, capitalist
-less	without	fearless, careless, hopeless, harmless
-ly	like; characteristic of	quickly, happily, briefly, gently, sadly
-ment	action or process	enjoyment, government, amazement
-ness	state of; quality of	kindness, laziness, happiness, goodness
-ous, -eous, -ious	full of	dangerous, joyous, nervous, curious, delicious, courageous

Greek and Latin Roots	Meaning	Examples
astr, aster	star	astronomy, asterisk
aud	hear	audible, audience, audio, inaudible, auditorium
tract	drag; pull; draw from	tractor, attraction, detract, subtract
spect	look	inspect
port	carry	porter, portable, export
dict	to say	dictate, diction, dictionary, edict, predict, verdict
rupt	to break	erupt, rupture, abrupt, disruptive, bankrupt
scrib, scrip	to write	scribble, describe, postscript
ped	foot	pedestrian, pedal
equi	equal	equal, equate, equation, equitable
pop	people	popular, population

Name _____

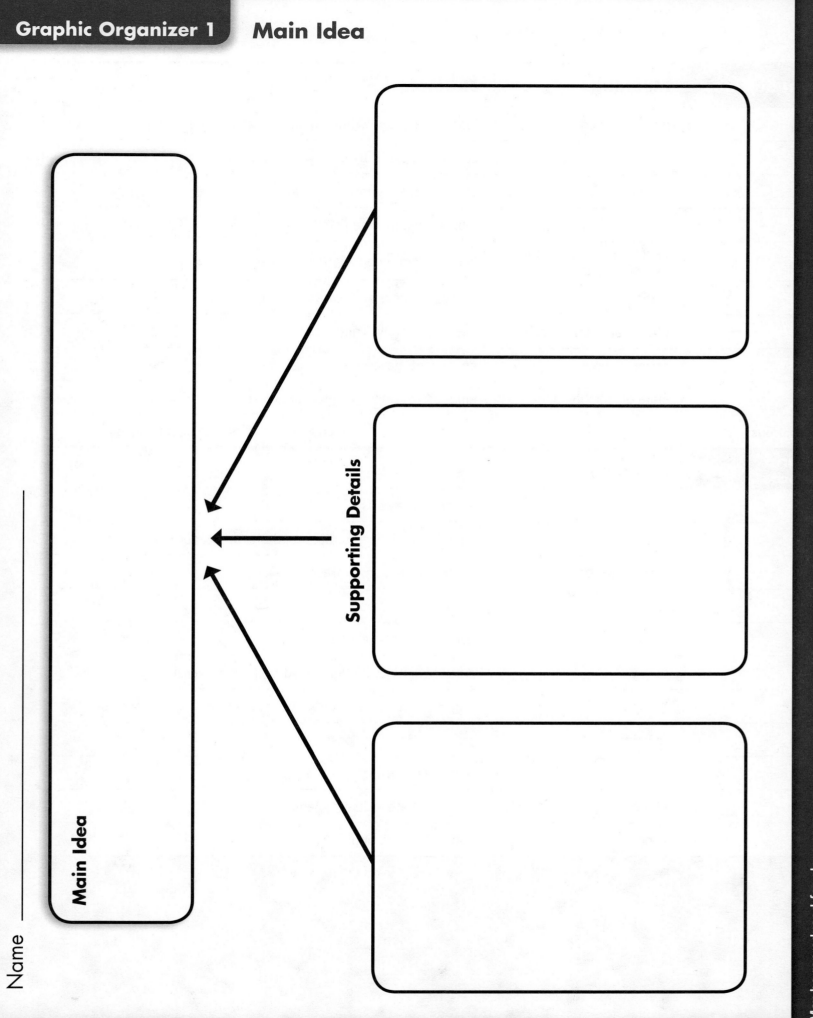

Main Idea

Supporting Details

Name _____

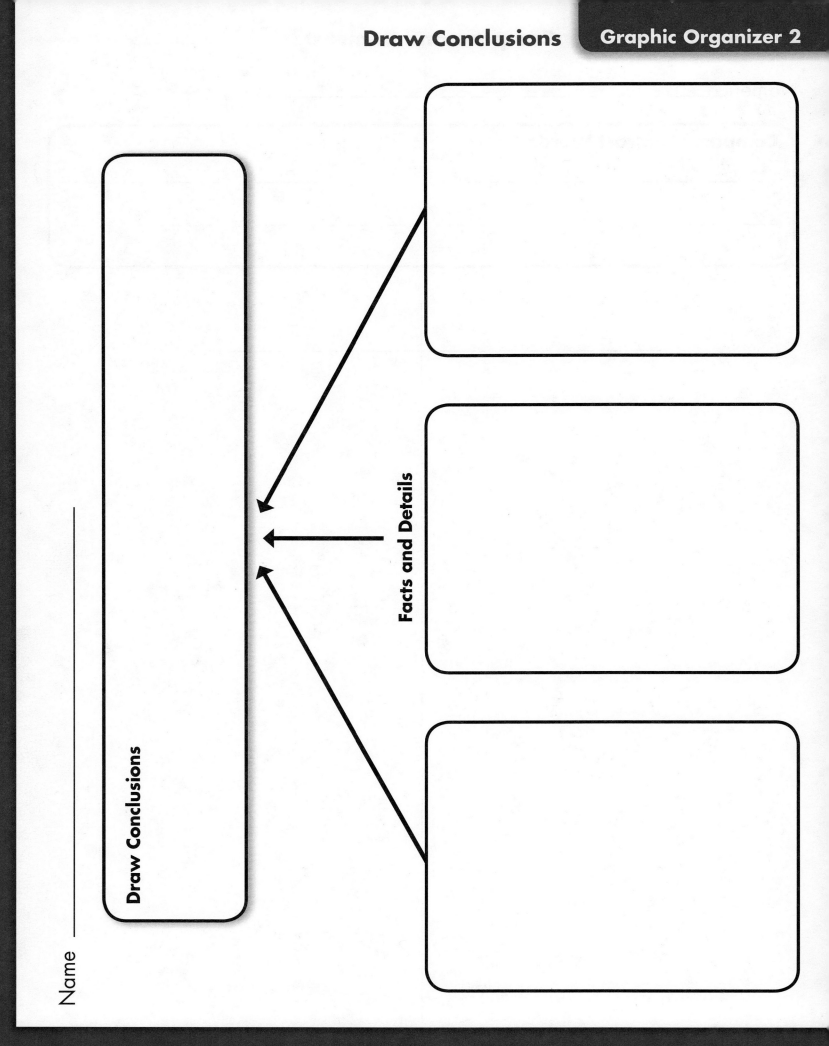

Draw Conclusions

Facts and Details

Name _____

Compare/Contrast Words

_____ _____ _____ _____

_____ _____ _____ _____

Name _____

Compare/Contrast Words

_____   _____   _____   _____

_____   _____   _____   _____

1

2

Both

Name _____

Sequence Words

_____   _____   _____   _____

_____   _____   _____   _____

Beginning

Middle

End

Name _____

Sequence Words

_____ _____ _____ _____

_____ _____ _____ _____

Steps:

1

2

3

4

5

Bookmarks

Fiction

- Who are the characters?

- Where does the story take place?

- When does the story take place?

- What is the problem or goal?

- How is the problem solved or the goal reached?

Nonfiction

- What did I learn?

- What is this mainly about?

Connections Between *My Sidewalks* and Scott Foresman *Reading Street*

My Sidewalks is designed to parallel essential elements in *Scott Foresman Reading Street*. Connections between the two programs are reflected in the indexes of the Teacher's Guides.

- Corresponding **priority skills** ensure that students receive instruction in the critical elements of reading—phonemic awareness, phonics, fluency, vocabulary, and comprehension.

- Parallel **concepts and themes** enable smooth transitions between *My Sidewalks* and *Reading Street.*

- Consistency of **scaffolded instruction** promotes familiarity with routines and terminology.

- Alignment of **before, during, and after reading strategies** reinforces successful reading habits.

- **Comprehension** skill links provide Tier III readers with additional instruction and practice with main idea, compare/contrast, sequence, and drawing conclusions.

- **Vocabulary** links provide Tier III readers with additional instruction and practice with oral vocabulary.

- Consistent procedures for **corrective feedback** promptly reveal and address student needs, providing guidance for error correction.

- Connected **writing** modes offer student opportunities to respond to literature.

- **Cross-curricular** links lay out the same science and social studies foundations for Tier III readers as for students in the core program.

Index

ask questions, *V1* 5, 10, 17, 22, 29, 34, 41, 46, 53, 58, 65, 70, 77, 82, 89, 94, 101, 106, 113, 118, 125, 130, 137, 142, 149, 154, 161, 166, 173, 178; *V2* 5, 10, 17, 22, 29, 34, 41, 46, 53, 58, 65, 70, 77, 82, 89, 94, 101, 106, 113, 118, 125, 130, 137, 142, 149, 154, 161, 166, 173, 178

concept development. *See* Concept development.

fix-up strategies, *V1* 5, 10, 17, 22, 29, 34, 41, 46, 53, 58, 65, 70, 77, 82, 89, 94, 101, 106, 113, 118, 125, 130, 137, 142, 149, 154, 161, 166, 173, 178; *V2* 5, 10, 17, 22, 29, 34, 41, 46, 53, 58, 65, 70, 77, 82, 89, 94, 101, 106, 113, 118, 125, 130, 137, 142, 149, 154, 161, 166, 173, 178

graphic organizers. *See* Graphic and semantic organizers.

graphic sources. *See* Graphic sources.

paired reading, *V1* 7, 11, 19, 23, 31, 35, 43, 47, 55, 59, 67, 71, 79, 83, 91, 95, 103, 107, 115, 119, 127, 131, 139, 143, 151, 155, 163, 167, 175, 179; *V2* 7, 11, 23, 35, 47, 59, 67, 71, 79, 83, 91, 95, 103, 107, 115, 119, 127, 131, 139, 143, 151, 155, 163, 167, 175, 179

picture clues, *V1* 5, 17, 29, 41, 53, 65, 77, 89, 101, 113, 125, 137, 149, 161, 173; *V2* 5, 17, 29, 41, 53, 65, 77, 89, 101, 113, 125, 137, 149, 161, 173

predict, *V1* 8, 20, 44, 56, 68, 80, 92, 104, 116, 128, 140, 152, 164, 176; *V2* 8, 20, 68, 80, 92, 104, 116, 128, 140, 152, 164, 176

preview, *V1* 5, 17, 29, 41, 53, 65, 77, 89, 101, 113, 125, 137, 149, 161, 173; *V2* 5, 17, 29, 41, 53, 65, 77, 89, 101, 113, 125, 137, 149, 161, 173

reader response. *See* Reader response.

recall and retell, *V1* 13, 25, 37, 49, 61, 73, 85, 97, 109, 121, 133, 145, 157, 169, 181; *V2* 13, 25, 37, 49, 61, 73, 85, 97, 109, 121, 133, 145, 157, 169, 181

self-monitor, *V1* 5, 10, 17, 22, 29, 34, 41, 46, 53, 58, 65, 70, 77, 82, 89, 94, 101, 106, 113, 118, 125, 130, 137, 142, 149, 154, 161, 166, 173, 178; *V2* 5, 10, 17, 22, 29, 34, 41, 46, 53, 58, 65, 70, 77, 82, 89, 94, 101, 106, 113, 118, 125, 130, 137, 142, 149, 154, 161, 166, 173, 178

set purpose for reading, *V1* 5, 17, 29, 41, 53, 65, 77, 89, 101, 113, 125, 137, 149, 161, 173; *V2* 5, 17, 29, 41, 53, 65, 77, 89, 101, 113, 125, 137, 149, 161, 173

story structure, *V1* 10, 22, 34, 46, 58, 70, 82, 94, 106, 118, 130, 142, 154, 166, 178; *V2* 10, 22, 34, 46, 58, 70, 82, 94, 106, 118, 130, 142, 154, 166, 178

character, *V1* 23, 35, 46, 47, 71, 82, 83, 95, 106, 107, 154; *V2* 22, 34, 58, 70, 82, 118, 154, 178

setting, *V1* 35, 46, 48, 95, 106, 155; *V2* 11, 34, 35, 70, 143, 178

summarize, *V1* 7, 12, 19, 24, 31, 36, 43, 48, 55, 60, 67, 72, 79, 84, 91, 96, 103, 108, 115, 120, 127, 132, 139, 144, 151, 156, 163, 168, 175, 180; *V2* 7, 12, 19, 24, 31, 36, 43, 48, 55, 60, 67, 72, 79, 84, 91, 96, 103, 108, 115, 120, 127, 132, 139, 144, 151, 156, 163, 168, 175, 180

think alouds. Think alouds and teacher modeling are demonstrated throughout weekly lessons as a basic teaching strategy.

text features, *V1* 108, 156; *V2* 12, 36, 48

text structure, *V1* 5, 17, 29, 41, 53, 65, 125, 137, 149, 161, 173; *V2* 5, 17, 29, 41, 53, 65, 77, 89, 101, 113, 125, 137, 149, 161, 173

Concept development

concept definition mapping, *V1* 4, 12, 16, 24, 28, 36, 40, 48, 52, 60, 64, 72, 76, 84, 88, 96, 100, 108, 112, 120, 124, 132, 136, 144, 148, 156, 160, 168, 172, 180; *V2* 4, 12, 16, 24, 28, 36, 40, 48, 52, 60, 64, 72, 76, 84, 88, 96, 100, 108, 112, 120, 124, 132, 136, 144, 148, 156, 160, 168, 172, 180

concept vocabulary, *Welcome to My Sidewalks,* 23; *V1* 2, 4, 6, 8, 10, 12, 14, 16, 18, 20, 22, 24, 26, 28, 30, 32, 34, 36, 38, 40, 42, 44, 46, 48, 50, 52, 54, 56, 58, 60, 62, 64, 66, 68, 70, 72, 74, 76, 78, 80, 82, 84, 86, 88, 90, 92, 94, 96, 98, 100, 102, 104, 106, 108, 110, 112, 114, 116, 118, 120, 122, 124, 126, 128, 130, 132, 134, 136, 138, 140, 142, 144, 146, 148, 150, 152, 154, 156, 158, 160, 162, 164, 166, 168, 170, 172, 174, 176, 178, 180; *V2* 2, 4,

6, 8, 10, 12, 14, 16, 18, 20, 22, 24, 26, 28, 30, 32, 34, 36, 38, 40, 42, 44, 46, 48, 50, 52, 54, 56, 58, 60, 62, 64, 66, 68, 70, 72, 74, 76, 78, 80, 82, 84, 86, 88, 90, 92, 94, 96, 98, 100, 102, 104, 106, 108, 110, 112, 114, 116, 118, 120, 122, 124, 126, 128, 130, 132, 134, 136, 138, 140, 142, 144, 146, 148, 150, 152, 154, 156, 158, 160, 162, 164, 166, 168, 170, 172, 174, 176, 178, 180

semantic map (concept web), *V1* 4, 12, 16, 24, 36, 40, 48, 52, 60, 64, 72, 76, 84, 88, 96, 100, 108, 112, 120, 124, 132, 136, 144, 148, 156, 160, 168, 172, 180; *V2* 4, 12, 16, 24, 28, 36, 40, 48, 52, 60, 64, 72, 76, 84, 88, 96, 100, 108, 112, 120, 124, 132, 136, 144, 148, 156, 160, 168, 172, 180

think alouds, *V1* 4, 16, 28, 40, 52, 64, 76, 88, 100, 112, 124, 136, 148, 160, 172; *V2* 4, 16, 28, 40, 52, 64, 76, 88, 100, 112, 124, 136, 148, 160, 172

Conclusions, draw. *See* Comprehension, Skills.

Connections, make, *V1* 13, 25, 37, 49, 61, 73, 85, 97, 109, 121, 133, 145, 157, 169, 181; *V2* 13, 25, 37, 49, 61, 73, 85, 97, 109, 121, 133, 145, 157, 169, 181

Content-area texts

fine arts, *V1* 11, 36, 53, 83, 91, 96, 144; *V2* 33, 131

health, *V1* 12

math, *V1* 127

music, *V1* 7, 65, 79

science, *V1* 17, 19, 25, 59, 60, 67, 125, 129, 137, 139, 143, 145, 149, 151, 156, 157, 161, 163, 168, 175, 179; *V2* 17, 19, 24, 53, 96, 113, 120, 173, 179

social studies, *V1* 29, 31, 35, 36, 37, 41, 43, 47, 49, 53, 55, 61, 65, 67, 73, 77, 84, 85, 89, 91, 96, 101, 103, 108, 113, 115, 119, 120, 121, 125, 127, 131, 144, 155, 163, 167, 173, 180; *V2* 5, 7, 13, 24, 29, 31, 36, 41, 48, 55, 59, 60, 61, 65, 67, 71, 72, 77, 79, 83, 84, 85, 89, 91, 95, 97, 101, 103, 107, 109, 119, 125, 127, 131, 133, 137, 139, 144, 161, 163, 167, 168, 169, 176

technology, *V1* 65, 72, 103; *V2* 36, 41, 43, 49, 180

Context clues. *See* Vocabulary, Strategies.

Contractions. *See* Spelling, word structure; Word Structure.

Contrast. *See* Comprehension, Skills, compare and contrast.

Conventions. *See* Writing, writing elements.

Corrective feedback

fluency, *V1* 5, 7, 9, 11, 17, 19, 21, 23, 29, 31, 33, 35, 41, 43, 45, 47, 53, 55, 57, 59, 65, 67, 69, 71, 77, 79, 81, 83, 89, 91, 93, 95, 101, 103, 105, 107, 113, 115, 117, 119, 125, 127, 129, 131, 137, 139, 141, 143, 149, 151, 153, 155, 161, 163, 165, 167, 173, 175, 177, 179; *V2* 5, 7, 9, 11, 17, 19, 21, 23, 29, 31, 33, 35, 41, 43, 45, 47, 53, 55, 57, 59, 65, 67, 69, 71, 77, 79, 81, 83, 89, 91, 93, 95, 101, 103, 105, 107, 113, 115, 117, 119, 125, 127, 129, 131, 137, 139, 141, 143, 149, 151, 153, 155, 161, 163, 165, 167, 173, 175, 177, 179

immediate corrective feedback, *V1* 5, 7, 9, 11, 17, 19, 21, 23, 29, 31, 33, 35, 41, 43, 45, 47, 53, 55, 57, 59, 65, 67, 69, 71, 77, 79, 81, 83, 89, 91, 93, 95, 101, 103, 105, 107, 113, 115, 117, 119, 125, 127, 129, 131, 137, 139, 141, 143, 149, 151, 153, 155, 161, 163, 165, 167, 173, 175, 177, 179; *V2* 5, 7, 9, 11, 17, 19, 21, 23, 29, 31, 33, 35, 41, 43, 45, 47, 53, 55, 57, 59, 65, 67, 69, 71, 77, 79, 81, 83, 89, 91, 93, 95, 101, 103, 105, 107, 113, 115, 117, 119, 125, 127, 129, 131, 137, 139, 141, 143, 149, 151, 153, 155, 161, 163, 165, 167, 173, 175, 177, 179

oral reading, *V1* 5, 7, 9, 11, 17, 19, 21, 23, 29, 31, 33, 35, 41, 43, 45, 47, 53, 55, 57, 59, 65, 67, 69, 71, 77, 79, 81, 83, 89, 91, 93, 95, 101, 103, 105, 107, 113, 115, 117, 119, 125, 127, 129, 131, 137, 139, 141, 143, 149, 151, 153, 155, 161, 163, 165, 167, 173, 175, 177, 179; *V2* 5, 7, 9, 11, 17, 19, 21, 23, 29, 31, 33, 35, 41, 43, 45, 47, 53, 55, 57, 59, 65, 67, 69, 71, 77, 79, 81, 83, 89, 91, 93, 95, 101, 103, 105, 107, 113, 115, 117, 119, 125, 127, 129, 131, 137, 139, 141, 143, 149, 151, 153, 155, 161, 163, 165, 167, 173, 175, 177, 179

paired reading, *V1* 7, 11, 19, 23, 31, 35, 43, 47, 55, 59, 67, 71, 79, 83, 91, 95, 103, 107, 115, 119, 127, 131, 139, 143, 151, 155, 163, 167, 175, 179; *V2* 7, 11, 19, 23, 31, 35, 43, 47, 55, 59, 67, 71, 79, 83, 91, 95, 103, 107, 115, 119, 127, 131, 139, 143, 151, 155, 163, 167, 175, 179

phonics, *V1* 6, 18, 66, 78, 126, 138, 162; *V2* 18, 42, 66, 78, 90, 102, 126, 138, 150

word structure, *V1* 18, 30, 42, 54, 90, 102, 114, 150, 174; *V2* 6, 30, 54, 114, 162, 174

See also Fluency; Phonics.

Creative/dramatic activities. *See* Fluency, Readers' Theater.

Critical thinking. *See* Comprehension, Skills.

Cultures, appreciating. *See* Multicultural connections.

Derivations, word. *See* Vocabulary, Development, etymologies; Word structure, related words.

Descriptive writing. *See* Writing, writing purpose.

Diagram. *See* Graphic sources.

Dictionary/glossary, *V1* 4, 16, 28, 40, 52, 64, 76, 88, 100, 112, 124, 136, 148, 160, 172; *V2* 4, 16, 28, 40, 52, 64, 76, 88, 100, 112, 124, 136, 148, 160, 172

Differentiated instruction, *Welcome to My Sidewalks,* 10–11; *V1* xiv–xv; *V2* xiv–xv

Discussion. *See* Oral language.

Drama. *See* Fluency, Readers' Theater.

Draw conclusions. *See* Comprehension, Skills.

During reading comprehension strategies.
See Comprehension, Strategies.

ELL

English Language Learners, *V1* xvi–xvii; *V2* xvi–xvii

Endings. *See* Spelling, word structure; Word structure.

Entertaining article. *See* Genres.

Error correction. *See* Corrective feedback.

ESL (English as a Second Language). *See* ELL.

Etymologies. *See* Vocabulary, Development.

Evaluation. *See* Assessment.

Expository nonfiction. *See* Genres.

Expository writing. *See* Writing, writing purpose.

F

Family involvement. *See* School-home connection.

Fantasy. *See* Genres.

Fine arts. *See* Content-area texts.

Fix-up strategies. *See* Comprehension, Strategies.

Flexible grouping. *See* Differentiated instruction.

Fluency

accuracy, *V1* 13, 25, 37, 49, 61, 73, 85, 97, 109, 121, 133, 145, 157, 169, 181, 184–185; *V2* 13, 25, 37, 49, 61, 73, 85, 97, 109, 121, 133, 145, 157, 169, 181, 184–185

assessment (WCPM), *V1* 13, 25, 37, 49, 61, 73, 85, 97, 109, 121, 133, 145, 157, 169, 181; *V2* 13, 25, 37, 49, 61, 73, 85, 97, 109, 121, 133, 145, 157, 169, 181

audio-assisted reading, *V1* 5, 7, 9, 11, 17, 19, 21, 23, 29, 31, 33, 35, 41, 43, 45, 47, 53, 55, 57, 59, 65, 67, 69, 71, 77, 79, 81, 83, 89, 91, 93, 95, 101, 103, 105, 107, 113, 115, 117, 119, 125, 127, 129, 131, 137, 139, 141, 143, 149, 151, 153, 155, 161, 163, 165, 173, 175, 177, 179; *V2* 5, 7, 9, 11, 17, 19, 21, 23, 29, 31, 33, 35, 41, 43, 45, 47, 53, 55, 57, 59, 65, 67, 69, 71, 77, 79, 81, 83, 89, 91, 93, 95, 101, 103, 105, 107, 113, 115, 117, 119, 125, 127, 129, 131, 137, 139, 141, 143, 149, 151, 153, 155, 161, 163, 165, 167, 173, 175, 177, 179

automaticity, *V1* 13, 25, 37, 49, 61, 73, 85, 97, 109, 121, 133, 145, 157, 169, 181, 184–185; *V2* 13, 25, 37, 49, 61, 73, 85, 97, 109, 121, 133, 145, 157, 169, 181, 184–185

corrective feedback, *V1* 5, 7, 9, 11, 17, 19, 21, 23, 29, 31, 33, 35, 41, 43, 45, 47, 53, 55, 57, 59, 65, 67, 69, 71, 77, 79, 81, 83, 89, 91, 93, 95, 101, 103, 105, 107, 113, 115, 117, 119, 125, 127, 129, 131, 137, 139, 141, 143, 149, 151, 153, 155, 161, 163, 165, 167, 173, 175, 177, 179; *V2* 5, 7, 9, 17, 19, 21, 23, 29, 31, 33, 35, 41, 43, 45, 47, 53, 55, 57, 59, 65, 67, 69, 71, 77, 79, 81, 83, 89, 91, 93, 95, 101, 103, 105, 107, 113, 115, 117, 119, 125, 127, 129, 131, 137, 139, 141, 143, 149, 151, 153, 155, 161, 163, 165, 167, 173, 175, 177, 179

fluency probes. *See* Fluency, assessment.

modeling by teacher, *Welcome to My Sidewalks,* 28; *V1* 5, 17, 29, 41, 53, 65, 77, 89, 101, 113, 125, 137, 149, 161, 173; *V2* 5, 17, 29, 41, 53, 65, 77, 89, 101, 113, 125, 137, 149, 161, 173

oral reading, *Welcome to My Sidewalks,* 28–29; *V1* 5, 7, 9, 11, 17, 19, 21, 29, 31, 33, 41, 43, 45, 53, 55, 57, 65, 67, 69, 71, 77, 79, 81, 83, 89, 91, 93, 95, 101, 103, 105, 107, 113, 115, 117, 119, 125, 127, 129, 131, 137, 139, 141, 143, 149, 151, 153, 155, 161, 163, 165, 167, 173, 175, 177, 179; *V2* 5, 7, 9, 17, 19, 21, 23, 29, 31, 33, 35, 41, 43, 45, 47, 53, 55, 57, 59, 65, 67, 69, 71, 77, 79, 81, 83, 89, 91, 93, 95, 101, 103, 105, 107, 113, 115, 117, 119, 125, 127, 129, 131, 137, 139, 141, 143, 149, 151, 153, 155, 161, 163, 165, 167, 173, 175, 177, 179

paired reading, *V1* 7, 11, 19, 23, 31, 35, 43, 47, 55, 59, 67, 71, 79, 83, 91, 95, 103, 107, 115, 119, 127, 131, 139, 143, 151, 155, 163, 167, 175, 179; *V2* 7, 11, 23, 35, 47, 59, 67, 71, 79, 83, 91, 95, 103, 107, 15, 119, 127, 131, 139, 143, 151, 155, 163, 167, 175, 179

Readers' Theater, *V1* 11, 23, 35, 47, 59, 71, 83, 95, 107, 119, 131, 143, 155, 167, 179; *V2* 11, 23, 35, 47, 59, 71, 83, 95, 107, 119, 131, 143, 155, 167, 179

repeated reading, *Welcome to My Sidewalks,* 28–29; *V1* 5, 7, 9, 11, 17, 19, 21, 29, 31, 33, 41, 43, 45, 53, 55, 57, 65, 67, 69, 71, 77, 79, 81, 83, 89, 91, 93, 95, 101, 103, 105, 107, 113, 115, 117, 119, 125, 127, 129, 131, 137, 139, 141, 143, 149, 151, 153, 155, 161, 163, 165, 167, 173, 175, 177, 179; *V2* 5, 7, 9, 17, 19, 21, 23, 29, 31, 33, 35, 41, 43, 45, 47, 53, 55, 57, 59, 65, 67, 69, 71, 77, 79, 81, 83, 89, 91, 93, 95, 101, 103, 105, 107, 113, 115, 117, 119, 125, 127, 129, 131, 137, 139, 141, 143, 149, 151, 153, 155, 161, 163, 165, 167, 173, 175, 177, 179

word reading, *Welcome to My Sidewalks,* 20

Fluency probes. *See* Fluency, assessment.

Focus. *See* Writing, writing elements.

Generate questions. *See* Comprehension, Strategies, ask questions.

Genres

animal fantasy, *V1* 23; *V2* 11

biography, *V1* 139, 151, 163; *V2* 7

expository nonfiction, *V1* 36, 43, 65, 67, 72, 79, 89, 91, 119, 125, 127, 143, 151; *V2* 29, 31, 65, 67, 72, 89, 91, 161, 167, 168, 175

fantasy, *V1* 95

historical fiction, *V1* 167

how-to article, *V1* 143, 168; *V2* 12, 36

humorous fiction, *V1* 95

informational article, *V1* 7, 9, 12, 19, 31, 55, 59, 60, 84, 103, 115, 139, 163, 175; *V2* 19, 47, 103, 120, 144, 180

legend, *V2* 23

letter, *V2* 155

mystery, *V2* 55, 59, 60

myth, *V2* 115

narrative nonfiction, *V1* 178; *V2* 96, 106, 163

photo essay, *V1* 96, 120, 144, 156, 179; *V2* 101

poetry, *V1* 132, 148; *V2* 108, 132

realistic fiction, *V1* 11, 35, 47, 71, 83, 107, 131, 155; *V2* 35, 71, 83, 95, 119, 131, 143, 179

science fiction, *V1* 24

Glossary. *See* Dictionary/glossary.

Graphic and semantic organizers

compare and contrast T-chart, *V1* 42, 44, 66, 68, 214; *V2* 30, 32, 66, 68, 78, 80, 174, 176, 214

concept web, *V1* 4, 16, 28, 40, 52, 64, 76, 88, 100, 112, 124, 136, 148, 160, 172; *V2* 4, 16, 28, 40, 52, 64, 76, 88, 100, 112, 124, 136, 148, 160, 172

draw conclusions chart, *V1* 18, 20, 78, 80, 90, 92, 150, 152, 213; *V2* 54, 56, 114, 116, 138, 140, 150, 152, 213

main idea map, *V1* 54, 56, 114, 116, 138, 140, 174, 176, 212; *V2* 42, 44, 102, 104, 162, 164, 212

sequence-steps in a process chart, *V1* 6, 8, 102, 104, 126, 128, 217; *V2* 90, 92, 217

sequence-story map, *V1* 30, 32, 216; *V2* 6, 8, 126, 128, 216

story map, *V1* 30, 32, 216; *V2* 6, 8, 126, 128, 216

T-chart, *V1* 42, 44, 66, 68, 214; *V2* 30, 32, 66, 68, 78, 80, 174, 176, 214

Venn diagram, *V1* 162, 164, 215; *V2* 18, 20, 215

Graphic sources

advertisement, *V1* 43

calendar, *V1* 127

chart/table, *V1* 165; *V2* 48

diagram/scale drawing, *V1* 149, 151; *V2* 7, 120, 179

illustration (photograph or art) and/or caption, *V1* 5, 17, 29, 41, 53, 68, 70, 77, 89, 92, 94, 101, 103, 113, 125, 128, 137, 149, 161, 173; *V2* 5, 17, 29, 32, 34, 41, 53, 65, 68, 70, 77, 89, 92, 94, 101, 113, 125, 137, 149, 161, 164, 166, 173

list, *V1* 119, 168

map, *V1* 31, 35, 91; *V2* 47, 48, 60, 103, 167

sign, *V1* 29, 55

time line, *V2* 43, 55

Greek and Latin roots. *See* Word structure.

Grouping students for instruction. *See* Differentiated instruction.

Guided oral reading. Guided oral reading is part of every lesson plan.

Health. *See* Content-area texts.

Higher order thinking skills. *See* Comprehension, Strategies.

Historical fiction. *See* Genres.

Historical nonfiction. *See* Genres.

Home-school connection. *See* School-home connection.

Homework. *See* School-home connection.

How-to article. *See* Genres.

Idioms. *See* Vocabulary, Development.

Illustrations. *See* Graphic sources.

Immediate corrective feedback. *See* Corrective feedback.

Independent reading, *V1* 7, 9, 11, 19, 21, 23, 31, 33, 35, 43, 45, 47, 55, 57, 59, 67, 69, 71, 79, 81, 83, 91, 93, 95, 103, 105, 107, 115, 117, 119, 127, 129, 131, 139, 141, 143, 151, 153, 155, 163, 165, 167, 175, 177, 179; *V2* 7, 9, 19, 21, 23, 31, 33, 35, 43, 45, 47, 55, 57, 59, 67, 69, 71, 79, 81, 83, 91, 93, 95, 103, 105, 107, 115, 117, 119, 127, 131, 139, 141, 143, 151, 153, 155, 163, 165, 167, 175, 177, 179

Inference. *See* Comprehension, Skills, draw conclusions. Inferential thinking questions appears throughout each lesson.

Inflected endings. *See* Spelling, word structure; Word structure, endings, inflected.

Informal assessment. *See* Assessment, classroom-based.

Informational article. *See* Genres.

Journal, *V1* 5, 17, 29, 41, 53, 65, 77, 89, 101, 113, 125, 137, 149, 161, 173; *V2* 5, 17, 29, 41, 53, 65, 77, 89, 101, 113, 125, 137, 149, 161, 173

Judgments, make. *See* Comprehension, Skills, draw conclusions.

Language, oral. *See* Oral language.

Latin and Greek roots. *See* Word structure.

Legend. *See* Genres.

Letter. *See* Genres.

List. *See* Graphic sources.

Listening comprehension

Read Together, *V1* 12, 24, 36, 48, 60, 72, 84, 96, 108, 120, 132, 144, 156, 168, 180; *V2* 12, 24, 36, 48, 60, 72, 84, 96, 108, 120, 132, 144, 156, 168, 180

Literal comprehension. Literal comprehension questions appear throughout each lesson.

Literary craft

author's craft, *V1* 83; *V2* 35

Literary devices

point of view, *V1* 71; *V2* 11

See also Sound devices and poetic elements.

Main idea and supporting details. *See* Comprehension, Skills.

Make connections. *See* Connections, make.

Make judgments. *See* Comprehension, Skills, draw conclusions.

Map. *See* Graphic sources.

Mapping selection. *See* Graphic and semantic organizers, story map.

Math. *See* Content-area texts.

Metacognition. *See* Comprehension, Strategies, self-monitor.

Modeling. Teacher modeling and think alouds are presented throughout the lessons.

Monitor progress. *See* Assessment, progress monitoring.

Multicultural connections, *V1* 4, 5, 7, 9, 11, 12, 13, 72, 167; *V2* 23, 47, 115, 149, 151, 155, 156

Multisyllabic words. *See* Word structure.

Music. *See* Content-area texts.

Mystery. *See* Genres.

Myth. *See* Genres.

Narrative nonfiction. *See* Genres.

Narrative writing. *See* Writing, writing purpose.

New Literacies. *See* Content-area texts, technology.

Nonfiction. *See* Genres.

Note-taking. *See* Comprehension, Strategies, fix-up strategies.

Oral language

discussion, *V1* 4, 13, 16, 25, 28, 37, 40, 49, 52, 61, 64, 73, 76, 85, 88, 97, 100, 109, 112, 121, 124, 133, 136, 145, 148, 157, 160, 169, 172, 181; *V2* 4, 13, 16, 25, 28, 37, 40, 49, 52, 61, 64, 73, 76, 85, 88, 97, 100, 109, 112, 121, 124, 133, 136, 145, 148, 157, 160, 169, 172, 181

questions, *V1* 5, 7, 9, 11, 12, 17, 19, 21, 23, 24, 29, 31, 33, 35, 36, 41, 43, 45, 47, 48, 53, 55, 57, 59, 60, 65, 67, 69, 71, 72, 77, 79, 81, 83, 84, 89, 91, 93, 95, 96, 101, 103, 105, 107, 108, 113, 115, 117, 119, 120, 125, 127, 129, 131, 132, 137, 139, 141, 143, 144, 149, 151, 153, 155, 156, 161, 163, 165, 167, 168, 173, 175, 177, 179, 180; *V2* 5, 7, 9, 11, 12, 17, 19, 21, 23, 24, 29, 31, 33, 35, 36, 41, 43, 45, 47, 48, 53, 55, 57, 59, 60, 65, 67, 69, 71, 72, 77, 79, 81, 83, 84, 89, 91, 93, 95, 96, 101, 103, 105, 107, 108, 113, 115, 117, 119, 120, 125, 127, 129, 131, 132, 137, 139, 141, 143, 144, 149, 151, 153, 155, 156, 161, 163, 165, 167, 168, 173, 175, 177, 179, 180

retelling, *V1* 13, 25, 37, 49, 61, 73, 85, 97, 109, 121, 133, 145, 157, 169, 181; *V2* 13, 25, 37, 49, 61, 73, 85, 97, 109, 121, 133, 145, 157, 169, 181

summary, *V1* 7, 12, 19, 24, 31, 36, 43, 48, 55, 60, 67, 72, 79, 84, 91, 96, 103, 108, 115, 120, 127, 132, 139, 144, 151, 156, 163, 168, 175, 180; *V2* 7, 12, 19, 24, 31, 36, 43, 48, 55, 60, 67, 72, 79, 84, 91, 96, 103, 108, 115, 120, 127, 132, 139, 144, 151, 156, 163, 168, 175, 180

Oral reading. *See* Fluency.

Oral vocabulary

concept words, *V1* 4, 6, 8, 10, 16, 18, 20, 22, 28, 30, 32, 34, 40, 42, 44, 46, 52, 54, 56, 58, 64, 66, 68, 70, 76, 78, 80, 82, 88, 90, 92, 94, 100, 102, 104, 106, 112, 114, 116, 118, 124, 126, 128, 130, 136, 138, 140, 142, 148, 150, 152, 154, 160, 162, 164, 166, 172, 174, 176, 178; *V2* 4, 6, 8, 10, 16, 18, 20, 22, 28, 30, 32, 34, 40, 42, 44, 46, 52, 54, 56, 58, 64, 66, 68, 70, 76, 78, 80, 82, 88, 90, 92, 94, 100, 102, 104, 106, 112, 114, 116, 118, 124, 126, 128, 130, 136, 138, 140, 142, 148, 150, 152, 154, 160, 162, 164, 166, 172, 174, 176, 178

Organization. *See* Writing, writing elements.

Organizing information. *See* Graphic and semantic organizers.

Paired reading. *See* Comprehension, Strategies; Fluency.

Personal narrative. *See* Writing, writing purpose.

Phonics

blend sounds to decode words, *V1* 9, 21, 33, 45, 57, 81, 105, 117, 129; *V2* 9

corrective feedback, *V1* 6, 18, 66, 78, 126, 138, 162; *V2* 18, 42, 66, 78, 90, 102, 126, 138, 150

multisyllabic words. *See* Word structure.

vowel digraphs

ai, ay, *V1* 126, 128, 129

ea, ee, *V1* 138, 140

ie, igh, *V1* 18, 20

oa, ow, *V1* 162, 164

oo, /ü/, *V2* 90, 92

oo, u, /ů/, *V2* 138, 140

vowel diphthongs

oi, *V2* 66, 68

ou, *V2* 42, 44

ow, *V2* 42, 44

oy, *V2* 66, 68

vowel patterns, less common

a, al, *V2* 102, 104

au, aw, *V2* 102, 104

ew, ue, *V2* 90, 92

vowels, long

e, y, *V1* 138, 140

i, y, *V2* 18, 20, 21, 150, 152

o, *V2* 150, 152

vowels, r-controlled

ar, *V1* 66, 68

er, ir, ur, *V1* 78, 80, 81

or, *V1* 66, 68

vowels, short

ea /e/, *V2* 126, 128

word parts. *See* Word structure.

Photo essay. *See* Genres.

Pictures. *See* Comprehension, Strategies, pictures clues; Graphic sources, illustrations.

Plurals. *See* Spelling, word structure; Word structure.

Poetic devices. *See* Sound devices and poetic elements.

Poetry. *See* Genres.

Point of view. *See* Literary devices.

Predict. *See* Comprehension, Strategies.

Prefixes. *See* Word structure.

Prereading strategies. *See* Comprehension, Strategies for specific strategies; Concept development.

Preview. *See* Comprehension, Strategies.

Prior knowledge. *See* Comprehension, Strategies, activate prior knowledge.

Progress monitoring. *See* Assessment.

Purpose for reading. *See* Comprehension, Strategies, set purpose for reading.

Questions, answer. *See* Comprehension, Strategies.

Questions, ask. *See* Comprehension, Strategies.

Reader response, *V1* 5, 7, 9, 11, 12, 17, 19, 21, 23, 24, 29, 31, 33, 35, 36, 41, 43, 45, 47, 48, 53, 55, 57, 59, 60, 65, 67, 69, 71, 72, 77, 79, 81, 83, 84, 89, 91, 93, 95, 96, 101, 103, 105, 107, 108, 113, 115, 117, 119, 120, 125, 127, 129, 131, 132, 137, 139, 141, 143, 144, 149, 151, 153, 155, 156, 161, 163, 165, 167, 168, 173, 175, 177, 179, 180; *V2* 5, 7, 9, 11, 12, 17, 19, 21, 23, 24, 29, 31, 33, 35, 36, 41, 43, 45, 47, 48, 53, 55, 57, 59, 60, 65, 67, 69, 71, 72, 77, 79, 81, 83, 84, 89, 91, 93, 95, 96, 101, 103, 105, 107, 108, 113, 115, 117, 119, 120, 125, 127, 129, 131, 132, 137, 139, 141, 143, 144, 149, 151, 153, 155, 156, 161, 163, 165, 167, 168, 173, 175, 177, 179, 180

Readers' Theater. *See* Fluency.

Reading across texts. *See* Connections, make.

Reading levels, *Welcome to My Sidewalks,* 14–15; *V1* xii–xiii; *V2* xii–xiii

Realistic fiction. *See* Genres.

Recall and retell. *See* Comprehension, Strategies.

Reference sources. *See* Dictionary/glossary.

Related words. *See* Spelling, word structure; Word structure.

Repeated reading. *See* Fluency.

Research

bibliography, *Welcome to My Sidewalks,* 30

research base for My Sidewalks, *Welcome to My Sidewalks,* 6, 18–29, 30

Respond to literature. *See* Reader response.

Response to Literature (written), *V1* 5, 7, 8, 11, 13, 17, 19, 21, 23, 25, 29, 31, 33, 35, 37, 41, 43, 45, 47, 49, 53, 55, 57, 59, 61, 65, 67, 69, 71, 73, 77, 79, 81, 83, 85, 89, 91, 93, 95, 97, 101, 103, 105, 107, 109, 113, 115, 117, 119, 121, 125, 127, 129, 131, 133, 137, 139, 141, 143, 145, 149, 151, 153, 155, 157, 161, 163, 165, 167, 169, 173, 175, 177, 179, 181; *V2* 5, 7, 8, 11, 13, 17, 19, 21, 23, 25, 29, 31, 33, 35, 37, 41, 43, 45, 47, 49, 53, 55, 57, 59, 61, 65, 67, 69, 71, 73, 77, 79, 81, 83, 85, 89, 91, 93, 95, 97, 101, 103, 105, 107, 109, 113, 115, 117, 119, 121, 125, 127, 129, 131, 133, 137, 139, 141, 143, 145, 149, 151, 153, 155, 157, 161, 163, 165, 167, 169, 173, 175, 177, 179, 181

Retelling. *See* Comprehension, Strategies, recall and retell.

Rhyme. *See* Sound devices and poetic elements.

Scaffolded instruction, *Welcome to My Sidewalks,* 9; *V1* 4, 5, 6, 7, 8, 9, 10, 11, 12, 16, 17, 18, 19, 20, 21, 22, 23, 24, 28, 29, 30, 31, 32, 33, 34, 35, 36, 40, 41, 42, 43, 44, 45, 46, 47, 48, 52, 53, 54, 55, 56, 57, 58, 59, 60, 64, 65, 66, 67, 68, 69, 70, 71, 72, 76, 77, 78, 79, 80, 81, 82, 83, 84, 88, 89, 90, 91, 92, 93, 94, 95, 96, 100, 101, 102, 103, 104, 105, 106, 107, 108, 112, 113, 114, 115, 116, 117, 118, 119, 120, 124, 125, 126, 127, 128, 129, 130, 131, 132, 136, 137, 138, 139, 140, 141, 142, 143, 144, 148, 149, 150, 151, 152, 153, 154, 155, 156, 160, 161, 162, 163, 164, 165, 166, 167, 168, 172, 173, 174, 175, 176, 177, 178, 179, 180; *V2* 4, 5, 6, 7, 8, 9, 10, 11, 12, 16,

17, 18, 19, 20, 21, 22, 23, 24, 28, 29, 30, 31, 32, 33, 34, 35, 36, 40, 41, 42, 43, 44, 45, 46, 47, 48, 52, 53, 54, 55, 56, 57, 58, 59, 60, 64, 65, 66, 67, 68, 69, 70, 71, 72, 76, 77, 78, 79, 80, 81, 82, 83, 84, 88, 89, 90, 91, 92, 93, 94, 95, 96, 100, 101, 102, 103, 104, 105, 106, 107, 108, 112, 113, 114, 115, 116, 117, 118, 119, 120, 124, 125, 126, 127, 128, 129, 130, 131, 132, 136, 137, 138, 139, 140, 141, 142, 143, 144, 148, 149, 150, 151, 152, 153, 154, 155, 156, 160, 161, 162, 163, 164, 165, 166, 167, 168, 172, 173, 174, 175, 176, 177, 178, 179, 180

School-home connection, *V1* 5, 17, 29, 41, 53, 65, 77, 89, 101, 113, 125, 137, 149, 161, 173; *V2* 5, 17, 29, 41, 53, 65, 77, 89, 101, 113, 125, 137, 149, 161, 173

Science. *See* Content-area texts.

Science fiction. *See* Genres.

Self-monitor. *See* Comprehension, Strategies.

Self-question. *See* Comprehension, Strategies, ask questions.

Self-selected reading, *V1* 189–192; *V2* 189–192

Semantic map. *See* Concept development.

Sequence. *See* Comprehension, Skills.

Set purpose for reading. *See* Comprehension, Strategies.

Setting. *See* Comprehension, Strategies, story structure.

Shared Reading, *V1* 12, 24, 36, 48, 60, 72, 84, 96, 108, 120, 132, 144, 156, 168, 180; *V2* 12, 24, 36, 48, 60, 72, 84, 96, 108, 120, 132, 144, 156, 168, 180

Sign. *See* Graphic sources.

Social studies. *See* Content-area texts.

Sound devices and poetic elements

rhyme, *V1* 157

Sound Pronunciation Guide, *Welcome to My Sidewalks,* 31–32

Spelling

phonics, connection to, *V1* 8, 20, 68, 80, 128, 140, 164; *V2* 20, 44, 68, 92, 104, 128, 140, 152

word structure, use to spell words, *V1* 8, 20, 32, 44, 56, 68, 92, 104, 116, 152, 176; *V2* 8, 32, 56, 80, 116, 164, 176

Story grammar. *See* Comprehension, Strategies, story structure.

Story structure. *See* Comprehension, Strategies.

Structural analysis. *See* Spelling, word structure; Word structure.

Suffixes. *See* Spelling, word structure; Word structure.

Summarize. *See* Comprehension, Strategies.

Support. *See* Writing, writing elements.

Syllables. *See* Word structure.

Synonyms. *See* Vocabulary, Development.

Tables. *See* Graphic sources, chart/table.

Taking notes. *See* Comprehension, Strategies, fix-up strategies.

Technology. *See* Content-area texts.

Tested Vocabulary Cards. *See* Vocabulary, Strategies.

Testing, formal and informal. *See* Assessment.

Text features. *See* Comprehension, Strategies.

Text structure. *See* Comprehension, Strategies.

Think alouds. *See* Comprehension, Strategies; Concept development.

Tiers of intervention, *Welcome to My Sidewalks,* 4; *V1* iv; *V2* iv

Timed reading. *See* Fluency, assessment.

Time line. *See* Graphic and semantic organizers; Graphic sources.

Trade books. *See* Self-selected reading.

Unfamiliar words. *See* Vocabulary, Strategies.

Venn diagram. *See* Graphic and semantic organizers.

Vocabulary

Development

antonyms, *V2* 46, 94

concept vocabulary, *Welcome to My Sidewalks,* 23; *V1* 2, 4, 6, 8, 10, 12, 14, 16, 18, 20, 22, 24, 26, 28, 30, 32, 34, 36, 38, 40, 42, 44, 46, 48, 50, 52, 54, 56, 58, 60, 62, 64, 66, 68, 70, 72, 74, 76, 78, 80, 82, 84, 86, 88, 90, 92, 94, 96, 98, 100, 102, 104, 106, 108, 110, 112, 114, 116, 118, 120, 122, 124, 126, 128, 130, 132, 134, 136, 138, 140, 142, 144, 146, 148, 150, 152, 154, 156, 158, 160, 162, 164, 166, 168, 170, 172, 174, 176, 178, 180; *V2* 2, 4, 6, 8, 10, 12, 14, 16, 18, 20, 22, 24, 26, 28, 30, 32, 34, 36, 38, 40, 42, 44, 46, 48, 50, 52, 54, 56, 58, 60, 62, 64, 66, 68, 70, 72, 74, 76, 78, 80, 82, 84, 86, 88, 90, 92, 94, 96, 98, 100, 102, 104, 106, 108, 110, 112, 114, 116, 118, 120, 122, 124, 126, 128, 130, 132, 134, 136, 138, 140, 142, 144, 146, 148, 150, 152, 154, 156, 158, 160, 162, 164, 166, 168, 170, 172, 174, 176, 178, 180

etymologies, *V1* 47

Greek and Latin roots. *See* Word structure.

idioms, *V2* 24, 47

synonyms, *V2* 61, 94

Strategies

concept definition map, *V1* 4, 12, 16, 24, 28, 36, 40, 48, 52, 60, 64, 72, 76, 84, 88, 96, 100, 108, 112, 120, 124, 132, 136, 144, 148, 156, 160, 168, 172, 180; *V2* 4, 12, 16, 24, 28, 36, 40, 48, 52, 60, 64, 72, 76, 84, 88, 96, 100, 108, 112, 120, 124, 132, 136, 144, 148, 156, 160, 168, 172, 180

context clues, *V1* 107, 141, 153, 165, 177; *V2* 93, 119, 141, 177

cumulative review, *V1* 12, 24, 36, 48, 60, 72, 84, 96, 108, 120, 132, 144, 156, 168, 180; *V2* 12, 24, 36, 48, 60, 72, 84, 96, 108, 120, 132, 144, 156, 168, 180

dictionary/glossary. *See* Dictionary/glossary.

semantic map (concept web), *V1* 4, 12, 16, 24, 28, 36, 40, 48, 52, 60, 64, 72, 76, 84, 88, 96, 100, 108, 112, 120, 124, 132, 136, 144, 148, 156, 160, 168, 172, 180; *V2* 4, 12, 16, 24, 28, 36, 40, 48, 52, 60, 64, 72, 76, 84, 88, 96, 100, 108, 112, 120, 124, 132, 136, 144, 148, 156, 160, 168, 172, 180

Tested Vocabulary Cards, *Welcome to My Sidewalks,* 20; *V1* 4, 16, 28, 40, 52, 64, 76, 88, 100, 112, 124, 136, 148, 160, 172; *V2* 4, 16, 28, 40, 52, 64, 76, 88, 100, 112, 124, 136, 148, 160, 172

unfamiliar words, *V1* 107, 141, 153, 165, 177; *V2* 93, 119, 141, 177

Web. *See* Graphic and semantic organizers, concept web.

Word reading. *See* Fluency.

Word structure

base words

    without spelling changes, *V1* 42, 44, 90, 92

    with spelling changes, *V1* 30, 32, 42, 44, 90, 92, 93, 106

compound words, *V1* 10, 21; *V2* 6, 8, 9, 33, 57

contractions, *V1* 150, 152

corrective feedback, *V1* 18, 30, 42, 54, 90, 102, 114, 150, 174; *V2* 6, 30, 54, 114, 162, 174

endings, comparative/superlative, *V1* 90, 92, 93

endings, inflected, *V1* 30, 32, 42, 44, 45

Greek and Latin roots, *V2* 70, 118, 130

multisyllabic words, *V1* 4, 9, 16, 21, 28, 33, 40, 45, 52, 57, 64, 66, 68, 69, 76, 88, 100, 112, 124, 136, 148, 160, 172; *V2* 4, 16, 28, 33, 40, 45, 52, 57, 64, 69, 76, 88, 100, 112, 124, 136, 148, 160, 172

plurals, *V1* 30, 32, 106

prefixes, *V1* 54, 56, 82, 94, 130, 153, 154, 166, 174, 176, 178, 179

related words, *V1* 106, 118, 142; *V2* 22, 34, 106, 142, 174, 176

root words, *V1* 22, 58, 178; *V2* 82

suffixes, *V1* 34, 70, 114, 116, 117; *V2* 10, 54, 56, 58, 114, 116

syllable patterns

    closed with long vowels, *V1* 18, 20

    closed with short vowels, *V1* 6, 8

    common, *V2* 78, 80

    consonant + *le*, *V2* 30, 32

    VC/CV, *V1* 66, 68

    VC/V; V/CV, *V1* 102, 104, 105

    V/V, *V2* 162, 164

Word study. *See* Phonics; Vocabulary; Word structure.

Writing

journal, *V1* 5, 17, 29, 41, 53, 65, 77, 89, 101, 113, 125, 137, 149, 161, 173; *V2* 5, 17, 29, 41, 53, 65, 77, 89, 101, 113, 125, 137, 149, 161, 173

response to literature, *V1* 5, 7, 8, 11, 13, 17, 19, 21, 23, 25, 29, 31, 33, 35, 37, 41, 43, 45, 47, 49, 53, 55, 57, 59, 61, 65, 67, 69, 71, 73, 77, 79, 81, 83, 85, 89, 91, 93, 95, 97, 101, 103, 105, 107, 109, 113, 115, 117, 119, 121, 125, 127, 129, 131, 133, 137, 139, 141, 143, 145, 149, 151, 153, 155, 157, 161, 163, 165, 167, 169, 173, 175, 177, 179, 181; *V2* 5, 7, 8, 11, 13, 17, 19, 21, 23, 25, 29, 31, 33, 35, 37, 41, 43, 45, 47, 49, 53, 55, 57, 59, 61, 65, 67, 69, 71, 73, 77, 79, 81, 83, 85, 89, 91, 93, 95, 97, 101, 103, 105, 107, 109, 113, 115, 117, 119, 121, 125, 127, 129, 131, 133, 137, 139, 141, 143, 145, 149, 151, 153, 155, 157, 161, 163, 165, 167, 169, 173, 175, 177, 179, 181

writing elements

    conventions, *V1* 35, 71, 91, 103, 131, 175, 179; *V2* 11, 107, 131, 151, 167

    focus, *V1* 23, 55, 107, 119, 139, 143, 155, 167, 179; *V2* 11, 35, 59, 83, 95, 119, 131, 139, 143, 175

    organization, *V1* 11, 35, 37, 83, 107, 115, 119, 131, 163, 179; *V2* 11, 35, 71, 107, 127, 131, 179

    support, *V1* 19, 23, 31, 43, 55, 59, 67, 71, 79, 83, 95, 127, 139, 143, 151, 155, 163, 167, 175, 179; *V2* 7, 19, 23, 31, 43, 47, 55, 67, 71, 79, 83, 91, 103, 115, 119, 127, 155, 163, 167, 179

writing purpose

    descriptive writing, *V1* 23, 43, 47, 71, 83, 155; *V2* 35

    expository writing, *V1* 35, 59, 95, 119, 131, 167, 179; *V2* 23, 47, 59, 83, 95, 107, 119, 143, 167

    narrative writing, *V1* 11, 107; *V2* 11, 131, 179

    personal narrative writing, *V1* 107, 143; *V2* 71, 155

Teacher Notes

Teacher Notes

Teacher Notes

Teacher Notes

Teacher Notes

Teacher Notes

Teacher Notes

Teacher Notes

2 Retelling Have students reread a Student Reader selection and retell it. See p. 186.

3 Unit Test Administer the Unit Test in the Assessment Book. Record scores for each test. See the Assessment Book, p. 16.

4 Unit Retelling Assessment Record students' retelling scores for each unit. See the Assessment Book, pp. 12–14.

Students may exit the program at midyear or at the end of the year. See p. 188 for exit criteria.

If . . . students are unable to use vocabulary words to answer questions or to add words to the concept web,

then . . . use one of these strategies.

- Model using the words to discuss the lesson concept.

- Provide word pairs, one of which fits on the web. Have students choose the word and explain why it fits.

- Provide cloze sentences for students to complete with vocabulary words.

- Brainstorm additional words for the concept web. Keep the web on display and add words throughout the week.

- Reteach words using the Vocabulary Routine.

- Provide a "starter" or "warm-up" to establish a sense of efficacy. Start by reading a sentence or a small piece of the text to show that it is accessible. Elicit student experience related to the text to show it is familiar.

- Provide choices whenever possible. I let students choose what selection to read first or retell. Let them choose which activity to do on the 4 You 2 Do page and how to do it when alternative responses are possible.

- Social interaction helps engage students. Allow students to work in pairs or teams, for example when reading aloud, when answering questions, or when retelling.

Concept/Amazing Words

Use this Routine to teach concept vocabulary.

1 Introduce the Word Relate the word to the week's concept. Supply a student-friendly definition.

2 Demonstrate Provide several familiar examples to demonstrate meaning.

3 Apply Have students demonstrate understanding with a simple activity.

4 Display the Word Relate the word to the concept by displaying it on a concept web. Have students identify word parts and practice reading the word.

5 Use the Word Often Encourage students to use the word often in their writing and speaking. Ask questions that require students to use the word.

Monitor Progress

Use these strategies to monitor progress on a regular basis.

- When reading, stop at the end of each paragraph or section to check comprehension and vocabulary.

- Monitor student oral reading fluency regularly.

- Assign and check Practice Book pages daily.

Choose from the following assessment options.

1 Fluency Each week, take a two-minute timed sample of students' oral reading. Record results on the Fluency Progress Chart, p. 185. Be sure each student is assessed at least every other week.

Using Graphic Organizers

Use the graphic organizers on pp. 228–233 to provide a visual framework for students to organize, comprehend, and synthesize information.

- Students can use the organizers both to record what they read and to plan their own written work.

- Model how to fill out each organizer and how to select only relevant information.

- Use a paragraph or the beginning of a selection to help students begin filling out an organizer.

- Have additional copies of organizers available for different selections in a lesson.

Motivating Students to Read

Motivating students to want to read is key to improving their reading skills. Use these strategies to motivate students.

- Establish a sense of purpose and relate reading to real-world experience.

- Do an interest inventory with each student. Does he like race cars? Is she fascinated by baseball? Direct them to books, magazines, and Internet sites at their independent reading level on topics of interest. See pp. 189–190 for ways to match students with text.

Routine Card 2

The Before, During, and After Reading strategies should be reinforced daily. Use this Routine to teach comprehension strategies.

1 Teach Describe each strategy explicitly, explaining when, why, and how to use it.

2 Model Think aloud to model applying the strategy with different selections.

3 Practice Have students practice using the strategy, with support and prompting.

4 Apply Independently Expect students to begin using these strategies independently.

Routine Card 1

Routine Card 4

Use these strategies to help children develop fluency.

• **Model Fluency** Model reading "as if you were speaking," attending to punctuation and phrasing and reading with expression (prosody).

• **Provide Corrective Feedback** Provide feedback on oral reading.

If... students misread a word,
then... help them decode it and have them reread the sentence.

If... students read at an inappropriate or unsteady pace,
then... model an appropriate pace, having children echo.

If... students lack oral expression,
then... model how to read based on the meaning of the passage. Tell students that their expression should show their understanding.

• **Monitor Fluency** See pp. 184–185 for assessment options.

Routine Card 3

To become engaged with the text, students need to understand what they read. How do we know when we understand what we've read and when we are only reading words without understanding? Model monitoring your reading.

• Think out loud frequently as you read, so students can hear how good readers make meaning as they read.

• Model fix-up strategies, such as rereading and summarizing, to use when understanding breaks down.

• Teach strategies readers use to hold their attention as they read, such as taking notes, stopping frequently to retell, or using a graphic organizer.

• Have students practice these strategies in small groups or with a partner.

Multisyllabic Word Routine

Teach students this Routine for reading long words.

1 Look for Meaningful Parts Think about the meaning of each part. Use the parts to read the word. Help students analyze long words for base words, endings (*-ing, -ed, -s*), prefixes (*un-, re-, dis-, mis-, non-*), and suffixes (*-ly, -ness, -less, -ful,* and so on).

2 Chunk Words with No Recognizable Parts Say each chunk slowly. Then say the chunks fast to make a word.

Comprehension Strategies

Teach students these comprehension strategies.

1 Preview Before reading, look at text features to determine the genre and get an idea of the topic.

2 Ask Questions During reading, ask questions:

* Nonfiction **What did I learn? What is this mainly about?**
* Fiction **Who is in the story?**
  Where/When does it take place?
  What is the problem or goal? How is the problem solved or the goal reached?

3 Look Back to Answer Questions After reading, look back in the text to find answers to questions.

4 Summarize or Retell Summarize the main ideas of a nonfiction selection or retell the main events of a story.

Reading Engagement

If . . . students do not appear to be engaged with the text,

then . . . use one of these strategies.

* Read chorally.

* Have students read in a whisper.

* Ask questions.

* Assign reading partners.

* Sit next to a student and alternate reading paragraphs aloud.

* Stop at designated points to check understanding.

* Read aloud while students echo-read.

Fluency Practice

Use one of these Routines for fluency practice. Provide corrective feedback as you listen to each student read.

* **Oral Reading** Students read a passage orally. To achieve optimal fluency, they should reread three or four times.

* **Paired Reading** Partners read, switching readers at the end of each page. For optimal fluency, students should reread three or four times.

* **Audio-Assisted Reading** A student reads aloud while listening to the recording.

* **Readers' Theater** Groups of students rehearse reading the parts of each character and the narrator until they can read fluently and with expression. Then they read aloud as a performance or radio play.